FROM MY HEART
A Memoir

FROM MY HEART
A Memoir

Sam Wanyanga

Copyright © 2013 by Sam Wanyanga
ISBN: 978-9966-1529-9-2

Published by Sahel Books Inc.
P.O. BOX 6451, South Bend IN, 46660
Or
P.O. BOX 770—00600, Nairobi, Kenya
www.sahelpublishing.net
Printed in the United States of America, the United Kingdom and India
Edited by: Sam Okello
Cover Design: Peter Omamo
Interior Design: Hellen Wahonya Okello

All rights reserved.

No part of this publication may be reproduced, distributed, or transmitted in any form or by any means, or stored in any database or retrieval system, without prior written permission from publisher and author.

To my beloved family and their families

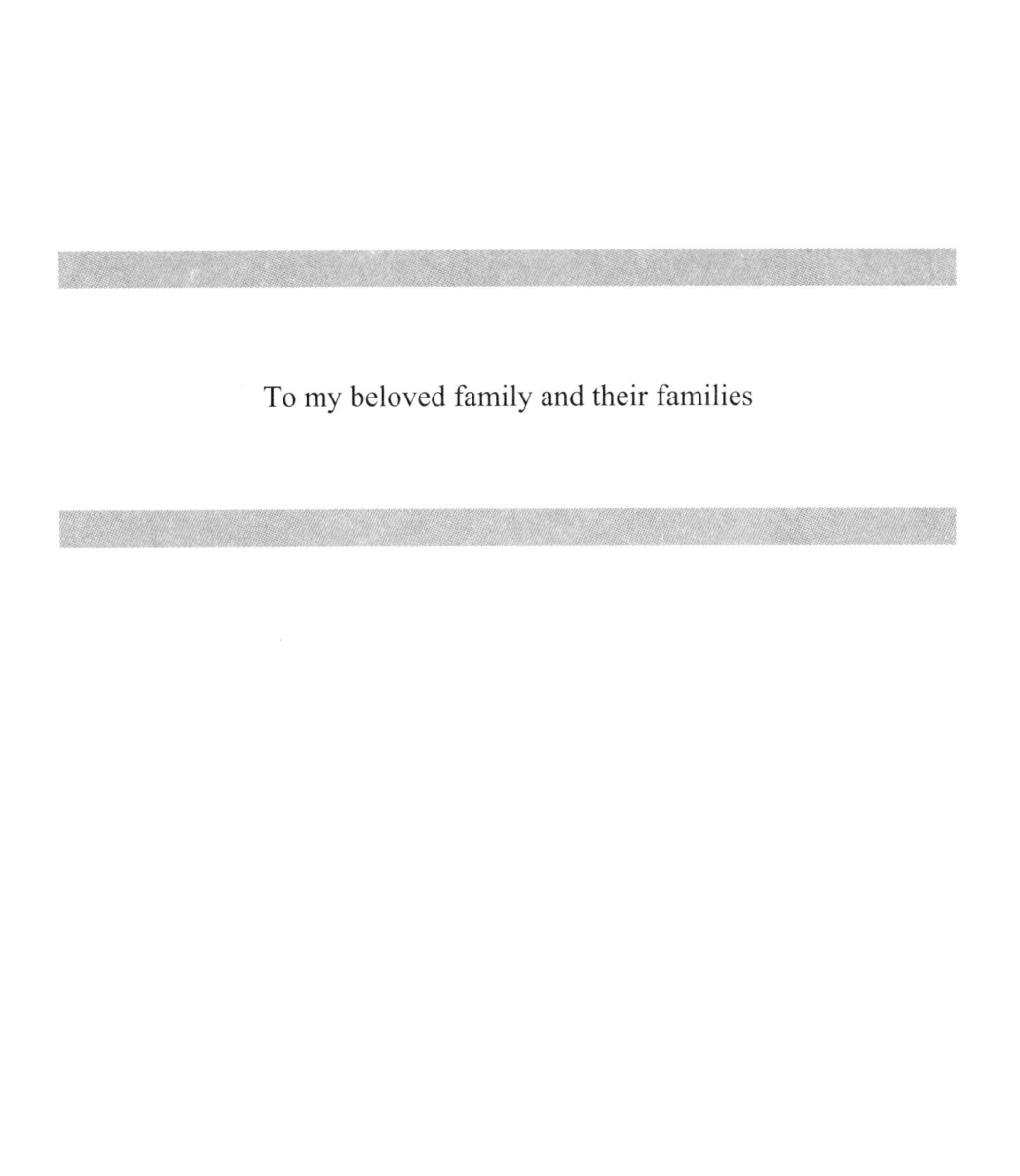

Contents

Dedication	7
Acknowledgement	11
Blessing	13
Omol	19
Cradle	30
Abisage	57
Nightmare	65
Jezebel	79
Deluge	92
Pedagogue	96
Tinga	105
Rose	114
Law School	124
Employee	148
Practitioner	170
Tanzania	184
Vision	195
Polygon	204
Disasters	221
Nuptials	241
Benevolence	250
Black Magic	266
Church	274
Politics	280
Liberation	304
Overseas	312

ACKNOWLEGDEMENT

I take this opportunity to thank the Almighty God for giving me good health and the wisdom to write this book. I thank all the people who made the publication of the book possible.I am indebted to my friend Mr. Francis A. Wodi, a retired Solicitor and Advocate, a retired Chief Superintendent of Police Force, Former Deputy General Manager and Legal Adviser /Company Secretary of Henkel Chemicals Nigeria Limited, Lagos, and Retired Legal Practitioner, for reading the manuscript in its entirety and making helpful suggestions.To Miss Linet Sophy Ombaka for typing and proofreading the manuscript. To the Director of college ministry, in the apiscopal Dioces of West Tennessee, an Anglican Priest ministering with small churches in Memphis area and adjunt Professor of religion at University of Memphis, Elder Willie Venter, the Senior Head Elder of Overtone Park S.D.A. Church in Memphis, Tennessee, and Nathaniel Nyagol, a Gospel Songs Evangelist in Kenya and USA for the words of encouragement which fired me to continue writing. To my nephew Philip Ogeya, my sons James and Ken for the valuable corrections they made. To my daughter Lydiah for the assistance she gave without which this project would not have materialized, and Everline for typing part of the manuscript and availing her computer and printer for the work.To Anthony and Lydia for provision of funds.

I am equally grateful to Hon. Sam Okello and Frasam Investments Ltd, home to Sahel Publishing, for working with me to avail topnotch editorial services and publishing this book. Lastly I'm indebted and indeed grateful to my entire family for standing by me while writing this book.

CHAPTER 1

BLESSING

The time is the first cock crow. My mother is in labor, expecting a child our family had been waiting five years for. Six years earlier my sister had been born. That was the beginning of the 2nd World War. The family had gone through famine and pestilence as a result of the war. The white man had arrived barely 30 years earlier. The need for education had not caught up in earnest among the Kavirondos (as the Luo were then called). Religious explorers, particularly from the Church Missionary Society (C.M.S), had opened up much of the Kavirondo area and our people had embraced their faith; they learnt to read to enable them to read the Bible. They also learnt to write. Our parents were not privy to the art of keeping dates as we do today. My sister Lewnida Choka's exact birth date could therefore not be ascertained. There being two major events occurring at the time (the war and the great famine), it helped determine her year of birth which was 1938. Our parents had no clocks or watches. Time was determined by the position of the sun during the day and the position of the moon, stars and cockcrow during the night.

At the second cockcrow, the spasms intensified. My father was not worried. He had been through this seven times before and he knew exactly what to do. He was thus not in a hurry to seek help. There were no trained nurses or midwives, but old women who were quite knowledgeable in the delivery of babies.

Ongoma, Omwala's wife, was a woman of few friends. She had refused to embrace religion and was deeply steeped in tradition. She liked my mother a lot as Mama would later admit. Whatever she lacked, Mama was always there for her. They bonded quite well.

At the third cockcrow my father quickly sought out Ongoma, who on realizing the reason for her early morning call, jumped from the traditional stool she was sitting on while warming herself—courtesy of a fire inside her hut—and made straight for our homestead.

During those days there were no lights because there was no electricity. There were no lamps because there was no kerosene. Light was provided by a burning log, tied grass or chaff of millet. It was still dark when Ongoma arrived. With the aid of a burning log, she proceeded to where my mother, Loice Mulure, lay and helped her deliver a healthy, bouncing baby boy. She tied the umbilical cord with a strand of a whisk obtained from a bull's tail, and cut it with a blade split from the stalk of corn (maize) or millet. It was a joyous moment for the whole family. The baby was then bathed in cold water to make it cry. If it didn't, the old woman knew straight away that something was wrong. But the hardest part, at least as far as my mother was concerned, was yet to come.

Traditionally, it was generally accepted that the father named the child. This was the reason my mother would get into trouble with my father. Naming of babies took four distinct patterns:

A baby was named after a deceased relative (ancestor) or the time it was born. For example, Otieno was a name given to a baby born at night—Atieno if it was a girl. Onyango and Anyango were named after those born in the morning respectively, and Odhiambo and Adhiambo were named after those born in the evening. Babies were also named after major events like war or famines or occurrences or even important persons. If a baby was born during a war, it would be named Olweny, or if born during famine it would be called Okech or Akech depending on the gender. Alternatively, it would be named after that particular famine. In Kenya, where I was born, we have persons named *Uhuru* meaning independence. We also have lots of Mandelas, Clintons, Reagans, Kenyattas, Nkurumas, Lumumbas and Obamas.

Having learned how to read, my mother read the Bible thoroughly. She recalled the past five years she had been in pain, waiting for this baby. She had prayed incessantly and God had answered her prayer. She likened herself to Hannah, the wife of Elkanah, whom she had read about in the Bible. Hannah was childless while her co-wife Penninah had children. Whenever Elkannah offered a sacrifice to God, he would give portions of the sacrifice to Penninah and each of her children as was the tradition. Hannah would receive only one portion for she had no children. Each time they went to sacrifice, Peninah taunted her and that made her cry. Hannah decided to pray that God would give her a child. God answered and she bore a child whom she named Samuel, meaning "asked of God." Like Hannah, Mother was determined to name her son Samuel. But my father realized that he had not named any of his children after his late father and he wasn't going to let this opportunity slip; so he told my mother off. He told her that the baby was going to be named Ohon, after his father. My mother reminded him of his Christian beliefs, one of which was the discarding of the traditional beliefs and taboos. It took a neighbor's intervention—and that of the well-wishers who had come to congratulate her—to resolve the sudden stalemate. By Solomonic wisdom, they managed to persuade them to compromise and name the baby Samuel Ohon. Both were happy with the names.

I was therefore born on the third cockcrow. The day, month or year I do not know because my parents were not literate enough to keep records. Our forefathers preserved information for generations by passing it down from father to son, but dates were never part of this scheme. Information passed down to me by my parents, together with my personal experiences, has been the source of information contained herein and the basis of this narration.

Through the same source I learned that I was the last born in a family of eight. My siblings were: Muhudhi, Okech, Sanya, Aduda, Okumu, Sijenyi and Choka. Sanya and Okumu died in infancy. The rest survived and left descendants. My father, Wanyanga, was the son of Ohon.

The following is my family tree up to the 12th generation:

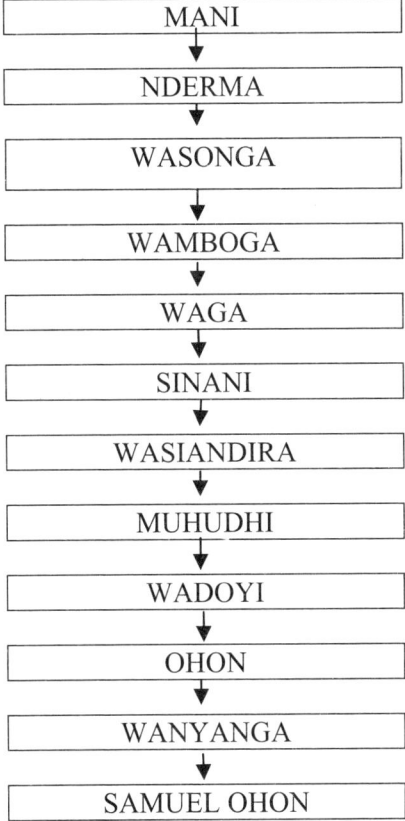

As was the practice then, my mother was kept indoors for four days. Had I been a baby girl, I would have been kept indoors for three days. Almost all the best food she ate during that time came from well-wishers who thronged the home with gifts of good food, particularly meat, green bananas, fish and chicken in adherence to tradition. Some brought pieces of old garments to cover the newborn and to protect it from the Gem cold, as children did not have clothes of their own.

If food had to be cooked for a mother of a newborn, it had to be done by someone who was post-menopausal. After menopause a woman was forbidden from having sexual relations with a man. Any woman engaging in sexual relations with a man and cooking for a mother who had just delivered was believed to bring bad omen to the baby and could lead to its death. So the choice of a cook was closely monitored by the elders.

The elders settled on Ongoma to be the cook. There were not many old women then of her age. She did her job well and I am a living testimony to that. Just as my birth was a bundle of joy to the whole family, so was my dedication in church—as I was told. Like all the babies during that era, I depended on my mother's breast milk. In fact, in my case, I'm told I extended this even after I was old enough to eat normal food. I could still demand to suckle and my mother gladly obliged. I later learned that she hated to offend me. Being the last born, as she was sure she wasn't going to get another baby, she wouldn't do anything to me that would hurt my feelings. So whenever I felt like suckling I simply made a little noise and I would be on her lap. It took the intervention of my father to stop that behavior. I actually feared my father from the day I saw him beat my sister. She had sneaked from home to attend a night dance in the neighborhood. How the old man knew defies my logic to date. But as my sister was sneaking back through the fence, there he was standing right before her. He got a hold of her and administered a few blows on her with his palm and said he wasn't done with her yet and would further sort her out at daybreak. My sister came into the hut where we were sleeping, shivering and knew that she had a date with a fixer. The following morning my father made good his promise. He got a hold of her, tied her with a rope to a post, brought four canes and did a job on her until she feigned passing out. My mother, on seeing that, ran to call the neighbors who persuaded him to stop beating the girl. From that day, I developed extreme fear of him and was frightened by his mere presence. Despite that I still loved him very much. As you can see, I was born of poor and semi-illiterate parents who had a large family to feed, clothe, provide healthcare for and educate. It was quite a task.

It was now 7:00 o'clock and my sister, Lewnida, had to go to school. James, who attended Lwanda Intermediate School, had already left home as early as 5:00 o'clock in order to arrive on time. My eldest sister, Pelesia, was already married. Absalom, who was my eldest brother, and Haggai, who was his follower, had cut short their education to look for jobs to help my parents run the home and were at their respective places of work. Absalom's wife, N'gon'ga, had travelled to Nakuru the previous evening to join him. That was the state of the home.

Ordinarily my mother would leave me under N'gong'a's care whenever she went out to attend to her many chores. But this day N'gon'ga was not available. My sister Lewnida and I were the only persons at home, but she too had to go to Maliera Primary School. My Mom and Dad had to work in the farm, faraway from home. They were not expected back until sundown. Short on practical options, my sister decided to take me with her to school. The year was 1952—as I would later learn. Arriving in school, she put me outside the door of a classroom and proceeded into one of her lessons. This would be my first day in school. My sister continued to take me along and placed me at the same spot every day. The classroom was a mud-walled structure with a grass-thatched roof. There were no shutters for doors and none for windows. A portion of the wall was painted black. This was where a barefooted teacher in a pair of shorts wrote using chalk. The medium of communication was the local dialect (sometimes called mother-tongue). I don't know whether it was by design or mere coincidence that from the spot where my sister placed me I was able to see and follow proceeding inside the classroom. If they were learning alphabets, I learned it with them. Whatever they were learning, be it numbers, mother-tongue or writing, I learned it too. I later learnt that the classroom, in front of which I was left by my sister, was actually standard one (1st Grade). During those days, there were no books to write on by the lower graders. They wrote on slates, at least they called them so, using specially made pieces of graphite.

Not to be left out, I borrowed my sister's slate and she got me some graphite to help me learn. Whenever the class was given a test, I did the same from outside the class and handed in my slate to be marked along with the others. At first the teacher was reluctant to accept my slate. But impressed with my first attempt, where I scored an A, he readily accepted it for the subsequent tests. I did my 1st and 2nd grade (standard 1 and 2) outside the classroom with the full connivance of the class teachers. During those days pupils went to school strictly on payment of a prescribed school fees. Some guy reported me to the school management that I was learning without paying fees. My father was summoned and ordered to pay for the previous two years before I could be allowed into third grade. Since my father pleaded with them to be allowed to start paying my fees from 3rd grade, they reluctantly agreed. In 1954, I was admitted into the classroom for the first time, but in 3rd grade and not 1st grade. I was not a genius, but I was a straight A kind of a kid. I worked hard for whatever grade I obtained.

Since I was in standard 3, in just another year I would be sitting a national examination—Common Entrance Examination (C.E.E), one of the many exams the colonialists introduced and used as hurdles to check the growing number of native elites. I had mastered the vowels, which was vital when writing in mother-tongue. I knew the alphabets; I could sing them in either direction, forward or backward. I could also count numbers and had knowledge of addition and subtraction. I had started picking up English words which would be the medium of instruction from standard five. In std. 3 we tackled Nature Study, Reading, Writing and Arithmetic. I was well prepared for these because I had a resident tutor in the person of my sister. The two years I would later take in class 3 and 4 proved to be eventful indeed. One particular event proved helpful in determining my age. But I'll get to it later.

The privilage of having something to cover my body with ended the moment I jumped out of my mother's lap. It was retrogression. I came out of my mother's womb nude, but with the help of well-wishers I got garments to cover my body. Henceforth I was going to move around completely naked, until I could go to school in my uniform. Kids those days had no clothes because parents could not afford them. There were no social functions for them, except church. While going there, kids wore their father's old shirts, which acted as shorts as well. At home they made a piece of cloth the size of one's palm or big enough to cover the private parts only. That piece of cloth was fastened to a string which was tied around the waist. The rest of the body was bare, including the buttocks (the rump). That was the standard attire for both genders, come rain or sunshine; but you know what…that did not bother me at all. My father was a Christian who frequented church and had lots of old shirts and even an old raincoat. Those became my clothes for going to church.

I was not spared retrogression in the bedroom as well. Leaving my mother's lap meant leaving the comfort of her bed too. Destination was the floor—with my father's old raincoat acting as a bed, a mattress, a blanket and sheets, all in one. But I was mistaken to think my bedding was the worst. A playmate from the neighborhood stopped me on my tracks the moment I started complaining loudly about the matter. He told me in my face that I was lucky I had an old raincoat. He said he was sleeping on a cow's hide with giant holes made by rats. He was sleeping on one part and covering himself with the other. I shut up and never complained about my bedding again. But again, because of bed-wetting I did not use that coat for long. Within a short time it was all torn up; then instead of getting a blanket I was given a sack. The idea was to put the sack on the floor, slip into it and sleep. From that day on I slept in the sack and cannot remember how long I used it. And since bed-wetting did not do much damage to it, it looked like eternity.

My luck to move out of the sack came with a misfortune. The so called house, the one in which I slept, was a grass-thatched structure with mud walls. The floor was not cemented, just ordinary ground plastered with cowdung. We slept on that floor with roaches, rats, all kinds of ants and sometimes even snakes. Those were the good old days. One night as I was sleeping, something bit my eyelash. Since it was dark I did not know what it was. My mother, however, knew what it was not; she was sure it wasn't a snake. She explained that snakes do not come where cattle are. We shared the room with a couple of calves and heifers. Secondly, she explained that a snake bite is quiet distinguishable; it leaves a mark. Thirdly, and that almost made me pass out, I would be dead if it were a snake. She sought some ghee and smeared it all over the swollen lash. That night was my last in the sack. I graduated to mother's raincoat. I used it until I was in 4th grade, when my father finally decided to do something about it.

When the present and future generations read what my peers and I went through in those days, they should realize one thing. That the affluence and good life we later lived, which they will inherit, did not come down like manna from heaven; we worked hard for it through school and at our work places. It was the culmination of perseverance, diligence, dedication and determination. Anyone willing to succeed and prosper in life should emulate those attributes. As mankind develops technologically, competition becomes stiffer and stiffer by the day. Only the fittest will survive and prosper. Indeed, just like during our youth, when we had to contend with pestilence, famine and ignorance, the present generation has to contend with Ebola, HIV AIDS and other technological challenges. These require divine intervention. So let each of us seek divine intervention for in it lies our survival and salvation.

CHAPTER 2

OMOL

When I was born, my father—Nickolus Wanyanga Ohon—was fairly old, but he did not know how old he was or when he was born. All he could remember was that the white man came after he had been born. Records available in Government archives show that the first white missionaries arrived in Kenya toward the end of the 19th century. So my father put his date of birth at around 1896. He was old enough and took part in the 1st World War of 1914-1918. He told us horrifying stories of his experiences in the war. He was a no-nonsense guy who hardly laughed. A casual look at him depicted a guy who was always stressed but was focused on whatever he set his eyes on. He had no formal education, but he could read and write, courtesy of the missionaries and the war. He was a teetotaler and never smoked any kind of weed. He hated anybody who smoked cigarettes and other weeds or drank alcohol. He referred to them as dead people (deceased) whose funerals had not been announced. Whether you were his brother, cousin, friend or even his own child and you were engaged in any or both of the habits, he avoided your company like plague, and literally cut you out of his life. This would be the cause of a rift between him and my eldest brother, Absalom, who took to drinking alcohol and smoking cigarettes as soon as he landed a job.

One day I asked Father why he did not drink alcohol or smoke cigarettes or opium (bhang) or tobacco—like his many peers did.

Dad said, "Look here, my son, your grandfather used to drink a lot."

I shrugged. "So?"

"It's a long story."

And it was. He went on to tell me how Grandpa attended most drinking parties in the neighborhood. During those days, people had mastered the art of brewing traditional alcohol from maize, millet or sorghum. Maize, millet or sorghum was ground into flour, put into a pot, mixed with water to form dough and left for a couple of days to ferment. The fermented dough was then removed from the pot and roasted in an open pan and then spread on the ground to dry in the sun. The resultant stuff was called *mbare*. Millet or sorghum was soaked in water and left for a number of days to sprout. The resultant staff was called *thowi*. *Mbare* was then soaked in a big container; *thowi* was dried, grounded then added onto it and stirred until it resembled porridge. It was left for a couple of days to brew. The more *thowi* was added to it, the stronger the brew got. The brew was then put into a middle-sized pot and specially made reed stalks (*oseke*) placed into it for drinking. Only old men were allowed to drink this brew with *oseke*. Men sat on three-legged stools around the pot. Apart from *mbare,* there was another form of brew known as *otia*. The brewing of *otia* followed more or less the same process like *mbare* except, instead of roasting and drying the fermented dough, the dough was just spread in the sun to dry. After drying, the dough, which was like flour, was poured into the pot of boiling water and prepared like *ugali*. The stuff was removed from the pot and spread out to cool. It was then put into a pot mixed with water and *thowi* stirred until it blended like porridge. It was left for a number of days.

An old woman who wanted to drink came and sat at the foot of her brother-in-law, who occasionally handed over the oseke to her for a few sips. As the contents of the pot diminished, women were on hand with hot water to add into the pot. They knew exactly what quantity to add. Sometimes there were not enough *oseke* for everybody so people took turns drinking. One could drink with *oseke* and pass it on to the next person. This way, everybody drank until they were all full. Women were not allowed to take the hard stuff. Theirs was the diluted stuff left after the old men had taken their fill. The stuff left in the pot was mostly sediments of flour. They took hot water, poured it into the pot and poured the contents into a bag made from papyrus leaves. They squeezed the stuff into another pot and used a bowl made from a dried shell of a calabash fruit to draw it and drink. This stuff was not strong enough to make the women drunk. They were not supposed to get drunk anyway since, traditionally, that was a taboo. *Oseke,* on the other hand, had spongy gauze on one end to filter the sediments and this was the side dipped into the pot. Using one *oseke* for drinking by several people was not only inhygienic, but for the criminally-minded persons, they used it to poison others. How they did it I do not know. When I asked my father about this, he told me they retained poison in their mouths, pretended to be drinking and then passed the contaminated *oseke* to the victim. They then excused themselves, went out and cleaned up before they came back and resumed drinking. To me this was still wrought with danger to the culprit, but I did not want to engage my father in an argument over this since I was not going to win. So I asked him how my grandfather was killed with alcohol. He told me that during their era, people were few and lived not far from one another. Only a few years back they had been living in clustered villages to ward off marauding cattle rustlers.

My grandfather, Ohon, was a fierce man. In fact I'm told my father took some of his traits. As a result of this character, he had no time for grudgers, begrudgers and liars. Naturally, he made many enemies. Those days, during harvest, the old men asked their wives to brew the traditional stuff and slaughter a big cock. The old men would then invite their peers from the neighborhood for a treat. The peers would come, eat drink and make merry until the wee hours. This was rotated among the peers until everyone had invited everyone else. One day my grandfather was invited to one such treat. He willingly went as usual, but unknown to him, it was only a trap to get him. Physically, no one would dare challenge him and no amount of witchcraft could finish him because he was impervious to witchcraft. The only possible way to bring him down was to lure him into a trap and unsuspectingly snap life out of him. The enemy did what he had to do. Then my grandfather sent for his eldest son—my father.

He said, "I am dying because of my greed for alcohol!"

"Dying?"

He was. He directed my father to proclaim to all his children and descendants to refrain from the evil drink. Three days later, my grandfather was no more after he cursed alcohol and to date his descendants who have not heeded the warning have been ruined. Majority of them are dead; their deaths being directly connected to alcohol. The rest suffer from diminished responsibility and bipolar disorder. We have seen the power of a curse in our family.

My father was five six and medium-sized by African standards. He was black in complexion. His eyes were black too. He had hair all over his body and he was bow- legged. His head was bald but his face was heavily bearded. Like everybody else in his era, his toes had been infested with jiggers, but unlike his peers his feet were not deformed as a result. In my estimation, he may have weighed 180-190 pounds. He was always in very good health. The first time I saw him ailing, old age had caught up with him. During my youth, he was a good sprinter. I realized I could not out run him, so whenever I made a mistake I did not attempt to run because he would nip me on the run. His face showed signs of having been attacked by chicken pox, but it was a handsome face nevertheless. He also dressed smartly and was well-groomed. He shaved his bushy beard and combed the remaining hair on his head regularly. Though his peers liked bathing in the streams, he preferred bathing at home and this he did regularly. His six incisors had been removed, courtesy of a traditional practice that demanded this. The practice had its origin in an epidemic. A long time ago there was an outbreak of tetanus. Peoples' jaws were locked and many people died, not from tetanus, but from the pangs of starvation. Once the jaws were locked one could not eat. Somebody, therefore, came up with a brilliant idea: "What if we removed six of our lower teeth, couldn't we pass liquid food through the opening?" They experimented and it worked and so the practice stuck. In modern times, however, the practice has been discarded, perhaps due to improved medical knowledge. Apart from the six teeth, Father kept the rest until shortly before his death. He had partial loss of eyesight. Because of this, he came to lose his two front upper teeth too. It happened this way. One evening he was riding his bicycle when a boy, also riding but in the opposite direction, appeared suddenly. Father crashed into him (he could not see very well) and fell. Years later, he was requested by his grandson, Henry Ndukwe, to acompany him to his father-in-law's place. On the way, the bicycle slid and he fell. This time he lost his remaining front teeth. He retained his remaining teeth until he died.

Apart from meanness and stinginess, Father was a harsh person. He brooded no nonsense and hardly laughed. The best he could manage was a smile, which was evident on his face most of the time. There were many incidences I observed in him and many more he narrated or somebody narrated about him. At a District Commissioner's baraza meeting at the Chief's Camp, in Mutumbu, he caused the D.C. to abandon his meeting hastily when he beat a certain old man with a stick because he was saying something Father did not like. It was a near stampede as the Government officer took off, followed by his security detail, causing the meeting to end prematurely. The one incident I witnessed was at the funeral of an old man in our village. There was this old man who was mourning. Strangely, when he was within ear shot he said nice things about the deceased, but when he moved away he was all curses and name-calling. Someone tipped Father about it and he followed the old man as he moved toward the gate. Not knowing that he was being followed, he started cursing the deceased again. Father caught up with him and heard him too. Right there, Father administered a couple of blows on him and he took off. It was this temperament that made his peers fear and respect him.

One day I asked him why he did not get along with his brother and cousins. He was very blunt in his answer.

He said, "Son, I hate drunkards, liars and people who say one thing and do the opposite. This is my problem with most people. They testify falsely against others. I have a problem with that. They don't go to church; I have a problem with that. They go to bed with other men's wives; I have a problem with that. So when they come to me and start talking as if I don't know them I get worked up."

With that explanation, I never revisited that topic.

Father was a devout Seventh-day Adeventist. He participated, along with Silfano Ayayo Mijema, Musa Adongo, Mathayo Oduma and others, in bringing S.D.A. to Maliera in 1939, and he remained a staunch Adventist ever since. He was a church elder of Maliera and Malanga S.D.A. churches for many years and was loved by members he ministered to. He took part in the establishment of Maliera Primary School and for many years served in the school committee. As a Christian, he proved to be a prolific debator, a good arbitrator and an impartial judge. He was in the team that participated in the emancipation of our people from oppression. He was a minister, a family man, an arbitrator and a politician, all rolled in one. He loved his children dearly and strove to give them the best education possible. I am indebted to him for my education and good family. He was morally upright. He never flirted with any woman as long as he remained married. As children, our very existence is testimony to his faithfulness to Mother. Socially he was full of humor. Whenever he met his adoring grandchildren, their wives or his sisters-in-law, laughter and happiness abounded. He was not as industrious as my mother, but they both managed to feed, clothe and educate us. As he grew older, he did less and less physical tasks and stopped completely later in life.

Dad was taken ill for the first time in 1966. He was admitted at the Kaimosi Hospital through the efforts of my brother, James. He was treated and he recovered rapidly. In 1982 he got ill again and was admitted for one week at Siaya District Hospital, treated and discharged. In 1984 he was taken ill again and admitted at Siaya District Hospital. The doctor diagnosed that his heart was weak and was not pumping as it should have. However, he was treated and discharged again. In February 1985 he was admitted again in the same hospital with similar symptoms. He was put on medication and discharged. In April of the same year he had another attack, but this time he refused to be taken to the hospital.

He said, "Son, old age cannot be treated even in the best of hospitals with the best doctors, so just be strong as you have always been."

"And what's that supposed to mean, Father?" I asked.

"Just let me be!"

I pleaded with him severally to allow me to take him to the hospital; told him that I still needed him and could not manage if he died on me.

He said, "I know your step-brothers will be your biggest problem when I'm gone because they are like snakes in the grass. You will need to be careful when dealing with them."

"Father, what's the matter?" I asked.

"The biggest problem will be land, but I called the elders in your presence and divided my land and gave them their portion which they will have to share. The other portion I left for Joka Mulure (meaning my mother's children). It is enough if you add the parcels of land you bought. As I have already given Absalom his land, the present home is left for Haggai Okech's children, but I will not go to the hospital."

I sighed. "You won't?"

"No, son, not this time"

I did not press this hospital issue further. On 17th June 1985, his condition worsened and he sent for me once again. When I went he repeated the same things he told me about land. I asked him about Absalom's land, part of which he had allowed his brother Musa Achual to till.

He said, "Look here, I only allowed him to till, I did not give him ownership. In any case I could not give him ownership because it is no longer registered in my name, but that is not what I called you here for. I wanted to tell you that should anything happen to me, I want you to give me a decent burial. I don't want music other than Christian either at my funeral or in my homestead at any given time after I am gone. Do you understand?"

"Yes, I do," I said.

"Good," he said with finality.

And so on the 19th of June 1985 Father passed on. When talking to me about giving him a decent burial, he did not know that I had liaised with my sisters and agreed on how we were going to take care of the burial expenses. Although the burial was attended by a mammoth crowd, we gave him a decent send off. That was the end of the man who brought me into this world. A man I considered my greatest friend. The man who taught me a lot, particularly in politics. He was the man who helped me reconstruct our home and inspired me to take care of our dependants. *He was a man and a half.* I lived with my father longer than I lived with my mother. I knew his likes and dislikes, dos and don'ts, his food preferences; knew when he was angry and when he had been quarreled with by my step-mother.

When my step-mother kicked him out of her house, he moved into my mother's house where I would have long night sessions with him, talking until the wee hours. I visited him frequently because I knew he needed someone to talk to since my step-mother could not avail herself. Sometime we had sharp differences but since I had learned to be patient and tolerant, I maneuvered the ship to the dock without a problem. We would agree in the end and I would insist he pray for me before I parted. Most of the disagreements came about because of my step-mother. She would feed my father falsehoods and in an effort to give a proper perspective, an argument would ensue. My father held his ground and I clung to mine. All these quarrels, differences and disagreements ended well, with a prayer from father.

Father was an introvert. He must have had very few friends, in fact none that I know of. He lost track of his close relatives; he knew neither his maternal uncles' villages nor the name of even a single one of them. He did not know where his sister Abisage's daughters were married. People came home to see and talk to him, but I never saw him visiting his peers or anybody else. I would later in life strive to connect him to these relatives.

There were six things that gave Father gratification: the first was his marriage. Before he met and remarried my step-mother, he was distressed, withdrawn and disheartened. After the marriage, he changed. He became more responsive and jovial. It was as if he had undergone complete transformation.

The second thing was when my brother James got a scholarship to study in Burma. He was elated.

The third was when James returned after graduation. Dad could not hide his happiness. It was like a crowning achievement.

The fourth was my graduation - the first advocate in the family, in the village and in the whole tribe. This was a joyous moment for him but his happiness was overshadowed by the events of November, 1971.

The fifth was my election as Councillor for North Gem. The old man was all airs. It was as if North Gem had be handed to his own son!

The sixth one was my election as Chairman of Siaya County Council. That was satisfying; it partially healed the wounds in his heart.

There were three things I knew devastated him. The first was the death of my mother in 1958. It took him time to adjust and find his stride. Normalcy returned when he remarried. The second was the death of my eldest brother, Absalom Muhudhi, on 2nd December 1968. He was down but I am happy he was not out. The last was the death of my brother, James Helekia Sijenyi, his wife and child and my first born, Beatrice Florence Akinyi. My father almost died from shock. Strong as he had always been, he picked himself up and surprisingly lived another 14 years after that tragedy. That was my father—strong, resilient, loving and highly religious. He never uttered a word to betray his love for his second wife.

Father was born into a very poor family. During those days, wealth was measured in terms of heads of cattle one owned, the size of land one occupied, and the size of the family. The size of the family depended, to a large extent, on the number of wives one married. The more the wives, the more land one acquired, as wives were used to acquire land. My grandfather was poor so he didn't have enough wealth to marry other wives. In those days one had to have at least fifteen cattle in order to marry one wife, and so my father inherited that poverty from his father. Whatever little he got from the war he used to marry my mother. He was not what one would classify as hardworking, but my mother was. To prove that he was the man of the house, he had to strive to put food on the table. He worked in the goldmines of Sakwa and in the beaches of Lake Victoria as a fisherman. He even tried his hand on business. Donkeys were the closest we had to trailers and trains. There were no roads. With his donkey, he traversed the wild west of Kavirondo, trading in maize, millet, sesame (simsim), sorgum, fish, cassava and groundnuts. He would be away for weeks or even months but on his return we had enough on the table for a while. He abandoned his comfort and good living in order for us to eat, go to school and have some rags over our bodies. Not all fathers did that for their children. I knew of homes in the neighborhood where parents were mean and drank a lot; they are now desolate.

My older brothers and sisters were among the very first to go to school when missionaries started schools, but there were pitfalls and barriers. The only school around was Malanga, sponsored by the Church Missioonary Society. Our people had embraced Anglican Church faith, so our children had to attend their sponsored school. This was not going to be easy. There was a bully who waylaid those going to school, beat them up and scared most of the children from going. The irony was that he was being sponsored and encouraged by a few bad grapes from his tribe including the Chief and the Padre of C.M.S. Between 1920 and 1938 nobody from my tribe was able to go to learn because of this sponsored insecurity. A colonial chief and a colonial padre literally denied us education in our own country. Only a few of our children learned, but away from home. The intervention of Benjamin Misango, a young strong boy at the time, and from our tribe, did little to help matters. He decided one day to take on the bully one on one. He beat the bully and humiliated him so much that from that day anybody who accompanied Misango to school was safe. But that brought only a short reprieve. With the way now cleared of the bully, they hatched another plot to stop our people from school. The only intermediate school at the time—within walking distance—was Maseno, a C.M.S. school 25 kilometers away. To be able to join Maseno, one had to get recommendation from the padre in charge of the area one came from. In our case the padre was a tribalist, a sadist and a totalitarian of the first order. One also had to pass a national examination. Whenever our people passed the exams and were called to Maseno School, the padre deleted their names and put the names of boys from his tribe who did not pass. That was devastating. My father and others, like Musa Adongo, Sylfano Ayayo, Andrew Ochola, Mathayo Oduma and other elders said enough was enough. They put their heads together and decided that if the problem was the padre, the solution was to have padres of their own, under C.M.S. Sylfano Ayayo and Andrew Ochola were chosen to go for training. My father would later team up with other elders to push for religious, political and educational empowerment of our people. I am a living testimony of that struggle.

My mother, Loice Mulure (popularly known as OMOL), was the daughter of Okech and Aduda. Okech was from Karariw in the house of Karadier. Aduda was the daughter of Wamwayi, from the Usuha sub-tribe. In the early 1920s her eldest sister, Dursila Onjare, was married to one Robert Ogola Omune. The couple was blessed with the first son, Isaiah Omune. Dursila sought her sister Loice to come and babysit her son, Isaiah. My father saw this young, robust and beautiful girl and fell in love at first sight. The relationship would later blossom into a booming love and later marriage. My father did not know the date or year of their marriage, but given the information which I have been made privy to, the marriage of my mother to my father must have taken place around 1922. I now know that my eldest brother, Absalom Muhudhi, was born around 1923. My mother was hardworking and generous. Her magnanimity was so great that she could prepare a lot of food and go out to call those who were hungry to come and eat. Because of this, God ensured we had a meal all the time. In fact, I consider myself blessed because of her kind deeds. She loved all her children and provided for them equally—but she reserved special love for me. She worked hard to ensure all the kids went to school. She even had a room in her house for other relatives. She worked all the time in the farm, in the homestead and in the house. She was what one would call a workaholic.

She was a devoted Christian. First as C.M.S. member and later a Seventh-day Adventist. She was the pillar of our home. She was outgoing. Villagers loved her very much. She was the epitome of a good Christian. The church members called her "Omol pon gi roye" (an old cow at ease in the company of heifers). Indeed that is what she was. She could sing and dance the Christian melodies with the enthusiasm and vigor of a young teenager. She could not write but was able to read the Bible fluently. She rose to become a deaconess in the SDA church. Her homestead was open twenty four hours to everyone including lunatics and destitutes.

Years of hard work finally took a toll on her. She started ailing. During those days medical knowledge was still primitive. There was no technology for proper diagnosis of some illnesses. From my reading of medical journals and books these days, I have come to realize that Mother died of diabetes. Once or twice I watched her relapse into what I now know must have been a diabetic coma. On those occasions, she did pull out of it. If it happened when Father was around, he gave her something to eat or drink immediately—a ripe banana or *sugared* porridge. I don't know how, but Father had known how to reverse the coma and I bet he did not get that knowledge from any medical practitioner. It was sheer trial and error.

It was in 1958, 34 years after my parents' marriage, that Mother boarded a lorry, along with other church members, to be at a funeral in Uranga, Alego. She was in jovial mood, I was told. The journey was safe and did not take long. They alighted and made for the grave, singing. Prayers were said, then they were shown seats prepared for them. They took their seats, then singing started again while waiting on the hosts to serve them tea. Just as suddenly as it had always been, my mother, I was told, collapsed and as usual started growling. Father was not there because he did not make the trip. Nobody present knew what to do. She just growled and growled and when the growling stopped, she had just passed on, as simple as that. They did not even send her body to the hospital for postmortem. But again, what would that have achieved? She was dead. Postmortem was not going to resurrect her and no foul play was suspected. What upset me most was that I was not present when Mother was buried. Actually, three of her children were not present. Lewnida and I were in Tororo, Uganda. My other brother was in Tanganyika. My sister's husband, Wilson Abayo, was working for Uganda Cement Industries, in Tororo. He received the message of my mother's death and impending burial in good time for us to travel and attend the burial; but he withheld the information from us. Why he did that I did not know and I was too upset and young to ask. The fact was—my sister and I came to the funeral three weeks after the burial. That was when my troubles and tribulations began. For the few years I lived with Mom and Dad, not even once did I see them quarrel or observe Father chasing Mom around, wanting to beat her. Maybe they quarreled, but they tried to hide it from me. If they did, on this they succeeded.

Mother was a wonderful cook. Anything she touched turned delicious. As we were not endowed financially, our meals tended to be vegetarian. Be it Kenyan dishes like kales (sukuma wiki), cabbage, *muto, Osuga, Omboga or aboka*, once Mom was done with it, you would be licking your fingers forever. Occasionally we ate meat or fish or chicken, but only when there was a visitor for whom that food was prepared and the visitor was good enough to eat and leave some for us. During that time, cooking oil was ghee from cow milk. Salt was ash from burnt chaff from beans. There was no salt as we know it today. Sugar had just been introduced and there were certain homes where it was still detested. Rice and wheat flour were the preserve of the rich. Mom and Dad lived simple lives and that is why—from their meager resources—they were able to save to take us to school. I remember five of us sharing one foot of a chicken for a meal. We could feed a whole week on half a chicken. In the situation we were in, the only meal we were sure of was supper (evening meal); lunch was discretionary. If it was there we took it, if it was not there we did not fuss about it. Breakfast was out of the question. We never had one. As I said, Mom was a devoted Christian, a Seventh - day Adventist to boot. I recall that every Friday evening and Saturday evening at sunset the villagers gathered at our home to usher in and conclude the Sabbath. Mom and Dad took turns leading the gathering in short sermons after we had sung hymns of praise from the *Seventh-day Adventist Hymnal*. It is from this that I developed vast knowledge of hymns. Today I can sing half of the hymns in *Nya–Gendia*.

Whenever Mom went to a camp meeting, devotional gatherings or Sabbath visits, she brought me along. At first I thought it was because she was scared of leaving me alone at home. If that crossed her mind, it must have been a peripheral reason. The main reason, when I sit back and ponder, was because she wanted me to know God, love the church and be a useful future citizen. I remember one evening Mama took me to Malanga Church to hear a white pastor preach. It started raining heavily and at the end of the sermon the rain turned into a storm. The pastor was advised to drive away to the mission station where he was staying while the storm was still on. If he waited until it subsided, the road would be impassable.

As the pastor was going to pass right in front of our home, the church elder requested him to give my Mom and I a ride and drop us off in front of our gate and he obliged. The experience of being driven in a motor vehicle was overwhelming. I could not sit still because I was scared. I stood there all the time thinking the car was going to smash into the trees by the road. The weather did little to alleviate my fears. Every time there was a flash of lightning, followed by a roar of thunder, I thought the whole world, at least the world in my little mind, was coming to an end. The pastor's sermon about the world coming to an end by being crushed by a huge stone cast by an unforeseen hand added fire to my anxiety. A ten-minute-ride seemed like eternity. I was relieved when Mom told him to pull up to drop us off. I heard Mom utter something in the local dialect which sounded like thank you. He answered in broken local dialect. I was indeed surprised because I did not know a white man could utter a word in our local dialect; more so because when he preached he did it through an interpreter. When the door of the car was opened for her, Mom came out, jerked me out and whisked me onto her shoulder. In the middle of that storm we made it home safely. That evening as I was warming myself beside a cooking fire, I felt proud and elated. The following day I would boast to my pals about the ride. It turned out to be quite exciting.

•
———

I was not what one would call a healthy child. Because of the deep love my mother had for me, whenever I got sick she started crying and continued crying until Father came and took me to the local health facility, Malanga Dispensary. A modern health centre now stands at the site where the dispensary once stood, serving close to 10,000 people. At the local health facility I would be given an anti malaria injection and would be back within two hours playing with other kids as if nothing had happened. This became routine—my mother crying, my father rushing me to the hospital. I had lots of these malarial attacks. I owe my life to God who arranged for my father to be available whenever I had a bout. If it were not for my father's quick action, I wouldn't have survived. At the time my mother died, I had not stayed with her for long, because of my school days and her busy itinenary. Cumulatively, I can put the total number of years at five only. That is a very short time to know someone well.

The only commandment among the Ten Commandments God gave Moses, which has a positive promise, is the fifth:

> *Honor your father and your mother, so that you may live long in the land the Lord your God is giving you.* (Exodus 20:12, NIV)

I honoured my father and my mother and God kept His end of the bargain. If it were not for Him, I would not have survived those recurrent malarial attacks; I would not have survived the turmoil and tribulations of my youth; I would not have had the will and strength to overcome the many disasters the devil placed in my way. Many people die even from simple accidents, but God saw me through five serious vehicular accidents, some with only minor injuries. He kept me off my brother's car wherein I would have surely died. He loved me and had a mission for me. I hope I didn't disappoint Him since I lived the lifestyle of my mother, OMOL.

CHAPTER 3

CRADLE

I did very well when I learnt from outside the classroom. I had not been subjected to school rules and routines. Because I was naughty, school days were not going to be a bed of roses. It soon dawned on me that school was boring, teachers were very strict; they whipped people and there was nobody to complain to. I suddenly started hating school. One morning, as I was going to school, there was a bulldozer grading the road in front of our home. A couple of other boys who were also going to school and I started following the bulldozer as it cleared the road. It was beautiful to watch it move big chunks of soil and toss them aside. I had not seen a bulldozer all my life. By the time I remembered school, I was a couple of miles away from school. I did not go to school that day. The following day I feared going to school. I knew I would be whipped and that was the last thing I wanted. I left home as if I was going to school, but instead went and hid in a cassava plantation near the road, where I could see the children coming from school for lunch. On seeing them, I would come out of my hideout and head home as if I was coming from school. I did this for two days. On the third day someone leaked to my father that I had not been going to school. As I was approaching home from my simple hideout, I heard Father discussing me with Mama. I immediately sensed what awaited me at home—caning worse than the teacher's. I made a quick u- turn, dropped my bag and dashed into the bush. I realized that I was in deep trouble. I decided to go to my maternal uncle's home, which was some three kilometers away, and made it there by dusk.

My uncle, Oyath Okech, was illiterate. His son, Okech, was slightly older than me. His daughter and youngest son, Oyudo, were still toddlers. His wife was also illiterate. They loved my mother immensely. In fact, the first time my sister took me with her to school, Mom and Dad had gone to till the land given to them by Uncle Oyath. I stayed with my uncle for three days. Back home, my parents searched frantically for me. My uncle was disturbed and suspected that I must have run away after doing something silly. He decided to make inquiries. After confirming his suspicion, he came for me, persuaded me to accompany him to our home; that he would talk my parents into pardoning me.

I agreed to play ball.

But on the way I got suspicious that he was probably leading me into a lair. Since I was walking in front of him, I doubled my pace. Upon realizing this, he moved hastily toward me. I bolted, with him in hot pursuit. But it was not long before I ran out of steam. He threw a stick he had, which got entangled between my legs, and I fell. He got a hold of me and gave me a few bashes with the stick. He then frogmarched me to my home. It was unpleasant.

On arrival, Mother was happy and relieved that I had been found. Father, on the other hand, behaved as if he was not done with me. My uncle kept his part of the bargain and persuaded my parents not to punish me again because he had done it on the way when I tried to run. The following day Father took me to school and talked to the head teacher, who allowed me into class without further punishment. From this incident I learned a very important lesson. *Never run away from a wrong since the world has become a small village; the law will eventually catch up and you will face the very consequences you feared. Be obedient to the law and listen to your mother and father. Honour them and be blessed. If you don't you will not live long or prosper, but will wither like a flower does from loss of moisture.* Therefore, young folks, do what the Apostle Peter says: "Show proper respect to everyone: Love the brotherhood of believers, fear God, honour the king." 1 Peter 2:17

———

When I grew up under the watchful eye of Mom and Dad in the tiny village of Magunda, in Central Kavirondo, there were no set rules to be obeyed or disobeyed. As a lamb finds the teats of its mother, so was one supposed to learn the dos and don'ts by instinct. This caused a lot of confusion in my mind. I said to myself that this was going to be tough because I was scared of caning. I was going to have to be extra alert to survive. But I had one disadvantage. Being the last born in a home where older siblings were away from home, I did not have playmates. This affected me and shaped what my later life was going to be. If it was building a mad house, I had to come up with the design, the materials and do the building myself. I designed and built a mud storeyed building long before I set my eyes on a storeyed building. I designed and built a lorry pulling up to twelve trailers long before trailers were on our roads. I kept on playing and discovering things by myself. I would occasionally have playmate, but this was the exception rather than the rule. I continued this playfulness and innovation into my early school days. In school, playfulness was not about playing in the rain or with mud or even inventing, it was about soccer and I got soccer-mad. If it was possible to play soccer $^{24}/_7$ I would have done it. Let me bring you along.

It was break-time in school. In my estimation we were over 100 boys and girls and everybody was busy. Some ran around, some jumped ropes, others wrestled and most girls played netball—and their daily favorite: *hop step and jump*. I was attracted to a group playing soccer at the corner of the soccerfield. As I made my way to join them, I bumped into Omolo Mwalo. He behaved as if he was trying to shake off everybody. He had something in his hand which I had never seen. The thing looked like a small pail, but with compartments. It was about one foot tall and six inches in diameter. Each compartment looked like a bowl and there were three of them. I got curious. Omolo's father, Elon Mwalo, was one of the few educated guys in the village.

He was a veterinary officer at the Kabete Veterinary Research Station. He was a man of means, wealthy by local standards. His wife, Anyango, made sure everybody noticed their privilaged status by making sure Omolo came to school in good clothes and carried fancy things, like this strange object he was carrying.

Omolo made the corner. Other pupils could not see him, but I followed him as I was determined to know what this strange object was. I arrived just when he was dismantling the thing. I confirmed that the compartments were actually bowls carrying food. This explained why he was hiding from other pupils. He needed a hidden place where he could enjoy his food without interference. There I was, standing right behind him and there was nothing he could do about it. I noticed the first bowl contained roasted meat, which had been stewed. It looked and smelled delicious. The second bowl contained pastry (chapati), and the third contained things I had never seen. They looked like pellets or granules of grain; they were very many in the bowl and they were whitish in colour. To me they looked like the eggs of red ants. When I asked him what they were, he said, "Very nice food. Sweet and delicious. Father brought them from Nairobi the other day."

"Can I taste?"

"Sure."

He offered some, which I put in my mouth. Finding them unpalatable, I threw up, and he burst into laughter. I said to myself he should have offered me a piece of meat or even pastry instead. At least I knew what they were and how they tasted and besides, it had been quite a while since I last ate meat. But these red ant eggs, no way, I wasn't going to eat them.

The bell rang and we dashed to class. Omolo did not complete eating his meal. Perhaps he continued at lunch break from where he left off. It was several years later that I came to know what Omolo had offered me was rice, the staple food for more than ½ of the world's population, and the small pail with compartments was a metal lunch box. So my first encounter with rice was all drama. I felt pity for myself, but blamed it on the poverty which engulfed our home—where rice, meat, chicken, fish and other foods for the affluent were non-existent.

But my formative years were just beginning!

*

Wherever there is a group of young people, like in a school set up, things tend to happen—some strange, others expected, some unexpected and others boarder on the ridiculous. In school, 3rd graders and down wrote on slates using graphite. Both items were provided by the school. Out of the blue, some boys started eating the graphite. The habit spread to the girls and soon members of the 3rd, 2nd and 1st grade chewed their pens. Eventually, school management could not cope up with the rate at which pens were diminishing. On realizing where the pens were disappearing to, they stopped issuing any more graphite pens and as a result pens became scarce. If one had a full one he shared it with his/her desk mate, if the desk mate did not have any.

One day Ombore had a full graphite pen his father had bought him. At break-time he left it in his bag. On returning, he did not find it. He did not report the loss to the teacher as he should have. Instead he suspected that William, a boy who sat behind him, stole it. He accused William of having stolen and eaten his pen, an accusation William denied. Ombore was strong, robust and well-fed, but William was lean and a weakling. Ombore appeared to be older than him. The argument got intense, prompting Ombore to jump onto William, knocking him down. In the process William threw up on Ombore's face. He was pulled off William and the matter reported to the teacher. When the teacher investigated the matter, Ombore narrated what he thought might have happened. The teacher demanded to see the vomit and asked Ombore to look at it to see if there were traces of graphite in it. Ombore and those who were there could not see any trace of graphite in the vomit. The false accusations earned Ombore a few lashes of the cane and a two-week suspension.

That's what one gets for lying.

―――

A part from soccer, the next thing I loved in school was concerts. As parents were invited to school to review the progress of their children, teachers prepared for the occasion. There would be drills, treasure hunt, songs, concert and soccer. By body size, I was tiny. Drills, treasure hunts, songs and soccer were for seniors. I was going to miss out in the fun, but some Good Samaritans came to my rescue. Salome and Beldina came up with a concert idea that required the participation of a very small person. In fact only a midget would have begrudged me that chance. The play was in two parts and both required a *smally*.

Let me explain.

There was a bird, common in Central Kavirondo then, black with long feathers protruding backwards from the head. They are now extinct or maybe they migrated elsewhere. During those days children used to play with them. Whenever it perched on a tree nearby, children asked questions and we believed it answered. For instance one would ask the bird to show him/her the direction of his maternal uncle's home. The bird would, by turning its head, show the direction. On several occasions I personally talked to the bird. The other part of the play required something that could dance to a foreign and unrecognized language. Salome and Belidina felt I fitted those two roles perfectly. I was not a bird. I did not know how the bird could tell all the directions it was asked to point out. But as an actor I had to do something similar to the bird. So we rehearsed. When the time for the play came, they put me in a sack and tied my hands above my head. My hands would act as the bird's head. To the amazement of the congregation, I pointed all the directions accurately. But this was just an appetizer; the main course was still to come, in the form of the next play.

The next play was similar in attire. I was not to be recognized or seen. I was supposed to be a dancing bird. I can only share with you the words, unfortunately not the tune. The words of the song were—*TTTATITA TIA TINGLI TATIA* (The words mean nothing). As these words were sung, I motioned my hands in rhythm with the music. They were repeated for close to two minutes. There was a standing ovation when the concert ended. Although we performed this concert more than 55 years ago, whenever I meet Salome or Beldina we usually sing the song. God worked wonders for them by giving them long lives and good families.

*

And during those formative years, something happened that helped open my mind. There was this boy that was just slightly taller than me. He must have been older too. One day, without the slightest provocation, he gave me a thrashing and from that day I made sure I gave him space. I avoided his company and made sure I never crossed his way. One morning, before we entered class, I notice blood oozing from his mouth. He was distressed and appeared to be in pain. I thought he had been punched by a colleague. But other than me, nobody else appeared surprised, though blood was there for everyone to see. Curious, I asked what the hell was wrong with the boy. I was told nothing was wrong with him, someone had just pulled out one of his milk teeth.

What?

I got even more confused.

Milk teeth?

I thought human teeth were strong; you could not just pull them out with your bare hands. This was confusion I needed an explanation for. I asked the first teacher to come to class that morning. She was articulate in her explanation. She said, "Babies are born without teeth, but after a couple of months they grow teeth while still suckling. These are the milk teeth you heard about."

I nodded.

And suddenly I knew that between 7 and 9 babies lose their milk teeth. The teeth just loosen and drop off or are forcibly pulled out once they start getting loose. I also learned an important lesson that would help me in the future, because a few months later, in 1954, I also started losing my milk teeth.

It dawned on me that I could use this explanation to calculate the year I was born. Father told me that my grandfather, after whom I was named, died in the middle of the 2nd World War and since that war started in 1938, this placed my grandfather's death at 1940 or 1941. I could not have been named after him if he was alive. Only the names of deceased relatives qualified to be used for naming babies, according to Luo tradition. So counting backwards and using the greater of the three numbers I was given by the teacher, I fixed the year of my birth at 1945. The day and month of my birth was determined by other events. My father could remember, and my mother concurred, that I was born during the weeding of crops planted in the short rains. Short rains start around July and ended in November. So I put my month of birth at September because that was the peak month for weeding. The day was arbitrarily fixed to give the benefit of doubt to doubt itself. Like rocket science, my date of birth was worked out by calculations and was a figure arrived at after those calculations. I therefore adopted September 15, 1945, as my date of birth. Because of my experience, I made sure all my kids got birth certificates showing their actual dates of birth.

―――

Oloo was a great friend of mine. We were in the same class and our homes were in the same direction from school. He was a partial orphan. He lost his father when he was still young. The mother was hard working, but she walked with a limp—sometime even with the aid of a stick. This greatly affected her mobility, which resulted in her low productivity. But this did not dampen her spirits and resolve; she was able to raise Oloo and his siblings and even gave them education and clothes. Twice or thrice, he had accompanied me home for lunch. Lunch at home was *ugali*—a mixture of cassava and millet ground to form flour. The hard part was the grinding.

Here is how it was done.

Two stones were used…one large and a smaller one specially made for the purpose. The large one was placed in a slightly slanting position and firmly secured. The person who was to grind knelt behind the raised side of the big stone. A mixture of millet and cassava was then poured at the raised end of the stone and, using the small stone, she or he was able to crush the mixture by pressing the small stone over the mixture against the big stone, with a downward and upward movement. Flour was produced and *ugali* could then be cooked. One could not grind maize (*corn*) using this method because maize grains are bigger and cannot be crushed by the force of the small stone over the big one. The big stone measured an average two feet long, one foot wide and one foot high. The shape looked more oval than rectangular. The small stone was like the shape of a pie or cake (cylindrical and six inches in diameter).

Now back to Oloo.

One day he asked me to accompany him for a quick lunch. We dashed to his home and a surprise awaited me there. On the table was what looked like *ugali*, only that it was white. In my home—as was in every other home—*ugali* was placed on *ogudu*. *Ogudu* was like a small basket. Vegetables were cowpeas leaves (boo) served in *tawo* (a bowl made from clay). It was the preparation of that vegetable that made it delicious. It was like what my mother used to prepare for us. The only difference, I was told, was that Oloo's mother used real salt on it and this improved its quality and taste. We partook of the meal and went back to school. Like rice from Omolo, this was the first time I tasted *ugali* made from maize (corn). But unlike Omolo's rice, this stuff was tastier and sweeter and I enjoyed it. I later learned that an Asian businessman had installed a mill in Yala, six miles away, for grinding maize into flour. Maize meal later overtook cassava and millet flour in popularity and this has remained true till now. I never lost the grinding skills I acquired, though. If I were to be in a situation where I had to, I can still kneel between the grinding stone and produce flour with ease, only that it has to be millet, cassava or sorghum.

*

Up till now, I had never gone to a sleepover anywhere. A part from a few lunch visits, I had only been to school, church and camp meetings. I had very few friends and among the few I had was Marenya. Marenya had a brother called Ariepa and both were the sons of Elkana Nyageya. We were in school together and attended the same church. Elkana, together with his wife, were devoted Seventh-day Adventists. As we were coming from church one Saturday, Marenya and his brother asked that I spend the night at their home. My parents agreed and I proceeded to their home, which was a short distance from Maliera SDA Church. On the way we played all sorts of games—chasing grasshoppers, flying kites and even hide and seek. As it was a Sabbath Day, we were forbidden from engaging in more vigorous activities like playing soccer. We restricted ourselves to the lighter stuff.

Soon we were joined by other boys and the home became a beehive of activity and a bit overcrowded for my liking. We, however, continued to play after Marenya and Ariepa changed into their home clothes, which were a pair of torn pants (short trousers). It was late into the afternoon, but I had not had lunch. It was a standard practice at my home that lunch was prepared on Friday and served on Saturday. The other days, lunch was optional. We continued to play. Then first, Marenya disappeared. Then Ariepa. Moments later, Marenya was the first to return. When he returned, his chest and mouth was greasy. It was quiet visible since we had been playing on dust—rolling, wrestling and running around. Ariepa returned later and like Marenya he was greasy over the mouth and chest. There was no doubt that they had been away secretly eating. They were sneaked into the backroom and given food away from the rest of us. My guess was that it was something with soup. From the smell I settled on chicken. This looked very strange to me. How could the homeboys be sneaked into the backyard and given food in secret away from other kids playing in the same compound, including me, who Marenya had specifically asked to a sleepover? To be fair to the parents, maybe the food was not enough. But just where did they expect me, as their guest, to get food if they did not give it to me?

I had to make a quick decision. If I stayed here I would go without food until I went back home the following morning. I decided to call it quits and sneaked. It was late in the evening, but I made it back safely. I narrated the story to my mother who was sympathetic and quickly prepared a meal for me. I never accepted any invitation for a sleepover again. As for the Nyageyas, they never returned my visit. I believe they must have felt embarrassed.

Going to school was only for the fittest. One had to be fit and combative to be able to make it. First one had to contend with ferocious weather, then wild animals and night runners. But the most dangerous was fellow humans. For my 1st, 2nd, 3rd and 4th grades, I attended Maliera School. This was a Seventh-day Adventist-sponsored school. During this time primary and intermediate schools were run by churches. In Central Kavirondo, there were 3 churches that ran schools—the Roman Catholic Church, (RC), Church Missionary Society (CMS), and the Seventh-day Adventist Church (SDA). Maliera was only 1½ miles away from home. To get there before 6:00 o'clock in the morning was frightening, though. That was the time night runners were returning home from work and there were many. The leopards, hyenas and foxes were also returning to their dens. Stories abounded of kids molested by night runners or mauled by wild animals. One had to be extremely careful and brave.

But the worst that awaited school-going kids was a bunch of miscreants lying in wait to beat them up. These were school dropouts or those who didn't go to school at all. There were two gangs—one led by Sigwa Ogola and another by Agano Obanda. These gangs worked independently, but sometimes in agreement. They were at their most lethal when they teamed up. They armed themselves with machetes, whips, knives and sticks and blocked the northern and western routes to the school. Their motive was to beat the life out of you or chase you back to your home. They were kids like us, but very ruthless. To avoid being beaten, we formed groups. They could not face a group. If you were late and the group left you, you were in trouble. You could not reach school. I had an unexpected date with them one day. All the groups went before I was ready. When I finally made it to the road, I could not see my guys, yet I could not miss school because tests were going on. I decided to make contingency plans for survival on my way to school. I put three stones in my hand bag and put two in may pant pockets. I then hit the road running. I encountered the Sigwa Gang at their hideout. When they saw me coming, they jumped into my path and blocked it—four of them, each properly armed. I faced Sigwa, intending to push him out of my way, but instead he shoved me aside. At this moment, I reached for the stone in my right pocket and with quick reflex action thrust it onto his face. This sent him on his back. One colleague, who rushed in to pin me down, also received a smash with the stone, on the nasal region. The rest of the gang fled. Sigwa and his colleague followed them bleeding. That was the end of this group or any other group harassing me on the way to school.

*

Alumba Osese was another boy who stopped them from harassing him. One day Alumba decided to arm himself with a machete. He hid it inside the shirt at his back. As he approached the gang, they blocked his way, but he did not panic. He just walked on straight to them. Like me, he also singled out the leader, faced him and pulled out his machete. The whole gang just took to their heels with Alumba in hot pursuit, to the joy of some of us who were watching. Whenever they saw Alumba thereafter, they just dispersed. Some boys who were not strong enough to face them saw hell on their way to school. Many dropped out or went to learn elsewhere. The problem was—you could not report these harassments to your parents. If you did, you invited beating from them. They did not want to hear that you were beaten by a boy or boys your age. You can imagine how proud my father was when he heard how I single-handedly dealt with the rascals.

If an adult or adults were involved in the harassment and beatings, my parents would have promptly intervened, but a boy like me and of my age, no way. I was expected to defend myself by standing up to the boys, and if I beat them, like I did, my parents were elated. It was survival of the fittest. I knew of boys my age who never left the safety of their home to herd, play with other boys or even go to school. For that reason, many dropped out of school, took to peddling drugs and drinking alcohol, thereby ruining their lives.

*

My growth was not stunted at all. I ate the best food—milk, ghee, *ugali*, vegetables, fruits, puree (mixture of boiled beans and maize), porridge and occasionally meat, chicken and fish; so it was not about stunted growth. It must have been because of my size and my age. Kids went to school when they were very old. Some went to school in their late teens, some in the middle teens, most in the lower teens, but I went to school when I was six. All along I was a tiny thing among them and they treated me with kid gloves. It was therefore not surprising that when, in 1955, I was to do my Common Entrance Examination (CEE), my father refused. He knew I would pass. That's what bothered him. You see, this examination was done at the end of the 4th year. All primary schools were up to class 4 (4th year). In the fifth year one went to intermediate school. In the entire Central Kavirondo, there were only five of them. Competition to join intermediate school was fierce. At my age—and my body size—if I passed CEE and was admitted to any of the intermediate schools, how would I survive? Father, in his his wisdom, knew I would not survive, so he decided that I do CEE in 1956. I had no choice but to oblige. In any case, I was still too young; decisions had to be made for me and this was one of such decisions. Just to illustrate how tiny I was, if I sat on a bench, the desk was too high for me...I could not write. If I had my writing material on the desk and wanted to write, I had to stand up. I obeyed my father's decision and repeated 4th grade in 1956. The year would prove quiet boring to me because there was nothing new to learn.

Common Entrance Examination was only weeks away now. It was about 6:00 o'clock in the evening. We were leaving Mutumbu, where we had been playing soccer. We continued to shoot the ball back and forth with Otieno Oringo. The ball we were playing belonged to him. Otieno was not my age mate; he was much older than me. This practice of shooting ball back and forth along the road after a game ended in the field had been our usual way of dispersing to our respective homes. Otieno shot the ball to me and I returned it with a hot shot, but the wind deflected it into a thorny thicket where it could not be retrieved. Otieno, realizing the ball could not be retrieved, got worked up and lunged at me with a knife, ready to thrust it into my belly. I deflected the knife with a small stick I had in my hand. He lunged again, this time aiming the knife at my face. I blocked it with my left hand and received a hard blow on my left wrist and blood gushed out. That was when I realized I was in real danger. The guy was fuming; his eyes were bloodshot and he was coming at me again. *I must do something fast*, I thought.

I realized I had very few options. He was lethally armed, I was not. He had drawn the first blood, I had not. He was older and bigger, I was younger and smaller. I did not wait for him to come at me full throttle. I decided to rush at him as if I was going to hit him with the small stick I had in my hand. This threw him off-guard and enabled me to use what I had practiced and perfected—kicking. I put my foot between his legs and smashed his balls so hard that he had to grasp them in pain. That gave me a chance to get an upper cut with my right fist on his chin, which sent him sprawling on his back. Moving fast, I hit his hand which had the knife and the knife dropped. I then started working on him with the piece of stick I had until the stick was smashed to pieces. Seeing blood gushing from my hand made me even more ferocious. He ran, trying to escape into a nearby home where I followed him and dragged him from a house with kicks and blows. He ran to yet another home, this time apparently seeking refuge. He got in and hid under a bed. The home belonged to my cousin and his wife was the only one home then. In terms of relationship, the woman's husband was closer to me in blood than Otieno.

At this juncture, Otieno was also bleeding from the nose and mouth, but my bleeding was more serious as it was caused by a sharp object. I was covered all over in blood. The woman stood at the door of her hut, and on seeing me asked, "Otieno, why is this dog beating you!"

Huh? My cousin's wife calling me a dog? I got so mad by this remark that I threatened to set fire on her hut if Otieno did not come out. Meanwhile word spread in the village that I was going to kill Otieno. Word reached his father, who after arming himself with a stick, rushed to where we were. Someone tipped my father who also came armed with a stick. The village elder, who was the person responsible for keeping peace, also arrived. They converged at my cousin's home as if it was pre-arranged. On being told that Otieno cut me with a knife—and seeing me covered in blood—Otieno's father called out his son from under the bed and started beating him as he frog-marched him back home. Father took me to the dispensary where I was stitched and treated. I did C.E.E. with a bandaged hand and in pain.

I passed Common Entrance Examination well and started looking for a school to do class 5. I had chosen Maranda Intermediate, in Sakwa, and Nyagoko Intermediate School, in Asembo, both in Central Kavirondo.

As for Otieno, since he was also learning at Maliera, he feared going back to school and that marked the end of his education. He lived to become a good artisan. He was a good carpenter and repaired bicycles too—skills he handed over to his sons.

*

Away from school, during those formative years, I would be back home and immediately embark on the usual routine—playing. I tried all kinds of games to keep me, not only busy, but entertained. One day I started to play with beans. Beans had been harvested. They were lying in heaps on the yard and had not been threshed. The work of harvesting beans was not a man's job. Women harvested beans, dried them, threshed them and even removed chaff from them. Our beans had not undergone this process. As part of my playing, I took the pods one by one, opened them up, looking for big beans. Once I identified the big ones, I put them together. A thought ran through my mind that I should further separate the beans which had been threshed to come up with real big ones. I reasoned in my small mind that the very big ones were the ones that could fit in my nostrils. I tried a couple of times to fit them into my nostrils but most of them were smaller.

As I tried further I found two that could fit. I put them aside. I then decided to look for some that could fit into my ears. I was lucky. I got these faster and pushed them into each ear and listened to determine if I could hear the songs of the birds around. I could not. Next I pushed each into my nostrils to see if I could breathe. I found out I could breathe alright, but through my mouth. I had difficulty breathing through my nose. When I eventually had to take them out, I had no difficulty removing the ones in my ears. But when I tried to remove the ones in my nostrils, I realized I was in real trouble. As I dipped a finger into my nose to remove the bean, my finger only managed to push it farther and farther in. I tried the other side, the result was the same. By this time the beans were lodged right inside my nostrils and were on the verge of dropping into the larynx. I got worried and suddenly realized I was going to die. I started crying, but stopped when I realized that crying pushed the beans farther inside. I had to do something, otherwise I would die. Since I was alone at home, I walked out in the hope that I would meet someone who could help me. I made sure I walked stiff—with the least movement of my head.

I walked into our neighbor's home but there was nobody. The same was true of the second and the third homes I went to. I lost hope. I knew if I had to live, I had to get help as soon as possible. I decided to return home and hoped that one of my mother's many guests might pop in and find me. As I was walking back, I saw my father walking towards me.

"Where have you been?" he roared.

"The bean, Father!"

"The what?"

"My nose!"

Father immediately realized the grave danger I was in. And usually this kind of escapism would have resulted in thorough thrashing, but this time Father took me on his shoulder and sent me to the hospital. A nurse at the hospital had no difficulty removing the beans. With the aid of pincers it was done in seconds. I brightened up and with a wide grin jumped off the bed and thanked the nurse. Without him I do not know how long it would have taken before one or both beans dropped into my larynx. Father and I made it back home. By the time Mama returned home, and having listened to Father narrate what had happened, she warned me against such crap, after which she prepared me a sumptuous meal. I never put beans or any other object in my ear or nostrils again. I learned a lesson I will never forget.

*

Those days children my age had no toys or other play implements. One had to create his or her own toys. In my case the situation was even worse because I had no playmates. My age mates in the neigbourhood had criminal mentalities and I did not want to associate with them. Whenever I tried, I discovered they were either doing something silly or were inclined to put me in trouble with my parents.

Besides, I was a poor eater. Unlike other boys in other homes who were many and scrambled for the little food available, our home was awash with food and I was alone most of the time. I had all the food I needed, so I did not learn the technique of eating fast—a technique which some of my friends had perfected. As a result of my mother's hard work, there was plenty of food in our home, which my parents did not know what to do with. This prompted Father to go to Mombasa to look for his brother, Moses Achual, who had not been home in many years. Some people even feared he had died. Moses was my father's only brother.

He was married and at the time had 4 sons—Ohon, Okoth, Mijema and Ouma. Moses came with his wife, Dorina Odiaga, and the four sons, and all of them lived in our home for a while. It was during this time that I learned I could not match the speed with which my mates ate. When maize cobs were cooked, Ohon and Okoth each beat me three to one. The same was true when sweet potatoes, bananas or even cassava was cooked. It was also during this time that Father perfected the art of thriftiness. When chicken was on the menu, Father served the five of us one foot of a chicken. The four toes of the chicken were served to four of us. One toe to each of us and the stick (leg) was always preserved for Ohon since he was older than all of us. In the middle was *ugali* on a small basket and chicken and soup in a bowl. There were no plates or dishes. And since there were no chairs, Father, who ate with us, sat on a traditional stool. The rest of us (children) sat on the floor in a circle. Women were not supposed to eat with men, so Dorina, Mama and the daughters ate in the kitchen. A traditional stool was curved from a tree trunk and there were only a handful in one home. Those were the chairs of the day. The foot of the chicken was served to us halfway through the meal. We were urged to eat just a little and save part of a chicken's toe for a later meal. If you did not save, you were not served any part of the chicken, which would be the chicken entails or head or neck. You would eat your *ugali* with chicken soup only. Children could only eat chicken head, feet, chicken entails or neck. Men ate the back, liver, gizzard and any other part. These three, women were forbidden from eating. So women could eat any other parts of the chicken except the preserve of the men and the children. I considered this not thriftiness, but meanness.

This was a period I had difficulty with eating speed. My sister Lewnida was married into a home where folks followed traditional eating habits. When I first visited her, I found a big contrast with what went on at our home. Unlike our home, the homestead was big and up to four families lived there. There was a hut built in the middle of the home. Each family was supposed to cook for men, including the boys, and bring food to the central hut. Sometimes there would be enough *ugali* if the accompanying dish was vegetables, but if it was fish or meat, the speed was doubled. I could not cope with the team during my first meal with them. The way to eat was to pinch a small piece of *ugali* from the basket, dip it into soup in the common small pot and put the soaked *ugali* into the mouth. In a normal situation, one would munch *ugali* and whatever was with it. This turned out to be the mistake I made. By the time I swallowed my first pinch, my colleagues were on their fifth. I learned later that after dipping *ugali* into the soup and putting it into their mouths, they never munched. They swallowed the stuff straight, and just went for another pinch. Given the number of those taking the meal and the size of *ugali*, I was able to pinch *ugali* only three times. Here the ratio was 5:1. If it were not for my sister's husband, Wilson Abayo, I could not have had a meal to write home about. He ordered my sister to prepare food for me to eat alone because I did not have enough.

Moses and his family lived with us for about one year, then he built his own homestead. He moved out because his wife Dorina and my mother were not getting along. I would not like to speculate why they never got along. I was still too young to understand what was going on, but she used to shout and say words to my mother, some of which were unprintable. Three months into his new home, he lost Mijema—and a month or two later, Ouma died, both from bouts of untreated malaria. I was a constant victim of malaria myself. Signs I saw on the two boys before they died were signs I used to have when I had malaria. They were never taken to the hospital. Dorina got hysterical on the death of her second son. She believed my mother bewitched her sons and she got loud about it. This really upset my father and mother and they stopped helping her with provisions. Since they could not survive on their own, they decided to move back to Mombasa, much to the relief of my parents. It would be close to twenty years before I heard about them again.

My father's cold stinginess and thriftiness was a contrast to my mother's magnanimity and free-giving. The two needed each other as a check and balance. My father to check on my mother's free giving not to get extreme, which could make us give out everything and starve. My mother to check on Father's stinginess, which if left unchecked could compromise our biblical belief that God blesses a giving hand. The two were a perfect match. No wonder they never quarreled. The fusion of these two distinct characters would shape and mould me into what I would be in future—a free careful giver. A giver who would not let his people and dependants starve because he gave out everything; one who would not turn away someone in dire need of help if he could be able to assist even halfway.

In Africa—when it turns moonless dark—there are lots of activities. This is the time crickets begin chirping and fireflies, in their thousands, emit incessant glow to illuminate the surface. Mosquitoes are not to be outdone either. They leave their day-time hideouts in swarms to attack human settlements across the land. Some of them are deadly as they carry malarial parasites, which account for close to half the deaths in Africa. There are no lights as electricity is unheard of ... no TV or computers. No cell phones, flashy Ipads or even land lines. This *was* the Africa of the day—wild and dangerous. Let me use *present tense* to demonstrate this point:

At night danger looms in every corner or thicket. Supper is served early, at least when the sun is still up. Who can eat with his body covered with mosquitoes? Even those preparing food need light to do so and what better light is there than sunshine? This is the time wild animals are on the prowl. Leopards hunt singly, but give the one with cubs a wide berth; it is dangerous. Hyenas hunt in groups at night. They might threaten, provoke or intimidate you when you encounter them, but stand upright facing them; don't panic and don't run, for if you do they will eat you up on their strides. The snakes, which could not move around during the day because of heat are out looking for food. Beware when walking along that small path; you may step on a puff adder's head. Many snake species in Africa are deadly. Porcupines and foxes are out there too. The hippos can just cut you into half. These are the patrons of an African night. But all these are not as feared and as awesome as the annoying night runner.

The origin of night-running is unknown. In the part of the country where I come from, night runners have been around since time immemorial, terrorizing the populace and sometimes being caught and killed. The practice caused migrations. If one was a night runner who at some point had been caught in the act and his or her identity exposed, he or she, with their families, often migrated to different parts of the country where they were not known. More often than not, they lived secluded lives away from people. Research is needed to determine whether the act was inherited or acquired. Folklore has it that a woman married into a night-running family could be taught, if she accepted to be a night runner. They also believed they could do certain things to trigger a night runner's condition before he or she went out to do the act. These, they say, included making him or her balloon and pass gas uncontrollably. It was like a convulsive sickness—once it was triggered one had to go out to run and do mischief before the convulsions could stop.

Again let me use the *present tense*.

The night runner's day begins at dusk. Once the sun goes down you will, if around him, see him change. He starts being withdrawn, talks less and less and fumes and becomes agitated. The body balloons and passes gas uncontrollably. When these signs are noticed, the time is ripe for him to go out and let off that steam. He does this in style—kicking doors, pouring soil into people's bedrooms, running around, sometimes nude, and even beating children. Night runners are a societal nuisance. They don't kill or maim, but they scare you to death. Some people are known to have lost their power to speak after being scared by a night runner. They have the power to domesticate fierce wild animals like leopards, hyenas, crocodiles, hippos or even snakes. They use them in their night activities. How they do this I can't comprehend. They roam the homes across the village. Sometimes they waylay people along the roads and paths that traverse the village. They know each other very well. If there are two or more in an area, they agree on their operational zones. You won't find one in another's zone. They don't attack adults, but they beat up kids.

Sometimes adults in a home lie in wait and catch them. When this occurs, they are supposed to be released before dawn to protect their identity. Nobody is allowed to reveal a night runner's identity. He may be a prominent member of the village, a church elder or even a respected village elder. If he is revealed, he or she would be thoroughly embarrassed. You are not to kill him when caught. This would be murder, and besides, your home would become desolate. I have personally seen this happen. A church leader one night went with her husband night running to a neighbouring homestead. They were ambushed and caught, but the husband managed to wriggle himself free by sheer force and escaped. They got hold of the wife and drove five inch nails into her skull. They carried her up to the gate of her homestead and dumped her there. She died a few hours later. The home where she was caught is now desolate. Everybody died, a guy even killed his own brother, and a daughter committed suicide for no apparent reason.

If the people who caught a night runner released him and did not reveal his identity, the night runner would give them a gift. The gift would take the form of cattle or any smaller livestock if the night runner was not well to do. He would be friendly to them permanently and would not harass them again.

A night runner's life is tough. He runs the risk of embarrassment because he never can tell when the urge and symptoms will appear. It may be when he or she is at a place of work or on visitation. Once the symptoms appear, he must go out and release the steam. They also run the risk of being caught and exposed or even killed. But by comparison those are not as tough and soul-searching as looking for a wife or husband. They cannot just marry or be married into any home. They try to marry from or be married into night-running homes. If that happens, the couple married will thrive and be blessed with many and good-looking offspring. If, on the other hand, the night runner cannot find a night runner and marries a non-night runner, that marriage will not survive. Once a non-night runner discovers that his wife or husband is a night runner, she will run away from him or he will chase her away. Night-running is a good ground for divorce in a court of law.

My first encounter with a night runner, or what looked like one, was at my homestead. There was a full moon and I was sleeping in my brother's hut. The moon was very bright since there were no overcast clouds. In my sleep I had a sound like the gongs of a bell in the background. As I continued to sleep, these continued in intensity. Suddenly I was awakened by a strong urge to answer a call of nature. I jumped from the bed and made it to the door. What I thought was a dream was actually happening. I opened the door and got out and discovered that the sound was within the compound, but I had not seen the source. The sound started moving in my direction. The hair on my head shot up and the urge to answer that call dissipated. I wondered if I was going to die. My heart threatened to stop and my terror was indescribable. My palm became moist and cold. I tried to shout but was so frightened that I managed only a string of strange sounds.

My father's homestead, like the homes built during that era, was 60 yards long and 50 yards wide. It was tightly fenced with euphorbia and had one narrow gate, a yard wide. Logs were erected vertically on the gate to keep out night runners and other predators. My parents' hut was about forty yards away from the hut I was sleeping in. It appeared they were sound asleep. If Father were awake, this sound would have sent him scurrying to confront whatever it was. There was dead silence in his hut. The sound was coming my way. I was standing in front of the door petrified. *Will I scream or will I bolt back to the hut?* I was sure it had seen me, whatever it was; it was just 10 yards away from me, in some tall grasses in front of the hut. I was convinced it would attack me whatever I did. I decided neither to scream nor run back to the hut. I decided to stand next to a pole supporting the verandah, on the shadowy side. This hut was fourteen feet long and twelve feet wide, with a verandah 3 feet wide running its entire length. The verandah was supported by four poles, acting as pillars. These poles were about eight inches in diameter and six feet high. The roof was grass-thatched and the walls were mud-plastered. The pillar's shadow was big enough to completely cover me when I hid behind it. That was where I took temporary refuge.

Emerging from the grass was a huge animal that looked like a cat. On the neck someone had tied a bell. That accounted for the gong gong sound I was hearing. I saw it with clarity. Yes, it was a big cat with a bell tied around its neck. I got more terrified. Several questions ran through my mind. Could this be a leopard? Who the hell *belled* it and how? A leopard is a predatory feline common in Africa. It is fierce and pounces on, and breaks the neck of its prey. It has been known to attack even human beings. The fact that I was seeing a leopard with a bell on the neck at close range was disturbing. I stood like a zombie, terrified. The urge to scream intensified but for what use? It would devour me in seconds if I did. My father would not have a chance to rescue me. The thing can be fast. I saw what a similar one did to our dog—Ometho. The poor dog did not even have a chance to squeak. Here I was, watching it as it strode by. I realized it scared me stiff when it had just breezed past my location, squeezed itself between the gate poles and gong gong it went away.

But I was wrong to think my nightmare was over. As the gong gong faded, I thought I had a cluck from behind the hut, in front of which I was standing. I was pretty sure this was a person calling something. It was the kind of sound you would make when calling chicken. This made me even more terrified. I returned to the hut shaking all over and was awake the remainder of the night. The first thing I did in the morning was to inform Father what I had seen. He was the one who made me understand what was happening. He said night runners tamed wild animals for their night-running activities. This particular leopard must have been with a night runner who was not able to get into the homestead, but the leopard did. For a brief moment, the night runner was separated from his cat. Father also explained the cluck sound I heard. This he said must have been made by the night runner, a call Father interpreted to mean the night runner was asking the leopard to join him. A night runner's preoccupation was to instill maximum fear in his victim. The animals they domesticated didn't attack humans; they only used them to frighten people. The animals would most likely protect them from attacks by other wild animals. This particular night runner had succeeded in his mission—instilling maximum fear in me.

But we are not done with the African night yet.

A night in the village was a day of activity. After supper, teenagers walked around looking for parties. Partying among the youth was widespread, particularly over the weekends and during holidays. Girls and boys engaged in this practice. Youth of both sexes, from Christian homes, socialized by organizing retreats, camporees and crusades. They also organized these meetings at the home of a bereaved colleague to sing and console them. Their singing and concerts drove the youth into the church in droves. But when I was growing up, there were no parties and no Christian gatherings for the youth, except in church on Sabbath or at camp meetings. So boys and girls retired early to bed. Boys slept in their grandfather's hut or their older brother's hut, where they were taught how to grow into manhood. Girls slept either in their granny's or an old woman's hut, where they were taught feminine stuff.

In our home, story-telling was the preserve of Ng'onga, my elder brother's wife. She was good and would leave you spellbound with every story. In the village, during this time, most of the people were awake by two o'clock in the morning. Those going on a journey hit the road; those going to till and cultivate the land were in their fields. This was the time those who kept quails went out to trap them. That was when the night runners also had a field day. Such was the village night, tense, frightening and exciting. Things have, however, changed since electricity; TV, computers and cell phones are now available even in the remotest parts. Old night activities are being forced out. A night runner, in particular, is an endangered species. Two o'clock tilling is also out. People no longer wake up early to make their journey as communication is eased by buses, trains and planes. And good parents tend to have a firm grip on their kids, keeping them away from the scourge of night activities. They can be allowed to console the bereaved, but under the watchful eye of a parent. They organize youth meetings, crusades and camporees but an older person's presence is conspicuous. They are left no room to behave silly.

The nights are left for rascals and miscreants. They roam about in gangs on the roads and in the villages with one purpose—to beat and rob their victims. They are heavily armed with daggers and machetes and sometimes even bows and arrows. They would not spare even a night runner if they bumped into one during their mission. So let's just say that like the old days, an African night in the village is still wrought with danger. Let me give a final example to nail this angle.

It was nine o'clock in the night. We took supper three hours earlier, but I had been out in the yard chasing fireflies. I got tired and went to my brother's hut where my sister Lewnida, my brother's wife, Selina Ayier, and I slept. Selina was the first to see it and screamed. Everybody in the home was alarmed. An adult rushed there to see what it was that had scared Selina. Selina was a tough rural woman. Before marrying my brother, she had been toughened by years of herding her father's cattle. It was because of her bravery that, young as we were, we were comfortable sleeping in that hut with her. My sister and I trusted in her ability to protect us. But this night Selina is yelling hysterically and nobody knows why. Omoro is the first to arrive at the door. Omoro was from Nyalgunga—Alego. He stayed with us—one of the many who benefited from my mother's generosity. He was a student at Maliera. Nyalgunga was twenty miles away, so he could not learn and go to his home every day. He arrived ahead of my father, but was cautioned by Selina not to enter the hut. Standing at the door, and with the aid of a lamp, he saw and drew everybody's attention to it. Coiled in the frame of the hut was a big black snake, flashing its tongue menacingly. Omoro was a strongly built man. He was in his mid-teens but too big for his age. Besides, he was fearless. Teaming up with my father, the two could ward off anything. Omoro fetched the machete he always used in clearing the garden for tilling. He had sharpened it for the following day's use. Armed with it, he returned to confront the serpent. The thing was huge. My father was standing outside the hut. This was his son's hut and tradition didn't allow him to enter the hut, particularly as was the case here, when the son was married and his wife used the hut. Omoro's presence at this hour was God-sent.

Amid shouts of leave it, leave it, Omoro dashed into the hut and in seconds pulled the dead snake from the hut. The thing was even bigger than I thought. It was 8 feet long and about three inches thick—very black. Father said it was black mamba and on further scrutiny confirmed it was pregnant. He said only a few days earlier he had bumped into another one like it, only that it was swifter and not clumsy like the one Omoro had just killed. He attributed the clumsiness to the fact that it was pregnant. Omoro had severed her head with one blow of the machete. The head was completely detached from the body. That night a big fire was lit inside the hut. We put cow dung in the fire to goad away any more snakes and went to sleep.

―――

Nobody in our home during this time took alcohol. I had seen people drunk but had not seen alcohol or how it was made. Stories were told of people who got so drunk and were eaten by hyenas on the way. I did not like that, but I was curious to see alcohol, what it was, how it looked like, and more so how it was made. On occasions when I was with them, some of my mates advanced a theory that alcohol was fermented fruit juice. To ferment, they said, all you needed was fruit juice in a container, which you then buried in the soil for four days. I was determined to experiment and brew my own using this process. Lemons and oranges were plenty in our home, so getting juice was not going to be a problem. The problem was going to be how to get a container. The containers around were too big. If I had juice in them, I would not be able to dig a hole deep enough to cover it. I therefore needed a small container. Under my mother's bed was an old basket which contained an assortment of items. I pulled the basket from under the bed and removed the contents—item by item. Halfway through the process, I came across an old bottle. It was a green bottle with a glassy cork of the same color. The cork had grooves at one end and was rectangular shaped at the other end. The grooved end was screwed into the mouth of the bottle, to close it up. I unscrewed the cock, cleaned the bottle and poured a mixture of lemon and orange juice into it. I added a little sugar and corked it, then dug a hole and buried it there.

On the fourth day I retrieved the bottle to taste my brew. I tried to unscrew the cork, but the cork failed to open. I remembered vividly that when I first opened the bottle I had unscrewed it in an anti-clockwise fashion and it had opened. This was exactly how I was doing it now, but it failed to open. I was on the verge of giving up when a thought crossed my mind. What if I took a stone and hit the cork anti-clockwise. That way, I reasoned, it would open and I would quickly straighten up the bottle to prevent the brew from pouring out. Yes, this was what I was going to do. I took a small stone, lay the bottle horizontally and hit the cork once--hard. Nothing happened. Twice...nothing happened. When I hit the cork a third time, the cork broke loose from the bottle and hit my face between my eyes, missing my left eye by a mere centimeter. Blood gushed from the wound and I was temporarily blinded. My screams brought my mother running towards me. I was in a thicket at the fence of the homestead. When my mother arrived, I was already covered in blood. She was relieved, she admitted later, when she discovered I had not been bitten by a snake. She cleaned me up, then sought my father, who rushed me to the hospital.

In childhood many things happened that at that age you took for granted and didn't think much about. But when the thing you didn't take seriously nearly landed you in jail then you woke up to the reality and magnitude of the matter at hand. Then you said, "Oh why did I do it?"

One day as I was herding goats behind Mutumbu Primary School, in the desolate home of Mzee Atina, I entered his dilapidated and deserted house. He must have vacated that home a couple of years earlier. The roof of the house had caved in and the walls were falling apart. It was an ideal place to hide something because nobody would bother to look. While inside, I noticed something that looked like a box and was instantly attracted to it. *A box in a desolate home? This can't be!* On closer look, I saw it was a carton full of textbooks. The side of the carton towards the wall was eaten by ants. As I stood there—wondering who might have put those books there—my cousin, Congo, emerged from nowhere and, clearing his voice to alert me that I had company, he said, "Hey, what are those?"

"Come closer," I said.

"What are they?"

I gave him a stern look. "I said come closer!"

He came, pulled the carton from the anthill which was forming and announced loudly, as if I had not known, "They are Mutumbu books!"

I told him we should inform the older people so they could return them to school. It was at that point that he branded me stupid. He said I was stupid to think of returning the books just like that. He wanted us to detain the books and demand compensation for finding them. That sounded good enough for me. If I could make a few bucks for finding the books, that was okay with me. He said since I was the one who found them I had a right to keep them until he sorted out the compensation issue. I told him I could not carry the books because I had goats to look after. He said he would take care of that. I further told him my father would cane me if he saw me with the books. He said he would wait until night, then bring the books to my home, where they would stay until compensation was negotiated. We parted ways, leaving the books where I found them.

Midday—the following day—askaris came to our home with Congo tied with a rope. It was a Saturday and I had gone out with the goats. I was told Congo took them to the spot he had hidden the books in our home and they collected them. Before they left, they instructed my father to come with me to Ndere Chief's Baraza. When I returned, I heard what had happened and got really upset. I seethed with anger when father arrived and demanded the truth. I told him what I knew and he appeared to agree with my explanation. He knew I could not have stolen those books. After all, the books were for classes other than my class. I was also told that after receiving a few lashes, Congo started talking to save his skin. He told them I was with him at the desolated house. He admitted hiding those books there and kept watch during the day to see who was going there. The askaris (Policemen), however, allowed him to return home when his father asked them to, promising to produce him at Ndere Chief's Baraza the following Monday.

On Monday, Father and I went to Ndere. Congo was not there, but his father was. Asked why his son was absent, he said he woke up in the morning and found him gone. The idea of being punished for an offence I did not commit haunted me. That weekend I could not sleep. I kept having hallucinations and nightmares, seeing myself being whipped or being led to prison. Sometimes I could shout in the middle of the night, waking up everybody in the room. But the hard part had yet to come.

That Monday, the Chief was not in a hurry to hear our case. The more he kept me waiting the more I suffered psychological torment. Thirsty and hungry, we waited. Finally at six o'clock we were called in and asked to explain what had happened. I could not. I just cried. My father intervened and told them what I told him happened. Congo's father told them what Congo told him happened, which contained a bit of incrimination of himself and a bit of incrimination of me. Father, who knew I could not have stolen the books, defended me vehemently as Congo's father defended his son. It turned out to be a vexing duel between Congo's father and my father. The chief and his elders exonerated me from the theft and the charge of handling stolen property because they realized I never handled those books at any time. They returned a verdict of guilty on Congo in his absence, arguing that what he told the askaris and his father, and his decision to jump bail, were strong enough reasons to conclude he was guilty. The askaris were asked to look for him. Since he never returned home, they didn't arrest him.

As I said earlier, my bedding comprised my parents' rain coats and a sack. I had no blanket, no sheet, no mattress, no pillow and no bed. These were luxuries enjoyed only by the rich. We were not wealthy. In my fourth grade Father decided to reward me with a bed after a sterling performance in third grade end-year examinations. Beds were made locally with trees to form bed frames. Ropes were tied on the frames by experts to form a flat. Those ropes were made from a certain type of local grass (osinde). The beds were uncomfortable to sleep on unless they had a cushion. Cushions were two sacks filled with grass and knitted together to form a mattress. Father bought me the bed. I made the mattress myself. That night was to be my first night to sleep on a bed. Father also gave an old blanket to top it up. What a joy!

I soon discovered that this bed was not going to be as comfortable as I thought. Within weeks there was an army of bed bugs in every joint and knot in the bed. They literally feasted on my blood. I could no longer enjoy my sleep. To kill them I had to squeeze them between my thumbs one by one, but this had very little effect. When I complained about them, my mother brought boiled water and poured on every crevice and knot of the bed and killed all of them. This provided me a short reprieve as the bugs invaded again. My mother then made a routine of flushing them out every month and this regimen worked.

———

Ibrahim Mujema was my nephew. His home and mine stood a short distance apart. Our parents were Christians—his going to Maliera Church and mine to Malanga Church. This Saturday, as I did not go to church with my parents, I decided to play with him in his home. Luckily he and his two kid brothers were home; they too did not go to church. When I went in, I found them cooking chicken. They were in such a hurry that I asked them what was going on. They said they did not want their parents to return from church and find them cooking chicken. I realized their parents did not give them the chicken…they must have stolen it. Mijema was older than me. He was bigger, maturer and knew what he was doing. His parents arrived before the chicken was ready. What a frantic effort it was to hide the chicken. In their hurry to hide the pan, they put it on *njendambewa* (the rat's path), or space between the roof and the wall. As it couldn't balance on *njendambewa*, it went tumbling outside, just as the parents were passing by. I knew the consequences would be grave on Mijema and his kid brothers and I bolted back to my home. I missed eating a stolen chicken by a whisker.

Two weeks earlier, it was Mijema and his two kid brothers cooking chicken. This Saturday my parents had gone to a distant church and I was alone at home when Ochol came purporting to have eggs—which he wanted us to fry. Ochol was also older than me. He and Mijema could be age mates. I was still young and manipulable. I had not got sufficient exposure to prepare me to handle manipulative criminals. I tended to trust all my play mates, not knowing that some of them could play safe but have ulterior motives. Ochol was one of them. He purported to have six eggs which he wanted to fry. I had to provide cooking oil, firewood, matches, flour and pans, both for frying eggs and making *ugali*. During those days hens laid eggs in granaries, and in our home we had two granaries, in one of which one of our hens was laying. As I entered our house to prepare the stuff, Ochol purported to return to his home to bring the eggs. Instead of going back to his home, he stealthily made his way into our granary where our hen was laying and took eight eggs, six of which he brought pretending he had come with from his home. We prepared the food and enjoyed the meal, then he went back to his home. I was naïve indeed. I believed my parents would not find out. I hid the pans, thinking they would not discover what had happened.

But as you entered the kitchen the aroma of heated ghee struck your nose like air freshener. There was nothing I could do to blow away the smell. Secondly, I had forgotten to put off the glowing fire. And thirdly, I had no time to wash the dishes before my parents came in. So hiding the pans wasn't going to help. Still, I believed I was safe. When Mama got into the kitchen, though, she was instantly suspicious. Smelling a strong aroma of ghee, her first stop was the ghee pot. Quite a bit of it had been used, she could tell. She knew the quantity she had left in the pot. Next thing was to find out what was cooked with her ghee. It didn't take long to find out. Under the bed, there was a frying pan and another pan used for making *ugali*. So it was not only her ghee, it was her flour too. From the frying pan she easily surmised that eggs were fried, which made her dash to the granary where her hen laid. All the eight eggs the hen had laid were gone. She had collected enough evidence to try and convict me even in a court of law. I had smelt a rat and was alert, but when I did not see her react, I relaxed. She went away for a couple of minutes and returned. Unknown to me, she had gone to brief my father, who was in a neighbour's home. She came back with Father, but left him by the gate, as if they were watching what I would do—and had agreed how to counter it.

As soon as she returned, she demanded to know where her hen's eggs were. As she attempted to catch me, I slithered away and bolted for the gate, not knowing that Father was waiting there. She pretended to run after me, but was running immobile, like a runner warming up for a race. On reaching the gate, Father nabbed me. He reached out for the cane he had prepared for that purpose. Believe me, I sang. I had to tell them everything including where I hid the egg shells. It was when they saw the shells that I knew Ochol only brought six eggs and went with two. He duped me into believing the eggs he brought were his, yet he stole ours and made it seem like I was the guy who stole them. Father led me to Ochol's home and demanded to know why he came to steal eggs from our home. He denied any wrongdoing. When asked why his chest was oily, he could not answer. Meanwhile I was seething. He had played with my brain to make me look bad and stupid before my parents. He was going to see me. Big or small, he was going to find out the stuff I was made of. I was punished for being stupid, not for stealing. My parents knew I did not steal.

When I met Ochol the following day, it was war. Old and big as he was, he could not match my fury. I was as furious as a wounded buffalo. My fury was aroused even more when I remembered how one day he came where I was herding goats and for no apparent reason beat and killed somebody's chicken and forced me to carry it for him; that he would come for it later. I left the chicken at the gate but he never came for it and I believe dogs helped themselves to it. Our fighting became a daily routine whenever and wherever we met until our parents intervened and called a truce. He never joked with me again. He later took to a life of crime.

A few months after my incident with him, he stole from somebody else who followed his footsteps up to his home. When confronted, he slipped through the person and ran away. Shortly thereafter, we heard shouts from the direction of his uncle Ongoro's desolate house which was not very far from our home. I ran there and found him being lowered down from the roof of the house unconscious. Someone saw him enter the vacated house with a rope in hand and alerted people who rushed there and saved him from hanging himself. A few days later, he disappeared from home and was never seen again.

Grazing fields were few and scattered and in all of them danger loomed. There would be boys waiting to beat you up or some brutes or sadists waiting to harm you. It was survival of the fittest. One day as I grazed in one of the fields with Steven Odongo, two boys emerged from a maize plantation. The elder one was called Kiche and was carrying a small stick. Its size was between a small stick and a cane. It was, however, as long as a cane. Kiche was with his brother, Godia. Whenever they appeared we smelled trouble. Odongo knew this and beat a hasty retreat. He led his cattle away. He was hearding Reuben Kwasu's cattle and I was left alone. I was not going to run because that was not my nature. Father had told me that only cowards ran when confronted with trouble. But taking on two boys—one clearly bigger and older—was going to be a tall order. The bigger one approached and demanded that I leave immediately. I refused and he started beating me with his stick. I got hold of the stick and wrestled him to the ground. His brother came to his rescue with another stick. He beat me at the back several times until I released my hold on Kiche and stood to confront him. He ran away. Meanwhile, Kiche picked up his stick and started beating me again. I used the same technique I had used earlier to subdue him. Again his brother came and belaboured my back with a stick. He again ran away when I confronted him. A woman who was watching the scenario from across the river shouted and threatened that she was going to call their mother, Anne Muguna. When they heard this, they left me. I had bruises all over my back but Kiche had a bleeding gum from a head-butt. There were many such unprovoked fights, but I was battle-hardened and faced them head-on.

Fighting among herders themselves was very rare, though; what was common was wrestling. This was just a sport. When we were not playing soccer, we were either wrestling or playing high-jump. In the process of herding, a part from peer fights, there were many troubles encountered by the herdsboy. We were in trouble when a cow was on heat. All the bulls in the neighbourhood converged and fought for supremacy. Whichever bull beat the others had the cow.

Brutes and sadists were also around, people whose main concern was to harm you. One could go to an anthill, dig it to expose the ants—particularly the male ones. He would then come and chase you until he caught you. Then led you to the anthill, removed your clothes, and held you tight as the ants bit you. This was what Agutu Nyariany did to me one day. He alleged that I left the goats to wander into his shamba. This was false; he just wanted to enjoy hurting me.

Among the problems herders had to contend with was the weather. It was bad when it was dry and the sun was on you directly, but it was even worse when you were caught up in a storm. One day as I was herding three miles away from home, it started raining. There had been no sign of any significant overcast, but there it was, rain. I thought it was going to be light and would subside quickly. This was not to be. This light rain developed into a thunderstorm. I had nowhere to shelter because homesteads were faraway. I was by the riverside and was the only one herding at that time. I tried to shelter under a tree, but moved away and stood in the open space, when I remembered a story my father told me once. He said one was likely to be struck by lightning if one took shelter under a tree. The cattle I had were driven a mile away by the strong winds. The storm lasted a very long time. It might have been an hour or so before it ended. It took me close to half an hour to locate the cattle. By the time I got them, my father had already come for me. He said when they saw how heavy the storm was, they prayed for me, but they also banked on the fact that perhaps I took shelter in one of the homes close to the grazing area. I told him the storm came unexpectedly and did not give me a chance to drive the cattle home. Father brought me a warm coat, so I removed the drenched clothes and slid into a warm *kabuti*. He took over and drove the cattle home, with me in tow. Mama was waiting for me with a calabash of hot porridge, which I drank by the fireplace.

As herdsboys we also developed some bad habits. This came as a result of peer influence. We picked up these habits from older boys. We could induce bulls to fight. This was done in three ways. One, when there was a female on heat they were going to compete for. In this case, all we needed to do was bring all the bulls together and lead the cow to them. That was the spark needed to start a fire. The other way was to take a tick which had sucked blood properly and had a bulging tummy, drain blood from the tick into some grass and lead two bulls there. A smell of blood would trigger a fight. The third way was just to coerce two bulls to fight. This habit was bad because sometimes one bull killed another and the loss was devastating.

The other bad habit was that of taking ripe maize from someone's shamba for roasting without his or her permission. The habit was tolerated so long as it was strictly for roasting while herding. This habit has since been abandoned. Today if you take somebody's ripe maize it would be theft and you could, if caught, be charged in a court of law. The same rule applied to ripe bananas, which herders could eat so long as they were herding. Since grazing fields have diminished due to overpopulation, folks no longer keep large herds of cattle. They restrict themselves to one or two cows for milk, but these they tether while grazing. For the same reason, farmland has also diminished. You can hardly find a plantation of bananas, where one can find ripe bananas and help himself to. Everybody now has his land where no one can send cattle to graze.

*

Speaking of hobbies, there were hobbies that were not connected to herding. Fighting itself was a hobby that many boys engaged in. There were roadside fights, which were actually "macho" type. After a good meal, one would walk onto a road. He would, without any provocation, start fighting a boy he met of his age or size. If he was overpowered, he would be thrashed. The other boys would just stand there cheering. They would cheer whoever was winning despite the fact that the winning boy wasn't from their village. Such were the hobbies of the tough old boys.

There was also "peke" playing. This was a hobby to some and a means of livelihood to others. It was a game played with money, real money. A small hole, one inch in diameter and one inch deep, was drilled into the ground. Six steps away from the hole, a line was marked. An agreement was reached between the two contestants on the denomination of the money to be used. Only coins could be used though. The denominations to be used were a cent, five cents and ten cents. Once the denomination was agreed, it was time to determine who played first. One of them tossed the coin towards the hole while standing at the six-step line. Then the next contestant did the same. If any of them was lucky to toss the coin into the hole, he automatically played first. The contestant whose coin was nearest to the hole played next. The next thing to be determined was how many cents to play. If two cents was agreed on, then each contestant would contribute two cents and hand them to the first person to toss. He would take all the agreed upon coins and toss them into the hole. The coins that dropped into the hole were his. The next player would pick up the coins which did not enter the hole and toss. He too would take only what entered the hole. The exercise would be repeated until all the agreed upon coins were tossed into the hole. If the first player tossed and all the coins dropped into the hole, he would take all the coins and the exercise to determine who plays first would commence again.

The money I used to by my first shirt and pair of shorts I got from this source. I saved up to Kenya Shillings fifteen (15/=). That was a lot of money. The disadvantage of *peke* was that once you got hooked to it, you wanted to play it all the time. Those who got deep into it dropped out of school. Boys who were really good at it saved close to Kenya Shillings one hundred (Kshs 100/=). Those days if you had Kshs 100/= you were considered rich. That was enough to pay dowry, which was what many boys targeted then.

One day I did not go to school. Auka Mugwa came to play *peke* with me. I was not in a very good mood that day. I cannot recollect what had depressed me, but I was really down. We sneaked into some thicket across the road that passed in front of our home. We hid there, made ourselves a playground and started playing. At first Auka was lucky. He scored on every move he made. He had taken almost all the coins I had. That was just not my day. I gave out the last coin I had and it was my move. I scored that move, and another and another. Lady luck was smiling on me and it was Auka's turn to worry. He was down to his last cents and the move was mine. I tossed all the coins into the hole. As I bent to pick them up, he hit me so hard on the back of my head that I fell face-down onto the hole. If his desire was to get me out of the way, pick up the money and run, he failed. My body covered the hole. I got up and engaged him in a vicious fight. We fought until he couldn't take it anymore and ran away. I collected the money and went back home—with a full pocket.

Every fight I was involved in I came out the victor—until I met Ogada. He and another boy I provoked on the road were the two that I can remember beat me properly. The good thing those days was that once you beat someone your fame spread and this instilled fear in other boys. Wherever you went boys feared you. This explained why it took Sigwa and his team some time before they waylaid and challenged me to a fight.

From the day I was thrashed by Ogada, I gave way whenever he passed by. He announced to everybody who dared to listen that he beat me. This embarrassed me a lot. Granted he beat me, but why broadcast to all and sundry? I was relieved when he dropped out of school. At least I was spared the bragging and embarrassment that he kept humiliating me with.

Such was my childhood. Survival of the fittest!

CHAPTER 4

ABISAGE

Maliera SDA Primary School, where I did classes one to four, had no class five. During those days, classes one to four were primary and classes five to eight were intermediate. Maliera did not have an intermediate school as intermediate schools were few and scattered, and were run by credible churches. However, any pupil could join any intermediate school regardless of his/her religious affiliation.

As one sat the Common Entrance Examination (C.E.E.) one chose the intermediate school to attend. When I did CEE, my choices were Maranda, in Sakwa, and Nyagoko, in Asembo. Maranda was 25 miles away from home and Nyagoko was 30 miles away. It was December 1956, after I had done my CEE and schools had closed for Christmas holidays, when Oloo Ogam and I set off to go and find out if I had been admitted to Nyagoko or Maranda. Oloo came from Sakwa and knew the way to Nyagoko and Maranda. He came all the way from Sakwa in search of a primary school to attend. Being a Seventh-day Adventist, he could only learn in an SDA-sponsored school; that was the religious policy. The nearest such school for him was Maliera. He stayed with us and my mother provided his needs through schooling days.

Although I was barely eleven, we had to walk 25 or so miles. There were no buses and no roads. Bicycles were considered the preserve of the rich. In our entire village, only Maganda had one. He protected it and looked after it as one would protect a wife. He could not give it to anybody, least of all a teenager who would carry a small boy on it. In any case, Oloo Ogam could not ride, so any bicycle available was of no use to us. We set off at the third cock crow carrying *nyoyo* (a mixture of maize and beans). This delicacy was easy to carry on a journey. Thirst would be quenched by asking for water from any of the many homesteads scattered along sections of the route we were going to take.

The plan was to go to Oloo Ogam's home, spend the night there, then go to Nyagoko the next day and to Maranda the second day. Oloo Ogam was in his mid teens, robust and had made this journey several times. He knew it was going to be tough on me, given my age, but he hid that fact from me. The idea that someone from my home was going to visit his was exciting to him and his parents. The journey took us through the jungle and wild animal tracks. By midday I was tired; my legs were heavy and my body was bathed in sweat. As I had lost water through sweat, I felt very thirsty. Oloo noticed this and we called at the next homestead to ask for water. Luckily, we found an old woman and sought her help. She seemed perplexed by our request. It was as if we had sought water from a stone. "Where have you come from?" she asked.

"Gem," we said.

"Gem?"

We nodded.

She gave us another strange look to ensure we had no sinister intentions, then offered us stools to sit on and went into a hut. She reemerged with two gourds, one in each hand. We were surprised to discover that the gourds contained porridge and not water. She told us that in that area it was very hard to find water; the only source of water was 15 miles away. Milk and porridge, though, were plentiful. We thanked the old lady and hit the road again.

It was dusk when we finally arrived at Mzee Ogam's homestead. My feet were sore and swollen. I was dusty and extremely exhausted. Oloo's parents were very pleased to see me, the son of a magnanimous mother who was taking good care of their son. Our arrival coincided with Oloo's older brother's marriage so there was plenty of food. We rested for three days before embarking on our mission. We first went to Nyagoko, where I didn't find my name on the list of those selected to join class 5. The following day we proceeded to Maranda, some 8 miles from Ogam's home.

On arrival at Maranda, I went straight to the notice board and found my name on the list. There was also another notice advising that interviews for admission into class 5 would be conducted in 2 days. We went back to Ogam's home elated. Two days later, Oloo and I made it to Maranda in time for the interview. There were 100 or so of us yet the school wanted only 40 pupils. I was the smallest and youngest among the interviewees. The interview was basically an aptitude test, which I failed since I didn't know anything about such tests. Matters were not helped by the fact that the teacher interviewing me kept mentioning my age and size. Luckily for me, the Head Master decided to admit me anyway.

But how was I going to fit in with boys twice my age? And the school being a boarding one, was I going to adjust to the routine at my tender age? Sharing my worries, my parents had discussed these concerns and a solution was arrived at. Aunty Abisage Okuom was married in Sakwa and her home was a mere $1^1/_2$ miles from Maranda School. It was decided that if I got admitted at Maranda I would stay with Aunty Abisage. When I informed the Head Master about this arrangement, he readily accepted me. He did not want me to miss my chance at Maranda. Having walked 25 miles at my age, he was determined not to let me down. As I sat and waited for my paperwork to be completed, clouds formed. It was going to rain big. We sought shelter in the Head Master's permanent house—brick walls, a concrete floor and corrugated iron sheets. I had never been inside a house like this before. All the houses back home were mud-walled with grass-thatched roofs. Whenever I sheltered in a hut, I only heard lightning and thunder to contend with, but this was going to be different. It started with a light drizzle, then torrents followed, then a mighty thunderstorm and finally a ruthless hailstorm.

The sound of rain beating the corrugated iron sheets was frightening enough, but coupled with the lightening and thunder, I thought the whole house would crumble on me. I tried closing my eyes to avoid seeing the lightning, but my ears still heard the terrible roar of thunder. This made me very apprehensive. I thought I was going to die. And just when I thought things couldn't get any worse, hailstones started dropping on the roof and deafening me completely. Scared stiff, I lay prostrate on the floor and eventually passed out. I later woke up and saw that people who were very tense were now relaxed and were talking. In spite of the quiet, though, my ears were still blocked and there was this continuous ringing tone in them. It took a lot of time before my ears finally cleared.

The rain having subsided, we made it back to Mzee Ogam's home and the following day we hit the road back to Gem elated because I had secured class 5 in a reputable intermediate school. We shot birds off the trees with catapults as we made the long journey home.

Schools opened in January 1957. Three days before they did, Father borrowed a bicycle and gave me a ride to Aunty Abisage's home in Sakwa. She received us warmly. This was actually payback time for her. A few years earlier, my parents had accommodated her only son, Jonah Otieno, who was a student in Gem. This time it was Abisage's turn to play host. She was elated. Father returned to Gem and on a Monday I was among the first pupils to register.

Aunty Abisage Okuom was a born-again Christian. Her husband, Jandara, was an atheist and a pipe chain smoker. Apart from their only son, Jonah Otieno, they had a daughter named Ngesa. Their homestead comprised the main hut that belonged to them, a kitchen, a kraal for goats and sheep and Jonah's hut, which was going to be my *maskan*. My aunt really loved me.

There was not much food then. Food consisted of *ugali*, made from the flour of millet and cassava, mostly with vegetables. More often than not, when there was a different dish, it was fish. In those days fish was harvested in Lake Victoria and there were more than 20 species of edible ones. Coming from the highlands, I couldn't eat most of these species. I could eat *omena* (dagaa), *ngege* (tilapia) and other local species like *ningu* and *fulu*. My aunty loved me so much that whenever she brought home any fish without scales, she made sure she bought *omena* or *fulu* for me. She could not let me eat vegetables when everybody else ate fish. If she forgot to buy alternative fish for me, she would slaughter a chicken for me. Because of these favors, I loved her very much. I enjoyed staying with Aunty's family because it was the only time I was never caned even if I messed up. She wouldn't allow it.

I started very well and loved going to school. Almost all the boys were in their teens and were boarders. I was the only day scholar. Life in boarding was tough. The dormitories were mosquito-infested and had no piped water. There was no borehole either from which water could be fetched; the only source of water was a pond called Kenya. The pond was a whole mile away from school. In the mornings and evenings boys streamed to Kenya with their buckets and basins and brought water for cooking. They were supposed to bathe in the thicket around the pond. During drought, Kenya just dried up and the boys had to trek for miles to River Yala to fetch water. These were some of the things the Head Master had feared I could not cope with because of my age. In spite of that age thing, though, I still enjoyed athletics and soccer.

One day, in the first week of second term, I was late for school. Our class master was Mr. Owaga, a man I feared very much. Two of the things I remember about him were: he was a stammerer and he was very harsh. The guy caned until kids bled. While at it, he shouted, "*KU KU KU KULRI WU O O O YI*—Bend, boy! Bend!" Since I was late, I was sure I had a date with him. The very thought of facing him scared me because I had not been caned in a long time. I decided to skip school that day. But by so doing I realized I had made the biggest mistake of my life. It was now no longer a few minutes lateness, it was truancy. What was I going to do? I decided never to go back to school. For the next few weeks I pretended to go to school each morning and coming back each evening but never really went. I only gave up pretence when Lwanya blew the whistle on me. He informed Aunty that I had not been going to school. Aunty tried to talk me into returning to school but I refused. Once or twice I joined a band of game hunters and returned with meat. My aunty's husband liked it and never raised a voice against my truancy as long as the meat was coming.

Suddenly I was struck by a very strong desire to read. I read every book that I could lay my hands on. I sought from Lwanya and obtained *Highway Book Five,* by Carey Francis. Highway was a series of intermediate arithmetic books for classes five, six, seven and eight.

While I still stayed with Aunty Abisage, Lwanya one day suggested we make a trip to Lake Victoria. The lake was about 15 miles towards Usenge. The idea of seeing the lake for the first time appealed to me and I urged him to seek permission for me. I had been told a lot about the lake—that it was an expansive water mass where boats, yatches and even ships sailed. It was the place where all the fish came from. I wanted to see the ship and have a feel for how fish was caught. I had fished back home using a string, a bait and a hook, but these only caught fingerlings in the streams back home. I wanted to see how real fish was caught. The expectation and a burning desire to make the trip as soon as possible was overwhelming. I wished Lwanya had not aroused my optimism by asking me to make this trip. Now it was my turn to pester him.

One weekend, after clearing with Aunty, we gladly set off for Usenge. Aunty released us with a word of caution to Lwanya. She said, "Beware of crocodiles!" This bothered me a lot. Crocodiles, did they live in the lake? I had heard very little about them and had not bothered to know where they lived, but from the pictures I had seen, they looked dreadful. Would I see them on this trip? And what did she mean we beware of them? I asked Lwanya if he had ever seen any alive; he said he hadn't, but he had heard that they were capable of catching a bull and tossing it several feet in the water then following it there to devour it. I sensed that if it was strong enough to toss a bull into the water, a human being, more so a small one like me, would be mince meat to it. Out of fright, I made a decision that once we arrived I would keep a safe distance from the lake and avoid being caught by any crocodile.

The home we went visiting was about fifty yards from the lake. I saw water as far as my sight could allow—water and the skyline. As we arrived in the afternoon, a cool easterly wind was blowing from the lake. I stood at the gate of the homestead and admired the vast water mass. It was just wonderful. The ripples of the waves landing majestically on the sandy shores were a beauty to behold. Within minutes, kids my age started driving herds of cattle into the lake to drink and themselves diving into the cool waters for a swim, oblivious to the danger of crocs. This encouraged me to move closer to the lake. I moved up to the edge of the water, with the last ripples of the waves splashing my feet, but that was as far as I could go. The fear of crocodiles still haunted me. When nothing happened to the kids, I gained courage and walked three or four feet into the water. If I were to go farther, I was going to swim, but I did not know how to swim. The best I had done by way of swimming was lie in storm water back home and crawl, pretending to swim. But real deep water with the waves splashing was a different matter. I loved the way the boys kicked the water and threw their hands left and right and moved in the water. If I stayed here longer, I would get the boys to teach me to swim.

I did not sleep that night because of the roars of the waves. We had been forewarned by our hosts about this experience. "Those who come here for the first time do not sleep because they are not used to the roars of the waves," they said. I did not see a crocodile but I was told how to detect one in the water. I was told that when I am at the lake and I see something like cow dung floating in the water I should run as fast as I could away from the lake. The croc held its nose out of the water while its whole body was inside. Its nose was what looked like *owuoyo* (cow dung). The following day we made it back to Maranda, sleepy but with lots of experiences to share. Although I did not see a yacht or steam ship, I saw many boats coming to the shore with the help of easterly winds—loaded with fish.

I returned to my books after the lakeshore trip and read *Highway Book Five* from one cover to the other and knew all the sums therein. But there was a single arithmetic problem in the book that I could not solve. After a teacher helped me solve it, I again asked Lwanya to get me *Highway Book Six*. He had trouble, but later managed to borrow one from a friend. I went through it meticulously.

One day, as I was sitting in a kitchen beside a fireplace warming myself, I saw something that I would remember for years to come. The door to the kitchen faced the door to Jonah's hut. From where I sat I could see who entered or exited Jonah's hut. The sun had just gone down and darkness was setting in fast. There was no moon to provide light. And since clouds were overcast, there were no visible stars that could illuminate the atmosphere.

Suddenly I saw a white thing emerge from Jonah's hut. This thing looked like a human being. I had never seen anything like it. I was sure it was not a white man. I believed white men never walked around without cars. Could it be a ghost? I wasn't sure. I had never seen a ghost before. I got frightened. If it was a ghost, I would be in real trouble. I had heard tales of guys beaten and left for dead by ghosts, or even scared to death. Others, I heard, had been swallowed whole. *A ghost in the homestead? Where was everybody?* Normally I would have been with Ngesa in the kitchen at this hour, but she was with Lwanya's sister in their hut. As it moved towards the kitchen, where I was, I wondered if it had seen me.

"Where is everybody?" I wondered.

If this thing reached me and did something bad to me and disappeared nobody would know what happened to me. On closer scrutiny, I noticed it had a head, arms and was walking on legs. It had the form of a human being. *Wait a minute, that looks like a dress it is wearing.* If it was a ghost—as I was convinced it was, it was a she-ghost. I was awestruck. But I could not just wait for this thing to come and catch me. I had to do something. I let out a loud scream that brought everybody scampering out of their huts. It did not expect this. It was surprised. My screams stopped it in its tracks. I ran towards my aunt's hut screaming and behind me this thing was screaming too. *"En ang'o? En ang'o?*—What is it? What is it?" Wait. *A talking ghost?* By the time I got to my aunt's hut, I was breathless and between sobs. I said, "Ne...ne—Look....look," pointing at the "ghost". I was surprised when everyone burst into laughter saying, *"Mano en Atieno nyar Owuor*—That is Atieno daughter of Owuor." I cooled down. I had never been so scared in my life. I screamed because she scared me. She screamed because she thought something was chasing me. Atieno was born albino. That was the white skin I saw. She had been married and that day she had come to visit her mother. I was not aware she had come and I had never heard of her. She came over to my aunt's hut and embraced me and even had a little chat with me. That was my first encounter with an albino. She was a sister to Lwanya and the girl who was with Ngesa.

At the end of the 2nd term, I went back to Gem during holidays. When school opened, my brother, James Helekiah Sijenyi, returned home around two o'clock in the afternoon, borrowed a bike and by four o'clock he and I were on our way to Maranda. Five miles into the journey, it started raining. It poured so much that my brother could not ride the bike. The mud made it impossible even to push the bicycle. There were sections of the journey where he had to literally carry the bicycle. We walked through the jungle in rain and mud and made it to my aunt's home at dawn. We did not sleep; he took me to school. John Hezekiah Ougo Ochieng was the Head Master then. He went to the Head Master's office and talked with him at length. I was then called in and told to explain why I absconded. I was truthful in my explanation, but the Head Master did not believe me that the fear of being caned by Mr. Owaga could make me run away from school. I was expelled from school that day, but only after the Head Master had administered a few strokes. Mr. Ougo and I were later to be buddies and comrades in the struggle for Kenya's second liberation. My brother and I returned to Gem the following day disappointed and exhausted. For a moment I thought my education, like that of most of the boys in my village, would end in class five.

The next time I saw Aunty Abisage was when she came to the funeral of my mother—a couple of months later. She came to see her brother on a number of occasions thereafter, but since I was not home I did not see her. I would not go back to Sakwa until her burial.

When she died, I mobilized her brothers, cousins and all her relatives in Gem and made several trips in my car to Sakwa to bring them to the funeral. The old men and women wailed in anguish. That was the era when relatives strived to outwit each other in wailing at funerals. The longer one cried the more people believed he or she loved the deceased. I could not help weeping too, when I recalled how she loved me and fed me on special food, which even my own mother could not. I broke down and cried. It was the fourth time I had mourned loudly and visibly at a funeral. The first was when my mother died, the second when my elder brother died, the third when my daughter and my brother died with his family. After the burial we returned home.

A couple of months later we were invited by Jonah to attend her memorial ceremony. I took the same group, including the wife of Uncle Isaac Ochieng 'Thuthu" to Sakwa. Her name was Aduda. Aduda was a drunkard whose morals were with the dogs. Uncle met her when Tausi Band, of Ochieng Nelly fame, performed at the memorial ceremony of my deceased brother and promptly married her. It was this marriage that made Isaac abandon S.D.A. and embraced New Apostolic Church, along with her. His first wife, Hulda Honje, remained a staunch SDA until her death in a car accident. During the night at the ceremony, Aduda disappeared with some men and when she returned in the morning she sought water, not only for bathing, but for washing her undergarments as well. It was such a shame!

Aduda continued her immoral lifestyle unmindful of the inherent dangers it posed to herself, husband, her co-wife and her sexual patrons. The first known casualty of her immorality was her husband, Isaac. He caught a cold which refused to go away. He got thinner and thinner, coughing heavily at the same time. He finally got a bout of diarrhea from which he never recovered. Initially he agreed and was taken to a hospital several times. but later he refused medication and just passed on. After his death we realized Aduda must have had sexual contact with virtually all the male members of her church. It is a practice in churches that when one of their members die at home, the men, if the deceased is a man, and the women, if the deceased is a woman, attend to a body by washing, grooming and preserving it for burial. It is also a belief, according to folklore, that if a man dies you cannot touch him if you had an affair with his wife. If you do, you die, sometimes instantly.

When Isaac died, the entire male membership of his church made themselves unavailable. None of them showed up to perform what was required of them—wash the body and prepare it for burial. It was also a taboo for the promiscuous widow to touch the body of her departed husband or *kupiga nduru*—to scream at his death. If she did, the body would blow up to the point of bursting and she may even collapse and lose consciousness until traditional herbs were administered to reverse her unconsciousness. If nobody with knowledge of traditional herbs was around, she would die. According to the same folklore, sons and nephews were prohibited to touch the body of a deceased uncle or even see it naked. As a result of Aduda's immorality, my uncle suffered in life and in death.

When it was apparent nobody would turn up to wash and groom the body, Jack, Aunty Wamwayi's son, and I decided to defy tradition. We washed, groomed and prepared our uncle's body for burial. But if we thought the worst was over, we were mistaken. Traditionally, young men in the village came together after prayer by the presiding church elder and took turns digging the grave. In the case of my uncle this was not going to happen. All the teenagers—who in normal situations would have been swarming the home—were nowhere to be seen. They had disappeared and were not even at their homes. The obvious explanation was that they feared they would die if they took part in digging the grave because at some point they too must have patronized Aduda. My uncle's grave was dug by Anania Ataro, Jack and I. What I saw, which perplexed me, was that after Aduda had touched the body of my uncle while covering it up with a sheet, it inflated just as tradition had said it would. It happened so fast that I feared it would burst unless something was done about it. The quick thinking of my cousin, John Wamauwa, saved the situation. "I told Aduda never to touch the body, why did she bring a sheet to cover it?" he thundered while removing the sheet. Just as fast as it had swollen, the body shrunk to its normal size. Only a few of us who were clean—Jack, Anania, my aunt's son, myself and a few others—carried the coffin to its final resting place.

After Uncle Isaac's death, the remaining uncles—Miyere, Achwal and Thuthu Ja Luth—who took her in levirate union died from similar symptoms. Their spouses followed in quick succession. She was indiscriminate and incredibly generous when it came to sexuality. She was credited with wiping out a father and his son and rendering a bunch of homes desolate. She will forever be remembered for having single-handedly caused more deaths in our village than any other cause in living memory. The hard part was that I had to shoulder 90% of funeral expenses of each deceased including herself when she finally died. By the time my uncle Isaac died, I had already known the promiscuity of his wife, Aduda, courtesy of the funeral remembrance ceremony of my loving aunt—Abisage Okuom.

CHAPTER 5

NIGHTMARE

While I was at Maranda, back in 1957, Maliera was granted authority to commence admitting intermediate pupils. Classes five and six were started that same year. The first batch of pupils would sit Kenya African Preliminary Examination (KAPE) in 1959. In 1958 my father, out of parental love, took me to Maliera SDA Intermediate School in class 6. Life in class six was boring as there was nothing new to learn; I had done class six stuff by the time I dropped out of school at Maranda. The subjects were limited: Arithmetic, English and Nature Study. I was so much ahead of my class that whenever we were given a test, the teachers asked me to help them mark other pupils' work. Position one, with straight As, was my preserve. But this time my family didn't stay with Oloo Ogam; he had left to stay with Mathayo Okelo. We now lived with Obumba Obara.

Obumba came from Seme in search of an intermediate school. Seme is twenty five miles away from Maliera. He was enrolled at Maliera and my mother took care of him. But it was not just my mother who took in boys and girls who went to school at Maliera, many Adventists, being true to the spirit of love for one's neighbour and being good Samaritans, and also in an effort to help Maliera SDA Intermediate School stabilize, lived with pupils whose homes were far away. There were pupils from South Nyanza, particularly Karachuonyo. Others came from Seme, Sakwa, Asembo, Imbo, Uyoma and Alego. Those were taken and accommodated by the SDA church members for the duration of their stay at Maliera. This happened because Maliera had no boarding facilities. Obumba Obara was in his late teens. He was mature and intelligent. He had very good pieces of advice for me. He had lost his mother when he was still young and was brought up by his father.

One day he opened up to us, Orege and I, and narrated the tribulations he had gone through after losing his mother. I blasted back that whatever he was telling us could not happen to me because everybody loved me so much that even if I lost my mother the other neighbors would take good care of me. Obumba cut me short and told me harshly that all the people who loved me only loved my mother and for a reason. I could not believe him because I thought people revered my parents—my mother in particular. I had to learn the bitter truth later. He told me how he got burned and that he got scars on his body as a result of beatings. He shared with us memories of the days he went without food, the names the step-mother called him and the nasty stuff one could experience in life as a young man. I was flabbergasted, but the story soon disappeared from my mind.

As the first term in class six ended, my mother and father decided to send me to my sister, Leonida Choka, during the holidays. They put me in one of the two buses that plied the route. One of the buses was driven by Thuma

Odiala and another by Wanyanga Osese. Both drivers were our relatives—they were *Jo Umani*, the sub-tribe I come from. Father handed me over to Thuma Odiala and instructed him to transfer me to a bus headed to Tororo when we arrived at the terminus in Busia. Thuma did as instructed and by 11:00 a.m. my sister met me at the Tororo terminus. She lived with her family in the suburbs of Tororo, a rural setting. The family grew food and owned a large sugarcane *shamba*. I lived with my sister and husband without any problem. Food was plenty and there were days we went to watch mobile cinemas. I really enjoyed movies. It was the first time I watched movies; very exciting.

One day, during my stay in Tororo, I started feeling tired and exhausted. I felt too tired to even eat. I was moody, irritant and withdrawn. Nothing appeared to go right for me at all. At night I did not sleep. I sweated profusely and scratched my body all over. It was as if my whole body had been invaded by fleas and mites. I was restless. When I woke up in the morning, I felt even more tired. I had a pounding headache which refused to go away. My eyes were red and they bulged. I did not know what was wrong with me. My sister and her husband got really worried. They decided to take me to a hospital, where an examination revealed nothing wrong. I was given painkillers and asked to return home. That night I slept well and woke up the following day refreshed. I did not realize that this was a premonition to my mother's death.

By the end of that month, when my holidays still had a week to run, my sister's husband called her and I and we sat with him. Whatever he wanted to tell us, I could tell he had difficulty doing it. I thought I saw him fighting tears. But he finally gained courage and blurted it out. Between sobs, he said, "Mother has left us."

We did not know what the heck he was talking about. Was it his mother or our mother? And what did he mean by "left us?"

His mother was old, fine, but hardly as old as mine. She lived in Nyalgunga, Alego. Noticing our confusion, he drew a deep breath and decided to clarify things. He said, "Your mother has died."

My sister screamed uncontrollably and for a while I thought she would not stop. I got transfixed, with tears streaming down my cheeks. But it would be another twenty four hours before we started our journey home. I parted with my sister on the way. Tradition required her to go to her matrimonial home, wail there a little, before coming to the funeral. All along I thought we were coming to the burial of my mother, not knowing that she had long been buried.

I arrived home expecting a large crowd of mourners. My mother had been the darling of the village; surely on her burial day everybody would be there to pay last repects—the relatives, the neighbours, the church members and the entire village. I was surprised, therefore, when I arrived and found nobody at home. Not even my father was there. It was as if the home had been deserted. Nobody was around to show me the grave my mother laid in. Traditionally, if the owner of a homestead died his body was buried on the left side of his hut. If the wife died she was buried on the right side of her hut. So my mother's grave should have been on the right side of her hut. I surveyed the possible burial sites but failed to locate the grave. I dropped on my knees and started crying. I cried with my eyes closed for about thirty minutes or so. It was then that I realized Aunty Dorsila was standing beside me. She reached out and lifted me up. She led me to my mother's hut, where I sat down. Soon after, Father arrived. He too consoled me. And when neighbours heard I had come back, they streamed into our home and each tried his or her best to soothe me.

Father led me to Mama's grave, which was some thirty feet away from her hut. It was on the right side, but next to the fence. I stayed by the grave until sunset, when I was called to dinner. Father explained why he had decided to bury my mother next to the fence. He said he did that because he was a Christian and was moving away from tradition. He said he wanted his body to be buried next to my mother's since he had designated that place a cemetery for the home. He also said, in his endeavor to disregard tradition, that he had allowed my mother's body to be brought home through the gate contrary to tradition which demanded that the body be brought into the home through the fence.The following day my sister arrived from her matrimonial home and discussed with Father how her husband and his team would be taken care of when they came to the funeral.

Two days later, Wilson Abayo came to the funeral. He did not explain to my father why we were three weeks late in attending the funeral despite father sending him word immediately Mother died. Later, when I came to realize why my sister and I did not attend the burial, I almost cursed Wilson. He told us that because he did not have money for our transport, he had to wait till month end for his salary. What I did not understand was why he could not borrow money for my sister and I to attend the burial, then make plans to come when he was paid. He did not even have the courtesy to inform us immediately he received the news. This was the most callous and heartless thing that anyone could do to another. Wilson did this, not just to anyone, but to his wife and brother-in-law!

Two days after Wilson had come and gone, some church members came to the funeral from Imbo. These people came with several baskets of fish, fresh and dried, maize millet and cassava. My father did his best to entertain them. He used almost all his meager savings to buy meat, chicken and flour. He even bought sugar and bread for their tea, which was taken with milk. He invited women to help with preparation of food. What surprised me was that whatever the guests left over was consumed by the neighbours. Not even a morsel remained. Worse still, whatever the guests brought was taken by the neighbors. Nobody realized that my father and I also wanted to eat. Of course we ate that evening, but it was vegetables instead of meat, fish or chicken. It was then that I remembered what Obumba Obara had told me. How could they have eaten and taken everything, leaving us nothing to eat? I knew my life, thereafter, was going to be full of turbulence.

From then on it was going to be just my father and I in the homestead. My father tried his best to be father and mother, looking for food while I fetched water and firewood. Father was not used to this type of lifestyle and he found it hard to cope. My elder brother, Absalom Muhudhi, realized this and released his wife, Sylvia Awiti, to help out. I was relieved. At least I had a mother-like figure to take care of me. Sylvia tried her best. Vegetables were in the garden. Mother had a cow which produced enough milk and ghee to satisfy our needs. We still had maize and millet from the previous harvest, so flour was not a problem. The problem was how to get sugar and salt. Sylvia did not know how to make traditional salt, so we had to buy salt from the *duka*. My father had no money to do so as he was unemployed. Suddenly a different problem arose—the cow started producing less milk and Sylvia did not have knowledge of ghee extraction, so we had no ghee in our vegetables.

We grew the forerunner of the present-day kales called *Bad Maro*. They had huge leaves with light-green colour. They were not easy to cook, but my mother used to make a delicious dish out of them. We had *ugali* with this unpalatable vegetable. We longed for meat or fish or chicken even if it was just a foot of a chicken.

My father was out most of the time; he rarely took meals with us. This was the time he was courting my step-mother. Towards the end of that year, 1958, he brought the lady home. Good food suddenly reappeared. Tea with milk, fish, meat and ghee for cooking was suddenly there in plenty. Sylvia stayed briefly with us, then she went back to her husband.

My step-mother—Loice Wandati—had two previous failed marriages. She left children at both places. She had been married in Sirembe, in Gem, and in Ugenya. She had been to Ugenya immediately before she met and married my father. She came to our home with a boy a year and a half old. His name was Charles Ochieng. When I started staying with my step-mother, all seemed well.

Laktar Ongoro was our neighbour. He was of my father's age or just slightly younger. He was the only man I knew who smoked cigarettes. The old Kingstock cigarettes he smoked had such a strong odour that the smell could pervade a wide area. He used to walk past our gate smoking and I liked the odour of his cigarette. I longed for a day when I would be old enough to smoke. When that time came, I would smoke Kingstock which Laktar smoked.

One day I came across a packet of Kingstock cigarettes under a big tree in front of the gate of our home. I did not know what to do with a full packet of cigarettes. I wanted to take it to Laktar, but decided against it. I thought he would think I stole it. I then decided it was time to try cigarettes. I hid the packet in nearby bushes, went home and stole a burning stick.

I stealthily made it back to the place I hid the cigarettes. I lit one stick, which I hurriedly smoked. I lit a second and smoked the whole stick. In the middle of smoking the third stick, I heard a buzzing sound around my head. At first I thought it was a bee. It persisted but I saw no bee around. I started waving my hand around my head, trying to chase away the bee or whatever it was. The sound persisted, growing louder and louder, until it stopped, or at least I thought it did. I must have passed out because when my senses returned, I found myself inside the hut where I usually slept. I was sweating heavily and beside me was a heap of vomit—covered in black soot. Standing at the door was my father with a packet of cigarettes in his hand. He was narrating to my step-mother what happened. He said I screamed like a goat whose head had been hit hard with a blunt object. He ran towards the noise. He found me lying unconscious. He then picked up the cigarette packet and carried me into the room, where I vomited soot. He assured my step-mother that I will be alright because I had vomited. That would be the first and last time I touched or smoked a cigarette. Maybe that was God's way of sending me a signal to desist from smoking. In my family only Absalom smoked. He passed down the habit to all his sons. Some of them only left smoking in adulthood when they saw the havoc it visited on their friends—and on their own health.

A couple of months—after experimenting with cigarettes—I got very ill. The illness defied all medications I received for it. Our local dispensary, which had been my savior before, was unable to help. I was bedridden; I could neither stand nor sit. I developed bed sores, and believed I was going to die. Everyone lost hope. I could neither eat nor speak and could only take water. For some time, I was in a state of sub consciousness. One time I felt like I was hovering over miles and miles of very fine sand. There was no sunshine, but it was not dark. It was neither cold nor hot and did not know how long I was in that state. When I gained consciousness, I found myself in a hospital surrounded by medical personnel, among them my brother James Helekia Sijenyi. He had come from Nairobi that morning and found me unconscious. He carried and put me in a bus that took me to Maseno Mission Hospital. I heard the doctors say they had reversed my state of unconsciousness by a slew of intravenous injections. By this time I was fully awake. My journey through the fine sands abruptly ended—just before I gained consciousness.

The journey was smooth and enjoyable, but the destination was not in sight. I don't know whether I headed to heaven or hell. Whatever the destination was, I did not reach it.

Since my brother had to go back to Nairobi that evening, he asked my cousin, Nehemia Onyango, to pick me up from the hospital and take me to his house to await the following day's treatment. With the aid a bicycle, my cousin took me to his house for the night. I was still ill and could not walk. My cousin gave me food and a place to sleep. In the dead of the night, I saw my dead mother in a vision approaching where I was sleeping. She came and stood next to me. I felt a very cold hand touch me while saying, *"Bed abeda jachir nyathina*—Just have courage, my son." In that moment, I let out a shrill, which woke up everybody. When my cousin inquired what the matter was, I could not talk. I had not been talking for a week and the shrill was the first word that dropped off my lips. I lay there shivering. The cold hand, and the cold from the cement floor where I slept over a thin sheet, made the pounding of my heart and the shivering worse. Everybody eventually went back to sleep, but I stayed awake the remainder of the night. The following day my cousin arranged for me to be taken to hospital for further treatment. I felt I was improving, but could not walk yet. I stayed in my cousin's house for a week, each day in the morning and evening venturing out to practice walking.

On the sixth day I felt I needed to get out as part of my get fit exercise. My cousin lived at the Maseno Government Training Institute. On the southern part of the institute runs a railway track parallel to the Kisumu-Busia Road. I slowly made my way to the rail track and started walking towards Kisumu. Out of the blue, a man emerged from a nearby thicket brandishing a long kitchen knife. He started chasing two boys, who were walking a head of me. He ran after them menacingly and almost drove his knife into the back of one of them. The knife caught the boy's shirt at the back and split it into two. There were no other people on the track. The boys scaled the embarkment that separated the track and the road and jumped onto the road. When I saw this I started hobbling back. He looked back and saw me—and the way I was struggling to run. He must have concluded I was easy prey. He started running towards me. I could not run, leave alone, fast enough to escape him. He was panting heavily and was within five yards or so away from me. If he caught up with me, I was dead. Just as I was about to succumb to severe pain and stop running, the guy tripped and fell. He appeared hurt because he did not stand immediately. This gave me time to surmount the embarkment and move to the road. I did not see this insane man again as I made it back to my cousin's house. Thanks to the forced exercise of running, I now walked better as I approached my cousin's house.

That night I had the best sleep in weeks. I still do not know whether the cold hand that touched me was hallucination or the spirit of my dead mother assuring me of protection. But I definitely saw God's hand in my resurrection at the hospital and my escape from the madman at the rail track. The following day my cousin gave me bus fare to return home to recuperate. My father was very happy to see me alive. I made quick recovery and went back to school thereafter. After end-of-year examinations, where I topped my class with straight As, I prepared myself for class seven, which I was looking forward to.

In 1959 school opened for the New Year with Samuel Ouma Boro from South Nyanza as the Head Master of Maliera. Being the pointman, he opened up Maliera for boys and girls from South Nyanza and elsewhere. Classes five, six, seven and eight were full. A part from Kamagambo, Maliera was the only SDA intermediate school at the time. Some of these imported pupils were actually adults who had done forms one and two in Uganda. Some were admitted to class seven and some to class eight. Competition was very stiff and I was in danger of losing my first position in class. Samuel Ouma was born a teacher and a gifted administrator. He loved me a lot and I do not recall any day that he ever caned me. Of the three subjects—English, Arithmetic and Nature Study—he could teach any. And the team he assembled to help him was excellent.

That was the year Maliera was going to do KAPE (Kenya African Preliminary Examination) for the first time. At the end of term one something happened that upset me. When the results of the term were released, I found myself in position three. One of the big boys was first, Felgona Achien'g was second and I came in third. Back at home, Father asked how I had performed. I told him the truth. He was furious. "How could you be beaten by a girl?" he asked. "Real men are never beaten in class by women." He ordered my mother not to give me food that day. This bothered me a lot. I knew of boys whose parents congratulated them because they made it to the top ten. Here I was at position three and I was being punished because a girl was a head of me! I made sure she never beat me again until we completed class eight.

Felgona was the daughter of Mzee Wilson Mbola. She was bright and smart. She was also beautiful—but far older than me. Her grade in class never dropped below ten. She maintained the units until we left Maliera, and was the first girl from Maliera to be admitted into form I.

Because I continued to shine, the Head Master approached my father and tried to persuade him to let me sit KAPE that year—1959—although I was in class seven. The Head Master and my father knew I would pass, but Father refused because I was too young and too small in body to cope with boarding life. He wanted me to bid my time by going to class eight. This would give me time to grow. Mister Ouma agreed with him and I never did KAPE that year. Teachers continued to ask me to help them with marking, which I did dilligently.

Back home away from school, life became tougher. I was only fourteen, a small boy by any stretch of imagination. My father woke us up at three o'clock in the morning to go out and either dig or weed depending on what season it was. He would come down to our hut singing. "Ichamo kuon gi ngege kiny piny noru... ara cham mana kingeyo, kingeyo ni oyaye kiny piny noru." (You eat ugali with tilapia, it will dawn tomorrow. Just eat knowing that it will dawn tomorrow). That was my father's wake up call. He was supposed to meet you at the door already dressed, failing which he would give you a few lashes to wake you up. We would rush back home after six, wash our legs, feet and faces, put on our uniforms and dash to school. There was no breakfast and no time for taking even a glass of water. This was the routine throughout the school days. We would come back for lunch, uncertain of ever getting it ready. The only meal we were sure of was supper. As I had graduated from eating the toe of a chicken to eating any part of a chicken, I enjoyed my supper, making sure I took double ratio to compensate for breakfast and lunch, which I missed to do physiotherapy to Charles Ochien'ng. At his age Ochien'g could not walk but kids his age could run. When placed to sit at a point on the floor he could not move. All his toilet needs he did right there. The mother got worried that he would never walk. So every morning and evening, Friday and Saturday I was on Ochien'g walking him on the cold grass dew despite his cries. I was sure, this was going to help him. I had seen kids like him helped to walk through the same exercise. It was not long before he started walking. Those days all pupils in S.D.A. schools went to school on Sundays but rested on Fridays and Saturdays.

As I continued to live with my father and step-mother, I started experiencing changes in her demeanor towards me. She had taken complete control of my father by now. Whatever she said was final. The problem was she could say things about me that I never did and when I denied Father sided with her. One time Lewnida was home visiting. My step-mother alleged that I had stolen food from the pot. I believed she was just making up this allegation against me to make Father beat me. Her son, Ochien'g, was the one who stole the food. Father lunged at me and slapped me so hard, I fell. He was all over me with kicks and blows. As he was preparing to drill his boot into my head, my sister shouted. "You want to kill him! You want to kill him!" This distracted him and he spared me the boot. If it were not for Lewnida, he would have crushed my head with that boot. From that day I knew I was staying with people who could harm me—one of whom was my own father who had been turned against me. My sister cried because she realized my life was in danger, but there was nothing she could do. She just packed up her stuff and left that very moment for her matrimonial home.

Back at school, I continued to excel, but competition from the other boys got stiffer. Even so, I spent long hours playing soccer. Sometimes classes started without me knowing. If I was lucky a class teacher noticed my absence and sent a boy to call me. They knew just where to find me—wherever boys were playing soccer. For such indescretions, teachers did not punish me. They knew I would make up for lost time and excel in exams anyway. Was my playfulness compensation for the many years of solitude in my formative days? Intresting thought!

Bicycles were owned only by well to do guys during those days and there were only a handful in the entire village. My father, in spite his financial inadequacies, managed to buy one. I could ride one, but I needed more practice to improve my skills. I usually took Father's bike and rode it without him knowing. I remember once when I took the bike to go to Nyangweso with a friend. On our way back a tire burst. It was so bad that the tube could not be repaired; it had to be replaced. Even if it had to be repaired, I had no money for it. My fear now was—Father was going to know I took the bike. Seeing no way to mend it, I returned it in that condition and the first whopping I received was from my mother. And I knew I would be in more trouble when Father returned. This time my fortieth day had come and I indeed suffered the consequences of my disobedience when Father returned. I never touched his bike again, but some persons could still allow me to ride their bikes.

My cousin, Mathews Okello, had arranged to go to Imbo-where his brother, Isaiah Omune, married. Isaiah had died before certain cultural rites were performed, but Mathews could not perform them. This time Mathews was planning to go to Imbo for a purpose I did not know. I requested if I could go with him. He asked me if I could ride a bike up to Imbo. I said I could. Of course I knew I could ride to Imbo, but riding there and back the same day I couldn't. Father agreed to give me his bike, so Mathew, Odondo and I set off early in the morning. We crossed River Yala, which divides Alego from Imbo, on a makeshift bridge of poles, ropes and papyrus. We arrived around noon. I was exhausted. I had never ridden that long before. I needed complete rest, which I knew I would get at night.

But by 4:00, Mathew said it was time to go back. I couldn't belive it. Back to Gem? But he insisted, so we set off. I could not keep pace with Odondo and Odondo could not keep pace with him. I was two km behind him and one km behind Odondo. When he reached the bridge, he waited for us to help us cross together. After that bridge, rain came down heavily. My quarter pin came loose and the right pedal malfunctioned and this slowed me down even more. With the rain over, mud set in, which I could not handle due to the condition of my bike. When I heard a tire bust I said hurrah because now they would have to take me to the nearest home to be accommodate overnight. But Matthew was a tough guy. He had been in the *oringi* (Ferrying fish from the lake) business for a long time and had been in situations like this before and knew exactly what to do. He tied my bike to Odondo's and had me ride with him as a pillion passenger. With Odondo towing my bike, we made it slowly to Gem and arrived at about 4 a.m.

Later, in adulthood, I learned why Mathew could not spend a night in Imbo. I learned that he had not fulfilled any traditional rites for his wives. He had not paid dowry and had not gone to any of his fathers-in-law's homesteads to eat chicken or perform any of the marital rites which would legitimize his marriages. He could not sleep at his brother's father-in-law before he slept in his father-in-law's place. But at what point, while we were in Imbo, did he realize he was biting more than he could chew? Was it after we had been served lunch? I did not see any chicken!

Chicken aside, if he knew we were going to ride back why didn't he inform us from the beginning? These questions bothered me in adulthood, but I never found answers to them. Mathew later died without setting foot in his mother-in-law's house.

In 1960 I moved to class eight. I was still the smallest and youngest among the boys and girls in the class. The teaching was superb and teachers were very strict. Discipline was excellent. The big boys and girls knew what they came to do and never caused trouble for teachers or fellow pupils. But there were, of course, exceptions. Like this boy, Bita, who wanted to feed me his feaces. He and I had gone to visit our mutual friend. He was bigger and older. The friend's mother prepared good food and we ate well. On the way back, he slipped into some bushes next to the road to help himself. He came out of the bushes with a stick at the tip of which was feaces. He got a hold of me and pinned me down. He was at the point of forcing the feaces into my mouth when some old lady, who was watching the drama from a distance, shouted. He left me. I ran as fast as I could back to my home. I reported the matter to the Head Master during the next day. He claimed he was just joking, but he was not believed. His joke earned him a few lashes. He ceased to be my friend.

Competition for good grades continued to be tougher, the older boys trying to dominate and I trying to resist. At this stage Felgona Achien'g had slipped and exams were just ten months away. I had to prepare but I did not have any text books. I relied entirely on teachers' notes, which more often than not, were inadequate. I also had this problem of being woken up at three to go to the *shamba*. If my mother were alive, she would have never subjected me to this forced child labour. I also had a problem of inconsistency in eating. Whereas I could do nothing about inadequacy of food, I could do something about the morning routine and the books. So on the sixth week of first term, Odungi Randa, Isaac Oluoch and I agreed to raise 12.00 shillings to purchase a tin of 20 litres of paraffin. Each person was to raise four shillings. I did not have this money, but I had to raise it if I was to pass KAPE. Someone agreed to give me five shillings if I tilled half an acre of his land. My friends agreed to help, so I got the five shillings I needed. We got a lantern and after buying paraffin, we agreed to go to school in the evenings to study at night on our own.

The arrangement was that we would go with our beddings into our classroom, study up to 11:00 p.m., then sleep right there in the classroom. In the morning we would wake up, fold our beddings and hang them on the walls of the classroom. The rest of the pupils would come in the morning and find us in school. When I started floating this idea to my friends, things had changed for the worse at home. We were not only going to the *shamba* to work from 3:00 a.m., but also go to the field at 5:00 in the evening when we came back from school. This was what prompted me to come up with the preps idea. In a twenty-four hour cycle, I had four hours of hard labour in the morning, and two and half hour of traveling to and from school. Then there was eight hours of school time and three hours of evening labour—a total of seventeen and half hours!

Only six and a half hours were left for my meals, personal grooming and sleep. This was an excellent recipe for failing an examination. I was not going to allow this to happen. I don't know if this work schedule was prepared by my step-mother in cohorts with my father or not. But whether it was prepared by step-mother, my father or both, I was not going to follow it. I knew I would be considered disobedient or even rebellious, but the bottom line was— I was not going to abide by this schedule. Period. Somebody should have considered that the schedule was too tough for a fourteen-year-old. If someone had worked out that program to make me fail my exams, that someone would be disappointed. I knew in my mind that the repercussions of my defiance would be serious, but I was not going to allow my life to be ruined at an early age.

I came up with a perfect idea to camouflage my intentions. This was going to be the beginning of my tribulations proper. This is how it worked. We were in school a whole day. In the evenings we returned home for a quick supper, then headed straight back to school for preps. On a twenty four hour cycle we were in school from 7:00 p.m. to 1:00 p.m.—sixteen hours, then from 2:00 p.m. to 5:00 p.m.—3 hours. Make that a total of nineteen hours in school. Yes, that was the winning schedule. Because of preps, I could not go dig at 3:00 a.m. and 5:00 p.m. This set me on a collision cause with my step-mother, who set in motion a retaliatory process she had to handle carefully since Father would not allow her to harass me openly for fear of a backlash from the neighbours. Whenever I returned home for supper and found Father absent, I returned to school without eating anything. This went on for months, but I chose to bear it in silence. Besides, I was always in a hurry to return to school before dark. I feared night runners. Sometimes I came and found *ugali* pot on the hearth with water boiling, ready to be cooked. But on seeing me she would instruct that the boiling water be turned into porridge. She knew the porridge would take longer to be ready and by the time it was, I would be long gone. It was devastating.

It came down to a choice between food and school. I chose school. I remember vividly the culmination of all these problems. I had gone for three consecutive days without eating. My father was away. I survived on sugarcane, which a sympathetic friend gave me. Sugarcane and water—that was it. I was so hungry that I believed I would pass out unless I got something to eat fast. I slowly walked to Aunty Dursila Onjare's home and collapsed at the doorstep, after barely making it there. She rushed to where I was and asked me what the matter was. I told her I was hungry and needed food right away. She went into the hut and came back with a piece of *ugali* five days old, covered in yeast and mould. She also brought cold vegetables, since there was no time to warm anything. I asked her for a knife to remove the mould and yeast. I munched the *ugali* and cold vegetables and—after drinking a full gourd of water—I thanked her for the food.

I rested a while, then told her my problems with my step-mother. She must have gone to our home and created a scene. She could be very nasty when upset. I was given food that evening when I returned home for supper. For the next one year, I was never denied food, courtesy of the intervention of Aunty Dursila. Dursila loved me as one of her own children, a love that intensified after the death of my mother. Hers was the only home I could visit and eat something. She protected me. I always called on her to intercede with Father whenever matters seemed crazy. She was feared by Father and my step-mother. Her only concern was my safety and proper upbringing. Later—when I had a job and money—I not only built her a house with corrugated iron sheets, but provided for her upkeep the rest of her life.

Before we sat KAPE, we were told to choose the high schools we preferred to attend if we passed. My first choice was Maseno High School. My second was Kamusinga High School. The third choice was Kamagambo SDA Secondary School.

We continued to study with my friends and our grades improved. One day one of our teachers ordered us to remove our beddings from the classroom. We obliged, but when the Head Master, Mr. Samuel Ouma, heard about it, he called the teacher for a thorough dressing down and ordered us to return our beddings to the classroom. That evening he commended us and said the school's performance in KAPE would double if all pupils did what we were doing. The following week he ordered all class eight pupils to come for evening preps. He told them to look for their own paraffin. He promised to ask the teachers to teach during preps.

A month into exams, two things happened that perplexed me. One day as I was going home with a box in which I had my books, I left the box next to the road and got into a bush to relieve myself. When I returned, the box was gone. Somebody had taken it. At first I thought one of the boys from my village had done it. But this was not the case. I searched everywhere but could not find it. The notes and few textbooks I had were all in there. As it was nowhere to be found, I did not go to school for three days. I was devastated and demoralized. I knew I would not do well. On the fourth day, when I had lost hope and given up, my father received information that the items were with Omele Okon'go. My father and I went to get the box from Omele. Initially he denied having it, but later, when Father pressed him, he admitted having it. He wanted Father to pay him before he released the items, but Father refused and Omele turned rowdy. He threatened to beat Father up.

I remember well what Father told him. It was loaded. Father said, "Jabar, let me have my sons school box, I cannot fight with you; one day you will meet a guy your age to fight with." At the intervention of Gordon Ondunga he released my school box. I was overwhelmed with joy. Omele Okon'go was a *chang'aa*-drinking, bhang-smoking, rascal who believed he could beat anybody. Nobody was stronger than him, he thought, and boasted that if he stretched his right arm nobody could bend it. On the day he took my box he was apparently coming from the same direction I was. He found the box near the road and took it in full view of other pupils. Because they feared him, nobody was ready to volunteer information for fear of retaliation.

Two weeks after I got my box, Omele went to a dancing party in Sirembe. He started pulling his usual antics. At first he appeared fairly successful, as reported by Waguma, who was with him. Nobody could bend his stretched arm. From a crowd, Onyata emerged and accepted his challenge. Onyata was six feet, five inches tall, heavily built and weighed close to 250 pounds. He was massive, strong and was not normal. He was insane. I had seen Onyata chasing other madmen in the day—Ogwayo, Ochilo and Akomo. He was fearsome. This was the guy Omele stretched his arm to bend. Bending Omele's stretched arm was no big deal to Onyata. He did it with ease. Instead of calling off the game, Omele, pushed by whatever weed he smoked, stretched his right arm again for Onyata to twist. He got hold of Omele's hand and turned it full circle as Omele screamed in pain. He twisted it another 360° as Omele passed out. The arm bone completely dislodged from the shoulder bone. It took ten men to release Onyata's hold from Omele's arm. Waguna said he gained consciousness and stayed there until the the next day. In the afternoon Gordon Ondunga arranged for a lorry to pick him up and take him to the hospital. He was taken to Maseno Mission Hospital where he was treated. But even with treatment, Omele lost the motions on his right arm completely.

After getting my school box, I started revising furiously. Then one week to KAPE another incident happened. I had gone to graze our cattle. I took my fountain pen with me. This was the pen I was going to use during KAPE. On arriving home, I discovered that the pen was not in my shirt pocket where I usually kept it. I retraced my steps back to the field I had grazed in and looked diligently everywhere. I could not find it. I got distressed. Only a few weeks ago I had lost my school box and now I was losing my only pen? The one I had arranged to do KAPE with? Very strange. To cut this story short, I bought another pen soon after to do my KAPE.

One year later—as I was grazing cattle at the same spot where I had lost the pen, I found it right there, but it could not be used since the forces of nature had rendered it useless. I could not comprehend how I lost it only to find it a year later at the very spot I searched thoroughly before my exams.

As I was awaiting the release of my results, Father advised that I go to Nairobi and start persuading my brother to pay my school fees if I passed my exams. My brother stayed in Majengo. That estate was the home of *chang'aa* and promiscuity; prostitution was the order of the day and my brother, his wife and children lived in a tiny room flanked by two brothels. Toilet was communal and it was a room fourteen feet by ten feet, with a trench filled with water running the entire length of the building and draining into some kind of septic tank. There were small cubicles inside the building where one could bathe in a basin.

My brother was a drunkard per excellence. He would be broke two hours after receiving his salary most of the time. He worked in a press as a printer and earned good money, but he had nothing to show for it. If I was around and needed fees, I would accompany him to his work place and ask his employer to pay him the balance after giving me fees. This was the reason my father asked me to go and stay with him in Nairobi.

KAPE results were released when I was in Nairobi. My brother arranged for me to travel back home to get the results. I had performed marvelously well. It was beyond my expectations. I had straight As…only that in that year they used numbers instead of letters. I had *one* in English, *one* in Arithmetic, and *one* in Nature Study. Besides, I was the second-best pupil in the entire province. I knew I would go to Maseno High School the moment I saw the results.

My cousin, Nehemia Onyango, who worked in Maseno School, came home and informed us that my name was on the list of those called to join Form I at the school. He advised that we wait for the letter. We waited for weeks— nothing came either from Maseno or my two other choices. Everybody who was supposed to be called had been called—even those with a mean grade of two or three. The other four boys with a mean grade of one had been called. Felgona Achieng, with mean grade of two, had been called. What had happened to my letter?

On the fourth week—after I had lost hope of ever being called—I received a a letter from Kamagambo. The timing suggested that I had been taken by Kamagambo on 2nd selection, since I had failed to take my chance at Maseno. The thing is—Maseno released me for 2nd selection and that is how I ended with a letter from Kamagambo. It is clear Maseno High school had released my letter. It was received at our home/village and whoever got it either sat on it or simply destroyed it. If I had to make an intelligent guess, given the bad blood between me and my step-mother, I'd say she must have received the letter in Father's absence and hid it from us.

I do not regret having been called to Kamagambo; I would have been a nobody if I hadn't gone there. Kamagambo shaped my life into what I would later be in life. In spite of the tribulations along the way, I believe I've lived a satisfying life courtesy of Kamagambo Secondary School.

CHAPTER 6

JEZEBEL

My father was about 62 years old when he got married to my step-mother, Loice Wandati. She was thirty five. She had been through two previous marriages in quick succession. Both ended in constructive desertion and finally divorce. Father knew the problems inherent in marrying a divorcee, more so one that appeared to be a rolling stone. He probably was prepared for the consequences. He was desperate and, like a drowning man, prepared to grasp even at a twig to save himself. He was old enough to be her father. That age-gap would definitely cause problems. Her daughter, by the first marriage, would be married in three years. She would soon be a grandma.

Father, despite his old age, was still robust. The marriage would be blessed with five children: Ondunga, Atieno, Omondi, Miriam and Ogola. That was the order of their births between 1959 and 1970. She would later have grand and even great grand children. Life continued and my brother James and I stepped in to help Father's second family. We knew the important role our step-mother was playing in his life, a role we could not play even if we were millionaires. She realized that Father had been desperate for a wife and started taking advantage of the special place she occupied in his heart. She demanded and got anything she wanted. She soon took full control of things in the home. Instead of consulting him on the goings-on, she by-passed him and did as she pleased. Eventually Father was rendered powerless. Everything he did or wanted to do he consulted her and kind of begged her. If she didn't accept, that was the end of the matter. I am glad she didn't demand that I be banished from home. I would have been rendered homeless.

During the initial moments of their marriage, I was the only child of my mother at home. I was thirteen years old when my step-mother came home. My eldest sister, Aduda, had been married in 1949 and Lewnida had been married in 1956. Both were at their matrimonial homes. My brothers Muhudhi and Okech were at their work stations. Muhudhi was in Nakuru and Okech in Moshi, Tanganyika. James was in Burma for further studies. Among my father's children, of both families, I was the one who lived with my step-mother the longest. I even outlived my father. I knew her traits well. I could tell when she had been back-biting someone. I could detect when she was pretending or lying outright. Things like baying, cursing and spewing absurdities were common knowledge in the village. When she picked a quarrel with Father, everybody in the village knew it. She would shout abusively, curse and threaten to leave him. He would be there alright, listening, but the man whose mere presence sent shivers down the spine of many would stay mute throughout the ambarrasing tirades.

Cursing was her trademark even though she was a practicing member of the SDA church. Soon after marrying my father she was baptized. She pretended to be an SDA member but inwardly she was not.SDAs don't curse, backbite or pinch. But my step-mother did all these yet still claimed to be an SDA. I knew her well. I knew what she liked and what she didn't like. I knew when she simply didn't want to talk and when she had a problem with me. In adulthood, she feared me. Wherever I returned home and found her cursing, she would stop and hurriedly dash to her house. Her characteristics were many and varied. There were some bad things she did to everybody including her own children—things like backbiting and setting up one person against another. She would later have a lot of problems over these with her sons and their wives. I was not spared either. She nearly ruined my wife.

She was the litmus that triggered the estrangement of my wife and I. Pinching was in her blood and—along with envy and eavesdropping, she passed them down to her children. All her children had these attributes embedded in them. She could pinch virtually anything, from utensils to my kids' napkins to my wife's dresses and underpants. Whatever I did for my family, she wanted done for herself. But this was impossible. Anything good happening in my family was anathema to her—the birth of a child, graduation of a member of my family or even marriage. She detested anything good, but God continued to bless us and added us more and more blessings.

Eavesdropping was one heck of a problem. At night she would stealthily come and stand behind my cottage and listen as my wife and I intimately conversed. This was one of the reasons I moved out of my father's homestead and owned my own home prematurely. When her children started doing the same thing, I said enough was enough and started making arrangements to move out of my father's homestead. Her lies caused me a lot of confrontations with my father. But those were nothing in comparison to what she heaped on me after the accidental death of her son, Ondunga. First she said I killed him. How I did it I could not comprehend. The guy died five hundred miles from home in a motor vehicle accident!

After I fired him as a matatu conductor when he stole money, he made his way to Mombasa, where he got a job with a transporting company as a loader. On the day of the accident, they had ferried cement from Mombasa to Turkwell Gourge. On their way back, the lorry driver stopped at a market to buy cigarettes and left Ondunga in the driver's cabin with the engine running. Ondunga did not know how to drive, and had no driver's license. In spite of this, he got into the driver's seat, engaged the gear and off the lorry went. The area was hilly and the road had many sharp corners. There were deep valleys and gourges on the sides of the road. The lorry started gaining speed and the guy had no idea what to do. It sped on uncontrollably and crashed into a valley one hundred feet deep. Everybody in that lorry died.

Lawrence Otieno, a police officer and a friend whom I retained to follow up the matter, briefed me on how the accident occurred. Which insurance company can pay compensation for an accident like that? Which employer can compensate a turnboy (loader) who unlawfully drives a lorry and kills many people in it? In spite of all these, my step-mother had the cheek to say Ondunga's death was compensated and I received the compensation which I failed to hand over to her. These were the white lies which she implanted in her children, who saw me as an enemy; one who got their brother's compensation money and never gave it to them!

My step-mother loved food, but she loved tea even better. Smoking ten cents and drinking tea was her life. She stayed awake late into the night to enable her to smoke and drink tea out of the sight of everybody, including Father. I suspect Father didn't know she smoked. Father had such a strong dislike for smoking that I shudder to think how he would have reacted had he known. The last twelve out of twenty seven years he stayed with her, he retreated to my mother's house and could not possibly be privy to lots of what was going on in my step-mother's house.

The one thing that contributed to retrogression and even the demise of some of her family members was lack of discipline. She had the capability but not the ability to discipline her children. The children grew by instinct. I tried to intervene to instill some discipline in them but this was frowned upon by her and when I discovered that Father was powerless to do anything, I stopped and the consequences became devastating.

Hygiene and tidiness were foreign to her. The house was always in a mess since it was shared with live chickens. This state of untidiness is one of the things she passed on to her children.

To her credit, though, she was highly industrious. Like my mother before her, she could work in the field (Shamba) and put food on the table. If it were not for this she would not have helped me reconstruct the home. She was like a big tree with a big shadow in our home. Everybody took shelter underneath it. She provided shelter for her children, my nephews and other relatives. I was particularly impressed with the way she looked after her grandsons—Opiyo and Odongo. Once she had money to buy food, making that food was no big deal. She could not stay put and wait for manna from heaven. She worked hard and only required supplementary support from outside sources. That was where Dunga, my family and I came in. Even after she had known her illness was terminal, she still continued to till and by the time she died, she had maize, which she could have eaten until the following season. The maize, chicken and other property she had in her house were taken by her son Omondi and daughter Atieno immediately after she died, unmindful of the rights of their surviving kin who had equal claim to the property.

When a mother died and was survived by offspring and a husband, the widower could marry another wife. The new wife had the dual responsibility of taking care of the husband as well as the children whose mother had died. All of my mother's children, except I, were adults. All had married or had been married, except James. I was the only child of my mother who was still young and needed, not only love and affection, but parental care. I believed that before they married Father explained to my step-mother his marital situation. She must have known that Father had children by the first marriage that she was coming to take care of. This was going to be her primary responsibility. The fact that I was the only small one lightened the load. But it did not take long before she started showing animosity towards my mother's family. Her disdain for my mother's family became so conspicuous and overwhelming, that things started happening to my mother's family, the sources of which could be traced.

First, my brother Okech returned from Tanganyika and stayed for a while. She disagreed with him and they exchanged some unsavory words. He went back to Tanganyika and never voluntarily returned. His family disintegrated; the wife deserted and his children were abandoned. That was the end of that family. That was the first step in the desolation of my mother's family after her death.

One day my eldest brother Absalom returned home from his place of work. He stayed home a whole week. Since Father disliked him because he was a drunkard, my step-mother followed suit and hated him too. His disagreement with my step-mother came as a result of her refusal to give him food. They exchanged bitter words and although he had intended on staying a fortnight, he returned to Nairobi after just seven days. That was the last time he came home alive. He died under mysterious circumstances in 1968. Shortly before he died, my step-mother left home to visit an unknown place. My brother died in Nairobi and his body was brought home after three weeks, for burial. My step-mother returned home one week after the burial. She did not appear surprised that there was a funeral at home.

My brother James and his wife Christabel had differed with her. They alleged that when she went to Kakamega, where he worked, when Christabel had given birth to her second child, she stole some napkins and Christabel's underpants. These under-pants were never recovered. Christabel never gave birth again. As a result of this they had a strained relationship. Whenever they were together it was war; incessant war. Later James and his entire family, except one, were wiped out in an accident that claimed the lives of five people, four from one family, my mother's family. When James had this accident, he had just come from home. Several other accidents would occur as victims came from home. Personally I experienced three accidents, all happening when I was coming from home. My son Benard had a vehicular accident, also coming from home. So long as one did not get into contact with her, there was no vehicle accident!

These, together with the curses, the persecutions and outright hostilities she exhibited towards members of my mother's family, were strong indicators that her main objective was to obliterate Mulure's family. In this mission, she almost succeeded had I not learned survival tactics. God gave me the wisdom to overcome pitfalls and stay in some semblance of peace.

My patience and tolerance almost snapped when I came home one day and found my mother's house demolished. On inquiry, I was told she ordered the house demolished because she wanted to use the corrugated iron sheets. I nearly hit the roof with rage. My mother's house was unique. It was a constant reminder that the home belonged to her. Father never built a homestead for my step-mother. Whenever the mother of the homestead died, her house had to be maintained. If it got old, a new one had to be built. This would be the case so long as people lived in that homestead. The demolition of my mother's house could be interpreted in two ways. One, that she did not want anything in the home reminding her of my mother's family. By this time I had moved out of the homestead. Second, she wanted to claim the home as hers. Whatever the motive, if God grants me life and resources; a better house for my mother will come up sooner rather than later.

I have mentioned a bunch of incidents which strongly indicate bias, dislike and resentment of my mother's family by my step-mother. These incidents are not exhaustive. There were many more. If I were to write about every one of them, I would need a separate book for that. There is, however, one incident which sticks out like a sore thumb. In 1961 Absalom's wife, Sylvia Awiti, came home from Nairobi to stay with us for a while. She got ill and the illness did not respond to any treatment that was thrown at it. Her condition continued to deteriorate. My father and step-mother were there, but they refused to take Sylvia to a hospital where she could be treated. I was away in boarding school. The husband was in Nairobi, three hundred miles away. Nobody bothered to inform him about the illness. When schools closed for holidays, I came home and what I saw shook me to the core. I was informed Sylvia was home but very sick. She had not been eating solid food for a whole week. She could not walk, I was told. I went to her house to see her. The stench emanating from inside the house was repulsive. You would think someone dumped rotten meat inside the house. I braved the stench and moved in. Sylvia was half-dead. She was on a bed lying on her back. She spoke, but inaudibly. I strained to hear what she was saying; she was disparately trying to communicate something to me. She was half-naked. Indeed she had not eaten for a long time. She looked frail and emaciated. I then noticed a wound on her belly, three inches long. There was a hole in the wound which was actually cylindrical. On a closer look I noticed it had been infested by maggots.

Maggots were feasting on the flesh around the hole. I peeped into the hole and saw what I thought was the outer lining of the stomach or intestines. Her breathing was in consonance with the in and out movement of the part of the stomach or intestine I had seen. She was definitely going to die unless something was done fast. I went out and fetched my father and asked him why they had not taken her to the hospital or even informed her husband. He said they had no money and there was nothing they could do without money. I told him she was going to die unless she was rushed to a specialist. He said she was beyond help and that she would die anyway whether she was taken to a hospital or not. I was still young and immature but I knew Father was not unable to raise money to take Sylvia to the hospital. He had just refused to try, maybe at the instigation of my step-mother. I went back into the house to talk to Sylvia and try to make out what she was struggling to tell me. With a strained and drowning voice, she said, "I should not be taken to Maseno or Kisumu. They will refuse to treat me. The wound you see is a busted surgical wound. After the surgery in Kisumu I was warned not to do hard jobs like digging or drawing water from the river, but I ignored the warning. What you see is the result of defiance." I left her and went out to think. I reasoned that if I had money, I could take her to the hospital, but which hospital? I went out of the homestead to the neighbours to inquire which hospital, a part from Maseno or Kisumu, I could take her to. Nangina Mission Hospital, they said.

Nangina was thirty miles away and was served by only one bus—Lolwe. Yes, I had identified the hospital but how about the money to transport me and the patient to the hospital? I went back to Sylvia to find out if she had any money. She had none. Then a thought crossed my mind. Couldn't we find something in the house which we could pawn and get enough money out of? After all, we only needed fifty shillings. Sylvia and I settled on the two blankets she was using. The agreement was that we take and pledge the two blankets and let her use my blanket that night. I then went out to look for someone who would accept blankets as a pledge for Kshs 50.00. I failed to find one. Just when I was about to give up, Enock Ongaya came to see Sylvia. When he saw the condition in which she was, he agreed to give us Kshs 50.00 on condition it was not going to be a pledge but an outright sale. Since we had no problem with that, we gave him the two blankets and he brought us the Kshs 50.00. Enock Ongaya was the son of Omwala and Ongoma, the lady who helped deliver me.

The following day, early in the morning, I cleaned up and groomed Sylvia for the journey to Nangina. I looked for a wheelbarrow and wheeled her to the road to await Lolwe. In good health, Sylvia weighed two hundred and thirty pounds. I was fifteen and small. I must have weighed about one hundred pounds. The disparity in weight would soon be a big problem. The bus came and the turnboys helped me get her in. We were finally on our way to Nangina Mission Hospital. The trouble was that I had not been to Nangina and had to rely on the turn boys for direction. They knew I was taking a patient to the hospital.

At Nangina there were two bus stages—one for the main hospital, the other for the dispensary. In fact, the stage for the hospital was called Mission Stage and the stage for the dispensary was known as Hospital Stage. The two stages were one mile apart. When I told the turnboys we would alight at the hospital, they dropped us off at the dispensary. The dispensary and the hospital were a mile and a half apart. Can you imagine what that felt like? I didn't know what to do. It was around nine o'clock, in the morning, when we disembarked, but did not make it to the hospital until four in the evening. I had no wheelbarrow, no bicycle nor a vehicle to carry the patient. I just had to make her walk or walk her. I passed my right arm under her armpit and firmly held her shoulder blade. I then shoved her up. It was obvious she was in excruciating pain. She only made four to five steps at a time before she rested. I needed to rest too. I tried to ask passersby to help, but none was able to tolerate the smell.

They made sure they kept a safe distance from us. It took us six hours to make the one and a half mile journey!

The nurses were good. Most of them were white. When they saw me with the patient, they rushed to meet us with a wheelchair. They rushed her straight to the ward. After admission formalities were concluded, I was asked where her husband was. I lied he was dead and that I was the only relative alive. They asked me if I could sign to authorize surgical treatment. I agreed and signed. I did not understand the implications, though. All done, I made it back to the road, hoping to catch any means back home. That was not to be. At the road, I was informed that the only public transport was Lolwe. It came from Kisumu in the morning and went back in the afternoon. I went back to the hospital and explained my predicament to the nurses. They understood my plight and gave me a place to sleep. The following day, I made it back home.

Three days later, I saw my step-mother preparing to go on a journey. On inquiring, I was told she was going to see Sylvia at Nangina. I could not believe my ears. *My step-mother going to visit the patient? No way!* This woman had said they could not take Sylvia to the hospital because they did not have money. Now that I had taken her to the hospital, where had the money come from for the journey to Nangina? That was the most selfish and incredible thing I had ever heard. *Give me a break!*

But it happened she went. Like Jezebel, she had no shame at all. She was probably going thinking she would find her dead, but God worked miracles on Sylvia. The operation went smoothly and she recovered fully and lived another thirty eight years.

When schools opened, I went back.

Then I came home for end of term holidays. As usual I was radiant and robust. The vegetarian menu at school had proved wholesome and healthy. I instantly became the centre of attraction to girls my age. They were afraid to make the first move though. I enjoyed the spectacle as I walked by and they giggled and hid their faces. I changed my pose and mode of walking. They liked it, some of them burst into laughter. I knew they were falling for me.

One Saturday evening—as I was strolling to Kodiaga—I met this beautiful lass. She was everything like me, except gender. She was my age, complexion and size. She carried herself around with confidence. She had a stern but lovely look. She must have rebuffed many boys who dared talk to her. As I greeted her, out of the blue, she stretched her hand to shake my hand. I was going to Kodiaga where she had just come from.

I engaged her in a conversation and her response was inviting. Five minutes of boy-girl talk is a long time, particularly if that talk is the first and the girl is hurrying in order not to offend her mother who had sent her to the shop. That was how I met Jane Osore, my first girlfriend. She was the daughter of Bernard Odera, whose home was half a mile away from ours. Osore and I would see each other during the holidays until the end of second term—in 1962. We were still naïve, but we loved each other a lot. Both her parents and mine did not approve of the relationship and for good reason—that we were still young.

One Friday evening, during the beginning of the second term holidays, she passed by my place. I had not eaten anything the previous evening because I had some friends visiting. I was expected to be going to eat at my parents' house. I could not take a whole bunch of friends to my parents' house to eat. The result was that I forewent my meals. This Friday evening was no exception. On Saturday I was tired and did not go to church. I was in an empty tummy. It was one o'clock in the afternoon and we were sitting around a table in the living room of James' cottage, which I used as my sleeping cottage. My cousin Jack, as he was popularly known, was on my right and Osore was sitting directly opposite where I was sitting, separated by a table.

To my left was the door, and directly behind her was a window. Since I was very hungry, she was peeling a paw paw for me using a knife I always carried for my personal protection. Suddenly my step-mother appeared at the door and, without uttering a word, rushed to Osore and slapped her a couple of times and they fell down together. I was transfixed and astonished and I did not know whether to pounce on her and beat her up or push her out of the cottage. In the heat of the moment, I decided to do neither. I could neither beat nor forcibly grasp my step-mother; that was taboo. At any rate, I knew my father would kill me if I laid my hand on her. As I was pondering what to do, Jack, in an instant, got up, grasped her and pulled her from Osore. He pushed her outside the cottage. This gave Osore a chance to stand, squeeze through the window and run, with my step-mother in hot pursuit, shouting, "*Malaya...malaya.*" Can you believe it?

I got mad. I had never been as annoyed in my life as I was that day. *My step-mother beating my girlfriend; chasing her out of the home and calling her a prostitute?* That was more than I could take. In those days, if you were a boy my age and did not have a girlfriend, your parents got worried. They got worried because they were not sure you could court a girl for marriage when the right time came. There was no wrong I had done. I had not eaten her food. And since it was a Saturday, Osore's presence could not be said to have prevented me from going to the *shamba*. It did not have anything to do with school either since schools were closed. To this day I don't know what triggered the animosity. I hate to speculate, but what immediately came to mind was that this was part of her grand plan to subdue me. Later in life, I watched with interest to see if she would ever do the same to her children. She didn't. Her sons did more heinous things than this and both her daughters got children out of wedlock. She could not even utter as much as a squeak.

That day I got so mad, I could not speak. I didn't know what I would have done to her had she stayed around; luckily she had run after Osore and had not come back. Jack and I left the cottage crestfallen. What would the village boys say? They would ridicule us, me in particular, for months. They would say I didn't have guts to stand up to my step-mother. I would be a laughing stock and a centre of village gossip. That's what ran through my mind.

Jack's presence worsened matters. He was known to have a loose tongue and could make up stories. I was in a fix. I walked into my step-mother's kitchen. She had not returned. Father had not come back from church either. In the kitchen, water for *ugali* was boiling on one hearth. On the other was a pot of meat, warming. In my rage, I smashed the pot of meat to smithereens, emptied the *ugali* pot and poured out flour into the water. Within seconds, the kitchen was a mess. Nobody was going to eat anything in that home that day. I then moved to the main house, where I smashed everything—chairs, stools and tables. Nothing was left standing. I did not, however, move into their bedroom.

As I was making my way out, satisfied with my payback, I met my step- mother and she gave me a wide berth. I had a big stick in my hand and my knife was inside its holster, which was fastened to my belt. I left the knife visible for all to see. As I walked past the gate, I saw Osore standing a few yards away from it. Apparently, after my step-mother lost track of her, and after ensuring my step-mother had returned to the homestead, she made her way to hand back my wristwatch, which she had when she was attacked. I had now cooled down and composed myself. She did not speak. She just handed over the watch. I told her to wait right there while I returned home to take care of some business. She obliged. I went home, locked up the door to my cottage and returned. That marked the beginning of the seven days Osore and I were going to stay together.

We hid in the bush nearby, waiting for darkness. I was sure Father had returned and was looking for me. I was determined to evade him. While I was sure he would not approve of my step-mother's beating of Osore, my subsequent actions, as a result of the consuming rage, were unforgivable and begged for punishment. In the cover of darkness, Osore and I made it to Jack's cottage. Here, we insulated ourselves from the rest of the world, except Jack.

For seven days we lived in Jack's cottage, attending calls of nature and bathing only at night. This night was the second I was going to sleep without food. Jack did not know we were coming so he did not make any arrangements for our meals. It would not be until evening of the following day before we ate anything. Jack sacrificed a lot for us. He did not reveal our presence in his cottage to anyone. What he did to feed us was—he took his lunch but forwent supper for us. Meanwhile, Father looked for me everywhere. He visited everywhere he thought I could be. What he did not know was that I was only one hundred yards away from home. He came looking for me at Jack's homestead but since Jack's parents did not know I was there, he went away satisfied I was not there. But there was a problem. School was to open in just three days, and since my brother had sent my school fees and transport, I had to go. I told Osore we had to leave our hideout. But she too feared to go back to her home. Her father would beat life out of her. Besides, my father's frustration didn't help her cause. You see, Father had gone to her home and gave her parents a piece of his mind.

"Go and look for your dog and bring her home and tether her," he roared.

This didn't go down well with Osore's parents. They got quite upset when my father referred to their daughter as a dog—I was later told. Makes me wonder to date what she thought when I told her I had to go to school. She eventually settled on her maternal uncle's home as the place to go. By the second cockcrow, on the eighth day, I escorted her towards her maternal uncle's home in Regea. When we got to the spot where we were to say our goodbyes, she held me and refused to let go. I told her it was important for me to complete my education and get a job then come take her with me. After what looked like eternity, she released her grip. We wished each other well and parted ways. That was the last time I saw her. I later learned she had married my maternal cousin, had a couple of children and later died.

By midday, I returned home and found Father and my step-mother eating *ugali* and vegetables. I did not talk to them and they did not talk to me. My hunger over shadowed my anger. I still wore a serious face to deter any confrontation. I then moved to where they were seated, grabbed the *ugali* and, with my right hand, turned it upside down onto my left palm and made a hole in it with my right fist. Done, I took the bowl of vegetables and poured the content into the hole, then walked away. I went straight to my cottage and found the door open. My father had broken open the door and removed my belongings. I perched myself on a table and enjoyed the meal. A real one in ten days. As I walked to my cottage, I left my step-mother and Father in a state of bewilderment. They did not know where I had been the past eight days. To them, it appeared as if I had just returned from the dead. They probably had given up hope of ever finding me alive. The following day and subsequent they gave me food. When the time came for me to return to school, I left without a fuss. Little did I know that a decision made behind my back would spell doom for my studies.

I suffered a lot when I was growing up. Those supposed to care turned against me. I lived with a very dangerous woman. Father had no idea what I was going through. But even if he knew, he could do nothing about it. You see, food was my step-mother's weapon of choice. She used it to inflict injury mentally and physically. A part from being denied food during school days, I remember a four-week break in 1962. I was denied food by my step-mother for the duration of the break. The reason was that I had overreacted when she beat up my girlfriend. To this day, though, I believe she had no business beating my girlfriend. This denial of food started after Aduda had come home with her sick children. She brought them for treatment at Malanga Dispensary. She stayed with us for a while. What upset me was that I was being denied food with the full knowledge and acquiesce of Father. They wanted to turn me into a thief; otherwise how did they expect me to survive? But Aduda came to my rescue. She had three small children. Whenever they prepared *ugali* for her and her kids, she divided it into three parts. She ate one part and gave the children another. The remaining third she kept for me. This went on for three weeks—

the time she stayed with us. But I still had one week before I went back to school. Luckily we were also staying with Absalom's son—Thuthu. Thuthu took over from where my sister left off. The small *ugali* he was given he shared with me discretely. This went on until I returned to school. I will forever be grateful to Aduda and Thuthu. If it were not for them, perhaps I would have been a jailbird.

The needle that broke the camel's back came in January 1963. I had gone to Nairobi in December 1960 to plead with my brother to be paying my fees. He agreed. Fees in Kamagambo were heavier than other schools, but he managed to pay my 1961 and 1962 fees. When school opened in 1963, I expected fees from him as usual. At the leventh hour, though, I was told that he was not going to pay my fees. I was shocked. I had completed form two and was going to form three. I had performed very well the previous year and was looking forward to a great year. But this was not to be. I later learned it was conspiracy of my step-mother and my brother's wife—again with the acquiesce of my father. I felt so sad.

Other than beating my girlfriend, I had difficulty getting them to provide food for my guests—not just girls, even the boys. The contrast was big. Mother used to prepare food and pass it for anybody who was hungry, but this time I was required to leave guests in my cottage and go to my step mother's house to eat. I refused. If I was not going to share my food, however little with my friends, I wasn't going to eat at all. Thus the standoff continued whenever I had guests. But the ultimate humiliation came when I had guests from Alego. This one I'll take to my grave!

My wives were fodder for my step-mother. She had perfected the art of manipulation. She could play one against the other with ease. In the presence of one the others were bad. When the bad one came, the good one was bad. This made them quarrel often until they learned her motive. She wanted to destabilize them, make them leave. She was reported to have asked one of them to leave me. My wife refused to play ball and I was not amused at all.

But the ultimate sin she committed was maltreatment of Father. The man she had come to take care of she was now running down. There were days I literally cried when I saw what she subjected Father to. The first heinous thing she did was to chase Father away from her house, thereby denying him love and affection. Father moved into my mother's house without a fuss. From that moment on, Father became a completely different person. He lost interest in life. He became moody and irritant. He lost three quarters of his sight and rarely went out. He could not even go to church. I don't know whether he made this up, but he suffered partial loss of hearing as well. But the saddest of them all was denial of food. When I lived in Father's homestead, he could not go hungry; my wife was there to give him food. When I left, he became vulnerable. He was at the mercy of my step-mother. It mattered little that I bought the necessary provisions. Father would sometimes come to my home and tearfully ask for food. One day we decided we would just give him breakfast, lunch and supper the rest of the time. After a while, though, he stopped eating. On inquiry I found out that she wanted us to send food to everyone, not just Father. We tried alternatives, but our efforts were frustrated by her. Painful as it **was**, we had to go easy for fear that she could make good her threats—leave Father or poison his food.

I had seen brutes, sadists or even downright hardcore criminals but not anything like this. I believe my father would not have died the way he died, if he could have had love, affection and proper care. The three corner stone of decent living which his wife failed to give him. Money to take care of my father was not a problem. In 1974 I arranged to give my father a monthly allowance for his out of pocket expenses and food for the family. He received this allowance until he died. In addition to that allowance we still provided the family with maize, millet, meat, fish, eggs, chickens to enable them eat well. Why my step mother could not give Father food, I couldn't understand. It was not that she could not cook. She was just being malicious and wanted to accelerate the demise of Father.

I hope Father—as a result of marrying my step-mother—will not suffer for her manipulative actions and sins as King Ahab did as a result of marrying Jezebel and succumbing to her sins, intrigues and manipulation. The parallels are too similar to ignore. Earlier on I said I learned survival tactics in our home. Living in our home, you had to be battle-hardened. I was hardened, but I saw the hand of God in it. Later, in my life, I realized that God allowed me to go through those hardships and tribulations for a purpose. He was preparing me for what awaited me in the future. I had to be focused and alert all the time. I watched every move of my foes. I even watched Father. But I tried to avoid confrontation with my step-mother. It was so draining.

Over time, I evolved seven cardinal rules. These would see me fend off waves of conspiracy, harassment and devilish onslaughts thrown my way or to members of my family. These tactics were:

- Don't disagree or be seen to disagree with my step-mother
- Don't show your disdain to step-mother
- Behave and carry yourself as if nothing is wrong even when something is wrong
- Provide assistance as before
- Be careful what you eat or drink and where you eat or drink
- Don't take alcohol
- PASTORAY

I held on to these cardinal rules until my step-mother died. And through the rest of my life, I have never deviated from them!

To close this chapter, let me leave you with the words of the Apostle Paul. He says:

Dear friends never take revenge. Leave that to the righteous anger of God. For the scriptures say, "I will take revenge, I will pay them back," says the Lord. Instead, "if your enemies are hungry, feed them; If they are thirsty give them something to drink. In doing this you will heap burning coals of shame on their heads." Don't let evil conquer you, but conquer evil by doing good. (Romans 12:19 – 21, NLT)

So my motto was and will forever be: OVERCOME EVIL WITH GOOD.

CHAPTER 7

DELUGE

My brother Absalom sent me school fees as he had promised. I joined Kamagambo SDA Secondary School in form one, in 1961. I was the smallest in the entire school. Luckily there was one student, Willis Asimba, who came from Gem. He took charge of protecting me. Willis was in the teacher training section, training as teacher. Before joining Kamagambo, I was warned that first year students were bullied. Because of Willis' protection, however, I was never bullied at all.

A few surprises awaited me though. At meal time, *ugali* with beans was served. I neither liked the smell nor the taste of beans. It was like *nyoyo* (maize mixed with beans and cooked) with a lot of soup added. I did not like the soup either. I had never eaten *ugali* and beans before. I told Willis I did not like the food. He said, "Oremo, if you don't like the food (pointing at my plate), you can give me the soup, but try to eat the beans. In two weeks you will be complaining if they don't serve you beans with soup." Oremo was a slang word for Gem. With those words, I felt disarmed, gave him the soup and tried to force myself to eat. This was the beginning of the vegetarian menu I was going to eat for 4 years. Breakfast was porridge all the time. Lunch was either *nyoyo* with porridge or *ugali* with beans or cabbage. Supper was *ugali* with beans, cabbage, kales, groundnuts (peanuts) *dengu* or greengrams *dengu*. Towards the end of my stay in Kamagambo, they introduced a special meal which was served only on Fridays—rice and beans. We cherished that one!

The school had a generator for electricity. By 10:00 everybody was supposed to be in bed and quiet. I did not know students were supposed to be quiet after lights were off. Willis did not give me adequate orientation. I continued talking that night to a student who was sleeping on the top bed. Because of my age, they did not give me the upper bed, although that was what I would have preferred—for fear of bed-wetting. Suddenly someone gave me a lash on my side and the dormitory went quiet. I did not know who it was. What I could tell immediately was that whoever he was, his presence meant danger. The following morning I asked Willis who it was. He told me it was the preceptor, Erastus Angienda, the man in charge of discipline in the dormitories. Needless to say, that would mark the last time I received a lash.

At 5:00 a.m. the bell rang and everybody jumped out of bed, except me. I did not understand what was happening. Willis, however, came to my rescue again. He said, "Oremo, wake up, time is up. You shower at once because at 5:45 you must be in class. Can you belive it? I thought he was joking. As I continued to lie in bed, I heard a commotion, as if people were scrambling out. In the background I saw the preceptor. I jumped off my bed and made for the door. I met face to face with him, only this time he did not lash me. I made it to the bathroom and forced myself to take a cold shower. We went to class and broke for breakfast at 8:00 a.m. By 8:30 a.m. we were back in class, with only a short break at 10:00 a.m. At 1:00 p.m. we went for lunch and at 2:00 p.m. students were given *jembes* and slashers and led to the *shamba* to slash and dig for two hours. 5:00 p.m. was time for games. Supper was served at 6:00 p.m. and by 7:00 p.m. students were in class for preps. This was our routine Monday through Friday.

On Saturdays things were quite relaxed. Breakfast was served and all students were to be in church by 8:30 a.m. Lunch was served at 1:00 p.m. and then students went for excursion at 3:00 o'clock and returned at 5:00 p.m. Supper and preps were at the usual time, except on Fridays when there were no preps because of the Sabbath. On Sundays, after breakfast, students went for a 5-hour work programme in the farm and around the school compound. There were Sabbath-welcoming ceremonies every Friday evenings at sundown and Sabbath-closing ceremonies on Saturday evenings.

The term was rather uneventful. Exposure to new things and adjustment to my new lifestyle took the greater part of my time.

In August 1961 the weather suddenly changed. It started raining heavily. Sometimes it rained through the day and night. Everywhere in the school compound was like a cattle kraal—wet flooded and muddy. Crops were washed away by gushing waters. Rivers overflew their banks, and bridges were washed away. The rains and the floods curtailed all outdoor activities including work programme and games. It was a trying time!

Kamagambo was a complex made of a teachers training college, a secondary school, a girls boarding school and two mixed primary schools. Of the mixed primary schools, one was for *Luos*, the other for *Kisiis*. These institutions were separated by barbed wire, fences

One day—as we were returning from student walk—I decided to jump over the fence that separated the secondary section from the road. I did not know the ground was that wet and slippery. I slipped and landed on my left side. I injured myself pretty badly on the barbed wire. I had wounds on my left leg, thigh and pelvic muscle. I also had wounds on my left arm and hand. I bled profusely. I was rushed to the school dispensary, where I was stitched, treated and discharged. I got very sick as result of this misadventure. I could hardly walk. But the hard part came when I had to go to the toilet. The toilets were the squatting type. Since I could not bend my knees, I could not squat. Using the toilet became a nightmare. I had to do it standing. You can imagine the discomfort. Luckily, within two weeks I was up and about. I never forgot the incident and the pain I suffered, as a result of the deluge.

The rains continued to come down. Rivers overflew and bridges between Kamagambo and Kisumu were washed away. Buses stopped running. As the December holidays drew nigh, we started worrying about how we would get home. There was no traveling between Kamagambo and Kisumu. We were told that anyone who wanted to travel to Kisumu had to go to Homa bay—25 miles away—and take steamship to Kisumu. But even if we managed to make it to Kisumu, we were not sure of reaching home because bridges between Kisumu and Gem were washed away too.

Regardless, when schools closed we walked to Homa Bay from Kamagambo and took the steamship to Kisumu. I sat leaning on a rail at the stern of the steamship and, as I had walked all night and had not had time to sleep, I soon dozed off. One passenger saw how precarious the place I was sitting was and got nervous. If I went into deep sleep I could slide and drop into the water. He came and took me away from there, explaining the dangers inherent in sleeping while seated there. I never went there again. And although it was my first ride, I never got seasick.

We arrived in Kisumu safely. On inquiry, we were told the bridges along the route between Kisumu and Gem were intact, but there was one bus (OTC) that plied the route. Out of the 5 students who took the steamship to Kisumu, only 2 of us—Jully Achieng and I—were traveling farther than Kisumu. Billy Opundo and his cousins decided to sit out the rains in Kisumu.

Jully and I took the OTC to Busia, but before we arrived at our respective destinations, the driver was warned that there was a section along the way that was flooded and muddy and could not be passed. The driver decided to take a diversion to avoid driving to the impassable section. By 8:00 in the evening we reached a section where it was very muddy. The bus got stuck. Since there was nothing we could do to proceed with our journey, we slept in the bus till morning. By 11:00 in the morning, when the road had dried a little, the driver started struggling to get the bus out of the embarkment. After about an hour of struggle, the bus got out of the rut and within a couple of minutes, we arrived at the junction of the main road, where we had to alight. I left my luggage in a shop at Sidindi and went home walking—a distance of 6 miles. It took me 2 and half days to make it home from the school.

Schools opened for the New Year. My brother Absalom sent me the fees and I went back to school. During the half-term break, I went to visit Uncle Fanuel Odhiambo Ndoya at Rombe, in Uriri, South Nyanza. Fanuel was an uncle who, along with Pastor Sylfano, had migrated to South Nyanza; though not at the same time. His son, William Otieno Odhiambo, was in Kamagambo at the time too. He was popularly known as Green. Green and I were in the same class. He would later come to my assistance in the hour of need.

Rombe was about 25 miles from Kamagambo. We set off walking to Rombe and it took 5 hours to make the trip. You can imagine how elated my uncle was when he saw me. He and his wife, Janet, were all-smiles. Seeing me reminded them of my deceased mother—and my father—with whom they were very close before they moved. To show his overwhelming gratitude, Uncle slaughtered a cow. The guy who was brought in by Uncle to slaughter and skin the cow did something that seemed out of the ordinary. After opening up the carcass, and in the process of cutting different parts, he cut a piece of meat, dipped it into the cow's chine and tossed it into his mouth. I had never seen anybody eat raw meat before. It was disgusting. He cut another, then another, repeating the process until he could eat no more.

Janet Ochere—Green's mother—was a wonderful cook. She prepared the tastiest *ojury* I ever ate. *Ojury* was a mixture of the internal parts of a slaughtered animal: heart, liver spleen, intestines and other softer parts of meat. Add salt, seasoning and bile and you got the best *ojury*. I ate my meal with relish. Everybody was happy. In the evening, as Green played a gramophone for our entertainment, Samuel Okumu kept repeating—at the end of every record—*Gino dhi gwaro leses* (that thing is going to scratch the license). Samuel was the youngest in a family of 8: Dan, Green, Enock, Elijah, Ongwen, Mary Ndedah and himself. He was about 5 at the time. During those years, what were played on gramophones were large disks. At the centre was a paper-like item that marked the end of the plain section. Okumu, in his small mind, knew it was a license. We thought it was humerous the way he worried about the license, but he appeared to mean it. Every time I met Okumu after that, even in adulthood, I would remind him what he kept repeating that night and we would laugh our heads off.

Two days later we were back in school. Green, along with Enock, became two of my closest friends.

I rode in a train to Mombasa for the first time. My cousin, Naboth Odera, had invited and sent me fare to visit him. It was during the second-term holidays in 1962. Naboth was in class 8 at Maliera when I was in class 7. He preceded me to Kamagambo, where he did not go beyond form 2 because he lacked fees. When I joined Kamagambo in 1961, he was in form 2. When I was in form 2, he had already left school, but luckily got a job with the East African Railways and Harbors. He was posted to Mombasa. I took the train in Kisumu in the evening and arrived in Nairobi in the morning. I waited in Nairobi until evening for a connecting train to Mombasa. I took that train and in the morning I arrived in Mombasa. My cousin was at the station to receive me. What stunned me was that even as early as seven, when I arrived, Mombasa was very hot. I had to remove my shirt to survive. At his Shimanzi residence, we talked about the past and the present. He even arranged for me to visit James Opiyo and his brother Onyango Opondo. I also visited Noah Sijenyi and his wife, Nya Uyoma. And later I visited John Okeyo and his brother, Samel Osembo. Everybody was happy to see me, including Jack Ogero, who was in Mombasa to train as a tailor. I enjoyed their company and envied their lifestyle.

When it was time for me to head back home, I was showered with gifts from Okeyo, Noah and Naboth himself. Those were the first gifts that I ever received from anybody. I was very happy and thanked them with all my heart.

I boarded a train to Kisumu and arrived in Gem by bus. Little did I know that the fate that befell Naboth in form 2 would befall me the following year. But I'll talk about that in the next chapter. For now let me just say that although the events of 1961, the floods in particular, left a permanent scar on my body, there was not a scratch left on my spiritual being. I remained steadfast in my resolve to be upright and focused. That's why the events of 1963 would be a litmus test like no other.

CHAPTER 8

PEDAGOGUE

On the eve of opening in January 1963, it became clear that what I was told, that Absalom would not pay my fees for that year, was true. I had not received my fees yet, which I should have received around that time. I couldn't talk to him because he was in Nairobi and I had no transport to go to the city. His wife, Sylvia Awiti, had just left home a few days earlier. Had I known my fate then, I would have dropped a line or two for my brother. You see, Absalom was very understanding. In my presence he rarely did anything that could hurt me. He adoringly refered to me as *Wuon Wadoyi*— The son of Wadoyi. Traslated literally, the words mean *the father of Wadoyi*. Being the last born in our family, he loved me a lot; so I was convinced that if I talked to him one on one he would have a change of heart. But I had no fare to take me to Nairobi. And Father would be the last person to give me fare.

Seeing how things were going, I became convinced that my step-mother and Father never forgave me for the events of 1962. And now Sylvia Awiti and my step-mother also had a common interest in seeing me drop out of school. Sylvia's was that she was to be the only recipient of my brother's income. Let me explain. With my brother's employer deducting fees directly from his salary, Sylvia's lifestyle drastically changed. She could no longer take care of her brothers, whom she felt obligated to support. She could not afford her cigarettes and drinks either. Meals reduced to *ugali* and kales. And tea was without milk and bread. The fact that she couldn't take this state of affairs explained her frequent visits home. And even though my step-mother was the mastermind of the scheme to keep me from school, she found a receptive heart in Sylvia. She drafted Sylvia into the scheme and they managed to convince my brother to stop paying my fees. How they did it—and even got the concurance and connivance of my father—I could not tell.

On the opening day, I stayed on my bed. Father did not know where I was, but I believe he was not bothered. After all, I had once disappeared for 7 days and still returned. Today I needed time for meditation. I loved school and had made good friends there. Besides, my goal was to make it to the university, not drop out in Form II. But there I was, dropping out of school in form II. I cried and prayed that God would forgive me my sins—known and unknown. It was at that point that Mama's earlier appaearance to me concretized in my mind and I was jolted.

I remembered the night she appeared to me in a vision. Her words were, "Just take courage, my son."

Take courage? This was clearly a time to put to test my tolerance and resolve. As I lay on that bed, something urged me to get up. *But get up to do what?* I tried to resist. *Get up, man, sleeping will not help you. Get up and start doing something. Don't just lie there.* The mind was willing but the body was weak. 48 hours on water and a piece of sugarcane had taken a toll. But defying my body—and in obedience to my mind—I got off the bed, dressed up and went out. As I walked out of my cottage, I decided that in an effort to exercise and have fresh air, I should walk along the road for a while. I walked towards Kodiaga.

Now, as you go to Kodiaga, the road passes Maliera Mission Station. This was the centre for Adventist operations in Central Kavirondo (Central Nyanza). It controlled Adventist churches in Gem, Sakwa, Alego, Yimbo and Uyoma. Schools under Maliera jurisdiction were Luanda, Maliera, Ngero, Naya, Nyalgunga, Wangarot, Kamnara and Sanda. The presiding mission director was the late Pastor Ephraim Odero, a dedicated minister from Wangarot, Asembo.

As I passed the gate to Maliera Mission, something urged me to call in and explain my predicament to the pastor. I walked in and knocked on the pastor's door. He ushered me to a stool at one end of a long table. This building housed Pastor's residence and office. He immediately realized I was weak and offered me a gourd of porridge. I took the porridge in a slow manner to hide the true state of my hunger. With his probing eye and deep voice, he demanded to know why I had not gone back to school. This gave me an opportunity to explain my woes. I tried to be brief—to keep my step-mother and Father out of my problems.

I said, "Absalom has refused to pay my school fees."

He knew Absalom. He had taught him during the formative years of Maliera School. He asked what my father had said about the situation. I told him my father could not afford fees for Kamagambo. He then stopped talking for close to five minutes; he just sat there staring at the table. It was as if he had been struck by a thunderbolt and burned to the chair. I never saw him blink. This made me afraid. Was he breathing? Was he okay? Terrified, I consoled myself that he was a man of God and could not just die. When he came back, he cleared his throat.

"Can you teach?"

"I can," I said.

He went dead silent again. But unlike the previous trance, he came back after a short time. He said, "Come here tomorrow morning at eight."

I left his office and went home. Was he going to raise my fees? Or did he ask if I could teach because he wanted to give me a teaching job? Or was this meant to give him time to consult his superiors to either give me money or offer me a teaching job? As you can imagine, I went home with more questions than answers. I was, however, grateful that he gave me audience on short notice and all indications were that he was trying to help. It made me have a semblance of joy in this storm of darkness.

Pastor Ephraim Odero Okemba was a likeable guy. He was magnanimous, straight forward and brooded no nonsense. Before being posted to Maliera as a pastor, he had served at Maliera for many years as a teacher. All early alumni of Maliera passed through his hands. He is credited with having single-handedly moulded his nephew, Joseph Okello Ombonya, to get the necessary education and train to be a minister for Christ's flock. Pastor Okello rose in the Adventist church hierarchy to become Station Director, Field Director and finally Church Ministries Director in the East African Union. It was this same Pastor Ephraim Odero, who was now on the brink of saving me from the abyss of darkness and doom.

That evening I ate well and slept soundly.

I was up early the following morning. I groomed and left for the station. I did not want to be late. I wanted to be there when the man of God opened the office. I am a strong believer in first impressions. One's appearance and demeanor on a first encounter always turns out to be a mirror through which his/her character is judged.

I arrived early and when the pastor opened the office, I was the first to be called in. After exchanging pleasantries, he reached into his office drawer and pulled out a letter. He told me to take the letter to Luanda SDA Primary School. I did not know what the letter contained, but it was addressed to The Headmaster, Luanda SDA Primary School. Right there, I knew God had given me a job. I was going to teach!

I did not bother to go back home. I went straight to Luanda Primary School. There were only two teachers manning a school of five classes. I was going to be the third teacher. I took the letter to the Headmaster, Mr. Joseph Okello Ombonya. After reading the letter, he said, "Welcome!" The second teacher was Samson Hadulo Oduma. As it turned out, this marked my first day in a job I never knew I would have just twenty four hours earlier.

Back home, I did not have to inform anybody of my happiness. Everybody noticed. Gloom had been turned into joy, desperation into hope. I knew my education had been saved by the pastor—but only if I worked hard and stayed morally upright. I was determined to do both. I was not going to let down the pastor. My parents' retrogressive and harmful schemes against me had not been pushed out of my mind. I had to be careful. But strangely, from that moment I never viewed my parents as enemies or my brother as working in conjunction with them. I was going to start a new life, a new beginning. I would no longer be a student, but a worker. I would have pupils addressing me with such lofty titles as "Sir or MR..." I wanted to clear my mind of the past and give room for the future. I knew God was on my side and I did not want to let Him down. I was going to forgive everybody who had wronged me—or whom I thought had wronged me—and live an hounourable life.

At the back of my mind, though, I was determined to pursue further education despite this hitch. What better way to psyche myself for a better future than to forgive the past. I forgave my father. He was a victim of circumstances he could not control. I forgave my step-mother for her ill feelings, hostilities and downright bigotry. I forgave her curses, shouts of absurdities,—all directed at me and at members of my mother's family. I hope God forgave her too, because if He didn't, all would not be well with her family.

When I started teaching, I did not have a bicycle, so I would walk the six miles to school and back every day. My salary was Kenya Shillings one hundred and forty one and fifty cents per month. Not enough, but good enough for my needs. But again, I did not get my salary for two months. When I eventually got the three months' salary on the third month, I saved some towards my fees and employed a *shamba* boy for my parents. There was finally joy and a semblance of cohesion. I cleaned up the home to make it look good with the meager salary. I was able to finance my parents' wedding to pave way for Father to resume work as a church elder.

The wedding was very successful. I provided both parents with wedding outfits and made sure there was enough food for the invited guests. With both parents back in church, I focused my attention elsewhere—my future. I continued to save a little every month for my school fees. I knew the year would end and I would want to go back to school. In fact, I had already written to the principal informing him of my inability to go to school that year and asked him to reserve me a place in Form III.

He wrote back. He would reserve a spot!

Since it was becoming more and more difficult to walk to and from school every day, I felt I was not giving the pupils my best because of tiredness and fatigue. I talked this over with the Headmaster. But due to lack of staff houses in the school, it was decided I approach the pastor-in-charge. Pastor Masio agreed and I moved in with him. The good thing was—his house was within the school compound.

Pastor Masio was old enough to be my father. He did not stay with his family at the time. He was friendly and always had good advice for me. Whatever I missed from Father, I got it from Pastor Masio. He was not only my spiritual father, but was my first mentor. Because of him, I longed for the day I would also be called pastor. He taught me independent living. He could not allow me to do his laundry or even shine his shoes. He did it all by himself. He did not allow me to buy food as long as he was present. He bought and prepared food for both of us. He treated me like his son. I liked him a lot. Sometimes he could be gone for months and I would be left to take care of the chores along with my teaching. I could not cope, so I sent for my nephew, Fanuel Ogutu Okelo, to stay with us while learning at Luanda.

The other reason I sent for Fanuel was fright. I feared sleeping in the pastor's house alone. The house was at an isolated place and was the only residence in the entire school. I was fearful that bad guys might hatch a plot beat me up at night. Fanuel Ogutu came and I took responsibility for all his educational needs that year—school uniforms, books and fees.

During this time, Mama Dorcas Omondi Oyolo approached me to help her take care of her two children—Digolo and Dugna. I was not able to financially, so I advised her to take them to her home of birth in Luanda, where they could stay while learning there. She obliged and I helped the two kids with admission, school uniforms and fees. All these I was doing despite the fact that my target was to raise fees for my education. God, however, continued to shower me with blessings while preparing me for future tasks. Later, I would buy a bicycle to easen my commuter problems.

As a mentor, Pastor Masio encouraged us to take up preaching. It was his wish that each of us—Okello, Hadulo and I—become pastors. But only Okello and Hadulo would climb that ladder, with Okello reaching the apex and Hadulo settling in the mid ranks as a church elder. I took a different path. This would actually be the second time fate would see me deviate from a goal. The first was when I missed going to Maseno High School. Had I gone to Maseno, I would have ended up being a medical doctor or an engineer of sorts. I had a strong bias for sciences. In Kamagambo, however, they did not teach sciences because of *Evolution*, a subject Advetists frowned upon.

But teaching was not my dream profession. I was doing it out of necessity. It was the thing that came my way to help me raise money for school fees. First I was assigned to teach arithmetic in class one. I had no idea how a class one child was taught. I never did class one. To This day I don't know whether the assignment was out of malice or it was a genuine assignment to lift the load off the backs of Okello and Hadulo. Only Okello was trained to teach. Hadulo, like me, was not traincd, but he had taught for sometime and probably knew how to handle class one pupils.

I started with numbers, 1, 2, 3...., which they mastered quickly. I then moved to addition. This was the area pupils had difficulty for two weeks. I laboured to teach that $1 + 1 = 2$ but at the end of two weeks they still did not know that $1 + 1 = 2$. I gave up and told the Headmaster to give me another class, particularly the upper classes, to teach. The Headmaster agreed and I was assigned class five. This was the Carey Francis stuff, which I had mastered during my days in Maranda Intermediate. I was finally at the right place. But I was also given other classes.

On the extracurricular front, I was made games master. Games compromised soccer (Football as it was popularly known), net ball and drill. My duty was to prepare pupils for the Adventist Schools Games in Ndere. But our pupils were young. They could not successfully compete with the more established schools like Maliera. When we went to Ndere, we did well only in netball, where we were beaten in the finals, though. We did not make it past the preliminary stages in soccer.

The Lord continued to bless the school and enrollment tripled.

One day Hadulo's brother, Okwaro Oduma, came to pick him up to help trace items which had been stolen from his house. Hadulo asked if I could accompany them and I agreed. Okwaro had a Land Rover. We took the truck and went to their home, where we picked up three more people. The six of us drove deep into the countryside to look for Wakolo. Okwaro had learned that Wakolo was the head of a gang that broke and entered his house and robbed him.

Wakolo was a notorious criminal. He had done some very bad things to his victims. It was said he kept bees on his head, which he unleashed against victims. He was an extremely dangerous man. To counter his threat, we planned our operations while driving. We were not going to involve law enforcement officers, because they would not do anything since they were scared of Wakolo. Okwaro said we were going to use the element of surprise. We did not reckon with the fact that the Land Rover would give us away. And it did!

But first, let me say this. On the way to Wakolo's home, we got wind that Mukuti might know where the properties were. We rushed to his home and found him. He tried to run, but we were prepared and quickly caught him. He led us to a home where some of the items were. We did not find anybody at home since they had all fled. Luckily, Okwaro found some of his items there. We tried to persuade Mukuti to tell us where the rest of the items were, but he appeared not to know. So having failed to locate Wakolo, we released Mukuti and returned to school.

It was a classic sting operation.

I had vowed to live an almost celibate life. Since I was a teacher in an Adventist school, I needed to be morally upright and a good role model to pupils. I was also staying with Pastor Masio. I did not want to desecrate his house. Back home, I had to be just as good. The director's office was just eight hundred yards away. I wanted to be seen to be upright to prevent word filtering that I was a disgrace to the church. I succeeded in carrying myself around with a sense of decorum.

I was therefore surprised when a girl I did not know bumped into me as we were coming from a camp meeting. She smiled and apologized. As we walked along, she engaged me in a conversation. Strangley, I don't remember her name. What I recall is that her father's name was Ohon Jonah.

"But how can it be?" I asked.

"It's true," she said.

"I am Ohon and you are telling me your father is Ohon too?"

"Yes!"

This was the thrust of our conversation. The following Monday I went to school as usual. This time I already had a bike and was home over the weekends; I rode to school Monday mornings.

On Wednesday, though, things took a surprising turn. Mr. Hadulo came over and told me that I had a visitor who urgently wanted to see me. I asked who the visitor was, and he told me a feminine name. He said she was at the gate. I told him to tell her to wait till after class. It was the last class before games. I finished class and went to the field with the boys for games.

She sent Mr. Hadulo again.

For the second time, I told him to tell her to wait.

When I had finally set the boys to play, I went to see my guest. I recognized her as the girl who had bumped into me the day of the camp meeting. I did not want to be rude, but I strongly felt whatever problem she had, if I was the one to solve it, she should have waited until the weekend, when I returned home. If people associated me with her, it was going to be demeaning.

I decided I would treat her with contempt, but not rudely. She deserved a hearing after all, right?

I asked her what was so presessing that she had to tell me at my place of work. She said she was going to see her sister, but did not have fare. I told her she should have just walked since the destination was a walking distance. And since I wanted to have as brief a contact with her as possible, I told her to wait for me...I would be back. I had a friend I knew in one of the camp meetings. He was an excellent soccer player like me. His home was around Luanda. Occasionally I would go to visit him. Once or twice he had been to my place visiting too. His name was Jonah. When I returned after sending the pupils home, I told the girl I did not have money, but would take her to a friend's home to wait while I went home to fetch the money. She agreed. I took her to Jonah's home and dumped her there. That evening I rode back home.

The following day was a Thursday. On Friday I reported to work and went about my business. I was determined not to see her, although I sympathized with Jonah because of the problem I had caused him with. I actually expected him to do the obvious—show her the door. It turned out he could not. Jonah and my guest—unknown to me, or to him initially—were close relatives. Jonah's mother and the girl's father were a sister and a brother, hence the similarity in their names. I avoided her the whole day. And in the evening I went home using another route to avoid her. But what happened thereafter would embarrass me even more.

It was a Saturday Morning. I went to Ori to preach. I preached from the book of Ecclesiates chapter 3. But while there, I kept having this feeling that something was wrong. Finally, in the evening, God impressed it upon me to return home.

It was around six o'clock when I made it back. What struck me instantly was the multitude of people stretching a kilometer—from Kodiaga to Mutumbu. I thought someone must have died. Only funerals attracted such multitudes. But at halfway mark, I met the girl, the daughter of Ohon Jonah, sandwiched between two bouncers, walking from my home. I felt threatened. I saw my whole life crumbling around me. I saw my dreams fade away because of the recklessness of this girl—a good education, a good job, a good wife. What was she up to?

Whatever it was, I knew this throng of people had been told the girl's version of what had transpired. I uttered a very short prayer: *God, don't forsake me*. A few yards to our home, I stopped to inquire what was going on. The answer I got from the first person showed I had supporters. He said, "These people have been going around selling their daughter as merchandise. They think they can sell her to you too."

I saw people nod in approval. Yes, this was blackmail. One of the bouncers was a guy I knew—Wandiga. Wandinga was in the team not just because he was an uncle to the girl, but because in the event of a fight between them and members of my village, he would be counted on to defend their side.

His role was intimidation. He was strong and fearless. If you picked a fight with him, you were doomed. He was rumoured to have killed somebody!

They got to where I was. Wandiga knew me very well. He asked that we move to our home and discuss the matter. He was supported by one or two elders from my village. The main concern of the elders was to avoid a scandal spreading. But I said a stern no. "Whatever it is, let's discuss it here and now."

My reason for saying no was that I did not want to give them an opportunity of leaving the girl in my home. Listening to the tone of my voice, they gave in and agreed to discuss the matter there and then.

"*Wuon Wanyanga*—Son of Wanyanga," Wandiga said. "We have brought you your wife. We found where you had hidden her. Here she is, take her home."

The silence that followed was deafening. You could hear a needle drop. Everybody eagerly awaited my response.

I said, "Did you ask her how she happened to be at the place you found her?"

Wandiga nodded.

"Then may I ask the girl some questions?"

The moment they agreed I could crossexamine her, I knew I had her. I would tear her testimony, whatever it was, into pieces and expose her for what she really was. I coached my questions in such a way that her answer would be yes, yes...

Did you come to Luanda where I teach? Yes.

Did you send Mr. Hadulo to come and call me? Yes.

Did he tell you that I was still in class and would come later? Yes.

Did you send him again? Yes.

When I came, did I take you to Jonah's home? Yes.

Did I tell you I was going home to fetch money for you? Yes.

Did I tell you I would come back to bring you the money that evening? Yes.

That evening, I did not come back, right? Yes.

The following day you sent several people to me to call me, but I did not come, right? Yes.

When I inquired from you what you wanted me to do you said you wanted fare to your sister's place, right? Yes.

I told you I did not have money, right? Yes.

Bingo!

When I finished the withering crossexamination, the mother gained courage and spoke. "What do you want me to do?"

My response was curt, sharp and derogatory. "You give her fare to her sister's place or take her home and tether her so she doesn't wander around."

This was too much for the old woman. She started crying and saying things meant to push her group to start a fight, but wise counsel prevailed on Wandinga. He said, "Wuon Wanyanga, it is our daughter who wants you, you don't want her!"

With those remarks, he got hold of the girl and started whipping her as they walked away. That was to be the first of many times I would be carried in triumph. God had indeed answered my prayer in the hour of need.

The rest of my life as a teacher lacked drama. I continued to serve the school with dedication. Pupils loved me and I loved them. They could come all the way from their homes to help me with work at my home…and they loved it. I was, however, going to leave them at the end of the school year. It made me sad, but it had to be that way.

Teaching transformed me from a playboy to a focused teenager.

CHAPTER 9

TINGA

I had saved enough money to pay school fees for a year—1964. I knew 1965 would find my brother James back from overseas. I knew he would not refuse to pay my 1965 fees. I made a calculation that once I paid 1964 fees in full, nothing was going to stop me from completing secondary education. I wrote to the principal informing him I had raised the requisite fees and and wanted to get back to school. I received his positive response not too long after. I returned to Kamagambo without a problem. By now I had grown up. I was mature in mind and strong in body, but I was still a teenager and had teenage problems to contend with. These problems would eventually snowball into real challenges and almost cost my education. Problems like omnipotence, defiance and omniscience were issues I had to face. I would learn to deal with these the hard way as I continued to be in Kamagambo. And unlike 1962, I was not the youngest student any more. The students I was with in class, in 1962, were now one class ahead. It was frustrating sharing a class with kids I called *monos* just a year ago. I was, however, determined not to allow these frustrations to distract me.

When I taught I played a lot of soccer. I wanted to continue playing. I enjoyed soccer so much that the first thing I did when I returned to Kamagambo was talk to the games master, Mr. Benjamin Ochieng, to get the boys to rehabilitate a pitch which was in a deplorable state. He agreed and two soccer balls were bought for us. I was then elected captain of the soccer team by the students. I immediately started planning how to popularize soccer in the school. The games master eventually came up with a tournament when he realized the boys loved soccer and some had exceptional talent. Every evening after work, unless it was raining, the boys would be in the pitch. I was there with them. I was a coach and a captain. In the process, Kamagambo developed a formidable soccer team with boys like Jimmy, Samuel Nyatome, Tom Obanda, Billy Opundo and Saisi. We were unbeatable. My fame spread far and wide because my role in that team was pivotal. I could score from any angle and by any means permitted by soccer rules. I was called many names. Some called me Tinga. Others called me Tinga Tinga. Then there were those who called me Tractor or Faro. As you might expect, I became the backbone of the team and liked my Tinga name a lot.

One day we landed an invitation to Homa Bay High School to play soccer. There was no team in South Nyanza District that had beaten them. They heard we were invincible and wanted to beat us and claim the title of the best soccer team in the district. We accepted the invitation and traveled on a Sunday with our cheer girls—girls in the secondary section. The Homa Bay team was coached by a snobbish white man. I can't remember his name. I remember that when he saw me in the field, he came, walked around me with a sneer—

laughing at my anatomy. I was born bow-legged and because of the size of my patellas, which were smaller than normal, I could only stand with my knees curved backwards. The snob thought I could not play soccer because of the anatomical defect. When the match started with me in the team, he knew his team would massacre our team. But that was not to be. By half-time, the score was nil-nil. In our dressing room, I shuffled the team.

Within five minutes of the second half, Homa Bay was two goals down—both scores from my foot. We went on to pump eleven goals, seven of them to my credit. Midway in the game, whenever I touched the ball in the danger zone, the white coach would literally cry, so I was told. He knew it would be another goal. They finally got one consolation goal. We boasted after the match—that we had given each player from their side a goal to take home. I never saw the white man again, even at the reception the school hosted for us. And when the match ended, I was carried shoulder-high in triumph by my team mates. It was the second time I had been carried in jubilation. More would follow.

The result of the Homa Bay match boosted our fame; we now had a respected and feared team. My nick name echoed across the hills and valleys of Gusii Land. Abagusi are soccer lovers. Maybe I got my soccer trait from them. I was told one of my great, great, great grandmothers was a Gusii. Her name was Mondo. I am a descendant of Mondo.

Kisii High School heard of our exploits in Homa Bay and asked if they could play us on our own pitch. After consultations with the games master and the principal, we agreed to host them. But we knew this was going to be a tough one. The Kisii High School team was "captained" and coached by Hon. Christopher Obure, himself a former student of Kamagambo Secondary School. Our disadvantage, hence, was that the coach knew our team. He had been part of it. He knew our strengths and weaknesses. Our advantage, though, was that he had not watched us play—with me—in the team. They came and the match started well. I retained the lineup that beat Homa Bay. Suddenly, in an aerial tussle in the danger zone, I got injured. I was unconscious and was stretched out. When I gained consciousness, I found myself in the dormitory alone. Everybody was in the field watching the scintillating match. I noticed blood on my uniform and remembered the tussle. I must have passed out when I got hurt. I went back to the pitch to watch the match from the sidelines. But this was not to be. As soon as the spectators saw I was up, they demanded I join the action. The match ended on a one-one draw.

My soccer playing would continue until the end of my stay at Kamagambo. Later, I joined notable soccer clubs where I exceled. But I stopped playing competitive soccer after I joined Law School in 1967. The rest of the team members, like Samuel Nyatome and Jimmy, joined big clubs and eventually made the Kenya National Team. Chris Obure joined Gor Mahia Club and later became a Member of Parliament and minister in the Kenya Government.

In the school, there were younger boys who had promising soccer talent and strove to practice with us. They too benefited from my instruction and ended up playing very good soccer. They were Johnny and Jimmy Ombado. They were talented and played soccer intelligently. They learned new techniques from us and perfected them. Jimmy ended up marrying my niece, Edwina Atieno (*Popularly known as Atie*) who also made history by being the first ever lady from our tribe to hold an executive position in parastatal. She was Senior Benefits Manager in the National Social Security Fund. She is astute and talented. God blessed her with five kids.

While still in Kamagambo, I decided to visit the parents of one of my friends. But this was not the first time I would visit John. John was the son to Pastor Christopher Odero. Pastor Odero had worked at Maliera as Mission Director for a long time. That was how I came to know the family. I visited at their rural home in Ranen. Although the pastor was away at the time, the reception I received was wonderful. Mama John slaughtered a cock for me. It was the first time somebody had honoured me in that manner. I was delighted. We stayed for the duration of the break, then returned to school. Later, I made another visit to the Oderos. This time it was end of the holidays. I arrived in school one day too early. Nobody had turned up and I felt I was going to be bored alone. I decided to spend the evening with John. But this time it wasn't at the rural home; they were at the mission in Ranen. Ranen had been granted autonomy from Kenya Lake Field and Pastor Christopher Odero was its President.

His residence was an imposing building on the slopes of Ranen Hills. It was a building one could not miss. The reception was fabulous. This time the pastor was around. And boy, what a house this was! Every room and every corner was a marvel. The polished floors, the seats in the living room, the curtains and the way things were arranged was splendid. But I would later mess up and feel ashamed of myself. You see, I felt this sudden urge to visit the toilet. I surveyed the surrounding; there was no pit latrine. I gathered courage and asked John to show me, if there was any. I had expected him to lead me out of the house and point at some place for me, instead he led me deep into the house and pointed at a door and said, "There you are!"

I opened the door and got in. What I saw was completely strange to me. There was no hole except for this structure that looked like a small stool with a space at the top fixed firmly on the ground. There was water inside the structure. I wondered what they used this thing for. Meanwhile, I was pressed hard. I decided to use or misuse whatever was available. I climbed onto the stool and squatted. What happened next was the mess of the year. The stench that ensued didn't make matters any better. I tried to clean the mess, but there was little I could do, especially about the smell, which now permeated the house. I was so embarrassed. I hate to imagine what my hosts said behind my back.

But that was just the beginning. A few minutes later, I had to rush back to the toilet. Another shame awaited me there. Instead of knocking the door, I just opened the door and found Mama John Sitting on the stool. I said sorry and shut the door. I felt this was the second time in fifteen minutes I had embarrassed her. I felt so ashamed and asked to be allowed to go back to school. I made it back to school that same day in spite the fact I had intended to pass the evening in Ranen.

Sometime in 1964, Absalom lost his job and came back home. But through that ordeal, he stayed in touch with friends in Nairobi, who were looking for a job for him. When I came home in December, I found him there. He was unemployed and looked miserable. James sent me my fees for the new term, which Father kept for me. At about the same time, Absalom got a job and was needed in Nairobi as soon as possible. Since he did not have, money he approached Father. As usual, Father said he did not have money. But Absalom needed more than just fare; he also needed money for rent and food for a month. Later, he heard about Father having my fees and approached him to borrow from it, but Father refused and told him to ask me. Father knew I would not give him my fees. He remembered that Absalom had been the cause of my dropping out of school in 1963. He also remembered how bitter I was and reckoned I would still be indignant and just tell Absalom off. In the end, Abaslom never bothered to approach me. I guess the weight of his earlier actions weighed heavily on him.

It was now a Friday. By Monday, if he failed to report to work in Nairobi, he would be out of that Job. I wondered if he remembered what he did to me. I wondered what was on his mind as he took steps towards where I was. Was he saying *Let me try if he can give me* or was he certain I would give him the money? My step-mother was there when Father said he did not have money to give and when he said he could not give Absalom my fees. She must have recalled the conspiracy of 1963. Absalom approached me nonetheless and told me his predicament. He had been out of a job for a long time and here was an opportunity he was going to miss because he could not raise fare to Nairobi and a little more for rent. I could see desperation all over his face. He said, "If you give me 500/= it would be enough for my needs. At the end of the month, when I get my pay check, I will send you the 500/=."

In that moment, it dawned on me that if I gave him 500/=, I would remain with 300/= for fees. That could present problems. Still, he pleaded with me not to let him down because his future depended on this job. When he said this, I almost interjected that my future also depended on the fees he refused to pay in 1963, but I held my horses. Instead I said, "Follow me!"

We walked to Father, who was seated in front of his house. Our step-mother was in the kitchen, following proceedings through the side of her eye. We got to Father and I said, "Father, give him 500/=; he promises he will send it at the end of the month when he earns his salary."

Step-mother had drawn nearer. There was a silence. She looked directly into Father's eyes. Nobody spoke. This turn of events was not expected, so they had not rehearsed a joint response. Once I said yes, he was obliged to comply. I had said yes, so no amount of unspoken intimidation was going to change anything. Father went into the house and came back with 500/=. He put the money in my hand and I handed it to Absalom. I had forgiven him. I was not going to retaliate. After all, retaliation is not for us—we mortals. That is the preserve of the Creator.

At the end of the month, Absalom sent me the 500=, which I promptly paid. He had learned his lesson. Years of suffering injustices at home had made me acquire certain survival traits. Having been a victim, I strongly detested injustice—whether at home, at work or in school.

Let me tell you what I did regarding injustice at school when I reported back a week late. When I got there, students had been given their shares of soap for laundry and bathing. My friend Billy and I were denied any soap. At the next distribution, we demanded two portions of soap to compensate the ones we missed. The storekeeper refused. That being the case, we said nobody was going to get any soap until we got our double share. There was a standoff, which almost degenerated into violence. We held back the whole school with knives until the master on duty was called to solve the problem. We got our double share before other students were given. As a result other students, who had never gotten their soap, received their double share as well. We suspected the storekeeper wanted to take the soap home. He never attempted to deny anybody soap again.

I also recollect an incident of yellow maize. The government, in an effort to assist *wananchi,* received yellow maize from the USA. Someone started a rumour in school that back in States, yellow maize was for cattle and this particular consignment was unfit for human consumption. The rumour spread like bush fire. In no time, I led student to boycott yellow maize. Word reached the principal, who came in person and persuaded us to eat because that was what was available. He, however, had unsavory words for me and other ringleaders. He even forced me to address the students, to urge them to abandon their boycott and eat the food. As a result of standing up against what students felt were injustices, I became a hero. Even the school captain (prefect) realized the important role I played among students. Whenever he wanted a policy implemented, he got my nod before introducing it. If he went ahead and introduced it without seeking my opinion, I would shoot it down and that would be it. Such influence made Micah Odongo Amayo recommend me for headship of the students in 1965 when his term ended in 1964.

Micah Odongo Amayo was born an administrator. He was the son of Pastor Luka Amayo. Pastor Amayo had done missionary work in Maliera. That is where I knew Micah. He was the school captain (prefect) who took over from Kamau. He was a Christian to boot. He knew how to work well with students. His MO was to identify troublemakers like me and convince us to be on his side; everything else fell in place. The good thing with him was—unlike other leaders before him—he was not a pretender. He would stand up and tell off the management if he felt a policy he was being asked to implement would not be acceptable to the students. Micah and I got along quite well. He was grateful that I helped him run his term in office without any major hitch.

Beyond our Kamagambo days, Micah and I would interact a lot in education circles, first as the pioneer headmaster of Nyabola Girls Secondary School and then as the Central Nyanza Field education secretary. While he served in the two positions, I was the chairman of Maliera Secondary Board of Governors (B.O.G). During his term as education secretary, Adventists opened branches in all non-Adventist secondary schools in Siaya and Kisumu. The gap left by his untimely demise will be hard to fill. Later I would meet his daughters Betty and Jemima in the USA.

Shortly after the yellow maize incident, students boycotted *ugali* again. This time the boycott was because *ugali* was not cooked well. There were weevils in it and it tasted bitter. Nobody could eat it—even the hungriest of us. The students required no prompting to trash the *ugali*. The authorities reacted quickly and prepared another *ugali,* with good flour, which we later took.

Mr. Ayonga was the nurse in charge of the school dispensary. He kept three grade cows in the school compound. His herd was healthy and produced a lot of milk. One day the herd evaded the herdsboy and ate *ugali* which had been trashed by students. They ate the *ugali* and all of them died. Since Adventists don't eat of dead animals, Mr. Ayonga buried the three carcases deep in the school farm. What I heard the following day surprised me. When the site was visited in the morning, the graves were empty. Some people had gone there and removed the three carcasses and disappeared without a trace. The night thieves must have considered Mr. Ayonga a big fool for burying meat fit for human consumption.

But my love for soccer was bound to land me in trouble. The only teachers who loved soccer in Kamagambo were Meshak Dawa, Esther Awino and Benjamin Ochieng. The three were members of the disciplinary committee. This committee was made of five people, along with the principal, Mr. Marx, and Mr. Tegler. That was a ratio of two whites and three blacks. It was a ratio that would come in handy to ensure I completed secondary education.

One day I woke up with a pounding headache. I could not go to class so I went to the dispensary for treatment. I was treated and went to dormitory to rest. I rested for a while and my headache subsidized. I did not go to the mandatory work programme that day. In the evening, my class was to play soccer against another. Without me, they were going to lose. Since I was feeling better, I decided to play. When we won, the white man on duty accused me of malingering. He argued that if I had been sick, I should not have been playing soccer. I think he had underrated the strength of an African to recover from a bout of malaria. He also failed to understand the resolve of an African. I was determined to help my class win, even if it meant straining under a bout of Malaria.

Seething, he decided to punish me. He did not report to the principal or any member of the disciplinary committee. He pointed at a eucalyptus stump, three feet in diameter, and asked me to dig it out. Look, it would take a whole month to dig the thing out if I were to do it. I refused and just went to class. He must have reported me to the principal because soon after, the disciplinary committee met and I was called to defend myself. This was my specialty. I explained what had happened and sought to know how he knew I was not sick in the first place or how he satisfied himself that I could not recover by evening to play soccer. This needed a medical doctor to determine; he was not a medical doctor. I don't know what they discussed after I left, but I was called and told that I would be punished—under supervision of the white guy. The following day he showed me a place to dig. I asked him, if he were in my shoes, would he dig that trench and how long would it take him? He just walked away.

I again refused to dig. I later came to know that the disciplinary committee was split into two. The whites insisted I be sacked, but the blacks in one voice saying no. The whites believe in democracy. The voice of the majority prevails. Blacks outnumbered whites 3-2, assuming the principal had a vote, as I believe he did. The three blacks could not afford to lose me. Benjamin was the games master. I had given him fame. Meshack came from Gem, my home location, and was not going to recommend the sacking of one of the few boys from Gem. It was not lost on him that there were only two of us from Gem in the secondary section—Billy and I. Esther was my sister-in-law, married to Cousin Okello Obonyo. I'm indebted to the trio for defending me in the face of a relentless white onslaught. Without them, I would not have completed my secondary education at Kamagambo. I was later asked to split a wheel barrow worth of firewood, which I did, and that standoff ended.

Shortly after that incident, the management moved me from cleaning toilets and dormitories to mowing. I liked cleaning toilets and dorms. It gave me plenty of time during the work hours to study. It would take me an hour on a week day and two hours on Sunday to complete the job. I had eight extra hours for studying per week. But this mowing thing became even better. The person who thought he was punishing me must have been disappointed. Within two weeks, I had mowed everywhere and was just resting during work programme. They sought to move me again, but I refused. It had become obvious their moves were punitive.

Mr. Marx, the principal, was from South Africa. He and his wife were the only white teachers that one could write home about in the secondary section. The wife was the best English teacher I have ever met. Mr. Marx was a good administrator; he understood the plight of the blacks. He never sent anybody home for school fees. Maybe having lived in South Africa shaped his character and mentality. He was full of humor, but stern like steel. He could sometimes go physical. But once he beat you, or you fought him, that was the end of the matter—no further disciplinary stuff. I liked him. He had saved my life by allowing me to return to school. He liked performance. He even took me out on Saturdays when he went out to preach. I believe he did not habour any grudge against me.

One evening I went to pick up my clothes from Mama Esther's house. She used to get her daughters to do my laundry. Her house was on the primary girls section. School rules prohibited the turning on of lights in the dorms during preps. Unknown to me, Esther was not in. The girls had to turn on the lights to fetch my clothes. Mr. Tegler appeared from nowhere and spotted me inside the house, but left. The girls urged me to run, but I refused. I was in a staff house, not a dorm. How could these whites insist in turning off lights in black staff houses while they left theirs on? I was going to right this wrong or make people know about it—discrimination against blacks.

Within no time, the principal appeared. Teglar had reported me. The man was furious; the little hair on his bald head stood straight. He shouted, "Ohon, Ohon, where is Ohon?" I had plenty of time to run and hide, but I decided against it. I was not in the girls' dorm. I was in a staff house and I had permission of the owner to be visiting. I was not going to run. My nieces, who were there, ran and hid inside the house. I am the one who opened the door for Mr. Marx. He pulled me out and started raining blows on me as the girls watched through their classroom window. I returned the blows, realizing he was the centre of attraction, he left me. I went to the dorm fuming. I was sure he had overstepped his bounds this time. He could not punish me for being in a staff house. There was no rule prohibiting that. And he could not punish me for the fight because he started it. I knew he must have been disturbed. I also knew the trio would want to know why he did not allow lights in black houses while whites had lights in their houses.

After a while, he sent a student to call me. I went and found him in the office with a two-edged knife, about eight inches long, on the table. He gave me some wise counsel, then he let me go. That night I did not sleep. I did not know what he was up to. He did not tell me that he had forgiven me. He did not say he would punish me either. First day. Second day. Third day. Nothing happened. Mr. Marx had just dropped the matter like that—the art of forgiving perfected.

Mr. Marx would be on top of the list of teachers who shaped my life, along with Mr. Samuel Ouma Boro, Meshak Amayo, Mr. Siage, Mr. Meshak Dawa, Mrs. Esther Awino Okello, Mr. Benjamin Ochieng, Mr. Erastus An'gienda, Mr. Dishon Agutu, Mr. Tukiko Koyo, Mr. Munro, Mr. Tudor Jackson, Mr. Mcatney, Mr. Otieno Kwach, Mr. GK Mukele and Mr. Kamunyori. Mrs. Marx would also make the list.

Other than Mr. and Mrs. Marx, the rest of the white teachers were hypocrites. They appeared to be Christians, but had deep resentment and hate for Africans.

I am now on my final lap in Kamagambo. The year is 1965. My brother is back in the country and my form four fees are paid, just as I had anticipated. I arange to stay in school during the holidays. The authorities agree and five of us remain, though for different reasons. Some have no fare, but others for the same reason as mine—to revise. All five are form fours. The authorities give us food and plenty of time to read. The only work we do is chop firewood for our cooking and clean up our dorm. We make the best use of this time.

I topped the class in the second term exams. When we closed for the holidays, I again wanted to remain in school. I asked and permission was granted. At the eleventh hour, though, I changed my mind when I heard Mr. Marx would be driving to Nairobi. He agreed to give me a ride when I asked.

James was in Nairobi and I wanted to see him. But by going to Nairobi, I squandered a golden opportunity to prepare for my national exams. It was a decision I would later regret. Let me explain.

I arrived when James had just been transferred to Kakamega and was preparing to relocate. We left together in a GK vehicle and arrived in Kakamega in the evening. He was to work in an agricultural research station there. Since he had just taken up posting, he was not expected to earn a salary at the end of August. When school opened in September, I had no fare to school. It would be another three weeks before I made it back. Meanwhile, I did nothing. I did not carry my notes or textbooks. This was a big drawback.

When I finally made it back to school, I had about four weeks of study—very little time indeed. I made the best use of the time, sat the national exams—Cambridge School Certificate. I did not perform to my satisfaction, but I had fulfilled part of my dream—completing secondary education.

So, would I make it to campus?

CHAPTER 10

ROSE

When school closed in December 1965, I went straight to Kakamega to stay with James. My brother had, in 1964, married Edith Christabel Atieno—daughter of Barnabas Oigo Miser. She was of dual ancestry, Koguta and Ramogi. Christabel was very cute—fair-skinned, five feet six—in her mid-twenties. She was what one would call "exceptionally beautiful." She loved my brother and my brother loved her. They did not call themselves by their names. Both called each other *sweety*. And they accepted me in their home. They always fixed good food. Breakfast was eggs with buttered bread. It was with tea, coffee, cocoa or milo. Lunch was meat and so was supper. Many times we had meat or fish, or chicken and vegetables.

A few weeks later, we were joined by her sister, Jane, who came for a visit. Rose, as she preferred to be called, was strikingly beautiful. Brown, five feet four and in her late teens. She was an arresting figure-eight. If the two were to attend the same beauty contest, she would beat her senior sister hands down. She was still in class eight. For her and I, it was love at first sight—which later blossomed into marriage.

A few weeks into our relationship, I started seeing changes in Christabel's disposition towards us. She started overworking Rose. She talked to me less and less. This did not bother me at first because I don't talk much. But when I started seeing strange behaviour directed at me, I was alarmed. Whenever she did laundry, she sorted mine and left it undone. If she prepared food while my brother was away, she would place food on the table and never bother to alert me. Like a dog, she probably expected me to pick the scent of the food and follow it. This was unacceptable to me. At least I deserved the courtesy of being invited to the table for a meal. I discussed this with her and Rose. Nothing changed. One day she did the same thing and I refused to go to the table. I slept hungry that night. I had no alternative but to complain to my brother. I didn't know what my brother told her, but I noted that she invited me to the table whenever it was set. Still, her attitude continued as long as I lived under that roof.

Rose left. She went back to Nyakach to continue her education. At about the same time, I went to Nairobi to look for a job. The thing was—I had to start shaping my future. Results had been released and I had strong credits. That being the case, I had expected to go to Maseno High School. But this was not to be because the principal flatly refused to admit me. I again saw the hand of God in this. Had I been admitted to Maseno High, I would not have been what I am today. I would have missed out on being a Christian.

On arrival in Nairobi, I did not go to my brother's place in Majengo. I hated the place. I knew my capacity to think would be inhibited by the environment. I decided to go to Jericho, where my other brother had stayed when he was in Nairobi. That other brother had stayed with his friend—Caleb Otieno Oyunga. Caleb was well-built, black, about five' six"; handsome but unmarried. I have never seen a kinder and gentler person in my life. He was so polite that I believed he could never hurt a fly. He was a kid brother to the famous, late Dr. Ang'awa.

As I walked to his place that morning—after arriving in Nairobi by train—I had mixed feelings. Would he accept me or would he turn me away? He knew I had a brother in Nairobi. My fear was allayed when I found Caleb. It was a Sunday morning and he had not gone to work. With his trademark disarming smile, he welcomed me home with open arms. But I would not be the only person to stay with him. He was already accommodating Sherry Wamwayi and Moses Ogoye, who were both looking for a job. Unwittingly, I had joined a team of jobless fellows in the house of a Good Samaritan. The three of us had no money and could not buy food. Caleb was a clerk with East African Posts and Telecommunication and didn't make much. Regardless, he made sure food was always available for him and for us. A few weeks later, we were joined by yet another jobless man-Ochilo.

Moses and Wamwayi later got jobs, which they did briefly before proceeding to Makerere University. There, Moses pursued medicine and Wamwayi pursued education. Ochilo became a musician.

Caleb's house continued to be a launching pad for many professionals. We are all indebted to him. On behalf of all of us I say, "Thank you, *wuod Oyunga*—God bless you."

For me, work was priority number one. I sent out many applications, but reply to each of them was regrets. It was frustrating but I did not give up. One day Caleb brought me a letter inviting me to an interview with the East African Common Services. On the day I received the letter, the interviews had been done two days earlier. *What bad luck! I have been looking for a job and for three months I have gotten regrets. Some even fail to acknowledge receipt of my application! Now I receive an invitation two days late? I am doomed!*

I discussed my dilemma with colleagues and they urged me to find out what happened. *Maybe they still need someone,* they said.

With this encouragement, I set off the following morning for the East African Common Services offices—to an office I was directed to. I knocked and entered. I explained to the gentleman in this office that I got the invitation letter two days late. He said, "No, no, no, don't worry about it, I know what happened."

With these remarks, I was relieved. This officer went on to engage me in a conversation for close to five minutes. In the end he told me to report to him the following day at eight o'clock with my Cambridge School Certificate or a result slip. I thanked him and walked away.

I hurried back to the house happy. I had secured a job. At least that was what I thought. I did not know that some obstacles still lay on my way. On arriving home, I turned everything upside down to look for my result slip. I couldn't find it. I searched all night; nothing turned up. I asked my colleagues if anyone had taken or seen it. They said no. But I also ruled out the possibility of one among them taking it. *Why would they?* It would be of no use to them. In fact, Moses and Wamwayi had more superior certificates or result slips, they would not even look at mine. Suddenly there I was, the morning of my first day on a job. I had neither the Cambridge School Certificate nor my result slip. *Should I go back to the office and tell him I had misplaced the result slip or should I chicken out and just fail to go?* My colleagues again came to my help. They urged me to go and tell the officer the truth. And since I knew my examination number and the scores, I should request him to call Mtihani House to confirm my results.

Tired as I was, I made it to E.A.C.O at eight o'clock and proceeded to the officer. I told him what I had been advised to say. He told me to wait outside the office. Fifteen minutes later, a guy came and took me to my work station. I was excited. This job opened a floodgate of job opportunities for me. I received many letters, but since E.A.C.O. paid higher, I decided to stay put. I earned my first month's salary, but would resign during the course of the second month.

During the first week of my second month at E.A.C.S., I received an employment and posting letter from an unlikely source—the High Court of Kenya. I had earlier applied for a job at the High Court but received regrets. In my hand now was a letter informing me that I had been offered a job as a clerical officer in the service of the Government of Kenya. Another letter informed me that I needed to report to the Thika African Court for deployment. The salary, though, was inferior to E.A.C.S. That evening, before I could make a decision, my nephew, Manase Oyolo, traced me to Caleb's house in Jericho and told me he had received information from Dick Okelo that he had secured a job for me and I would be receiving a letter any time. He said I should not turn down the job. I discussed the matter with my colleagues, who in one accord urged me to accept the appointment. On that basis, I took the clerical officer job.

On the 1st day of July 1966, I reported to my work station. Thika African Court was one of the few colonial court systems that were still in place. My job description was to register cases—both civil and criminal—and prepare returns. I could tell the job would be challenging enough.

But I'm getting ahead of myself. Let me begin from the beginning. When I arrived in Thika, I did not know anybody and for a few days had to commute between Nairobi and Thika. This was not only expensive, it was tiresome as well. One day, in the court, I noticed a familiar face. The man was an *askari* (prison warder). He had brought remandees to court. I could see he recognized me too. After telling him I had been posted here but the government did not have accommodation for me, I asked if he knew of any available accommodation. Instead of answering yes or no, he said, "Why don't you come stay with us?"

That evening my trips to Nairobi ended. I stayed at Elijah Owambla Kwasu's house. After a month, though, I moved to government housing.

Elijah was a fierce man. He was 5'8" and in his mid-forties. He hardly laughed, but smiled a lot. Behind that smile was terror. No wonder he was a prison warder. He terrorized the remandees and did not spare his wife or children either. In his presence, everybody was tense. To me, though, he was a docile man. He maintained that posture for the duration of my stay with him.

When I stayed with Elijah, he and his wife shared the bedroom while I slept in the living room, where his children slept. He exhibited animosity towards his wife. His hostility was such that whenever he stepped out of bed he deliberately kicked his wife Jemima Asiko. Jemima slept on the floor. Everytime her husband kicked her, she would scream loud enough for us to hear. The only thing Jemima was now safe from was constant beating. He did not beat her for the duration of my stay. I was told beating Jemima was his hobby. But, man! She could cook! Her food was delicious. The menu was healthy and balanced. I enjoyed staying with this family in spite of the tribulations they had.

Jemima cried when she heard I would be leaving. For the first time in her marriage, she had lived with her husband in a semblance of peace. Now that I was leaving, things would move back to square one. I had a talk with Elijah about abusing his wife, but I never made a follow-up to know if things improved.

I moved to a dilapidated house. The two-room structure had a living room, a bedroom and a large veranda, which was also used as a kitchen. A pit latrine and a bathroom stood outside, about fifteen yards from the house. I had no furniture, utensils or beddings. I borrowed a bed, a mattress and utensils from Elijah and Jemima to start my new life. Trouble was—I had neither cooked nor budgeted for food before. Things got tough. With my first pay, I bought a bed, a mattress and a chair. I returned the stuff I had borrowed from the couple. The second month I bought a table and purchased a radiogram on credit. I also hired house help.

One day, while still at Elijah's, I went to watch the Prisons soccer team play a team from Gatuanyaga. Within a few minutes, they were three goals down. I asked the coach, who was my nephew—Henry Ndukwe's father-in-law—if he could let me play. Surprisingly, he did. Within five minutes we had reduced the deficit to one goal. We ended up beating them five to three. From that day, I became a regular in that team and ended up being picked by Abaluhya Football Club.

After coming to Nairobi—and now to Thika—I was in communication with Rose. We communicated through letters. She told me she would be in Nairobi in August 1966 to visit her sister, Janet. Janet and her husband—Enos Obunga—lived at Makongeni. Enos worked for EAR & H, while Janet was a homemaker. We agreed with Rose to meet in Nairobi—at Caleb's. Caleb made food for us. Rose came with Janet and we enjoyed our stay. We ate and drank. When we parted, the two went back to Makongeni and I went back to Thika.

We met again in Kisumu at the end of that month and proceeded home to see my parents. We had left Kisumu in the evening for my home, but the bus we boarded had a mechanical problem. We then walked at night from Yala to our home—a distance of about six miles—arriving there in the wee hours. We talked to my parents, rested a little and made it back to Kisumu. We parted ways in Kisumu when she returned to her home and I came over to my work station.

At the beginning of October 1966, Rose wrote to me—she wanted to see me. I wrote back suggesting we meet in Kisumu on Kenyatta day 20:10:66. When we met in Kisumu on Kenyatta day, she was carrying my baby and she said she didn't know what to do. I told her that, if she didn't mind she could come with me to Thika that very day. After soul searching for a while she agreed. That evening we were in a bus headed to Thika. The following night we would be husband and wife. We arrived in Thika safely and 21:10:66 was the official date of our marriage.

I was barely four months old on a job. I was ill prepared for marriage. I had a total of two chairs in my house and one bed and two mattresses—one mattress for the house help, the other mine. And utensils were makeshift; with plastic mugs as cups. Only three small cooking sufurias (pans) were in the house. Besides I had taken a friend to accommodate, who like me, came to Thika to work when he did not know anyone. I and him agreed that I provide during the current month and he would provide for us the next month. So I spent most of my money on buying food for three of us. By the time Rose arrived I had no money. The first thing I did to alleviate the situation was to ask the friend to leave but since he did not have anywhere to go, he stayed on and left at the end of the month. Meanwhile, I continued to stay with the house help, pondering what to do with him now that my wife was going to do the house chores. Things got really bad in the ensuing month of November—but Jemima chipped in from time to time. Our life style did not help to easen up the pressure on our finances. Both Rose and I had lived with James. We tended to be copying the lifestyle of someone being paid ten times our income. We needed to change our lifestyle ASAP.

Just as I was about to despair, my brother Absalom called to request me to allow my wife to go to Nairobi to help his wife Sylvia, who had just given birth to a baby girl. I jumped on this opportunity because it was going to give me the break I needed. The following day I took my wife to Nairobi—Ziwani—where he had moved his family. My wife stayed with Absalom's family for about one month, during which time I got myself organized.

On my wife's return to Thika, my father came to visit us. We stayed with him for a week then he returned home. But before he left for home, he discussed my marriage in general terms and probed the seriousness of our resolve. I think he got satisfied that we were serious and would not bulge. On his first day of the visit, my wife prepared chicken for my father and I. While she served a rump, she offered us other portions. This was cultural sacrilege. Women did not eat rumps and I was not going to allow her to disrespect my father—eating chicken rump in his presence. I asked Father to say grace, to bless the food. As he prayed, I reached out to my wife's plate and exchanged it with mine. If my father noticed anything, he never mentioned. Later, I had to explain to my wife that in my village, a woman does not eat chicken rump.

Our marriage was opposed by many. Different people had various reasons for opposing it. Some said it was a taboo for me and my brother to marry from the same family. But others countered; they had observed such marriages prosper. My brother James resented the marriage, others said. He never said anything to me though. Some folk said we were ill prepared. They were damn right. I was twenty one and my wife was eighteen at the time we got married. We were novices and naïve.

In the African culture, especially our culture, the validity and legality of a marriage is determined by a number of factors. Chief among them—*"Keny, Kisera, Riso and Teno"* ceremonies. *Keny* is a ceremony of paying dowry after the bride has been betrothed. Once the bride has been identified, the parents of the groom and the parents of the bride meet to discuss the terms of the marriage. How many cattle will be paid and whether or not there will be a wedding. This meeting is held at the bride's home and plenty of food is prepared and eaten by the father of the groom and his team. Dowry is paid either in cash or cattle and part of their discussion focuses on the value of cattle in cash. Once this is agreed upon, the father of the groom pays what he brought then departs. The father of the groom at a later time sends either his son or messengers with cattle to take to the bride's father. This process is repeated until all the cattle are sent to the bride's home.

After the entire dowry is paid, or if and when the two parents agree the remaining cattle will be paid later, the groom and his team are invited to the bride's home *(Kisera)*. He spends the night there—not in any house but in the makeshift structure constructed in the homestead—for that purpose. If it is raining, he is not supposed to move from that structure. On the following day, in the wee hours, an animal is slaughtered. This may be a bull or a bullock or he goat or ram depending on the social status of the bride's parents. The groom or any member of his team or anybody requested by him slaughters the animal, but the bride's family does the cooking. The table is set in the mother-in-law's house. But before they eat, the groom is required to cough up some money to his mother-in-law who will have prepared a special dish—*(Tap Maro)*—for him. The mother-in-law sometime asks for high amounts of money, but the groom and his team, through their official spokesman, must enter negotiations with them. There must always be an official spokesman for the groom. Traditionally the groom should not be heard. He can smile or grin, but not laugh. He can clear his throat, but not speak. Inside the mother-in-law's house, the groom sits upright. If he crosses his legs, he would be in trouble and is to be fined—the price, a goat. These negotiations, can take a lot of time with each side holding its ground. Should there be an impasse, the spokesperson for the mother-in-law, after consulting with the mother-in-law and her team—who will be hiding somewhere within the vicinity—will step in and accept the groom's last offer. If food gets cold, it is warmed.

In case there's a wedding, *Kisera* ceremony falls on the eve of wedding day. In some cases, it is held a few weeks to the wedding.

Riso ceremony on the other hand, is held after marriage. Assortment of food including, a goat is brought by the wife's sister from the wife's parent's home. The goat is slaughtered and with other food brought; is prepared by the wife and her sisters. The prepared food is served to the husband and his brothers.

The final ceremony is *Teno* and it is performed after *Riso*. The wife of the brother of the husband who had wedded or had performed a similar ceremony would lead the wife in this ceremony. The two women go out in the woods and fetch firewood along with three stones. On return, they make a hearth—they place the stones to hold a cooking pot, then light fire and prepare food brought by the husband. The food is served to the husband, his brothers and parents.

Teno ceremony marks the culmination of a major traditional marriage ceremony. If any of these ceremonies is not done, then the couple would not be considered married. When a couple wedded, all these ceremonies formed part of the wedding preparations and were done either on the eve of the wedding or on the wedding day.

I performed all these ceremonies for my customary law marriages and my father did his part as was required of him. In the case of Rose, she was as good as wedded, since I paid the requisite dowry *(Keny)* and preformed *Kisera*, *Riso* and *Teno*.

Jane Roseline Adongo or Jane Rose Adongo, as she later preferred to be called, was the sixth child in a family of eight, and the third and last girl. She did not go far with education because of our marriage, but she had drive, initiative and almost unparalleled determination. Rose was the kind of woman you would lock in a room without a window and upon return, she would be gone. Such was her determination. She believed in doing things and doing them well. She understood her educational limitations and would later do something about it. She had some unique attributes and characteristics which were the backbone of her checkered life.

Rose was exceedingly magnanimous. She was a free giver; she never looked over her shoulder when she wanted to help. She gave without second thoughts, many times leaving herself nothing to use. *The hand you stretch to give is the very same you stretch to receive*—so our Lord who gives blessed her abundantly. She had a good, caring husband and wonderful children. Later, some of our children died. Florence Beatrice Akinyi died at the age of five, in 1971; Barnabas Oigo died at 6, in 1981; Benard Onyango died at 24, in 1994; Kenneth Otieno died at 28, in 1997. Of the living kids Edyth Atieno got married, but is now divorced and is taking care of her four kids; Lydia Awuor married, but is now divorced and is also taking care of three kids; Martha

Akoth is married and has kids. Violet Akinyi is also married and has kids. She takes care of her extended family as well.

Through God's blessings, Rose was able to pay fees for several orphaned kids. She was never envious. She grew up in a polygamous environment. This taught her to live an envy-free life. She did not harbour ill feelings at all. If you crossed her, she would be pissed off for a while, but that was it. She was athletic and loved sports. She ran and played netball during her school days. She continued to play netball for the Post Office team where she worked.

Cleanliness was her hallmark. She would pass for a woman in her thirties when she was sixty. She showered twice a day. She taught her kids the art of cleanliness. She was friendly and amiable, particularly to her kids, neighbors and visitors. People loved her; visitors loved her; and colleagues at work adored her. In social circles, she was loved by all. I loved her too.

She was a workaholic. Once she set her sight on something, she did her best to achieve it. No wonder she moved through the ranks of KPTC from a mere telephone operator to a postal officer. Women of her day did not make good wives. They were not women worth talking about. They were promiscuous and immoral. They infected their husbands with myriads of ailments. They did more harm than good to their husbands. Not my Rose. She was clean and morally upright. In our marriage life, I never caught her in a stagnant delicto (a compromising situation). If she ever had any extra marital relationship, she did it discreetly.

And Rose loved church. She was not born SDA. She converted to SDA— Adventism, when she came to our home. She was Anglican by birth, like her mother before her, who was SDA and converted to Anglican and became strong in her new church. So was Rose. She was deaconess, church elder and leader of Dorcas. Her resolve to be in church in soul and spirit has earned her blessings from the Lord. And her strong surviving kids continue to be strong in church. When I appeared to slacken in my faith, she urged me on. She was a founder member and pillar of Magunda SDA church and worked hard overseas to raise funds for the construction of the church.

Her love for the church was strengthened and reinforced by her love for God. And Rose loves to pray. She prays several times a day—meal time, break time, departure and arrival, bed time and wake up time. Rose is a prayer warrior…she even had a three way morning cell phone prayer session with Sister Mary and Sister Wood. I loved it. She prays for her kids, grandkids, husband, church and church members, friends and even her clients. To her, prayer precedes everything else. If prayer were the main criteria of inheriting the Kingdom of God, then Rose will inherit it along with her kids and grandchildren who have chosen to bond with Christ. I believe I can be saved through her.

Rose maintains her stature, physic and health through healthy eating. She refrains from drinking alcohol and smoking any weed by whatever name. She refrains from red meat and most dairy products—she drinks soya milk and she eats a lot of fruits and vegetables. She eats mainly Daniel's diet. The result has been unbelievable. She is radiant and healthy and looks thirty years younger. Yes, she loves eating, but healthy eating.

Her love for her kids is unmatched; she loves her kids and grand kids so much that she would do anything within her power for them. They also love her. When we lost our son Bernard, she almost cracked. In fact, my greatest fear at that time was that she would go nuts, but through prayers, God counseled her and led her out of that tragedy. The loss, was the reason she flew to the USA—to rest her mind and body.

Where other women recoil and chicken out with stage fright. Rose stood and spoke without any fear. She loved to be seen and heard. Whether in broken English or broken Kiswahili she would be up delivering a speech.

While still in Thika our first child came on the 10th May, 1967. I named her Akinyi—she was born in the morning. She was christened Florence Beatrice. She had health problems during infancy—swollen teats. This made her have excruciating pain. We massaged them with hot water and squeezed…whitish stuff; milk-like flowed from them. She got temporary relief after the massage but the following day, they swelled again. When our first line of treatment didn't work, we took her to hospital where she was put on treatment. This helped her recover and the condition never recurred. Unfortunately, we lost Florence at the age of five, in 1971.

Rose was not an angel or a celestial body. She was mortal and human. Like every human being, she had her weakness. She had an "I" disease—*me, myself and I*. Bottom line, she loved herself.

As years went by, she became forgetful. She forgot basic things—like, where she kept money or cell phone or information. Perhaps it was old age, but it ran havoc in her life. She liked talking and anybody who likes talking will not have self-control—they will exaggerate, deny the obvious or make up stuff. Much as I liked her bravery, I chilled when she got up to speak and sometimes, I got embarrassed.

She was also a highly suspicious lady. This was one cause of our differences, sometimes. Any woman I greeted or talked to was, to her, my lover. This was her greatest weakness. It was not only me, she was suspicious with everyone. Once I realized it was her nature, I learned to live with it, but after I had made decisions which would impact our relationship.

One thing that she found hard to discard was her belief in traditions, cultural rights and taboos. These are the things Christianity does not condone, but she was knee deep in them. If she ever misses the Kingdom of God, it will be for this reason. During her early years in marriage, she had one hell of a temper; she got annoyed on simple matters and fumed with anger. These bouts of anger fizzled away as quickly as they came. I remember one such occasion when she became so furious with me that she left our home screaming and went to the graves of James, Christabel, and Florence. She rolled and wreathed on the graves crying that they *(The dead)* should come and get her. This did upset me a great deal.

Rose was easily swayed, that was why she was minced meat for my step-mother and my step-mother used every trick in the book to make sure she deserted home.

Her budgeting ability was handicapped. She appeared extravagant and she could not make ends meet most of the time. And nagging, negligence and rivalry was her soft underbelly. These almost caused us the life of one of our daughters—Lydia.

During the early years of our marriage, Rose was downright dishonest. She could squander school fees for the kids. She misappropriated rents she collected from our tenants and even ran down our Sub—Post Office. I was glad she pulled out of these mischiefs, apologized and became a good Christian. Whenever she reminisces about that past, she regrets and prays for forgiveness. My Rose is now a staunch Christian. I thank God for you Rose.

CHAPTER 11

LAW SCHOOL

During my working life at Thika, my dream of making it to the top was not extinguished. I continued to send applications to institutions of higher learning and to work places. I was invited for an interview by the East Africa Railways and Harbors for a position of Marine Officer Trainee. There were over 400 applicants who showed up to be interviewed among them, a gentleman—Odhiambo Marcelus Titus Adala—who would become a confidant and best friend. By elimination, the applicants were reduced to 40. Mr. Adala and I made the final list. We were both interviewed. I was among the 8 taken for vacant positions. My friend did not make it. The 8 were asked to wait for the paper work. I was extremely happy. I had secured a job as well as a training opportunity. This joy was, however, short lived.

One section on the forms required the applicants to state their marital status. I checked it and indicated that my spouse was expecting. I thought this was an advantage over my single counterparts. Little did I know that I was writing my obituary. Once we filled the forms and handed them over to an officer, we were instructed to wait. Later, someone emerged from the office and called me in. When I entered, the huge brown guy with a moustache asked me to take a seat. He looked at me inquisitively and said "Mr. Wanyanga, we are afraid we cannot take you. You see, our training involves long stints in high seas, sometimes up to 3 or 4 years. Being newly married and expecting your first child, you cannot be taken away from your family. Please go in peace and pass our regards to your wife". I was awestruck and felt as if my heart skipped a beat. That evening, I returned to Thika a heartbroken man. Although I was my own enemy, I had to tell the interviewers the truth.

And one month later, I received another shocker. A letter came by mail indicating that my application to the Law School was unsuccessful. *I felt my world crumble.* I wrote back to the Law School and requested that they consider me for the next intake. In the meantime, I continued to work at the Thika Law Courts—this gave me experience in law; particularly the procedures in civil and criminal law.

Towards the end of June 1967, I received another letter from the Law School. *Could this be the break through God had been preparing me for all this time? First, I fail to get a calling letter to join Maseno Secondary School; then I fail to secure admission to Maseno a second time and this keeps me in mainstream Christianity. Amazing indeed,* so I thought! *And again, I resign from EACSO and take up a lowly paying job at the High Court of Kenya; then I lose my spot at EAR&H as a marine officer under circumstances that are pitiful. Could this be the breakthrough?* I wondered!

I made it to the Law School for the interview and to my surprise, I encountered O.M.T. Adala. We bonded and commenced a friendship that lasted the rest of our Law School years and beyond.

Our Law School classes began on the 1st of August 1967. Mr. Adala and I shared a cubicle. The Kenya School of Law then, was like a 5-Star Hotel. The rooms were neat. Bedsheets were changed every day. Bathrooms had both cold and hot water. A bathtub was also available. And the food was awesome.

Breakfast was a three course meal—cereal, milk, eggs—fried, boiled or scrambled. We had bacon or sausages. Juice was in abundance. Bread and butter were on the table at every meal. We topped it up with a cup of tea or coffee. And we were prohibited from entering the dining hall without a tie and a jacket. We were expected to sit at the table and wait for the servers (attendants).

At ten o'clock they served tea and biscuits. And lunch and supper; we had either fried or boiled liver, ox-tail or steak or tongue… fried chicken…or stewed fish or fried fish. Vegetables were in abundance. English potatoes and rice was the staple. And at 4 o'clock it was tea with cakes, or sandwiches. Life in terms of food was at its best.

Laundry was done every day. We left dirty clothes on the beds with our name tag; by evening they were returned, pressed and tidy.

When we arrived at the Law School, there were only 13 of us—we formed a supplementary class. We filled vacancies of those who failed to report. In one month, we covered what the regular class did in 3 months. This was a heavy load. Accounting was a new subject to me and we were informed it was a tough subject and no one had passed it in the previous class at a first sitting This terrified us.

Examinations were arranged in such a manner that one could clear his first year exams and move to Articles by July of the following year. At that time one was expected to have passed all the 5 first year subjects. Examinations were undertaken in March, July and December of each year. First years could opt to sit for either 3 or 4 subjects. One could not sit for all 5 subjects in one sitting. One had to secure passes in 3 subjects taken in one sitting to secure an effective pass and move to do the remaining 2 in July. If in July one failed one or both subjects, he/she had to repeat and pass one or both in December examinations.

When I joined Law School, I moved my daughter and wife to Kakamega to stay with my brother James. After a short time, my brother's family and my family moved to stay with my brother in-law—Thadayo Dianga—in Athi River Railway Station. Then again, my family moved in with my mother-in-law in Nyakach for three months. Mr. Angugo sublet part of his house in Hurlingam, to my brother. My brother was kind enough to invite my family to live with them. Over the weekends, I visited with them. And they also visited me at the Law School—a walking distance from Hurlingam.

My sister in-law Christabel's attitude towards me had not changed. To her, I was a hindrance to the full enjoyment of her husband. She had 2 kids and in addition to my wife and daughter, she felt she hosted a crowd. Things came to a boil when my step brother Ondunga, 7 years old, came to visit with them. *His visit had coincided with my vacation.* For two days, neither Christabel nor my wife washed Ondunga's clothes. They left them soaked in the wash-basin while they washed the rest. I could not take this act in kindness. I exploded and said a few nasty words. My brother, whom I had expected a scold from; was silent about the incident. My wife did the clothes till Ondunga returned home.

At the Law School, we did the crash programme and were later joined by the rest of the students. And we switched to the regular class schedule.

We were honored to be visited from time to time by dignitaries like, the Attorney General, whose brainchild the school was. He invited the President of the Republic of Kenya to eat dinner with us; the menu stayed the same.

In April 1968, we were ready to take the Council of Legal Education Examinations. After exams, we went on vacation. Upon return, the results were ready. I was one of the few guys who had passed accounts. Since I had passed the other two subjects too, I obtained an effective pass. The following term, I was going to study only two subjects upon which I would be examined. In July 1968, I was examined on the two remaining subjects and I passed. I was ready to tackle the next stage—Articleship.

As students of Law School, we were entitled to a monthly allowance of about Kenya shillings 50. To others, it was booze—they drank themselves silly. To some like me, it was movie time. I liked movies and I also had my family to assist. Such was the imperial life we lived at the Law School. Institutions of Higher Learning in Kenya would later be a far cry of what we enjoyed at the Law School.

Amon Onyango and his wife—Teresa—were family friends to my brother James. Amon and James were bossom buddies. Both went to the University of Rangoon in Burma and were both scientists. I came to know the Onyangos through my brother. They were a lovely couple. They lived a half a mile from the Law School. When I was not at the Law School sweating it out, I was either at the Onyangos or at my brother's. One day, I went to visit with them and as they saw me off, some staggering fellow approached us. As he drew near, I noticed he was drunk. He got close to me and muttered words I did not understand. We ignored him. But instead of walking by, he suddenly turned and slapped me; almost sending me crashing down. He was ready for a fight. And just as he was about to give me another blow, I angled myself and gave him a double left right in quick succession which sent him sprawling on the ground. By the time he landed on the ground, he was 3 teeth less. He was down and out. We walked off quickly as if nothing had happened. *Nobody will know I beat him,* I thought. I walked away with a dislocated index finger which is deformed to-date.

In September when the school opened, I was one of the few guys who had completed year one successfully. I was ready to be attached to senior advocates—to start internship. I was attached to an Asian advocate downtown.

From day one, I realized that this guy was not a good master to me. *Or was it a racial thing,* I thought.

I arrived in his office and he instructed his office boy to lead me to an old abandoned office, almost 20 yards away. The room was secluded and to access it, one had to clear cobwebs along the way. The corridor leading there had not been cleaned in ages. As the office boy opened the door, rats on the floor spurt around competing for the only emergency exit—the door where we stood.

There was no furniture in the so-called office. For those with allergies, this was a death trap. I was told to report the following day when the office would be ready. It was not ready when I returned the following day...a Friday. When I came the following Monday and found the office was not ready, I said, *enough is enough.* I went and complained to the Principal. He told me he would look for someone else if I did not like the place. The following day, he summoned me to his office and asked if I would mind doing internship in Kisumu. He said, *if you intern in Kisumu, you will be eligible for payment of living out allowances.* He added, *as a family man that ought to be an advantage.* I got hooked on the idea and the following day, I was on my way to Kisumu. It would be 6 months before I got a single cent from Nairobi in the form of living out allowance.

I had a letter for M/s Kohli, Patel and Raichura advocates of Kisumu. I presented the letter to their office and was ushered in to see a Mr. Raichura. *Mr. Raichura will be my master,* I thought. From my observation, he was doing the bulk of the work at this Law Firm. And so, I commenced my two years stay in Kisumu.

This was a firm of three advocates as the name suggested. The three were humble guys. They had ¾ of the Asian business in town. Kohli dealt with criminal defenses; Patel, conveyance and Raichura was a master in civil procedure. They were a big contrast to my Asian master in Nairobi. And since they didn't have a spare office, they placed my desk at the registry. This was a strategic spot. That was where I wanted to be. At this spot, I would see and talk to the clients and even hear the three partners speak to clients. This exposure would be the experience I needed for my future endeavours.

When I arrived in Kisumu I did not have any particular person in mind who would host me. I did not know anyone in Kisumu. The decision to push me to Kisumu was arrived at so fast that I had no time to make my accommodation arrangements. And I could not book into a hotel—I did not have money. My brother had given me fare to Kisumu and that was it. My previous month's allowance had been used in commuting to and from town during my fruitless efforts to secure a master in Nairobi. *I had no money.* I had taken a bus from Nairobi and arrived in Kisumu around 5 o'clock in the morning. We had to wait in the bus until day break before we could disembark. I wandered around the bus stage and wondered who would host me in a city where I didn't know anyone.

At the entrance of the bus stage, I spotted someone I knew—Edward Ochieng was a lad from our village. He was born in our village but brought up by his aunt in Alego. The first time I saw him was in 1963 when he and other boys had friends who had come to visit them from Alego. They came to ask me for my gramophone—to entertain their guests. I gave them the gramophone without any fuss. That night, around 11 pm, a boy came to my cottage and banged on the door, *open, open,* he screamed. *Jo-Ulugano are smashing your gramophone.* I jumped out of bed, opened the door and there he was standing in front of me panting. I hurriedly dressed up, took up my spear and machete and took off to Ochieng's home. On arrival, I did not find Jo-Ulugano. The gramophone had not been smashed. I was informed a group of people came and demanded to enter the cottage where the guests were. When they were denied permission, they threatened to forcibly enter and smash the gramophone. I was told they must have heard when the boy was sent to call me and they disappeared into darkness. So that is how I came to know Edward Ochieng (the guy who called himself *Jadak Kende*—meaning one who lived alone). He later became popularly known as Jadak.

Edward was a newspaper vendor and a shoe shiner. On this day, Edward sat under a tree which was his place of work at the enterance of the bus stage. I walked up to him and explained my plight. *I'm in Kisumu for a while. I have no place to go and no money for food.* He said, *that is not a problem.* And added, *you can stay at my place.* Little did I know that he was himself being accommodated by a good individual whose wife was the stingiest woman I have ever met.

We arrived and proceeded to the servants' quarters where he was staying. When the owner of the home returned from work, he went to ask him if I could stay with them while I looked for a place of my own. The owner of the house agreed, but his wife did not. That evening, the *Ugali* which the wife prepared for the 3 of us was the same size she prepared for her husband and Jadak. I starved the whole night. And Jadak later confided in me that the same size *Ugali* is the usual size the woman would prepare for them. I had to move out for fear of starving to death and Jadak was kind enough to invite me to move in with him when he found a place of his own at another estate.

While waiting for my living-out allowance, I lived on a starving diet. My brother James chipped in from time to time, but this was not enough. He was providing for my family, which I was most grateful. He also provided for my father's second family. He had his hands full. In spite of all these, he helped me move to an affordable single room at Shauri Yako, in Kisumu. But my brother could only afford to pay my rent and not provide funds for food. Were it not for a friend and cousin—William Otieno Odhiambo(Green)—I would have starved to death. William and his wife Mary, whom I nick-named *Chiela,* stepped in to help me. We both lived in the same neighbourhood. Their house was a stone throw away from mine. William worked with the Government of Kenya and was stationed at the District Commissioner's office in Kisumu, while Mary was a stay home wife. This lovely couple offered me supper during weekdays and breakfast, lunch and super during the weekends; whenever I spent the weekends in town. I will forever be grateful to the couple.

Meanwhile, my brother James spoke to an old friend at my behest, to offer me accommodation elsewhere at an affordable rate. I knew Mzee Esau Donde, when I stayed with my brother James in Kakamega. He was, then the Provincial Information Officer for Western Province. My brother and I visited him at his residence in Kakamega. He was intellectually alert with a lot of natural wisdom. We loved his company and the ease with which he imparted knowledge to us. I particularly remember him telling me this—*the high school level I had reached was only a stepping stone, a mere spring board to greater things but only if I was focused. I could go down the ladder into the drain or climb the rungs to the top, the choice was mine,* he said.

Mzee Donde had a rental house in Makasembo when he was transferred from Kisumu. He then moved his family to Makasembo. Three of his children, George, Joe and Mary were left behind in Makasembo because they were in school, and Mzee was looking for someone responsible to move in and stay with them. *This was my opportune moment.* He gave my family one bedroom and we had access to the livingroom, kitchen and bathroom. The rest of the house was occupied by his 3 children. I was responsible for payment of the bills. His family lived independently of my family. His sons George and Joe, particularly George, who was the eldest, became a friend, a friendship that continued into later years.

It was while at Makasembo that my wife and I had our first serous brawl. A brawl that made me walk out on her and our daughter. I went to stay with a friend, Samuel Otieno, at his residence in Upper Railways. I was away for a week. And Samuel incessantly talked to me and convinced me to return to Makasembo. I went back and tried to make the best of the situation. I realized it was her pregnancy that made her react emotionally to most situations.

While in Makasembo, we expected our second child—Odongo, named after my late brother, but my brother James convinced us to name him after his friend and mentor—Otieno—popularly known as Otieno Simba. He was christened Kenneth. This was the friend James worked with at Agricultural Research Office in Nairobi immediately he returned from Rangoon University. His wife, Pauline, would later support my political ambitions.

Joab was not only a friend, but a relative too. He hailed from my maternal grandmother's hometown. In the African context, that was a close relative. Neither I nor my son or descendents would marry a girl from Joab's place. When I came to Kisumu for my practical, he was one of the few people I knew. So we struck a rapport. I visited him at his house and chatted into wee hours. And he reciprocated.

One day, he came over and told me that there was a girl in his house whom, he was serious about. His intention was to elope with this girl, but he had a snug—*the father was too harsh and the moment he realized his daughter was cohabiting, all hell would break loose and that would jeopardize his chances of marrying the woman,* he had confided in me. We weighed the pros and cons of the matter and decided to have him hide the woman and inform her father he would like to meet him at a venue of the father's choice. The venue was the girl's home. Joab asked me to accompany him…meanwhile; he alerted the woman's father that he would be accompanied by a lawyer. He figured a lawyer's company should slow his high-tempered future father-in-law. And since the man also worked in Kisumu, and resided in the same estate as Joab, we walked just a few blocks to the house.

Samuel Odiembo was a no nonsense guy. He was harsh to the point of being cruel. He was not young and he could be in his mid-thirties, but had the physic of a late teenager. If it were a matter of thrashing, he would thrash both of us with ease. He had a commanding voice. No wonder Jaramogi appointed him to be in charge of his finances at his transport company—Lolwe Bus. He had such piercing eyes that when he looked at you, one would wish to hide from him. He talked to us with so much rage that we thought he would pounce on us. In fact, when coming to the house, we positioned ourselves in a manner that would not impede our quick exit should that become necessary.

When I introduced the topic for discussion, he said I was wasting time and that I should go straight to the point. According to him, as we were to learn later, he wanted us to tell him how much we brought as dowry because we already had the wife. *And how could we pay without money? We were not here to pay dowry.* Even if we were to pay dowry we were not going to do it in Kisumu. Tradition demanded we go to the girl's father's countryside home. To our surprise, we compromised on one thing—Joab would have the girl and arrange to go to Asembo as soon as possible to pay dowry. His future mother-in-law offered us a cup of tea; which we took under a relaxed atmosphere. It was at this moment that we knew that deliberate leaks had reached him. He wanted to know where I was working as a Lawyer. *I am still in training but will soon be done,* I had said. He got us to commit to a specific date Joab would go to Asembo.

Joab picked a date four months away. He had to raise money within 3 months and use his pay for the 4th month to cover for expenses during the trip. Three weeks to the trip, Joab informed me he had cancelled the trip because they had an argument and a fight with his wife and even sent her away. *And so there is no need for the trip,* he had added. I insisted he explains the abrupt change of mind. He said his wife is unreasonable and nasty and could no longer make a good wife to him. I still wanted to know what caused the sudden change of heart. Just a one time fight would not warrant his cancelling a payment of dowry; save walking out of the marriage. He refused to tell me and I never pursued that line again, but I insisted on him making the trip. I had to involve relatives to convince him to take his wife back. He finally relented and we made the trip to Asembo.

Joab, his friend, *Mwalimu* Owala and I were in the team that travelled to Asembo. *Mzee* Samuel gave us a high class reception and entertainment. Everything was articulately arranged—from the seats to the coffee table and the huge dining table. The food was excellent—befitting a King. *Had Joab made good his threat not to come, it would have been devastating to this father because he cherished his daughter*, I thought. The marriage thrived and was blessed with children some of whom were very bright and one of whom later became an assistant chief of their area. They later died, the wife surviving the husband.

Mzee Samuel became a friend. We shared a lot in common. We were harsh and entertained no nonsense. And we were development conscious. For both of us, our kids were our world. We loved them very much. And Mzee Samuel became a Councillor and my staunchest supporter in my bid to become a Chairman of Siaya County Council.

While still staying at Makasembo, someone accused me to Mzee Donde that I was conspiring to take his house. *This was a false acusation*. He asked me to vacate the house with immediate effect. I moved my family back to Nairobi and another friend agreed to host me at Pembe Tatu. Evans Opot Ologo had a big house at Pembe Tatu, where he and his family resided. He gave me one room. Like Makasembo, we shared the bathroom. I cooked in the room which doubled up as my bedroom and livingroom. It was while staying here that I encountered my brother Absalom's estranged wife—Mary Achieng. She was living in Kisumu at the time.

Back home in Gem, I had no house. I did not have the priviledge of building a *Simba. Simba is the house a son builds at his father's homestead before marriage.* But now, I was married and needed a house for my family. Traditionally, I would be prohibited from building a house when married before building *Simba*. Bottom line, is if I had to do it the cultural way, I had to build two houses: *Simba* and another house for my family. Building the *Simba* would precede building the family house. I wanted a house but I was in a fix because of culture. Since I was still a student, I could not build two houses either concurrently or consecutively. I had to choose, either to obey culture and traditions, or my pocket. I opted to obey the latter.

I had just received a lampsum payment of my living out allowance, three quarters of which I deposited in a fixed deposit bank account. I intended to build a house and settle debts with the balance. In building my family house, I would be defying traditions in two ways; one, I would build a house with corrugated iron roof, while tradition demanded I build a house with grass thatched roof. Two, I would not be building *Simba,* but a family house. I built a family house big enough for my small family.

My wife's lifestyle and mine were as divergent as East is from West. We did not court long enough to learn and understand each other. We courted for about two months; subsequently, we eloped and rushed our marriage—she had conceived. I struggled to tolerate her behavior. She wanted to be in-charge—was also outspoken and overbearing. Her intellectual inhibition made her feel insecure and threatened. She suffered from what one would call inferiority complex. Once I realized this flaw, I started working on it to improve her intellectual image and confidence. I lowered myself to her level intellectually and encouraged her to further her education. I also encouraged her to join me in lectures and professional parties. My wife loved to party. I had Jadak accompany her to these joints, and I stayed home to nurse our kids—I changed diapers, fed them and sang a lullaby. God used me at this point to prepare me for more challenging tasks ahead.

A colleague at Law School made me abandon an interest in weekend dances. They would party to extremes to a point his wife would sneak with other men to restrooms—*you know what happened in those restrooms.* This made me nervous. I had to be stern with my wife. I insisted she quit going out to party over the weekend. She had no choice but to abandon the dance halls. I didn't want my woman to be everyman's piece of pie.

While still in Kisumu, I decided to make a trip to Ugenya. My estranged brother Absalom's wife—Sylvia Odera—was remarried there. I wanted to bring home my brother's son, Obuga. Mzee Justo Wamboga, an uncle, accompanied me to Ugenya. I presented to Obuga sweets and a vest that I had bought along the way. The boy bonded with us. When the elders in the home noted we had an ulterior motive, they disappeared into houses nearby to arm themselves. *We were gonna be beaten for wanting to steal Obuga.* Uncle Justo demanded we live right away. We exited and made it home safely. But the condition of Obuga disturbed my mind. Poor thing—two big wounds on his right leg; his body blistered and rashes spread all over his emaciated body…ringworms painted his scalp. I thought, *if he had his wish, Obuga would have come home with us.*

Absalom Muhudhi or Odongo, as he later preferred to be called, was born, according to him, in 1923. Absalom was the first born in our family. He attended Maliera SDA Primary School. My parents could not afford to pay his school fees any further than primary level. My brother Absalom had a gift—singing. He was a prolific singer. And he loved church. Once he was done with school at primary level, he had to find a job to help support his parents and siblings. He worked in Nakuru press. He initially intended to marry Nyar Jeje, but the arrangements flopped. He engaged and married Sylvia Odera, popularly known as Ng'onga, with whom he sired two children—Edda Odinga, named after our grandmother and Obuga, named after a prominent member of our tribe. Sylvia was older when they married; she was illiterate; old fashioned and a traditionalist. She smoked not only cigarettes, but a pipe as well. She was a good entertainer. She narrated to us scary night time stories while we slept at her house. What I missed from my grandmother, who died when I was still a toddler, I made up for from Sylvia.

Being a staunch Christian family, smoking was a taboo at our home. Anyone who smoked was considered strange and out of place. Although Ng'onga smoked, she did it in private. She concealed her smoking pipe so well that for a long time I did not know she smoked with a pipe. When she came to our home, I was still young and hardly four years old. With age, I observed her. One day, I discovered her smoking pipe neatly tucked at a corner in her grass-thatched roof. I pulled it out, used a stone to smash it to pieces—then I went to report to my parents. My mother was not amused. She felt I should not have taken the law into my own hands; *you should have brought the Kiko to us to confront Ng'onga,* she had said. This earned me a wallop from her. Ngonga never knew what happened to her *Kiko*.

But Ng'onga was most of the time dumped at home by my brother; even in my small mind I suspected something was amiss between them. I was not surprised that my brother later married another woman. It was this subsequent marriage that made Ng'onga to desert the home.

My brother courted and married Mary Achieng, popularly known as Abiba, alias Merab Achieng from Ugenya Kager. This was in 1950. The dowry paid for my sister Pelesia was taken to Abiba's home by my brother Absalom, as the dowry. Like Ng'onga, she was a cigarette smoker, but unlike her, she was young and never smoked with *Kiko*.

The couple got three children one of whom died young. Those who survived were: Thuthu and Ohon Dunga; both named after our two grandfathers. Like Ng'ong'a, Abiba did not stay long with Absalom. The crunch came when Abiba went to a party with a one month old baby, Dunga's follower. The child caught pneumonia and died and a short while later she stole school fees for my brother James. She denied this vehemently. It took my father's ingenuity to recover the money from her by which time she had spent part of it.

My brother got fed up with her. Obviously, he had an element of bad luck in his marriages. First he had an old pipe smoker and when he tried again, he got a dishonest whore. He kept on trying. His fourth attempt at getting a decent wife led him to Sylvia Awiti, whom he met and married. When my brother married Awiti, Abiba who had literally been abandoned at home, took off with Thuthu and Dunga. For a long time nobody knew where she was. One day, Father heard that she was working at Siaya Hospital and that the two boys Thuthu and Dunga were about to die from malnutrition and kwashiorkor.

My father did not waste any time. He set off on a bike for Siaya and took me along with him. Abiba was home, but we were unable to see the two boys. She hid them from us. When Father told her the purpose of our visit, she got into fits and turned ballistic. She called my father unprintable names in my presence and in the presence of a crowd which had gathered. Everyone present was embarrassed, including her fellow staff; the patients and even those who walked by. Her main contention was that Father should not have gone to collect the children and leave her. We returned home, but along the way, Father never said a single word. He was convinced his grandchildren would die.

Abiba had sealed her fate with the Wanyanga family by disgracing Father. *Asiye fundishwa na mamake hufundishwa na ulimwengu*—The world will teach whoever has not been taught by his or her mother.

Three months later, two children were abandoned by someone by the neighbour's home. The children were emaciated and malnourished. They lay on their backs and could not speak a word. Their condition was critical. Fortunately, someone gave a description of the individual who abandoned them. It fit Abiba.

My mother took the children home and for months, she labored to feed them on a balanced meal. In a matter of weeks, they were back on their feet and on their way to full recovery. If it were not for these kids grandmother—Loice Mulure—Thuthu and Dunga would have not survived another week. I thank God for Mother. Bless your heart Mom and R.I.P.

And one evening, I came home from school and everyone appeared worried. They had looked everywhere, but they could not trace Thuthu and Dunga. My parents concluded that they must have been kidnapped by Abiba. They didn't get unduly worried. *What goes around comes around.* They knew she would one day get fed up with them again and just drop them by as she did when they were at the verge of death. They were wrong and right. Wrong—because she never dropped them anywhere in the neighbourhood again; right—because she later dropped Thuthu at her aunt's place in Malanga and Dunga at another relative's home in Ulumbi. *With a mother like this, who needs a mother?* One could prefer going to hell if heaven was patronized by the likes of Abiba.

Later, I personally struggled to locate Thuthu and Dunga. As for Abiba, she was sacked from her job and became a whore in Kisumu. I located her and sent Thuthu to live with her in Kisumu. Unfortunately, Thuthu abandoned school and vanished. Abiba was *a good for nothing* mother.

The woman in my brother's life and his fourth attempt, Sylvia Awiti, was the daughter of Naaman Ogeya of Seme Kakelo. She had two brothers, whom I knew very well. Henry Ouma, a gentleman of the first order and Odero the musician.

Serious attempts by Abiba to reconcile with my brother and come back to him were fended off by Awiti. Some ended in exchange of blows in my brothers Nairobi house. The black spot and a dent on her life was a conspiracy to keep me out of school in 1963. I helped save her life and hoped she appreciated, although the first payback came in the form of a donkey's kick. In spite of warding off Abiba's return efforts, she did not prevent my brother from helping his other children, if they sought his help. There were others like Odinga, Obuga and Thuthu, whom he didn't assist at all. He assisted Dunga for only a brief period of time, but only at the intervention of a third party for he had become incapable of managing his finances. His wife Sylvia Awiti had to be in his employer's office on pay day to be given a share of his salary, to enable her feed the kids.

Absalom was a drunkard and a chain smoker. He drank both beer and *Chang'aa*. It was normal for him to reach home penniless on pay day. On the day of his death, the second day of December 1968, he had been to a drinking spree when suddenly it started to rain. *A storm followed and for a long time rain was just pouring,* so I was told. My brother didn't make it home that evening. And since that was not the first time he failed to make it home in the evening, nobody seemed bothered or even worried. The following day, word went around that someone was lying on a water trench. The guy was identified as Absalom. Police were called and the body was moved to city mortuary where a post mortem released, indicated death by asphyxia.

His body was brought home for burial three weeks after death. *You are killed by what you love.* My brother loved alcohol, but his death could also be attributed to my grandfather's curse. His estranged wives Ng'onga and Abiba did not attend his burial or funeral. All my brothers, sisters and step-brothers and step-sisters attended the burial. My step-mother however, was away— allegedly in Uganda where she had gone posterior to my brother's death. Before burial, we arranged for Obuga to be brought from Ugenya to attend the burial. He never returned to Ugenya after the burial.

After the death of Absalom, my brother James took over the responsibility of Absalom's widow and eight children; Okech's three children and our father's four children. This would continue until November 3rd 1971.

Again, while still in Kisumu doing my internship, I went home one weekend to see my parents. While there, my nephew—Dickson Otieno Misango—came to inform me that Richard Ogwayo was seriously ill and needed medical attention. Ogwayo was staying with his grandmother—Dursila Onjare—my aunt. Ogwayo was the eldest son of Mathayo Okello—the second son of Dursila. Mathayo had migrated to South Nyanza but Ogwayo refused to go with him. He preferred to remain in Gem and for a long time, he lived alone in the homestead which was vacated by his father. He dated girls within this homestead and had not built a *Simba*… he was single. When the Kitchen hut he slept in came down, he moved into one of his father's houses where he stayed for a while. When he got sick, his grandmother took him to her home and did her best to get him medical attention. But his illness defied treatments. Dickson approached me then. Ogwayo was in critical condition; he had a recurrent cough; and he was not eating any solid food. He was emaciated to a point his ribs were visible. Dickson and I decided to take him to the hospital. We put him on a wheel barrow and pushed him to Kodiaga bus stage. Most buses and the matatus heading to Kisumu just drove by. They feared the gentleman would die enroute to the hospital.

After a while, one matatu driver agreed to take him and I. Dickson did not make the trip. A few miles into the journey, he started throwing up. I had to remove my coat to put near his mouth to prevent vomit from spilling over. I also cleared his vomit from the matatu floor using my coat. On arrival in Kisumu, a handcart operator wheeled Ogwayo to the hospital where he was diagnosed and admitted for treatment. I was assured his condition would be stable after treatment. I left him in the hospital and went back home.

A week later, my brother James drove home with his wife from Nairobi. I asked them for a ride back to Kisumu. On the way, I told him he must call and see Ogwayo at the hospital. His wife refused and she was adamant about it. My brother, who had not said a word throughout the trip, on arrival in Kisumu, drove straight to the Municipal market and asked his wife; *"didn't you say you wanted fish?"* *" Oh yes,"* she responded. *"Then go and get fish,"* he said.

And she went off to purchase fish. My brother drove to the hospital. We proceeded to the ward and when we inquired about the patient, we were told he had died that morning. I was shocked. It was as if I was acting under a premonition. My brother was in worse shock. He confided in me later…"*what if I had listened to my wife and just drove off to Nairobi? What would people have said?"* He had wondered.

We wanted the body to be transported home but my brother didn't have money to hire a vehicle. The hospital staff advised us that the body had not developed rigor mortis—since the individual had passed on just hours earlier—and could be squeezed into a VW Beetle and driven home. My brother's wife never uttered a word as we transported the body home. And the fish she bought would be the first meal the mourners would relish on. They proceeded to Nairobi the following day without me as I had to help with the funeral arrangements.

On arrival home, everyone was shocked. We did not know where to take the body. We were not sure whether to take it into his grandmother's home or their deserted home. We had to stop and ask. We were directed to take it to their deserted home. The elders came and removed the body from the vehicle and took it home. The first thing was how to get the deceased parents to come and attend the funeral. It was agreed one of the relatives who knew where they lived, be sent to fetch them. The burial went on without a hitch, and I went to Kisumu thereafter.

One day, while still living in Pembe Tatu, I met Mzee Wilfred Indakwa Ogwel. Like Mzee Donde, he had a house in Moscow Estate in Kisumu where he was staying with his children. He worked with E.A.R &H as a mechanic. He was not home most of the time and needed someone responsible to stay with his kids in the house. I was on the other hand looking for a decent place to stay with my family. He allowed me to move into his Moscow house with my family. At this point, we were a family of three. He gave us a room and allowed us the use of—kitchen, sittingroom and the bathroom. We lived in peace with my wife, but then a second serious brawl ensued. I had gone home to see my parents, but missed the evening bus. So I spent the night at home. My wife was expecting and with her mind fixed on my imagined immorality, she tore into me and called me names, upon my return the next day. I lost my temper and got physical; it was her turn to move out. She did, but left me with our small daughter. The Wilfred daughters helped with preparation of food and grooming of the baby. My wife was away for almost a month. Her relatives had spoken to her and asked her to return. She did. I would not have managed if it were not for my nieces…the Wilfred daughters. I will forever be grateful to Mzee Wilfred Indakwa for the hospitality.

We later moved the family to Nyalenda, where we got our own house; the area had a rural setting. Benard Onyango our third child had just been born. It was still a single room with an outside pit latrine and a bathroom. And a small cubicle acted as a kitchen. For the first time since I came to Kisumu, I did not have someone staying with us.

One day, Benard fell sick at night. He was gasping for air, and behaving as if he was chocking. *I have never seen anything like this,* I thought. In fact, his big sister and big brother had never had any serious ailment. A cough here and a cough there…that was all. The attack, turned into a convulsion. I got scared and felt a strong urge to visit the latrine. When I returned to the house; we reached a decision to look for a taxi to transport Benard to the hospital. I went out and came back with a taxi. On our way to the hospital, we could smell human waste. We wondered what the source was. We blamed the taxi driver…turns out, when I had gone to the restroom; I stepped on my own waste. It was embedded on my shoes and I had not a clue. Anyhow, Benard recovered well after he had received treatment.

My house was built. I furnished it as far as my finances could allow and I also bought a pressure lamp with part of my living out allowance. During those days, only wealthy people owned Safari lamps. To own a pressure lamp, you were one of the few at the top. Mine was the only pressure lamp in the entire village. My brother James had just completed building his semi permanent house (A house with mud wall but corrugated iron roof) and he prided for being the first son of the village to build a semi permanent house. I took a first for purchasing and bringing home a pressure lamp.

One day, both of us were at home with our families. As night fell, we retreated to our respective cottages. I looked for our pressure lamp to light, but it was nowhere. I searched everywhere, I could not find it. Earlier, I had seen a pressure lamp light in my brother James' house. I knew it was theirs; given his financial status, I couldn't imagine he could own a car and fail to buy a lantern, leave alone a pressure lamp. I called my wife to find out where she had kept the lamp. *I took it to Jame's house,* she said. I compelled her to go and bring it. And to make matters worse, during those days, there were no candles. And even if there were—no shops were open at nine o'clock in the night. There were no extra tin lamps either. The only one in the home was being used by our parents and there was no way James or myself was going to take it away from them. So the choice was simple, either I stayed in darkness with my family while James and his family used my pressure lamp, or I had to take my pressure lamp and force James and his family to stay in darkness. I took my lamp and left my brother in darkness.

At that time, I did not realize how selfish I was. *I should not allow my pride to get the better of me,* I thought. James and his family deserved a better treatment from me. This was one of a few occasions my wife had a better judgment than me. Here I was, burning the hand that fed me. James had been everything to me and to my family—he was a man who saw me through high school, when I had been abandoned by everyone; a man who allowed me to marry his sister in-law when many people were opposed to the marriage; a man who hosted my family. Yes….I might have felt a sense of pride and satisfaction. *I had a lamp and he didn't. After all, why couldn't he buy a pressure lamp or Safari lamp? He was working and had enough money to buy a lamp, why didn't he?* Those thoughts running through my mind at the time showed how selfish and stupid I was. The most callous thing one could do to his senior brother. I will forever be ashamed of myself for this action.

The following morning, I had this victorious aura around me…*Yes! I had shown him how to come home prepared. Next time they will be better prepared.* These were in my imbecile mind at the time. On the other hand, my brother woke up and carried himself around as if nothing happened the night before. Sometimes, I wondered how children from one womb could have so different and divergent characteristics. My brother Absalom, sister Pelesia and Brother James had similar traits and characteristics. They were of docile dispositions—smiled a lot, laughed louder, joked a lot and were less confrontational and full of humility. On the other hand my brother Okech, Sister Lewnida and I were live wire type. No nonsense. *Fellows, if you stepped on our toes, you got us there and then.* We were however, truthful and our integrity was beyond reproach. We were also reliable. Our *No* was a *No* and *Yes* was a *Yes*. No ifs or buts…

Whose children—Caleb Ohon, popularly known as Lebo; Christopher Odhiambo, popularly known as *Mambo Yote* (Know it all) and Loice Omol—were staying at their maternal grandfather's home in Umgore. Their grandparents had brought them from Tanzania where they had been abandoned by their mother and later by their father. I wanted them home…so one day, I asked my cousin—Joash Diemo—to accompany me to the Mriga's home to see the kids. I had bought shirts for the boys and a dress for the girl. On our way, we bought sweets; taking a cue from my Ugenya visit. On arrival, we found the grandparents and the kids…I gave the gifts to the kids and they were happy. Unlike Obuga in Ugenya, these kids were healthy and well nourished. We were told they were in fact, attending school. This was relief to me and this initial contact would be critical in the days to come.

The Mriga's on the other hand were not as enthused; they felt I was making baby steps to take the kids and they did not hide their dislike of our visit and they said as much. Just before we departed, they were on my brother with a barrage of accusations. They placed their daughters and grandchildren's predicament squarely at my brother's door step. I did not urgue with them because I did not have my brother's part of the story. Because of this contact, the kids would later come to our home for visits; they noticed that their grandparent's attitude toward them started changing. They were no longer treated with *Kid Gloves*. When *Mambo Yote* revealed their ordeal to me, I said to him, *come live with us*. He said he could not speak for his brother or sister, but would go back and talk with them. On his part he said he was ready. A day later, before I went back to Kisumu, he came back to inform me that his brother and sister were willing and were ready to come. They were to come the following weekend. And during the week, I made arrangements on their living plans. I went with them to Kisumu and later took them to Nairobi to live with my brother James.

The Mriga's, I believed never forgave me for what I did, but I did what I had to do, those were our kids and I was not going to let them wander the country side homelessly. They had a home and I wanted them to be at their home. I also wanted to lessen the Mriga's burden by taking care of them. The children failed to take advantage of the opportunities I gave them along side with my own children—to go to school and learn. Although all of them on their own volition dropped out of school, I struggled to help them live decent lives.

My final year in Kisumu as a student was 1970. By this time, the family had grown to five. When we came to Kisumu in August 1968, we were three.

The Law School, throughout my stay in Kisumu, had sent me lecture notes through correspondence to enable me to keep up with my colleagues who took practicals in Nairobi. Life in Kisumu was not conducive for learning and the living out allowance came only during school days. During vacation, I had to look elsewhere for my rents, bills and food. James kept chipping in, but this was not sufficient to cover all the expenses. I sent my family to live with him during school vacations . This meant changing residences particularly paid residences every term.

I finally left for Nairobi in July 1970, together with my family. When school opened in August 1970, I buried myself in books. I was aware of my disadvantage. My colleagues had a head start—but as they say *Kutangulia siyo kufika*. (The first to start doesn't always finish.) Buoyed by this saying, I sweated on…day in day out. I was determined not only to catch up with them, but to beat some or all of them in the final examination. I cut out all my outings and did not attend students Kamukunjis. The movies and TV were out. I had no time for idle talk. I made sure I read a head of the lecturer and revised daily. I covered everything they did in my absence and was still able to keep up with them. My focus and determination were at their best.

During school vacations, I had a tight schedule—breakfast at seven; lunch at one and supper at eight; and retired to bed at eleven. Between six and seven in the evening, was my work out time. This paid, as was reflected in my exam results.

And with time, examinations format had been slightly changed. The final year students could opt to take four out of five subjects in the first sitting. Effective pass was still three subjects in one sitting. And exams would be in July 1971.

Lecturers were superb, like Mr. Kwach, Mr. Mukhele and Mr. Kamunyori. The African pioneers at the Law school—Mr. Munro, Mr. Meartney, and Mr. Tudor Jackson were superb in their presentations. If you wanted to fail you could. Laziness, drunkenness, idle talk and lack of concentration were the right combinations for failure. I decided to take advantage of the liberalised format of the exams and sat four subjects. *You reap what you sow*, I sowed success. I harvested success; my grades were one of the best in the class in all the four subjects. Land Law and Conveyancing—a very tough subject, I had to tackle next. When the results were released I was elated.

But throughout my School of Law days—1970/71 academic year, my wife and children continued to reside with my brother's family in Woodley, in Nairobi. From time to time; my brother's wife and my wife quarreled, but my wife always let her have her way. She was a difficult woman who could only stay with my brother James. My wife was virtually the house help, but that was just a small price to pay for the marvelous hospitality we got. One day, they got into an intense argument over a trivial matter. She gave my wife an ultimatum and threatened to leave Kawanyanga. I consoled my wife. I said, *sooner rather than later we will be on our own...so forgive your sister,* I added.

This incident gave me motivation and I discussed with my wife the possibility of going back to school—this was her only way to venture into the job market. My brother James held the keys to my wife's return to school. When we shared our plans with him, he was more than supportive. The following week, my wife was at Church Army School doing class eight. With determination, she did KAPE and later got KAPE certificate. With KAPE certificate, she was eligible for a job in a competitive job market. We hunted for jobs through relatives and friends. For a while, she almost despaired. Our breakthrough came when she got a job with East African Posts and Telecommunication as a Telephone Operator—courtesy to Mrs. Mikal Olando and Mr. Gadd Owiti. The family will forever be grateful to Mrs. Mikal Olando and Mr. Gadd Owiti.

She worked diligently in her job and rose through the ranks to become a Postal Assistant. She worked for twenty three years until a forced retirement in 1994 under circumstances beyond her control. Up to the time of her retirement, she was undergoing a training that would have seen her promoted to a Post Master. And throughout her working years, the family never depended on her income. In fact, I don't remember her giving me a single cent except where she coughed up a little for property development. She also didn't contribute any funds toward the kids' school fees. Maybe this was because I never asked her to give me money or to pay fees. Things would change for the better after she retired. She became responsible and paid fees not only for her kids, but other kids as well.

According to my brother—James Helekia Sijenyi—he was born in 1935. He was the fourth child. He was five feet, six inches—of medium built; dark complexion with gorilla-like earlobes. He was the first in our family whose six lower incisors teeth were not removed. He learned at Maliera Primary School, Luanda Intermediate School and Maseno Secondary School, before proceeding to Rangoon University in Burma; where he graduated with Bachelor of Science with honours degree majoring in soil chemistry. He was a brilliant boy and went through his education with ease. My brothers Absalom and Okech alternated in paying his school fees.

Because of his ears, he was nicknamed—gorilla, a name he hated. He was also nicknamed *Otenga* because of his brilliance (Otenga is a kite). The sharpness and ease with which a kite spots and picks a chick was likened to his sharpness and brilliance...hence his nickname. Like all my mother's children, he was healthy and robust in his infancy and youth days. The only health problem I noticed was a constant oozing of pus from his ears. I remember him joking about it. My sister Pelesia used to tell him that his ear stunk. He composed an interesting song about it for humour and to deflate the embarrassment. He would sing:

> *"Peli Aduda Nyisa ita ng'we....ita ngwe."*
> (Meaning; Peli Aduda tells me my ear stinks)

He would repeat this several times and we would laugh and join in the song. It was simply hilarious.

In 1958 after the death of our mother, James flew out of the country to Burma. He returned in 1964 and was employed by the Ministry of Agriculture as a research officer. He worked briefly in Nairobi and was later posted to Western Research Station in Kakamega. He left Government and joined Maize Marketing and Produce Board. The board sponsored his Cambridge University attendance where he obtained a diploma in entomology. He later went to Australia to study more pests and how to control them, again with the sponsorship of Maize Marketing and Produce Board.

He met Christabel Edyth Atieno in 1964, and tied the knot with her the same year. They were blessed with one daughter—Caroline Loice Amondi, born in October 1966. Christabel had a daughter—Nelly Atieno, whom she got out of wedlock.

I was told by my brother that a few weeks after the birth of Caroline, our step mother visited with them in Kakamega for two days. After she left, my brother and his wife noticed a few clothes missing—among them, my brother's underpants, and his wife's one knicker; one brazier and two underpants. As no one else came to their house during that period, they were certain my step-mother had stolen the missing items. Later, they traveled home to find out if indeed their clothes had been taken by her. His wife found her knickers, but her underpant and those of my brother were never recovered. This created bad blood between my brother's family and my step-mother. The animosity continued until the end of time—for my brother and his family.

Towards the end of October 1971, my brother planned a trip home, but a week earlier, he hosted a witchdoctor in his Woodley estate house. They had wanted another child, but all was in vain. They strongly felt they had been bewitched by my step-mother. They took to consulting witches and sorcerers so they could fight fire with fire. They consulted witches far and wide, but were unable to get a child. So a week before this Thursday, a witch had come all the way from Gem to begin a process of treatment that would take them home and to the witch's home in Gem. I witnessed the witch slaughter a hen and she uttered some inaudible words as the hen did its last kick. She took the hen's blood and mixed it with some ash, stirred and gave it to my brother and his wife to drink. My wife and I refused the offer. The witch dug a hole and buried the hen. The following day, she returned home.

I had just received my final year results. I was a happy man. *And what better place to relax than away from the city.* So, when I heard my brother's plans of going home over the weekend, I approached him and asked if I could ride with them. Since the trip would be over the weekend, it would not affect my studies for—Land Law and Conveyancing, which was the only subject I had to be examined on.

On Wednesday evening that week of the trip, my brother said to me, *you may not make it if my friend, Sherry Wamwayi, comes along.* Then he added, *don't worry, I will confirm with him then get back to you tomorrow.*

Friday morning, the day they were travelling home, Sherry Wamwayi called to say he was travelling and should be picked up from Nairobi High School. I knew I could not travel. I had psyched myself for this trip and failing to travel was a disappointment to me. I slumped on the sofa.

In the team was my brother, his wife, his adopted daughter and his daughter. My wife, I and our daughter were to stay behind. But my daughter threw tantrums. She wanted to accompany her playmates home. My brother said he would have room for her in the car. I tried to convince my wife to prepare our daughter for the trip. *My wife was hesitant.* We finally convinced my wife and my daughter accompanied James and his family home. I stayed in Woodley that Friday and Saturday and returned to Law School on Sunday.

That Sunday night I did not sleep. It was the Tororo feeling all over again: sweating, scratching and restlessness. On Monday 4th of November 1971 at two o'clock in the afternoon, Mr. Adalla approached me. He was not his usual self. It was as if something was disturbing him. As he did not want to look me straight in the eye, I knew there was something bothering him, but whatever it was, he had difficulty speaking. He gathered courage and said, *Wuo Nyakwenda, something has happened. I have received information about an accident at Uthiru along Nairobi-Limuru road. The description of the car involved in the accident fits your brother's car.* He couldn't tell me more because his eyes were teary, but I suspected he knew a lot more.

Considering how I felt the night before, I knew something terrible had happened to my brother. I felt like the whole world was crumbling around me. *If my brother died, I am doomed.* As I did not have any money for transport, I asked Mr. Adalla to give me money to travel to Uthiru to visit the accident scene, but he didn't have any. He said, *no point visiting the scene. The accident scene must have been cleared by now,* he added.

We managed to get some money which I used for transport to Woodley. I broke the news to my wife. Friends and relatives who had heard the tragedy started streaming in. On Tuesday, a police officer informed us that contrary to the news going round that all the occupants of the car perished—one small girl was found alive, but with serious injuries and was recuperating in the hospital. He had come to look for the next of kin of the injured girl. Only that morning, I had been told that everybody in the car perished…so hearing this news somehow consoled me. *Maybe, it was my daughter who was alive.* Whoever died or survived was not my preoccupation at that time.

What occupied my mind was the realization that had I made the trip, I would have also died. I started crying—because I was alive and at some point, I thought I was dreaming. I talked to myself. I became easily irritable and uncooperative.

When later I started wailing uncontrollably, the policeman advised that someone be assigned to watch over me. From that time henceforth, I had an aid watching over me until the funeral was over. The policeman took someone else to the hospital to see the injured girl and on his return, we learnt it was not our daughter, but my brother's daughter—Caroline. In my heart, I became more relieved that it was my brother's daughter, because God had spared my brother's seed for posterity. The dead were: my brother, his wife, my daughter, his adopted daughter and Sherry Wamwayi. My family lost a total of four people in that accident. I read in the inquest depositions that my brother had ran his car into a stationery lorry on the night of Sunday the 3rd of November 1971, as they drove back to Nairobi. I also read that there were witchcraft paraphernalia inside the wreckage. The inquest concluded that my brother was to blame for the accident. As a result of that finding, the insurance company did not and could not pay damages for the occupant's car. We took the four bodies' home for burial in a hired OTC bus.

After the burial, I tried to find someone who could help me retrace my brother's journey from Nairobi home and back. I could not find anyone with all information I needed. I gathered information from different persons. I got someone who narrated to me what happened at our home. Along the way, after dropping Wamwayi, my brother picked some provisions for my father and step-mother and also for his mother-in-law in Nyakach. While they were at our home, they offloaded the home provisions and left the Nyakach ones in the car. My step-mother noticed the imbalance between their stuff and what was heading to Nyakach. *The Nyakach package is larger,* she thought. She felt my brother was taking too much provision to his mother-in-law and she complained to my father. Father was supportive of her complaints. They felt that the mother-in-law should take their share and they take the mother-in-laws. This pushed my brother's wife to the edge. She quarreled and laid everything bare—*you are the reason I cannot sire children,* she said to my step-mother. The exchanges became so heated that my brother and his family had to give way and spend the night at my cousin, Joash Diemo's place. I was also informed that the following day, they picked Sherry Wamwayi from his home and together they went to see the witch who had returned to her home in Sirembe, from Nairobi. They were given herbs and witchcraft paraphernalia. They proceeded to Nyakach where my brother's wife narrated the incidence in our home to her mother. She advised them—*travel to Nairobi by another means and do not travel in the same vehicle,* she added. Apparently, they did not heed the old lady's advice and travelled back in their car.

My folk ensured the aid I was assigned was always by my side. They had feared I could commit suicide. Their fear was not misplaced because that possibility crossed my mind at some point. Everywhere I went, someone was with me. Even when visiting the bathroom (toilet), someone was at the door. People took turns to check on me. When I did not want to eat, they used persuasion. They kept me out of the funeral arrangements since I could not be of any use. I could contribute neither money nor ideas—the two things that were in great demand at the time. I had lost a daughter and a brother and his family. The grief, the sorrow and sadness I had was nothing compared to my father's. My father needed consolation, pity and sympathy more than I did. He was the one who needed an aid. He lost his wife in 1958, his son in 1968 and now his son, daughter in-law and grandchildren. If there was one who could think of taking his own life it was my father. And they did not allow him to come to Nairobi…so I didn't have the privilege of seeing his repose at the spur of the moment. When the funeral procession arrived home, I saw him wail like everybody else, but that was it, nothing extraordinary. He was surrounded by Christians, who sang tunes to console him.

The sight of four bodies being lowered into their final resting place was unbearable. Many fainted; my father and I had two people each holding us on both sides. I asked my aids to take me back to the house as I could not withstand the grief and my father's sight. In my father, I saw a body as good as dead. All the sacrifice that he had made for his son, proper education and a nice family, he was watching being buried, going down the grave.

In an African context, people educate their kids for two reasons: one; to enable the kids to be self-sufficient; to take care of themselves and their families and to be able to help the parents—kind of insurance cover or pension scheme. My father's expectation of a good life in old age was gone. As I knew my brother, he was definitely going to ensure my father had a good life. James was better than Absalom or Oketch. Both tried to help Father, but later abandoned him. I believed he would not have abandoned him. Absalom was dead; Oketch was nowhere to be seen. Who was going to take care of their kids? As he stood there watching the bodies being lowered into the grave, one after another, he must have thought of his own children, one of whom was only one year old. *With the death of James, who was going to help him take care of them? Who?* I am sure he must have taken consolation in the scriptures as written in Mathew 6:26-34. He must have stopped worrying. I believe Christians who surrounded Father must have expressed these virtues to him as they calmed him down. I knew life would never be the same for him, but being strong in the faith, I knew he would overcome the grief and settle down sooner rather than later.

At the burial, my step mother was present. Like everybody else, she was wailing and running around. She was shedding tears, but I don't know whether they were genuine or crocodile tears. Of course it was difficult to tell. *You cannot tell genuine or crocodile tears by simply watching the tears roll down one's cheeks.* I wondered what was going through her mind at that time. *Was it guilt and triumph or grief and sorrow?* Whatever it was, she kept it to herself, and she did all she could to hide it from everybody, including her husband.

Being a sweet talker, it was not easy to discern her motives from the way she talked. You had to be in hiding when she thought everybody was away to know her true colors. On the day of the burial, however, she did not betray her feelings toward us by exhibiting any such attitude. She was at her best and I commended her for that. Had she behaved otherwise, the situation would have turned catastrophic.

Tribute to James

I salute you James. Had you killed my mother at birth, I would not have been born. If you had not been born, I don't know what I would have been. If you did not whip me when I refused to help you carry grass for thatching your house, what would I have learnt? If in the middle of rain and thunderstorm, you did not lead me back to Maranda in your quest to get me back to school after absconding, what would I have been? If you did not drop by when I was sick and at the verge of death and took me to Maseno Mission Hospital, where would I have been? Where would I have been if you did not out of humility, kindness and magnanimity, provide my school fees for the final part of my high school years? The books, the learning aid, the transport to and from school, if you did not provide these, where would I have been? Had you refused to accommodate my family when I joined Law School, where would I have been? If you decided to abandon me and my family when I moved to Kisumu for my internship by refusing to accommodate my family and give financial support to us as and when we needed it, where would I have been? If you had refused to take up the financial responsibility of taking my wife back to school, where would she have been? Had you refused to extend your kindness to us by allowing my wife to stay with you in Nairobi when I was in my final lap in Law School, what would I have done? I would have been nothing without you. I would have been nowhere without you. So, Rest In Peace Wuo Nyakwenda.

After the burial, I left my family and my brother's surviving daughter at home and moved back to Nairobi via Kitale. I was told my brother had a retail shop in Kitale. When I visited the so called shop, there was nothing except a few packets of salt and match boxes. My brother had been staying in a tenant-purchase house in Nairobi, which was owned by the National Housing Finance cooperation. I had to arrange how the mortgage was going to be paid and find alternative accommodation for our relatives who stayed with us in Woodley. I also had to arrange where my family was going to live while I was still at Law School. It was a whole month before I went back to school. Exams were only two weeks away when I reported back to Law School. I ploughed into books and our lecturer, Mr. Mcatney, out of sympathy, agreed to give me extra couching every evening. I will forever be grateful to him for that gesture.

I sat for the examination and the results were exemplary, in fact, I was second best in class. Meanwhile, my family came to Nairobi and we continued to live in Woodley after paying two months' mortgage with the little money we were given at the funeral. We later moved out of the Woodley house to enable us to rent it to get enough money to pay off the mortgage. These measures were taken in the best interest of the estate and our family. As Jokawanyanga, we had to work together to overcome the grief of the enomous task that lay ahead.

Still at Law School and without any income except my fifty shilling monthly pocket money, and with a family to take care of, I assumed the responsibility of taking care of my brother's and Father's children, besides my father, step-mother and Absalom's widow, Awiti. I was 26 and ill prepared for the enormous task. Being the last born in the family, I did not even dream that one day fate would thrust on me such responsibility. I knew such responsibility could get down to me only when I would be old but the death of my brothers and then disappearance of another forced me to take up big responsibilities sooner rather than later.

After securing my family, I moved to the next stage, relocating the people who lived with us at Woodley. I let go of the house help with his full dues. Peres popularly known as Nyowange, my sister Pelesia's daughter moved out to stay with another relative. Dunga, Lebo, Odhiambo, obuga moved to Ziwani to stay with Awiti together with their other siblings. Omol and Thuthu were left at home with my step-mother. I asked Dunga and Ogeya who were at Nyabondo Secondary School in form one to come to Maliera where I knew the Administrator. The idea was to get them to be day scholars. The other reason I wanted them in Maliera was that it was the only school I could go to and ask the management to allow them to be in school while I was still looking for money to pay their fees. Dunga agreed and came, but Ogeya refused. I lost contact with Ogeya for the next two years. As for Dunga, that marked the beginning of his staying with my family. I divided the entire Wanyanga family into three groups: some were under my father, others in Ziwani under Awiti and the rest in Jerusalem, Nairobi under me. The heads of these groups had to provide food, clothing and accommodation to all the people under them. This arrangement continued until I got a job.

At the time of the funeral, my wife was expecting our fourth child and she came soon after the burial. We named her Christabel Edyth Atieno after my late brother's wife. Her birth increased the pressure and the burden on us. We just had to learn to cope. Although I was disturbed in mind a lot because I didn't have a job and I had not been admitted as an advocate, I prayed earnestly—for God to show me the way. Then I recalled Pastor Masio's words: *the distance between you and your God is the distance between your knees and the ground*. I continued to pray.

In Ziwani, Awiti took to trading in chan'gaa and drugs to support the family. My father back home benefited from the farm produce as they had taken farming more seriously to get them food on the table. On my part, although I was still looking for a job, my wife had a job and we helped ourselves with the little she got. This arrangement enabled us to feed and get fed.

I was still skeptical about my ability to feed this big family even if I got a well paying job. The number of dependants was too big for one person. Then I remembered that God helps those who help themselves. I realized that God had spared my life for a purpose. *I would have been dead along with my brother James. The 1958 sickness might have killed me but I was alive. The bean in my ear drums or nostrils would have killed me but I was alive. That alcohol making experiment bottle, the honey, the cigarettes or even the mad man on the railway would have killed me, but I was alive. The pangs of hunger, would have erased me from the face of the earth but thank God I was alive.* The purpose—*to take care of the orphans and partial orphans of Jokawanyanga*, I thought.

God had taught me tolerance, kindness and forgiveness. He taught me to be upright and honest; to be harsh but reasonable. God built in me an irresistible desire to bring my father's scattered family together and to provide for them. That was the time to test my ability and resolve. God gave me the wisdom and the finances to realize this purpose. I will forever praise the Lord for that.

We moved to Jerusalem from Woodley and stayed on top of a butchery. We lived in my wife's meager salary. Friends and relatives kept chipping in to assist us. I got a temporary job with the Ministry of Land and Settlement, where I worked for three months. This provided the much needed finances. I was sworn in as an advocate of the High Court of Kenya on the 17th April 1972— Advocate number 640. I therefore became eligible for employment. On the 18th April 1972, I hosted a graduation party where I invited friends and relatives. Chief among the guests was my friend, Adalla and Omondi Mbago. Omondi was hired by the Government of Kenya and rose through the ranks to become Kenya's 3rd Registerar - General. Mr. Adalla remained in private practice where he made a name. I believe this was the profession God had all along been preparing me for. I would not have succeeded in life and looked after my many dependants if I had not trained as a lawyer and ventured into private practice of law. Despite my handicaps which included stammering; platform (stage) fright; inability to think on my feet—God held my hand and I overcame these handicaps. I would not place myself in the category of the best lawyers because I was not, but I was determined; dedicated and diligent—three Ds which make the corner stone of success.

Above all, I was available.

CHAPTER 12

EMPLOYEE

I had not fully recovered from the shock of the accident of 1971. I had a lot of worries and was green in handling catastrophic situations like this one. The fact that I had no steady job made the situation worse. My wife was earning peanuts at her work place and the contribution we received were exhausted. I had to get a job fast, otherwise I was going to be homeless and without food. So it was a big relief to me when I received an invitation to attend an interview at the Attorney Generals chambers. I got a job of Legal Assistant in the Registrar Generals office in April, 1972. My docket included the administration of deceased's estates. The only problem we had with our employer was low pay. What we were paid was far less than our expectations and even lower than what other professionals earned, but we were paid promptly. We drew the attention of our employer to those concerns and when they didn't listen or act, we resigned enmasse. Almost all the newly recruited state counsels and Legal Assistants resigned. I had worked for only four months and enjoyed the work, but I lived in Kibera with my family. I was able to pay some of my debts and school fees for my growing extended family. I was also able to assist Father in taking care of the children I placed under his custody.

During the month of June, 1972, I read an advertisement in the local dailies of the position of an advocate in Municipal Council of Kisumu. I applied for the job and was called for the interview. Out of the eight who attended the interview, I was the only one hired. I was to report to work on the 1st of August 1972. So, when I resigned from the Attorney General's Chambers, I was not going to join the unemployed on the streets. I had secured a much better paying job than what I had. In fact, I was going to earn twice as much—*I had just been recruited as a Municipal Advocate.*

I reported to my new work station on schedule and underwent the initial orientation. The council offered me a house at Argwings Kodhek Estate—a three bedroom town house; with a large living room, a kitchen and one bathroom. I returned to Nairobi to bring my family from my brother in-law, William Waga's house, where I had left them. But my wife could not accompany me because she was working in Nairobi and it was not easy to get a transfer that fast. So I came to Kisumu with the kids—Kenneth, Bernard, and Edith, who was only eight months old. Benard was 2 years old and Kenneth was 3. In the team was also a maid to take care of them. And for the next four months, I was the father and mother of my three kids. Because I was not with the kids most of the time, I was compelled to hire another house help—to assist with the laundry, cleanliness of the house and preparation of food. I started a new life as a single working parent.

Meanwhile my uncle, Justo Wamboga approached me to allow his son Kenneth Ayayo (popularly known as Masi) to stay with us. Masi was learning in a secondary school in Kisumu as a day scholar and had been chased from where he was staying. Considering the number of people I was living with at that time, and what I had gone through, it was not easy to take another person in. Besides, Masi was a drunkard and also smoked cigarettes. I did not want my kids to deal with these. Reluctantly, I agreed to take him in on condition that he stopped the vice. When Masi came to stay with us, I warned him that if he ever smoked or drunk; I would not only whip him, but show him the door. He took that warning seriously and for the duration of his stay with us, he neither smoked nor drunk alcohol.

While at Argwings Kodhek, we were to accommodate yet a nephew, Martin Edson Ojwang Muger. Martin's father was my cousin. Martin got into trouble at St. Mary's School Yala. They were in the same class with my cousin, Congo, who stole some students' mattresses from school. Martin not only helped him ferry them home—he took two of the mattresses for his own use. This theft was discovered by school authorities while I was still with M/s. Kohli, Patel and Raichura Advocates in Kisumu doing my practical. They called in the police whose investigation led them to Congo's and Martin's homes respectively; where the mattresses were recovered. Congo and Martin were arrested and arraigned in court with the offence of stealing. Whereas the parents of Congo did not bother to do anything about his arrest, the parents of Martin came to me for assistance. I talked to Mr. Kohli who agreed to represent them in court for free. They were discharged with a warning not to repeat the offence and to be of good behavior. The court also recommended that they be readmitted to school. Martin went back to school and completed Form IV, but Congo, out of shame never went back to school. So, here was Martin wanting accommodation as he looked for a job after he had completed his high school at St. Mary's School, Yala. Although we were already a crowd, but because there were enough bedrooms for all of us, I accepted him into our fold. Martin stayed with us until a combined effort of Michael, Green and I secured him a job at the DCs office where he worked until he died.

At my work place, I had a handful. I set up a complete new department; did all conveyancing work; represented the council in courts—including valuation court, collected debts and negotiated the rescheduling of payment with councils' creditors. I enjoyed the work. I did my best to help the council amidst intrigues perpetuated by the easterners (people from Kisumu district) against westerners (people from Siaya district) where I came from. The easterners wanted all the jobs in the municipality to be held by themselves at the exclusion of everybody else. But this was not possible because they did not have enough man power.

Still, at Argwings Kodhek Flats, my friend and cousin, Enoch Genga, drove all the way from Mombasa to come and visit with us. We decided to drive to my home to say *jambo* to my parents. On arrival, my step-mother came out of the house screaming: *uwi! uwi! Not again, not again!* We were embarrassed.

When we returned to Kisumu, I borrowed a car to go and see a friend in Nyalenda. Jadak sat in the front passenger seat of the VW Beetle. I was still learning how to drive, but Jadak was already a licensed driver. This friend we had visited with, insisted on driving us. He took the steering and as the car moved on, the accelerator pedal got stuck and could not release. I was seated in the front passenger's seat with Jadak at the rare seat. The car started moving uncontrollably. We lost control and rammed into a bolder. The impact sent me flying through the windscreen. What happened thereafter was news to me...I was unconscious. It was around 7pm when the accident occurred. When I woke up from unconsciousness, I found myself in New Nyanza General Hospital at 4 am. I was badly injured. I had a deep cut on my nose and several other cuts on my head. The pain was excruciating. The pain was made worse by a nurse who stitched the cut on my nose without anesthesia. She complained aloud that the needle she was using was blunt. A blunt needle, no anesthesia and the fact that she appeared not to know what she was doing made the stitching take 2 hours. *Two hours of severe pain.* I almost passed out again by the time she was done with me. To my surprise, I was the only one in the car who was injured. While I was seriously injured and unconscious for 10 hours, the other occupants escaped unscathed. And coming in the wake of the 1971 accident, only eight months earlier, the accident scared me. I realized that my life was in danger. The devil was after my life. Like my brother James, I would look to the witches and sorcerers for a solution.

The first thing I did when I regained consciousness was to give instructions to those around—*no telling my wife about the accident*. I did not want her to know because she could not withstand the shock. I wanted her informed after my discharge from hospital. Despite my instruction not to tell my wife about the accident, someone called her and informed her. By evening, she was in Kisumu. We were hardly one month in Kisumu when this accident occurred. Whoever called her, told her things about Jadak that made her mad. So on arrival, the first person she fetched out was Jadak. When she linked up with him, she did not hesitate to give him a dress down. Jadak managed to beat her to hospital and narrated how she verbally attacked him, alleging that he was responsible for my accident; allegations which Jadak rightly denied. This information from Jadak did not go down well with me and when she made it to the hospital, I was furious. I demanded to know who had telephoned her about the accident—of course she refused to disclose this. I also wanted to know why she confronted Jadak. When she refused to answer me, I ordered her to go back to the house.

Unknown to me, before she came to the hospital, she had sent packing, the girl who was helping the maids take care of the kids, while I was in hospital. When I learned about this, I sneaked from the hospital ward raging with anger; went to the house and forced her to return to Nairobi. *Her coming had done me more harm than good,* I thought. This was the time I needed consolation and a shoulder to lay my head. Instead of thanking Jadak for having ensured I reached the hospital as soon as possible after the accident and for arranging for someone to stay with the kids in my absence, she started a war with Jadak and the girl. To me, this was primitive and obnoxious. She returned to Nairobi and three days later, I was discharged from hospital.

Before the discharge, an X-ray of my skull revealed a small fissure which the doctors said they could do nothing about. The point about the fissure still bothers me a lot; particularly during the cold weather or when I knock my head on a hard object. And I carry an ugly scar on my nose as a result of the incompetence of the nurse.

And the Saturday following the day of the accident, I came home in the afternoon and found a guest whom I did not know. She was welcoming and appeared as if she knew me well. I suspected she could be one of my nieces from Migori. I was reluctant to ask her name, for fear of exposing my ignorance. So to avoid any embarrassment, I carried myself around as if I knew her. And as we were about to take supper, Jadak walked in—we took supper together. After supper he asked if I knew the guest. *I think I know her,* I said. Jadak interrupted...he said, *I don't think you know her.* As he could not remember her name; he asked the guest to introduce herself. *I am Jane Rose Aluoch Musando. I come from Yiro but we live at Sidada*, she said. At that moment, it dawned on me that I had been mistaken to associate her with my Migori nieces. Jadak went on to explain that after he had closed his work, he went walking through the bus stage, and came across a beautiful girl; standing alone and looking desperate and worried. He approached her and asked; *can I help you?* She told Jadak she was supposed to meet a friend at the bus station. "I'm attending their wedding as the best maid. The wedding is tomorrow. I can't believe I missed her at this bus stage," she complained. Jadak informed her of a cousin who worked with Kisumu Municipality who could help. We did everything in our power to help locate the wedding venue. And she joined the bridal team.

After the wedding ceremony, about seven in the evening that same Saturday, she came back to my house having failed to get transport back to her hometown—Sidada. And we couldn't have asked for more. She was a lovely lady. She appeared mature because she knew her boundaries in a married man's tuff. And we also didn't disappoint, we treated her with high regard. Martin and Masi tried to be at their best in mannerism. And the kids were awesome. *She loves my family,* I thought. I also explained myself—my clean shaven hair...she felt pity for me. She recalled the accident—*the year was 1971, I heard Mother talk about it.* And she opened up more to us. She said she attended Highlands Girls' High School and added; *I will be sitting for my final exams for Form VI in November.*

Early Septermber on her way to school, she visited with us. I started feeling something special for her. *Can she make a better wife? Less nagging; thrifty and morally upright?* I wondered. She had however; passed the test on moral uprightness, on the three occasions I had a chance to test her. She proved unshakable on her resolve to maintain her dignity. That marked the beginning of a relationship that reluctantly and quickly grew and finally blossomed.

And what happened between my wife and I after the accident, was the beginning of our estrangement. Shortly after the accident, I took advantage of the Municipality's car purchase arrangement to acquire my first car, a Peugeot 404 saloon. I had learned how to drive by watching drivers and did not attend any formal driving school. I drove for pastime and I drove for more than a year without a licence.

One day, Caleb Otieno and I decided to drive to Siaya show, in my new car. I had not had much practice on marrum roads—all my driving skills were restricted to tarmac roads. The road, as you approach Ngiya, had a sharp bend to the right and another feeder road from the market joined the main road at the bend. As we approached this bend, I did not reduce speed. I was doing about 50 M.P.H.; then suddenly, a cyclist emerged from the feeder road at full speed. I could not swerve to either direction because I did not understand his intention. I was going to run into him regardless of the direction I swerved. I decided to press on the emergency brake; it sent the car spinning in the air...then landed on its top. There was a thicket at the point it landed therefore, we did not suffer any injuries and the car had only a few dents. We did not reach the show ground and instead went home to inform my father about the accident. We later drove back to Kisumu.

After repairing the dents on the car, it was payback time. My cousin Green and his wife Chiela, who fed me when I was stranded in Kisumu during my internship, had his father-in-law admitted at New Nyanza General Hospital. The doctors gave a grim prognosis on his survival and adviced that he be taken back to his home. Green asked me to drive the patient home. I fueled the vehicle and safely drove the patient. Unfortunatley, he died a few days later. Green and I still bumped into each other on several occasions after this incident.

When I lived in Siaya, Green got a temporary assignment—lecturing civil servants in Siaya. These lectures were scheduled for short periods; once a month...Green didn't need to rent a house in Siaya. We hosted him during these lecture stints. My wife Rose was hospitable, the goodwill had to be recriprocated...whenever I had no money when I lived in Kisumu, Green's wife was always there for me. *When you do a good deed to someone, you do it to yourself.*

After a few months stay at Argwings Kodhek Flats, the council moved me to Milimani to live among other council bosses. I was still staying with Masi, Martin, the workers and the children. My wife was still in Nairobi—unable to get a transfer. I defied traditions and moved to Milimani without her. The Milimani property was a big bungalow situated on a half acre land. It was not completely fenced, but had a lockable car garage. The house had a big livingroom and three spacious bedrooms. All rooms were ventilated to allow free flow of the lakeside breeze. All windows and doors including the verandah were mosquito-proof. It had one bathroom; and a kitchen. There was an outside self-contained servant quarter—with two rooms which could be used as a livingroom and bedroom. It also had a kitchen and bathroom. I moved Masi and Martin to the servant quarter.

It was payback time again. My friend—Caleb Otieno—who offered me accommodation in Nairobi needed my help. He had been suspended from his work place. He requested me to accommodate him and his family at my Milimani home. I was there for this brother until he secured independence.

Even before my wife joined us from Nairobi, our home in Milimani was open to all relatives and friends. We had visitors virtually every day. When I had frog matched her to the bus stage…for her to go back to Nairobi—out of anger—I had informed her I would marry the woman she called names and sent away. *She is kind enough to take care of my kids and so she will make my woes vanish,* I thought. I needed not only a wife, but a friend too. One in whom I could confide. A woman, who could raise our children and provide for the extended family. I needed someone I could trust; whose honesty and integrity was beyond reproach. I needed someone who could not push me into immorality by constantly portraying me as immoral. I needed a strong character whose mind was not easily swayed. I thought; *someone will influence my wife to poison me.* I became alert around her as a precautionary measure.

My wife finally moved to Kisumu in October 1972, when I had already made up my mind that our marriage was irredeemable. *This marriage is flawed and it's heading to the rocks,* I thought. In fact, those past few months my wife was away, I had been relatively peaceful. I focused on bringing up our children. It was my wish that this time around, *she is changed for the better.* That was not to be. The extravagance continued…the nagging, stubbornness and blatant lies increased. She misused any amounts of money I offered her. She demanded more because she was convinced I was a moneybag and spent on other women. As we continued to live through this failed marriage, I communicated with Jane. I wanted her to meet my wife. We set the date to coincide with Kenyatta Day that year. She came and my wife at first received her with open hands…prepared good food and a place for her to sleep. "She is the woman I intend to marry…the one you sent away never made it to the list," I said in a brusque tone. My wife became furious. The following morning, my wife went ballistic. She cursed Jane. Jane cried uncontrollably and my wife spewed more unprintable words. I was embarrassed. I could not understand my wife's change of attitude as she bellowed at Jane that morning. Jane gathered courage, took a deep breath then said, "I did not want to befriend your husband or even marry him, but because of your insults, I will henceforth befriend him and God willing marry him." Jane was right, she had resisted all my advances to her and I was almost giving up, my wife had unknowingly given me a life line.

I drove to our rural home in Gem and presented Jane to my father who was happy with the prospect of me marrying a second wife…as far as he was concerned; my marriage to my wife was irredeemable. I kept him in the picture at every stage—many times he had presided over meetings to find solutions to our problems. He knew precisely the source of the problem. One time, my father and my mother-in-law arranged to meet me in our house—in Milimani—

to try and solve the impasse, but the meeting flopped when my mother-in-law decided to be impartial and sided with her daughter's blatant lies. From that day on, my father realized our marriage could not be saved.

The following day after visiting with my father, I drove Jane back to Eldoret, Highland High School, but I still harbored some hope of redeeming our marriage. I kept in touch with Jane by correspondence throughout the term. Through the letters, I discovered the idea of playing second fiddle was worrying her. And with pride to hold onto and discouragement from friends, I had an uphill battle to win Jane over. She was a proud girl who had the total confidence of her parents; particularly her father whom she thought would not accept her being married as a second wife. Unknown to me at the time, her father was a polygamist, *he cannot be a hinderance to our marriage,* I thought.

When schools closed, I requested my cousin—Joash Diemo—to accompany me to Eldoret to pick Jane. When we arrived, Jane's attitude toward me had changed. She refused to ride with us. We had to plead. My cousin Joash was the man of the hour. It took his wit to convince Jane to ride with us. And Jane stayed in Kisumu with me for a few days and then she left for her home.

After seeing Jane off, I literally deserted my family. I was convinced beyond reasonable doubt—from the company my wife kept—that she was about to poison me. *It was a matter of time,* I thought. I decided to have meals in hotels… And I slept in lodges. I did this for about a month. When I ran out of money for hiring lodges, I slept in the car. My favourite spot—a packing bay in front of the Post Office opposite Nyanza Cinema, Kisumu. *The marriage was broken and there was no turning back.* It took the intervention of my cousins—Michael Meso and Wilfred Indakwa to call a truce between us.

During these turbulent years, I did not turn my back on my children. I was out of the home for fear of being poisoned, but my children attended school and they had food on the table. I also paid rent promptly. And I give myself a pat on the back because with this determination and drive, I have educated all my twenty-two children. I believe sometimes; God allows temptations and problems in one's life before He intervenes. In my case, this marriage turbulence was a precursor to what God had planned in my life—to prepare me for the plan and vision which he was about to launch to save Kawanyanga. The steps God put in place would be clearer as the years wore by. I cannot take pride and say it was my vision, because it was not.

In December 1972, members of Mutumbu Sports Association—an organization my brother James helped found—sent word that they wanted to pay their last respects to James and his family. They requested me to assist them with transporting drinks and food from Nairobi. I informed Jane of my plans to drive to Nairobi. She had planned to visit with her cousin in Nairobi; she asked if I would give her a ride. With two members of Mutumbu Sports Association in tow, we drove to Nairobi. Throughout the trip, Jane never said a word. *Something seemed to bother her. What could it be?* I wondered. Whatever it was; she kept it to herself. I dropped her at her cousin's hotel and proceeded to Kahawa. The following day after loading, I drove back to Kisumu and that was the last time I saw Jane that year.

The famous band—Tausi—of Ochieng Nelly graced the occasion. There was—dining, drinking and dancing. I had to keep away rascals who were out to cause trouble. This was it—there would be no more last rites performed at my brother and family's funeral. And Father held onto church from this point forward.

Shortly before Christmas, a friend, Ibrahim Onyango Ogola, who had travelled from Momabasa; requested to use my car to his home town. I met Ibrahim at Law School and we developed a liking for each other—we shared lots of secrets. He was the one who gave me orientation when I was employed as Legal Assistant in the Registrar General's office. He had been employed a year earlier and at the time of my hiring, he was heading out on a transfer to Momabasa. He had also witnessed the tragedy of James and family in November, 1971. Being a traditionalist to core; as soon as he was settled in Mombasa, he had arranged for me to meet a Sheikh—medicine man. The Sheikh gave me some *Dawa* and an expensive ring. "Wear the ring on your right dominant finger at all times," the Sheikh had directed. "That will keep off the demons and ill luck," he said. I wore the ring for many years until one night; it slipped out of my finger. I looked for it that night and even the following day, but never found it.

So I gave Ibrahim my car, but on his way back to Kisumu, the car rolled and was extensively damaged. He called me to convey the sad news. I arranged for the car to be towed to a garage in Kisumu. He never paid me a cent for the repairs. *What goes around comes around,* I thought.

Previously, I had borrowed Enock Genga's car.... Enock had come from Mombasa to visit. I was involved in an accident and the car was dented badly. I never gave Enock a cent for repairs.... Not even towing charges. *God must be punishing me for my inconsiderate and unkindness to Enock,* I thought. What I was going to spend was twice as much as what I would have spent on repairing Enock's car.... Like we say in Luo, *Ondong' mipimoye ema ipimoniye* (Do to others what you would like them to do to you). Boy, didn't I learn this the hard way! And as the saying: *Gima ogen jabare* (meaning: you can miss what you hope to get or have); I looked forward to enjoying my first Christmas riding around the neighbourhood in my car; and visiting with Jane. That was not to be. In fact, I spent the dullest X-mass ever. I did not know whether Jane had returned from Nairobi. If only I had access to my car, I was going to drive to her home and find out. "I will not attend Mutumbu Sports either," I mouthed.

Just about 7:00pm in the evening, a young; beautiful girl came to our home. I was struck by her beauty and she was not familiar. She walked straight to my cottage, her handbag dangling on her right hand. "Can I keep this bag here?" She asked, "I don't want to carry it along to the dance...I might lose it," she said. *How can this stranger entrust me with her belonging? She doesn't even know me. Why me? Why doesn't she entrust Mum and Dad?* I was bothered by this. I also decided to go to the dance.... Not to dance, but to find out more about her. She danced with nobody and everybody. She did not allow anyone to touch her; not even Isaac Thuma, whom she hang with. I concluded she was sly and had no time for men. *She could be around sixteen years old,* I thought.

Despite her beauty, I did not like her attitude toward alcohol. She drank like fish in water; any brand, including *Chang'aa*. I returned home to enjoy my sleep that night. Seven o'clock in the morning, she returned home to pick her handbag. Before she left, I took a close look at her, of any sign of drukardness—she was sober. *Where did the pombe she had been gulping go?* I wondered.

I was told she came from *Ka* Meshak Aduol and her name was Pamela Apiyo. This was my first contact with Pamela (popularly known as Pam). Ka Meshak was one kilometer away on the way to Maliera School.

Potentially, I was born a monogamist. The idea of having more than one wife did not appeal to me. I was not exposed to families with many wives. My mother was the only wife of my father. My elder brother although technically had four wives; only had one at a time. So the idea of marrying a second wife was not in my mind. Had my first marriage been successful, I would not have imagined a second marriage.

Things worsened when guys started mocking me that I did not have a wife; that the one I had was my brother's and that; if I wanted to be considered married, I ought to get my woman. I shut out these tirades to give my marriage a chance, but when my marriage did not work; I considered marrying a second time. And there was no impediment to a second marriage in my culture. My first marriage was a customary law marriage—I didn't need to dissolve it to enter into a second one. Immediately following the Nyalenda accident; I started dating women. I dated Rebecca (popularly known as Becky), but my friends felt she was mean, domineering and her morals were questionable. When I met Jane; I tested and watched her to see if she had the qualities I was looking for in a wife. She was not quite there, but was eighty percent close. I was determined to get her as a cure to my marital woes.

It was not only a cure I was looking for, I needed a helper—an aid; a woman I could sit down with and discuss things. I needed one with the potential to bring in resources, to assist me in caring for the twenty seven plus members of Wanyanga Family. Rose and I were already overwhelmed.

I had not met Jane since I left her in Nairobi in December 1972. She had shut off all avenues of communication. Her rebuke by Rose still echoed in my ears...*I did not want to befriend or even marry your husband, but now I will. Could she be the second woman in my life?* I wondered. Also, I knew she could make a good wife. She was an introvert like me, but unlike me, she was a bookworm. She was a complete opposite of Rose, who was talkative and outgoing. She was also calculated and focused. She treated me courteously and respectfully—a mannerism she maintained throughout our courtship.

Sometime in February 1973, I went to Nairobi on an official duty. On my return, I received information from my cousin; "you must see Jadak immediately," Joash Diemo had said with urgency. I went to Jadak's place and he told me that Joash brought Jane and since I was not in, they could not take her to my home in Milimani. They checked her in a hotel for the night. He led me to the hotel and we checked Jane out.

Rose was home that night. She had seen it coming and prepared herself psychologically. She knew our relationship was beyond saving and she could no longer stop me. In fact, it was her turn to fight to stay. On my part, I could not care less if she packed and left.

From the moment Jane stepped into my house that evening, she became my wife. She was twenty one years and I was twenty nine. *Age disparity does not matter. Life must start for Jane and me,* I thought. So came into my family and unto my life a woman who would be pivotal in the reconstruction of my father's family and home and the unity and prosperity of my own family.

One day, as I drove from work during rush hour, I stopped to pick up a friend. As the lady made her way to the car, there was already traffic jam. The occupant of the third car in the rear was a man of Asian descent. He got out of his car and ran toward me. He got to my door just as my passenger was getting in. The Asian tried to pull my ignition key to turn off the engine and I hit his hand. In that moment, I pulled off, but he hang on the door. When I realized he could fall off and get injured; I stopped the car and in that instant, he said he was a police officer. "I'm arresting you because you are causing obstruction," he said. I was not amused because as a matter of fact, there were other cars stopped ahead of me. *The days an African can be intimidated by an Asian are long gone. Twelve years after independence and an Asian still throwing his weight around suggesting an African is inferior! He must be living in Disney land,* I thought.

I was prepared for a legal face off. Someone must have whispered to him I was a lawyer.... Suddenly; he stopped manhandling me. He called a junior officer and commanded him to ride with me; he trailed us.

At the police station, he instructed the police on duty to book me in the OB and release me on bond because, "I hear he is a lawyer," he said.

I hired services of a Lawyer and when the case came up for a plea; I pleaded not guilty. The Magistrate, the Chief State witness and my Lawyer were all Asian. My friends persuaded me to plead guilty on the day of hearing because this Asian police had reasoned; *my case was a misdemeanor punishable by a fine only.* I refused. *He will do the same to another African. I must stand my ground and have the case heard,* I insisted. *And he has no other witness, but himself. How is he going to convict me on the strength of his own evidence and of the guy who booked me in the OB and who rode in my car? He is the complainant, the investigating officer as well as the arresting officer. This is a slum dunk case for my lawyer,* I thought.

I also knew the hearing would expose him to embarrassment. He uttered some words to me at the scene of my arrest which were racial, derogatory and demeaning to an African and he knew my witness and I would bring these up. I had him cornered.

On the day of the hearing; I still pleaded not guilty. They adjourned the proceedings briefly to consult in the chamber. A few minutes later; I was called in. A truce had been worked out. I was discharged. I walked away a free man. And I never saw the Asian again.

Martin Edson Ojwang Muger after moving out of my home in Milimani got his own house and settled. He met and married a lady from Nyahera in Kisumu. As was the custom, he had to go to his father-in-law's place to pay dowry. He requested me and a friend of his to accompany him.

The girl's home was fairly affluent. The food was A-class and the entertainment was classic. Being that we drove and we looked sharp in our suits; the hosts had high expectations of us. *That is exactly what I would do if I were the father-in-law. I would expect money enough to pay my expenses for entertaining the guests and to buy several cattle,* I thought.

After tea, I requested our hosts to excuse us. We took a short walk. *How much do you have on you Martin?* I asked. When Martin mentioned the amount he had, I became furious. I was not happy. *How could he bring us all the way to face embarrassment? If only he requested for our help before the trip, we would have definetly chipped in,* I thought. We walked back to our hosts and presented the little we had. *They were not amused,* I could tell by the looks on their faces. From that day, I vowed never to take anyone to his in-laws without first knowing how much money he had saved toward dowry.

Staying with two wives under one roof proved tough. I had to readjust my life. I put my two spouses to test. I had to determine each of their strengths and weaknesses in financial management. I decided they take turns in running the home. I gave Rose enough money for the month. Before month end, Rose, the spend-thrift had spent all the money and was ready for more. Jane on the other hand was conservative in her spending. The same amount I had given out to Rose is the same amount she had at her disposal to run the home for the month. At the end of the month, she had a surplus. And Jane proved to be an asset in our home.

And the responsibilities in the home doubled when Jane was expecting our first child. Just then, she received a calling letter inviting her to join Kenyatta University. The baby came before the university opened and Jane joined a few weeks later. She left us a three month old baby boy—James Helekiah Sijenyi—named after my late brother James. Jane brought her sister Peres Atieno to help me take care of the baby. Rose on the other hand, was also expecting our fifth baby—Lydiah Awuor. I was not a stranger to caring for babies. I did a superb job when Rose was still working in Nairobi. And on occasions she would abandon home…I stepped up to the call. I was an office-home guy; I never socialized and even cut down on my movie watching. I had ample time to ensure my children grew in the direction I wanted them to take. But I also knew my wife Jane was a worried woman, leaving a three month baby at home—more so if that baby is your first baby; was definitely disturbing. It affected her performance. On my part, I was occupied with running affairs of thirty-plus family members. Never once did I visit Jane at the University. We were united during vacation days.

I lost Ogeya's contact in 1971. I did not know where he went and I didn't care because he had refused to listen to my advice. One day, I stumbled into Ogeya in Kisumu. *Where have you been and what have you been up to?* I asked. He told me he had been learning at Ngere Secondary School where he did Kenya Junior and passed, but could not go on because of lack of school fees. He said he was just at his uncle's home doing nothing. *Do you want to go back to school?* I asked. He was enthused about returning to school. *Go back where you came from and bring your belonging to my house,* I said with finality. Two days later, my nephew—Adams Muger—facilitated his coming to my Milimani home. Within a short period, I secured admission for him at Pe-Hill Secondary School, in form two. I gave him the fees and a condition…*you can never go back to Ziwani during school vacation.* I wanted him to come to my house during those vacation days to enable me to monitor his progress. He did as I directed, but second term holidays of Form VI; he decided to test my resolve and determination to keep my word. Instead of coming to Kisumu, he went to Ziwani. When schools opened, he came to Kisumu to pick up fees. I was enraged. I bundled him back into the bus to Nairobi to go and get fees from whoever asked him to go to Nairobi for vacation. I never saw him again until the death of his brother. Later, he managed to return to Pe-Hill. He did his O-level and passed. He would again request for my help to further his education.

Meanwhile, Dunga the obedient one, after a short stint at Maliera, came and joined us in Kisumu. During those years it was difficult to get a place in a Secondary School…so I arranged for him to go to Kisumu Polytechnic while searching for a secondary school. Eventually, I secured a spot at St. Paul's Amukura High School, where he enrolled in Forms III and VI. Despite his slow learning, he managed to obtain a certificate which proved beneficial in the job market. My nephew—John Okeyo Muger—assisted him to secure a job with Customs and Exercise Department. He later met and married Esther with whom he had three sons—two of whom excelled and made it to university. And he became an alcoholic but sobered up and became the first in the village among his peers to build a magnificent home and also own a car. *Patience and obedience are a good virtue.* Dunga was a living testimony.

Sometime in 1974, I took the boys—Obunga, Dunga, Lebo, Omondi, Ogeya, and Mambo Yote—from Nairobi to our home in Gem. The idea was to have them at one location. I figured this could reduce the cost of living. I also wanted them to be all rounded in terms of being a jack of all trade. They needed to learn in school, at the same time get involved in farming. The training was military like. Those of them who were lazy cursed the day they were born. They also learnt poultry farming as well as horticulture. They worked hard on the farm and produced enough to feed the family. It was during their stay at home that my marshal plan was conceived and born. It soon became a vision.

One day, one of the boys—Simon Omondi—who was learning in STD six at Mutumbu, decided enough was enough. His mother Awiti, who felt her son was being overworked; sent him transport to travel to Nairobi. Simon packed Dunga's blanket. Dunga was determined to intercept him before he boarded the bus to Nairobi. Dunga caught up with him at Kisumu Railway Station...he took his blanket and returned home. But while in Nairobi, Omondi was unable to get admission into any school and sadly, that brought an abrupt end to his education. He married and sired children and worked for Nairobi City Coucil as a garbage collector. *He had sealed his destiny.*

Obuga on the other hand persevered and did his class seven at Mutumbu Primary School. He did well enough to secure a place in Form I. I talked to Benjamin Ofula, who was then the assistant Director of Education. He helped place Obuga at Machakos Technical School. I provided the funds and he joined Machakos, but before he left, I warned...*steer clear of Ziwani. They will steal your school fees.* He followed these instructions diligently during the first year and the first and second terms of second year. When schools opened for third term and I gave him transport and fees for the term, he passed by Ziwani and gave his step-mother Awiti his fees for safekeeping. I was told that when he asked for the money the following day, his step-mother claimed that someone had stolen the money. He didn't go to school and he had no guts to tell me about his school fees being stolen. That was the end of his education. He later moved to Mombasa; got a job, married and sired children. He died in Mombasa and I brought the body home for burial.

Lebo also did his class seven at Mutumbu Primary School. He was not brilliant therefore his performance was dismal. I was determined to take him to a secondary school. I secured a form one place for him in Mwer Secondary School—a good school. He did form I and II without major issues; except his grades were below average. Subsequently, in form III—third term, I gave him fees and transport. He left home for school. Unfortunately, I heard from the village rumor mills that he did not go to school. He was spotted at a home in Maliera village cohabiting with a widow. *Ain't this a height of stupidity or what? Why would he ruin his future so casually?* I organized a group of physically strong men who accompanied me to the supposed home. But he was too cunning for our unsuspecting team. He welcomed us. *Hold on here,* he said as he made his way to the bedroom—apparently to pick up his belonging. We waited in vain. The man had outwitted us and vanished into thin air of the black night. He escaped through the bedroom window. That was the end of Lebo's education. It would be years before I saw him again—at Ziwani making traditional brew for a certain individual. He was at the verge of death, emaciated and weak. His hair was red and he had a swollen face. It was as if he was suffering from kwashakior. *Do you want to return home?* I asked. That was the last time Lebo was in Nairobi.

After recovering well, I gave him a job with Siaya Country Council where he worked until he was fired because of drunkardness. He lived a life of turbulence; doing odd jobs and whatever money he got, he squandered in drinks. He experimented with marriage and discovered he could not cohabit with a wife. Like his father, he neither laughed nor joked

When James died, *Mambo Yote* was at Highway Secondary School. James had paid his fees. After James' demise, I took over. The year following James' death, *Mambo Yote* dropped out of school, but he carried himself around as if he was in school. At the end of every term; he brought me end term reports showing the scores he allegedly received. Satisfied that he was in school, I kept paying. I paid the fees for a year until I discovered he had absconded school. I tried to talk him into going back, but since he could not be re-admitted at Highway, I had to look for an alternative—possibly a school in the countryside. I talked to the Principal of Sawagongo High School who reluctantly agreed to take him in form three. He lasted there two weeks before he was expelled. He had made an illegal trip to the Nairobi show when he was not among the students selected to attend the show. That was the end of his education. He chose a life of crime and was in and out of jail a couple of times. He left Nairobi when he was warned he would be shot.

One of the main prerequisites of a marriage was the payment of bride price, which has to include but not limited to cattle. I had paid Roses' bride price, but I had not sent cattle. I needed to pay something for Jane, but I couldn't until I had bought and sent cattle to Roses' home—that was tradition. Despite our differences, I bought the largest bull at Sondu market and sent it to Roses' home. I made arrangements for it to be driven to her home. I was told, the following day, it cut loose the rope by which it was tethered and ran back to Sondu. When they tracked it down, they realized it had been slaughtered by a butcher. I was safe because according to tradition, the bull had to have spent the night at the girl's home; which it did. I din't have to repay.

That paved way for me to pay Jane's bride price. There was still a snag. Jane was expecting a baby. Cultural tradition prohibited payment of dowry while the woman is pregnant. On further inquiry, I was told I could pay dowry as long as I did not pay cattle. I organized without involving my father. I had also been warned...*your father-in-law is a no-nonsense man.* I had married Jane immediately she completed Form VI and this didn't go down well with my father-in-law. And so he looked forward to the day I would show my face so he could show me what he's made of. This is the reason I didn't want my father involved. I did not want to expose Father to the indignity of being harangued.

I prepared cash and felt I was ready for the trip, but then, a friend approached me that he needed to borrow money for something urgent. He promised to return the money soon enough before I took the trip. Two days to the D-day, this friend called on me and said he would not pay me on time. *Something came up,* he said. I was in shock. *How could he?* I approached relatives and friends to help me raise atleast half of what I required. They couldn't come through for me.

On the eve of the visit, the friend whom I had lent money brought a quarter of what I had given him. *I will bring the balance tomorrow,* he reassured. I waited for that money the following day up to five o'clock. When he failed to show up, I decided to go anyway. I had to fetch my cousins Joash and Wilfred who had to accompany me. They had given up hope of traveling and left for their respective homes. I encouraged them to just come along albeit night time was approaching. By seven o'clock, we had arrived at my father-in-law's home. Our delay had greatly inconvenienced them, but they were happy we made it.

My father-in-law did not know me before this visit. He was told that a short-fat-black man from Mutumbu had taken his daughter. He assumed it was a short-fat-black man who was his drinking pal at Lana. It was until he saw me that he realized I was not his drinking pal from Mutumbu. Later, I made other dowry payments for Jane, including Kisera.

Driving a motor vehicle without a valid driving license is a serious offence. If one is charged and convicted the penalty is huge. On the other hand, getting a driving license during that time was a nightmare. Corruption abounded and those who did not want to part with *Kitu Kidogo* (bribe) were disadvantaged. You could do the driving test forever, failing every time. It was against this back drop that I avoided going for a driving test. I drove my own car and had learnt to drive well. A whole year on the wheels perfected my driving skills. I was a fast driver and I thanked God I never had an accident involving a third party during that time. And police hardly flagged me, but if they did, I cheated that I left the license at home. They believed me.

Finally, it was time to make legal my driving. I paid the requisite fees and took the test. The practical portion of the test, I knew would be a slum dunk. I worried about the table part. As expected, I passed the practical and was told to return in the afternoon to repeat the table part. That evening, I had a provisional driving licence.

Mutumbu Sports 1973; sports officials had arranged with Tausi Band to grace the occasion, but the band never turned up. One official approached me and requested that I drive him to Siaya so we could trace Tausi Band. The officials did not want the fans disappointed and so we had to find Tausi Band.

We drove to Siaya, but we were out of luck. The band was out of site. We went to Kisumu and reliable sources informed us the band was out of town. We sourced for a different band in Nubia. Dr. Adams Nyahone, a band leader, agreed to come to Mutumbu. *Boy, did they deliver.* The following year, Dr. Adams composed a song for me—Advocate Wanyanga, which he recorded in a studio and placed in the market for sale. In 1974, he was again invited. He never disappointed.

Meanwhile, Ochieng Nelly visited me a number of times in my office and we developed genuine friendship. Mutumbu sports officials invited his band which came and played for us on several occassions. He too, composed two songs for me and were a hit of our time. Those were the days I was tottening on the realm of indecisiveness. They were the days I started toying with an idea of alternative option—an idea which was hell bound but unknown to me then.

The advent of Christianity ushered in a new era—traditional practices gave way to Christian values. Some traditions however, survived the onslaught of Christianity—most of which are practiced in parts of Africa today. In the part of the country I come from, *Nyawawa*, *Tero Buru* and *Jimbo Koth* are still widely practised. And some Christian homes are drawn into them. There are myths which only traditionalists believe. To some, they are archaic and out dated.

Nyawawa is a ceremony to drive out evil spirits. The practice of *Nyawawa* had defied modernization and western civilization and folks continue to participate in it. When it starts and where; nobody knows, but once it starts, it spreads *like bush fire*—people beat drums and anything which can produce a sound. Within no time, your neighbour works on his tin or drum. While they drum, they shout *Nyawawa*. In some parts it is called *Nyangore*. It is a favourite of children. They pour out of their mother's houses in droves with whatever tool they lay their hands…they drum, dance and shout *Nyawawa*. Women are not left behind. They join the children in dance and drum beating. Men however, don't take part in *Nyawawa*. Only those who are mentally disabled do. The devil worshippers and those who believe in ghosts also do. Basically, it is intended to drive out ghosts and evil spirits which would otherwise invade homes and strangle children.

Most people engage in *Nyawawa* at full moon when the dogs bark incessantly. Some believe the dogs spot those ghosts and evil spirits at full moon. But nobody knows for sure if this is the case. Just as suddenly as the drumming started, so it will end in the neighbourhood, but echoes from where it is going will continue as far as the ear can pick. Then silence engulfs the neighbourhood. Not even the barking dogs will be heard. Folks retire to their houses to have undisturbed sleep after the evil spirits are pushed into the water.

Nyawawa happens during the short and long rain seasons…so folks participate in *Nyawawa* twice a year. They believe, apart from chasing the evils away, it gives them good tidings and if done correctly and at the right time, it gives a bumper harvest to both believers and non-believers.

Nyawawa was a phenomenal occurrence that was religiously performed. I witnessed several of them while staying in the rural area (country side). Those who believe in the myth say that it started after *Nundu* (small pox) plague. Folks believe *Nundu* was brought by evil spirits which moved in packs along the road and pathways, sometimes singing in the dark of the night. If encountered by anyone, one is struck by Nundu. Folks then learnt to scare these evil spirits away by drumming.

Another tradition that has defied Christianity, modernity or science is *Jimbo Koth* (rainmaking). In my part of the country, we have a family line which professes this knowledge. They have the power to make rain fall or disappear. The knowledge is passed on by a father to his favorite son. In the olden days, these rainmakers denied people rain until they received payment in form of cattle, sheep or goats—depending on the status of the village. If the village had rich folks, he demanded a bullock or a heifer, if not, he settled for a ram or an ewe or a goat of any gender. Sometimes, he went to the village to solicit for those payments. If one village cooperated and paid the ransom and the other refused, the defiant village' still got rain, but with devastating hail-storms.

I was one of those who believed man could not make or disperse rain. *How wrong I was.* During the year I was involved in sports, I witnessed firsthand this phenomenal. I drove one of the officials to the rainmaker to pay him some money to disperse rains in our area. One day, we decided to hire services of a rainmaker instead of our usual one. One of our sport members leaked information to our previous rainmaker. He came to the sports ground and walked around, then proceded to the local market, where we were entertaining our new rainmaker. He quarreled with our new man, threatened to strike him with thunder and warned; *I will ensure he loses his powers to disperse rain.* The overcast which was light; thickened with rain making clouds and within one hour, rains came down. The irony—the torrential rain only covered an area a mile in diameter at the sports venue. No sports were held on that day. And it rained throughtout the night. The band didn't play either.

The next time we had a band, we were smart enough not to engage a different rainmaker. Our man dispersed the overcast clouds as it started to rain by picking a few blades of grass at the front of the restaurant; then spat twice on the grass while holding them toward the direction of the rain. In an instant, a strong wind blew and the imminent storm roared past and not a single drop fell thereafter.

I also had a chance to take my friend to a rainmaker's home. He wanted the rainmaker to assure him it was the right time to plant his crops. *Plant tomorrow because the rains will come down,* the rainmaker had said. To convince my friend, he took us to the edge of the fence at his home and showed us a pot half buried in the ground. He poured water into the pot and put freshly chopped bark of a tree into the water and spat in the pot. The water foamed and he said rain would fall the following day the moment foam bubbled over the pot. He explained that the more the bubbles overflew, the more it would rain. So the following day, there was heavy rain and I got convinced that an African has the technological knowledge to make or disperse rain.

In 1974, my nephew, Sed Onginjo Demba informed me he was going to marry his fiancée—Betty, in Kisumu. He requested me to avail my home for the-after-party reception. He wanted the church ceremony to be preceded by a small reception at Kisumu hotel and thereafter move the after-party to my Milimani home. My family contributed a ram and the after-party turned out to be the gist of the ceremony. That is how I came to know Sed, his wife Betty and Betty's father—Mzee Nondi. I later interacted with Mzee Nondi and his son David, on several occasions. At my Milimani home, I also met, Mr. and Mrs. Ogot Obudho. Mrs. Ogot was incharge of food preparation. To my surprise, Mr. Ogot was a nephew I had never met until this wedding. We became friends with the Ogots.

Six months later, times were tough and I could feel the weight of the family on my shoulders. I supplemented my income with a taxi business. I worked in the morning and did taxi in the evenings.

One day, a gentleman hired me to drive him to Hamisi. On my way back, the car stalled at Kiboswa. I was alone in the car and night had just set in. This area was notorious for thugs and so I was a worried man. I flagged vehicles from both directions, but neither stopped. I pushed the car across the road towards Kiboswa market and parked it at the bus stage. I continued to flash for vehicles coming from Kisumu side to stop. I had all kinds of imaginations as night fell. *I should walk to the watchmen and spend the night with them,* I thought *or maybe I should just stay in the car.* I stayed in the car. I tried to start the engine. The battery was dead. I still hoped some Good Samaritan would stop by and help me.

As I dozed off, I heard a vehicle approach from Kisumu direction. When it appeared on my view, I tried to flash. I was fortunate the battery had gained some power. This vehicle branched off into Kiboswa road and stopped a couple of yards away from the main road. *Who could it be? Could it be thugs?*

When the car eventually drove toward me, my breath stopped. The driver pulled the car on my side and asked, *what is the problem?*

The engine stalled, I explained. He turned off his ignition and opened the door then came up to my window. *Open the hood (bonnet),* he said. He touched a few places and asked me to start the car. It couldn't start. He went back to his truck and pulled out a tool box. With the spanners, he went to work. After a couple of minutes, he had me start the car. This time, the car started.

It was almost midnight and the gentleman had parked his car by the roadside. I had dropped off Mrs Ogot to her countryside home and was driving by when the man flagged me down. I drove on because I feared it could have been thugs or any such evil characters. But on second thought, I drove back and asked the man what he needed. He said he had run out of gas and wanted a ride to Kisumu to pick up some gas. *I have some spare gas in my car,* I had said. I helped him gas up and he drove off. I drove behind him and we parted ways in Kisumu.

So for this Good Samaritan, instead of finding out how much I would pay him, he asked, *do you know me?* I said no. *I am the guy you helped with petrol at Rae, and I cannot accept a single cent from you,* he said. I thanked him and we parted ways.

As they like to say in the part of the country I come from. *Adita mipimoe ema ipimoniye* (What goes around comes around*). If you do good, you do it for yourself and if you do bad you do it for yourself.*

While residing in Kisumu, Mama Esther Awino's daughter, Loice, lost her husband. Esther approached me to help with the planning of the funeral, which was to take place in Kendu-bay. Esther wanted a show at the funeral. I mobilized our folk in Kisumu and we collected funds and organized how we would travel to the funeral. Everything was in place and we proceeded to

Kendu-bay. But on my way to the funeral, my car broke down. I had to borrow a car from a friend. My cousin Sila drove it.

At the funeral, most of us dined, danced and drunk. Sila was still drunk the next day. He insisted he was driving us back. No one wanted to get into a car driven by a drunk. We tried to snatch the car keys from him and he threatened to go physical. We gave up and Sila drove off with his wife Nyasembo and left many of us who needed a ride stranded.

Without a car of my own and with the one I borrowed having driven off, my wife and I were stranded. The main road where we could get means to Kisumu was five miles away. I approached Green and asked if he could drop us off at the main road. He refused. I pleaded and he wouldn't give in. I gave up. *This was the man I had driven his dying father-in-law from the hospital to await his death at home. He had paid me nothing for this and now he's refusing to offer me a ride to the main road?* Disgusted and annoyed, I informed my wife we would just walk to the main road.

On the feeder road leading to the main road, I saw a car approach. It was my colleague's car. We worked together at the municipality. I flagged him down and he agreed to give us a ride. When we arrived in Sondu, he helped me check out my stalled car. The engine started and we drove off with him in tow.

A couple of months later—late in the night—while coming from Nyakach, I ran into boulders which some thugs had placed across the road. I punctured a tire and fearing an ambush I drove two miles on a flat tire and stopped. Just as I stopped I saw headlights of a vehicle coming behind from the direction I came. I flagged it down and there he was, the same friend who had helped me from Kendu-bay to Sondu. He helped me change the tire and again drove on tow until we reached Kisumu.

After returning from Kendu-bay visit, Mama Esther came over to my house and thanked me for everything. I had also expected Sila to return the car.

The following day, I went looking for him. Sila had not been home. His wife told me she had forced him to drop her off at the main road because he was driving in a recklace manner. He did and she boarded a public vehicle. Two days later, I tracked Sila down. I returned the vehicle and I apologized to the owner then walked away. Sila was not remorseful for his behavior and instead he just laughed at me.

My father-in-law had died. I also had the family's financial burden still wieighing on my shoulders. I had also made some stressful trips to Tanzania. My body could not take this any more. I started feeling lethargic. In the night my body perspired. And my eye sight started failing.

I visited Dr. C.S Patel, my family physician. The doctor after examing me, and carrying out a several tests informed me I had diabetes. He also referred me to an eye specialist—D.R. Bhardwaj. For Glucose tolerance test, he referred me to new Nyanza General Hospital. After eight hours, I brought the results and Dr. C.S. Patel said, *the disease is till at its infancy and does not require medication. Just watch your diet to control this,* he added. He advised me to avoid sugar and sugar products from my diet, and eat lots of fruits and vegetables. This was 1974.

I did as the doctor ordered and I have never taken any medication for this diabetes.

Our daughter Lydia almost died around the same time. She had diarrhea in the night and I had advised the mother to take her to the hospital the next morning. She instead proceeded to work and left Lydia under the watch of the maid. I received a call at work that my daughter wasn't doing good. I rushed home and the mother had also come home. We rushed Lydia to Patel and his team. Dr. Patel had referred Lydia to another hospital. With a team of Dr. Patel and four other doctors, Lydia was revived from the coma she had slipped into. God healed her through Dr. Patel and his team. We are in the USA courtesy to Dr. Patel and his team of Doctors.

Lydiah grew to be one of my best loved children. She could get anything from me and I never disappointed. I tried to give her the best in education and I borrowed to aid her trip to Germany. In Germany, she met a black American doing a conscription stint with the medical Corps in the US Army. She was naïve by then. She ended up marrying the man. By this marriage, she kind of, signed her obituary. She would lead a turbulent life in the USA and end up becoming a single mother to her three lovely kids—Shahid, Asha and Tariq. May God bless them.

In 1974 general elections, one of my cousins, Sila Mayienga, presented his candidature for election for North Gem Ward. If he won, he was going to be the first from my tribe to become a councillor. He had what it takes—education and charisma; he was development conscious and commanded stage presence. And he was fluent in three languages—Luo, English, and Kiswahili. No one could be a match to him. But he lacked four things. First off, he was not a people person and so the tribe was not psyched to rally behind him. If every adult from my tribe registered as a voter had used his suffrage to vote for him, the results would have been different.

Second, he lacked drive to raise funds. Several times he attempted to have friends and relatives fund his campaign but it was futile.

Third, he was not politically astute. He didn't know how to run a campaign and fend off opponents.

Fourth, he didn't have a means of transport. How could he transverse North Gem on foot. This was by no means a failed campaing from the start. I was compelled to release my car to aid in his travels during the last phase of the campaign, but this was too little too late. With only one car he could not monitor all the polling stations on the voting day. Against all odds, he did well and finished a close second.

I feel proud and honored to have associated myself with his campaign. After the election, he returned my car, like any other campaign car, it was in a deplorable condition. I spent a fortune repairing it. But that was only a small price I paid for the process of emancipation of my tribe. It would take a lot more sacrifices from me for the tribe to finally remove the yoke of bondage and be considered a people like others.

At work, I registered tremendous success in executing duties. I had set up a fully operational department; complete with letter heads. Titles and leases had been centralized and were under lock. Revenue was abundant in our kitty due to relentless pressure on our debtors and creditors nolonger breathed fire over our necks. Suppliers breathed a sigh of relief. And cases were disposed of, some of which were major and critical to the survival of the council. Valuation court matters were attended to using external assistance and criminal cases involving council employees were handled successfully.

I tried to improve the financial base of the council, but bottlenecks arose through the treasurer's department. There was no mechanism for checks and balances on how revenue was collected. The audit department was the main culprit. There was chaos in the collection of revenue in the market section; this laxity caused the council to lose millions in stolen revenue. As a result, some staff, including those who were innocent lost jobs.

During the course of 1974; Okwach, Odongo, Andere and I started a poultry business—Nyakuno Poultry. Our objective was to raise chicks for sale and keep hens (layers) for eggs. We planned to raise high breed cocks. And capons for sale. We turned Nyakuno into a limited liability company and sought and obtained an undertaking of foreign aid as we planned to do this on large scale. We pooled our resources together to raise the equity the foreign financier required. Among us, we raised enough in kind and cash. I bought an incubator for hatching chicks as part of my contribution towards the capital share of the company. After we completed the paperwork, the foreign financier asked us to seek permission from the District Development Committee before they could release instalment funds. That was in line with the Government requirement at the time.

We prepared a report showing viability of the enterprise and that within a few years, it would be a multimillion business enterprise. In the report we stressed the viability of the project. And the social economic impact it will have on the community. We noted it would provide jobs. The report was by itself convincing and needed no further explanation.

When the report reached the committee for discussion and approval, it was shot down by politicians who argued...*a bunch of small time employees of the council cannot have resources to launch a multi-million project.* They were partly right, but to me, the main reason was envy and selfishness.

Immediately the District Development Committee rejected our project proposal, the council launched investigations on the four of us. The one who was a market revenue collector was nailed. When the council started to harrass him, we rallied behind. We had little knowledge to the extent he had embezzled council money. He was charged, convicted and for the three of us; we were suspended and later dismissed. We never benefited from the proceeds of the theft and therefore as far as I was concerned, I was wrongly dismissed. I had to do something fast to remove this stain on me.

When I had gone to Nairobi to purchase the incubator, a member of Nyakuno poulty had accompanied me. The council felt I spent money stolen from the council. I had to prove my innocence before the council. I provided a receipt bearing my name and proof of the source of money.

I moved to the Industrial Court which was the right court then to file such a dispute. The court took a while to hear my case, when they finally did, they ruled in my favor. My lawyer, Collins Omondi, saved the day. He presented the facts of the case in an ariticulate manner. The court ordered that I be compensated for the wrongful dismissal by the council but stopped short of ordering my reinstatement. I was nolonger interested in working for the council. I was dully compensated.

Meanwhile, our foreign financier pulled out and notified us of their decision. The attempts by the big guns to start a similar project flopped because they could not raise the equity the financiers wanted and the financiers had learned their antics and intrigues. So then, they wanted nothing to do with these politicians. And also my dream of becoming a millionaire was clipped on the bud by selfishness.

During my entire working life in Kisumu, the town had more elite from Siaya than from Kisumu District. South Nyanza also had several. In the Council we had councillors from both Siaya and Kisumu Districts. In fact, only the town clerk and town treasurer were from elsewhere. This was viewed with a lot of concern by the indigenous folks. They had concerns that should the town clerk vacate office, I would be hired since I was the only one in the council qualified to fill the post. *They would not allow me to be a town clerk,* so the rumor mills said. They did not hide their disdain. Even before the poultry fiasco, I had already started making contingency plans to leave. *I would work on the poultry farm if it succeded and then I would get into private practice.*

After receiving my dismissal letter, I made arrangements for my family to move to Arina in Kisumu, as my wife Rose still worked there. On suspension, I had moved back home to concentrate on farming and poultry keeping. Jane Rose, on the other hand, taught at Rang'ala where she lived with our three children. And at this point, Pamela was at the door waiting to come in. Soon, she was going to be done with secondary education.

CHAPTER 13

PRACTITIONER

I spent the year 1975 in Gem. I used the time to expand my poultry house and arranged for the entire homestead to be fenced with barbed wire. I also sank a shallow well which never produced any water and planted sugarcane on my five acre farm in Sidada. God continued to bless me. Anything I touched prospered. The sugarcane grew yielded tons which I delivered to a sugar factory. The factory however, failed to pay me for most of the deliveries.

In between farming, I started to plot my next move. The Nyakuno option was out because it had been dissolved and no member wanted to be associated with it even though they struggled to make ends meet. Farming alone wasn't going to sustain me and my family, extended family and dependents, I had to look elsewhere. *I have a profession and practicing certificate from the Law Society.* I decided to make use of it.

Since she left her handbag in my cottage, Christmas of 1972, I had not met or seen Pamela. Her beauty; easy going—tough mannerism; left an impression on me. She was about five feet and about eighteen years; light complexion, well built and appeared to be in a hurry all the time. She wore a grin which I thought was permanent. Idid not get to know her sober side because I had not interacted much with her.

Her beauty struck me as exceptional and her grin reminded me of my mother's. With such a grin, my mother had disarmed many and won many friends. People just loved her. *Would she be like my mother?* I did not pursue this line of though then because I had no reason to. She was just a sojourner. This would not be for long.

Sometimes in 1974 during a school vacation, I organized a party for youth at our home. It was purely a dance party. No food or drinks were served. The youths came. Among them, was a young girl—striking in beauty. I thought, *I had seen her some place before.* She appeared to be in charge of a group of girls. As music played, she shouted orders at them. If you held your partner too close for comfort, she ordered you to stop dancing and take a seat. The girls obeyed her like a commander. I enjoyed the scene from a safe distance. I sent for her and on second thought, she came over. *Why are you so strict on these girls,* I asked. *They came to dance, not to impress boys,* she said curtly. I then asked her for a dance. She agreed. She held me tight but kept an eye on her girls.

It was at this dance she formerly introduced herself to me. *I'm here on vacation,* she said, then added, *visiting with an aunt at Kodiaga.* She explained, *I live in Kisumu with my sister Grace and I attend Nyakach Girls' Secondary School,* she explained. The dancing continued till early morning then they returned to their respective homes.

Shortly before Christmas that year, she passed by to ask me to give her friends and her, a ride to Malanga. I obliged. And every time I spotted her at a dance, she was always in a group, with girls. The group never flirted with boys; they were tough ladies.

We developed a close friendship over the years...so she would drop by my Milimani residence or home to say hallo. She became known to the members of my family and my parents liked her. My step-mother claimed she was a friend to Pamela's mother during their youth.

She also loved children; and was a fast learner.

Those were the humble beginnings of a relationship that would later develop in intensity and mature into marriage. This came barely three years after marrying Jane. *This will bring a rift between Jane and I,* I thought. I became reluctant. *But how long would I resist the charm of Pamela?* Meanwhile, we got our sixth child with Rose and named her after my father-in-law—Barnabas Oigo Miser.

While I was in financial doldrum, Jane had been posted to Sawagongo High School for her teaching practice. I had no money at the time to rent her a house near the school. Earlier, I had started building her a small cottage in my father's homestead but was still incomplete. With compensation money I received from Kisumu Municipality, I finished not only her house but that of Rose. With the cottage in good shape, she decided to stay home and commute to Sawagongo. She, like Rose, had not lived in our Gem home before. It was going to be the first time she stayed at home. Her teaching practice coincided with my stay at home. So the two of us stayed home and experienced things together.

Throughout my stay at home everything was my responsibility. I provided food for everybody. When she was not at school, she was home cooking and doing house chores. We learned a lot during that time. The pilferages and eavesdropping were still the norm. She could not afford to be careless with her knickers and innerwears. She had to watch what she said, how she said it and to whom or else Rose would be told everything and hell would break loose. She survived those trying moments because, like me, she learned survival tactics. She successfully completed her practicals and went back to the university.

I had stayed home in Gem for over six months when awaiting the decision of the court. I could not take up any job because technically I considered myself an employee of the Municipal Council of Kisumu, and until my case was heard and finalized, I did not want to jeopardize reinstatement chances. When it was finally over, I started private legal practice in Siaya. I considered Siaya because of its proximity to home and I had just started operating several projects at the countryside home. I wanted to be close by to run them. Kisumu was over thirty miles away and I could not start my legal business there.

Siaya District had been created a few years earlier, curved from the former Central Nyanza District. It had its first headquarters at Ukwala, in Ugenya, but later it was moved to Siaya. Siaya County Council had been created alongside the district with its inaugural chairman, Hon. Mathews

Ogutu, who presided over the commission which created it. The first elected chairman was Joash Odhialo. Both the District Headquarters and County Council offices had been constructed where all government departments and County officials were housed. I was particularly interested in the lands department, police station and the court. These were the departments that would be pivotal in my successful legal business.

The town was but a glorified marketplace. Its centre had one or two buildings constructed with permanent material, but that was it; the rest of the buildings were mud-walled structures that stood no chance in the event of a catastrophic storm.

The Post Office was housed in one of the permanent buildings and the hospital was still as it was during Abiba's days, with just one additional ward that was not enough to accommodate more than fifty patients at a time.

The roads were gravel with potholes everywhere; and since there was no electricity, entertainment joints were a thing of the past; only one small recreational ground where kids and adults played soccer existed.

Protestant churches were just moving in. Anglican and SDA had taken the lead. Roman Catholics had been around for over fifty years and had big cathedrals in Mbaga and Karapul-Ramba. The Adventists used the old courthouse as a church when they moved in.

I surveyed Siaya Town several times and concluded it had potential for rapid growth. I wanted to grow with it. It had good schools and there was frenzy in buying land from the indigenous people to build residential houses. To the west there was Lake Kanyaboli, Lake Victoria and Yala Swamp—sleeping financial giants.

I moved to Siaya and secured an office space in the County Council's former mabati offices. I opened my legal practice on the 1st day of December 1975. With a borrowed table, chairs and a typewriter, I hired Anjeline Oloo as my first employee. From that day on, sky was my limit. *I have to to succeed where others fear to tread,* I said to myself. *I won't allow myself to fail!*

Earlier, while in Kisumu, my two wives, Jane and Rose, decided it was time to settle the name confusion. We agreed that Rose should use Rose and Jane Rose should drop Rose and use Jane. This was to be a temporary measure until the children came up with a style of referring to their mothers. On my part, I moved from Rose and Jane to Nyasondu and Nyairo respectively.

I got a house at Pandi in Siaya and moved in with Nyairo's two children—Sijenyi and Odhiambo. I hired two maids—one for house chores the other a babysitter. I moved these children because I wanted to be in their lives. I checked on them frequently during work hours because I had little faith in the househelp and the babysitter; they were young and inexperienced.

*

Starting a private legal practice is no picnic. It takes courage, money and good organization. Mine was no exception. The only thing I had at inception was God, my brain, letterheads and a car. I applied these four tools and thrust into mainstream legal practice. God was always on my side. Whatever I did—though I did not realize at the time—God's hand was in it. He gave me good ideas and helped me achieve. He protected me from my friends and foes. I later backslid and disappointed Him, but as long as He was with me, everything went smooth.

My personal letterheads were distinct from the municipal advocate ones. God allows everything to happen in our lives for a purpose. *Who knew three years earlier, when I made personal letterheads, they would be the launching pad into my law practice?* They did and I thank God for having given me the idea.

My car was also a necessity in my legal practice. I needed the car to transverse courts. The Siaya court was a small one, headed by a District Magistrate; and so was Bondo, Ukwala and Maseno. The cream of legal work was at the Resident Magistrate Court level—in Kisumu. So again, my car became my tool of trade and helped me to stabilize and run a successful legal business in Siaya.

I had to contend with stress from my family and the extended family—I had to provide basic needs for them. Nyairo was at the university and she too needed financial help. Nyasondu was earning peanuts and needed my attention too. I was in a financial crisis, but I believed the Lord, who allowed all things to happen, was not about to abandon me. He was going to see me through this as he had done in the past.

In the first month, the gross income from the business was not worth mentioning. It took faith to move on. In the second month, things started to look up. The profit margin doubled. *I'm on my way to great things,* I thought. God opened doors and I received crème de la crème clientale in the region. I was finally in business!

My business name spread across town and to the countryside. Clients streamed in and Angeline could not cope with the workload. I recruited a lady from Alego—Consolata Awino—to assist Angeline. Anjeline and Consolata would be popularly known as Nyalego *Maduong* and Nyalego *Matin* respectively. These two ladies worked with dedication and their level of professionalism was unquestionable. I owe my success to the duo. But I cannot forget Joseph Otieno, who joined this team of dedicated workers. God Bless them!

When I eventually received compensation from the Municipality, I relocated my offices to the building owned by Kenya National Union of Teachers, Siaya Branch. The building was magnificent. I expanded the office and brought in new furniture and returned whatever equipment I had borrowed. I secured an office big enough to enhance advocate confidentiality. I also cleared all the debts from the previous office. *I was destined for big things!*

I bought two pieces of land for development of residential housing units since Siaya town was becoming *the* hub of business. Tenants stood ready to occupy these units.

In late 1975 to mid 1976, when I was going through tough financial times, my family in Kisumu was on the receiving end. I could not give the support they needed to survive. Nyasondu—who was not used to planning and budgeting—failed to provide enough to sustain Edyth, Lydiah and Kazee (Barnabas Oigo Miser). Kenneth and Bernard were at Mumias Boys Boarding School. Nyasondu reached out to politicians, workmates and my colleagues. One day one of them said, "I'm telling you this in confidence, my friend."

The way he said it made me freeze. "What is it?"

"You ought to stop your wife from causing you embarrassment!"

I frowned.

"Well," the friend said. "You can frown all you want, but your wife begs money from politicians. A prominenet politician just whispered these same sentiments to me. I've told you as a friend, that's all!"

"Thank you," I said.

Later, I decided to lessen the burden on Nyasondu. I removed the kids from her care and hired a lorry to ferry most of our heavyduty stuff home. I was angry and full of rage when I did this.

Let me explain.

Earlier, I had allowed her to collect rent for our two houses in Kisumu and pay the mortgage. I had been wrong to entrust her with this. I ended up suing one of the tenants for non-payment not knowing the tenant had made payments to Nyasondu. In court, I was humbled and embarrassed when the tenant produced receipts as proof he was up to date with payment. What I did was damn. I should not have believed Nyasondu's lies. I should have spoken to the tenant before taking the matter to court. I learned a lesson.

I also failed to understand why Nyasondu had to beg for money. The money she collected from our tenants, added to her salary, was enough to pay her rent in Arina and also put food on the table. Maybe that was her fate and destiny... *if you take care of the cents, the shillings take care of themselves, but she took care of none.*

And to add insult to injury, she surrendered the Arina rental house where she lived to her employer to enable her to reside without paying rent. We lost the house to K.P. & T Cooperation. The council also demanded I surrender the rental homes I had bought since I was behind in mortgage instalments. I moved in swiftly and re-negotiated a payment plan and saved my houses.

Meanwhile, Dunga, who had been seriously ill and was admitted at Kisumu District Hospital, got discharged and headed to Arina. Omol also joined Nyasondu in Arina.

In the meantime, I took over collection of Okore rents. It was expensive to drive from Siaya to Kisumu every month to collect rent then proceed to pay the mortgages, but I had no alternative. I did this until the mortgage payments were cleared.

As for Rose (Nyasondu), I would entrust her with another assignment after we reconciled and she was vintage Rose. I regretted this again.

I kept an eye on what went on at the poultry farm in Gem. After the brief interruption, occasioned by my suspension from the council, business picked up. High- ranking government officials visited the farm, including the then Nyanza Provincial Commissioner, Isaiah Cheluget.

The population was then at 1250 chickens (layers and cocks). I had acquired a substantial number of Okwach's layers. And due to constant interruptions, the hens were not laying at 80%, which was the optimum capacity.

The Agricultural Finance Cooperation, which gave me a loan to improve the farm, declined to release all the funds in lumpsum, so I could not expand and improve certain facets of the business, especially completion of a shallow well.

Enoch Ong'aya, whom we hired to take care of the poultry business, did a heck of a job. Everyday he ensured his chores were done to my expectations. He made sure the water vendor delivered daily, sixty gallons as required. He ensured the birds were vaccinated, fed and sick ones isolated for treatment. He fed the birds pellets and greens twice a week as was required of him. He collected, counted and stored eggs. Whenever foodstock ran low, he promptly informed me. I'm grateful to you, Enock, and God bless you!

My parents, the kids and Thuthu, who were at home, did fine too. They had enough to eat and every school-going kid was in school. Everything appeared to be moving as planned despite a few drawbacks.

Sylvia, on the other hand, was barely surviving in Nairobi. Upon discharge from Nangina Mission Hospital, she was instructed to avoid hard duties and concentrate on light work. *The consequence of hardwork is surgical rapture,* the nurse had said. So Sylivia avoided home for fear of hardwork and continued to stay in Ziwani with her kids. With the little benefits she received from her deceased husband's employer, she did drugs and brewed *chang'aa* to survive. Syliva looked pathetic. Well-wishers and social organizations chipped in and she maintained the girls—Loice and Achienge and the boy, Otieno, in school. Then I took over. She also got into a marriage of convenience for financial security.

Ogeya did odd jobs and contributed to Sylvia. Omondi was there alright, but unemployed. The girls didn't disappoint. They became the backbone of the family and helped their brother and mother until her death.

And after overcoming family drawbacks, I realized some financial stability and took over the Nairobi responsibilities...as was envisaged in the initial plan. I helped the kids until they were done with education and got married. Meanwhile, Jane (Nyairo) was at Kenyatta University. One day, as she was going to town by bus, she lost balance and fell out as the bus negotiated a corner. She suffered bruises, but no limb was broken. This incident added to my worries, but I thank God she lived.

As I continued to stay with the kids and the maids in Siaya, Nyairo spent her vacations with us. The kids were not familiar with her because of her absence. Instead, they bonded with the babysitter.

In 1976, her final year at the university, she was pregnant with our third baby. One evening she walked in from college without notice. She appeared lethargic and in pain. She had sneaked from college because she wanted to have the baby at home, in Siaya. I left for Kisumu early morning to work while she rested. Upon return from work, Jane lay on the bed, her belly flat, but I didn't see a baby. The househelp did not say a word. Neither did Jane. I had to break the silence. "Can someone tell me what's going on here?"

Jane said, "I checked myself in at the hospital after you left for work; had the baby in twenty minutes, then I requested someone to take care of the baby for me while I came home for a shower."

I felt a chill.

But she went on. "They don't have water at the hospital."

"Does that mean the baby is alive"

"Of course!"

"At the hospital?"

She frowned. "What's wrong with you?"

"Nothing!"

I finally relaxed. I had just brought another life into this world. A bouncing baby boy. We named him Omondi, because he was born in the morning.

Jane and I proceeded to the hospital, picked our Omondi and returned home. I had to salute Jane for being strong. *Boy, she was tough!*

Later, she was due to sit for final exams and had to leave the three-day-old boy under my care. Jack Omondi was not breastfed. Sijenyi, on the other hand, had been breastfed for just three months; Odhiambo for a week. The thought of a three-day-old baby being left under my care was no big deal. I had a wealth of knowledge and experience. Previously, I had taken care of Kenneth, Benard and Edyth when they were young, and so I was going to do my best to help this three-day-old toddler survive until its mother returned.

I hired another babysitter, just for Jack. Otieno Obange, a peadiatrician, also availed his services to my kids twenty-four-seven. And Father and Stepmother visited twice. Mother-in-law, sisters—Pelesia and Lewnida—were also at hand. An Asian friend advised me on the right medicine to administer to the baby to avoid gas in the tummy. The support system was enormous, I could not have asked for more.

Two weeks after Jack's birth, Pamela paid me a visit in Siaya. When she walkled in, I had the tiny babe on my lap. She stepped in and took care of the little ones for me. When I was away in court, I returned to find she'd already sent a sick one to Otieno Obange for treatment. I was relieved of a very significant responsibility while she was in Siaya. My father and step-mother took note of her gentleness toward the kids. They were impressed. Pamela once said, *I take care of these kids as my own.* And she was right. She did care for them like she was their biological mother.

Pamela became the rose-flower in our home. She was hospitable to guests who visited. The kids loved her, but the maids were sort of uneasy around her because of her strictness; although they liked that she could come to their level and speak to them. She was simply nice.

She had mood swings once in a while—she was expecting my baby. She did not let these moods affect her personality, though.

Nyairo had a stellar performance in her practical teaching. Upon completion of her exams, she arrived home. Pamela was home with us. I explained to her how Pamela came in handy for the kids. "She has cared for them like her very own," I said.

Nyairo was a class act. She didn't appear to mind Pamela at all. She treated her respectfully, unlike Nyasondu who threw a fit when she had come from Nairobi and found Becky in the house taking care of the kids. She was grateful to Pamela.

Pamella and I discussed the possibility of getting married—to avoid the stigma of her carrying an illegitimate child. We agreed she would stay after Nayiro's coming home. Pamela and Nyairo were no strangers. They had known each other since my days in Kisumu, but had not lived under one roof. Later, Pamela had a change of heart—she left the following day and I would never see her for another year.

After a few weeks, results were released. Nyairo did very well. The Teachers Service Commission posted her to Chulaimbo Secondary School, twenty five miles from Siaya. I needed her close to Siaya. We requested the commission to consider a school closer to Siaya Township. They considered our request and granted. Nyairo was reassigned to Rangala Girls Secondary School. I drove her to school most days as my schedule permitted. Other days she commuted to and from school. After the school allocated her a house, we relocated the family to Rang'ala and stayed there for thirteen years. Anthony, Akinyi, Oduor, Loice and Celestine were born there.

While Nyairo worked for six months without pay, the financial burden lay on me. Finally, Teachers Service Commision paid her a lumpsum amount which we used to construct seven rooms in Mutumbu plot—a plot we acquired in 1974.

*

By 1977 the poultry farm was still competitive. A few hundred had been killed, egg production had dropped, but not at an alarming rate. Every three days, I drove home, picked eggs and sent them to Kisumu for sale. I then bought feed and medicine for the chickens from the profit margin.

One day I sold all thirty cartoons of eggs in Kisumu. I was a lucky guy and a happy one too. I passed by my Arina home to see Nyasondu, then proceeded home, to Gem. I had wanted to go all the way to Rang'ala, but I thought of stopping in Gem to see my father briefly. The road was good as it had just been tarmacked, but had not been marked. It had rained. Visibility was poor.

A few minutes after I got behind the wheel, from my home in Gem, I spotted the headlights of a vehicle in the rearview mirror. It closed in on me fast and I pressed on gas, then gained a comfortable distance. Suddenly, at a bend, he flashed full lights again. I pressed on gas and left him about a mile behind. When I looked in the rear mirror, to determine how far he was, the left tyre skid off the road. In an instant I lost control of the vehicle and the impact sent the car airborne. I was thrown off the vehicle and landed fifteen meters from it.

I picked myself up. I felt my head hurt and noticed blood on my palm. Immediately, I sensed I was in danger. I flagged vehicles heading to Rang'ala to transport me to Rang'ala Mission Nursing Centre and vehicles from Busia to bring me to a hospital in Kisumu. The first vehicle to stop was from Busia, with a Sikh at the steering. He agreed to give me a ride to Kisumu, but also was kind enough to stop by my home so I could inform my folk of the accident and organize boys who would watch over my accident vehicle.

On arrival in Kisumu, the Sikh dropped me at New Nyanza General Hospital, where I was examined and X-rayed. I had no serious injury—only a minor cut on the head and a bruise. After treatment, I walked home to Arina. Nyasondu was stunned and almost became hysterical when she saw me.

The following morning, I traveled back to the accident scene. What I saw was unbelievable. The car had been vandalized—the battery, starter and other parts were gone, stolen. *The home boys had lied to me. How sad.* I towed the car to a garage where it was fixed and sold to a third party. I then acquired another car for my use.

After completion of the construction of the plot in Mutumbu, I started several businesses at the location. The main one was a retail shop. This shop enabled me to operate off-license bar and lodging and I hired my cousin Caleb Thuthu to manage the lodging part. He served me with dedication and I was impressed. I would later give him more demanding responsibilities, from which he would earn a decent living.

But I had not seen Pamela close to a year. One evening, as I sat in the shop chatting with the customers who were taking beer, I heard shouts and whistles from the direction of the entrance to the shopping centre. *What may have triggered the whistles and shouts?* Still in the wonder mode, I spotted a woman, dressed to kill. She walked briskly toward my shop as she walked past a crowd. The shouts and whistles were approval of her. *She is awesome,* I thought. When she walked into the shop, I realized Pamela was back to me. I introduced her to the customer at the shop, but I had long lost interest in her because I thought she'd abandoned me. *We agreed you were to stay in Siaya with us and we would legalize our marriage,* I recalled in silence. She had not even attempted to make contact with me. This made me furious with her.

We stayed in the shop until customers left at midnight. I needed time to talk to her, alone; to find out what she was up to. I needed to know what happened to the baby and what she had been doing with her life since leaving Siaya. I wanted to know if she was married. I had many questions I wanted her to answer. My parents had blamed me for letting her go when she came to Siaya. I had said to them then, *I have no chains to tie her,* but right now, I needed to know if she was back to be mine.

That night, we talked. She had come back to be mine.

"But when do you intend to come officially? I asked.

"Tomorrow," she said.

Pamela had given birth six months earlier and she said baby Victor Otieno had Daddy's eyes. *That means this boy is a replica of me,* I thought. The next day we drove to Kisumu to pick up our son, Victor, and returned home to Gem with my new family. Pamela had left Victor at her sister's house in Kisumu.

With her arrival I entered the league of polygamists proper. Vintage Nyairo never complained about her new co-wife. She went on her business as if nothing had happened. Pamela would be known as Nyamwalo and Victor would be Simu.

Nyamwalo, like Nyasondu, was a twin and like Nyairo, she was related to Jairo. Twins, according to culture, were named Opiyo and Apiyo or Odongo and Adongo, depending on the order of birth. The first to come out, if a boy, was named Opiyo and a girl was named Apiyo. The boy who followed was named Odongo and the girl was named Adongo. Nyamwalo was Apiyo. She told me her twin sister, Adongo, died. Nyasondu, who was named Adongo, also lost her twin sister, Apiyo. So I have a set of twins in my household although from different ancestries.

Nyairo means the daughter of Jairo and Nyamwalo means the daughter of Jamwalo. Nyairo's parents are Joiro and Nyamwalo's mother was Nyairo, meaning she came from Yiro to be married to Jamwalo. Tradition prohibits marrying a daughter along with her mother. Since Nyairo and Nyamwalo's mother came from Yiro, Nyamwalo technically and traditionally is Nyairo's daughter. In the traditional context, a daughter of your brother, brother-in-law, sister-in-law, cousin or cousin-in-law is your daughter. But the prohibition was only a general rule since for every rule there is an exception. Nyamwalo's case falls within the exception. Nyamwalo was a sosoral sister to Nyairo, so there could be no impediment to the marriage, the elders declared.

Jomwalo—Nyamwalo's folks—are deep in cultural tradition. Nyamwalo gave me extra coaching in their customs. When I went to *Kisera* at her home, several of these cultural norms still amazed me. The morning of our departure from her home was the climax. We were in the *Siwandha* and had just been asked to move to my mother-in-law's house. Suddenly, women sang, danced and ululated in the house. They stepped out, led by many sisters-in-law who sang and danced. We witnessed acrobatic dances—styles I had never seen in my life. One of my sisters-in-law took the dance to a brand new level. Her right leg swung in the air and she frog-jumped with her left leg. Then everybody's one leg was in the air swinging to the rhythm of the singing as they marched toward us. It did not matter what type of dress the woman wore—short or long, legs were in the air.

My cousin Oluoch Okello, from experience, told me to join in the jig as he started swinging his leg in the air, trying to emulate the dancers. Twins had been borne in my cousin's family so he knew something about twin tradition. Trying to emulate the dancers, I joined the dance and did my shake up as if that was what they were waiting for. In a second, the *charms girl* changed the song and hell broke loose. It was now a few steps forward a few backward all in rhyme with the music. Everybody joined in the music, old and young, women and men. I was relieved when it finally ended as suddenly as it had started because I wasn't getting my forward and backward steps right. We got into the house and were entertained as tradition demanded, and I was later to learn that the dance was called *Miend Rut*—a dance for twins.

Getting Nyamwalo into my life concluded God's plan for salvage and recovery of my father's home. With Ng'on'ga and Abiba back home and Nyasondu, Nyairo and Nyamwalo in, the team was complete. If everybody played his or her part diligently we were bound to realise positive results.

Nyamwalo, as a person, was likeable and accommodative. She was the kind of woman you would wish to have around you when a visitor was home. She would treat the visitor with such keenness and devotion. She was quick in response, usually at her best in emergency. *A person is sick who needs to be rushed to the hospital, a visitor is home unexpectedly and at odd hours, she would be there to turn a bleak situation into hope.* She was sly and fearless. She could confront any problem or anybody and knew her way around things. Like me she was so smart that she was able to get bosses and employers to hire friends or relatives. She loved children, especially hers dearly. My parents, who saw this quality in her, were not mistaken. She loved her husband. She could do anything to protect me. She reminded me of my mother. She could have been my mother's first choice had my mother been alive.

But for every positive there is an equal measure of negative. A person is considered good when his or her good outweighs his or her bad. Nyamwalo was no exception. She exhibited some characteristics which were bad. She could be stubborn and obstinate to the point of being rude. If she didn't want to do something she wouldn't do it no matter what pressure was put on her. She lacked the ability to do or get things done either because of laziness or just shear carelessness. She was loud and quarrelsome, a live wire you could not step on. In old age she became moody and showed signs of bipolar. She was so secretive that sometimes she could present an untrue position of a situation to protect her secrecy. But in spite of her shortcomings and complexes, she was a wonderful wife and a loving mother to all our 22 children.

She was blessed with nice kids—two boys Victor and Kennedy (popularly known as Ken), and four girls: Betty, Loice, Dorothy (popularly known as Acheche) and Linda (popularly known as Grandy). Her greatest weakness would be her inability to be on her feet while pregnant. She could lie on bed 24/7 with short breaks for meal, bath and the toilet only.

I took Nyamwalo home, where she stayed in Nyasondu's house. Traditionally, when a man married another wife before he built a house for her, she lived in the first wife's house. And given the financial constraints of the time, it would be some time before I would be able to build her a house. When I brought in my properties from Anne, I stored them in one of the vacant living rooms of our buildings in Mutumbu. So when Nyamwalo was home I took my best furniture home for her use, and that was when her carelessness started showing. The executive furniture would later be reduced to tatters under her care.

And since she was doing nothing at home, I decided to keep her busy by letting her run our retail shop. Instead of running it to success she ran it down and out. Anything she touched did not prosper. Anything left under her tutelage flopped. May be that was her destiny!

I did not have the honour of seeing my mother-in-law, Nyamwalo's mother. She passed on in 1974, before I knew I would live with her daughter. She was the only mother-in-law I did not meet. I saw Nyamwalo's sisters, Grace Sijenyi and Achieng, and cousin Shade. I met her father, Mzee Bita—a soft and amiable mzee. Her sister Grace was like a mother to her. Whatever she knew or did not know was the work of Grace. We become close to the Sijenyis, helping each other financially and materially. Her cousin Shade was like my kid brother. He was there for me when I needed him. We loved him very much and he helped us a lot. He was a gracious giver and for that God blessed him abundantly.

Nyamwalo did not appear to have professed any Christian inclination before she came to our home. When she found a strong Christian base here, she reluctantly started to embrace the faith. Her faith was lukewarm. She did not take the church seriously. She only went to church when she liked and often without devotion. Even when in church, her concentration was questionable, but all these changed later. She embraced the faith more vigorously. She took a leadership position in church and urged her children to be serious with their faith. The moment she started doing this, things started falling in place for the better for her children. She got two degree and three tertiary graduates in her stable, one of whom became a lawyer.

As our children grew older, I decided to change tact in the way I related to them. Instead of giving orders, I started to involve them and their mothers in decision-making. I wanted to hear their views on petty matters of the home. I talked things over with Nyasondu, Nyairo and Nyamwalo and we agreed on three things:

- Eating together when all of us were together.
- Having evening devotions not only when we were together but also when we were in our respective residences.
- Consulting, planning and brainstorming together. The eating together posed no problem at all, because I provided the food and the mothers prepared it in turns. The devotion part was the

tricky part, whereas Nyasondu and Nyairo had no difficulty participating along with the children. Nyamwalo could not. She could not deliver a short sermon or pray as was required.

All our children could give a short sermon and we, as adults, were supposed to encourage them by doing what we wanted them to do. Nyamwalo could not do this, much to the embarrassment of the children. But the most intriguing part was the consultation, planning and brainstorming sessions. All adult members of the family participated in this session, except Nyamwalo. I could introduce the topic and invite everybody to comment, beginning with the youngest. In ascending order, all kids participated. The parents participated, except Nyamwalo, who said she had nothing to say. Whatever it was, advice or caution or warning or admonishment to the kids, she had nothing to say. A business venture we wanted to start or a construction work to undertake, she had nothing to say. Visitors coming so we had to prepare a budget for their entertainment, she had nothing to say. Whether it was a complex or indifference bothering her, nobody knew. Good thing was—Nyasondu, Nyairo and I were on hand to help the kids deal with the issues in their lives.

I believed every member of the family benefited from eating and praying together. A family that eats and prays together stays together. We planted the seeds of unity that would be enjoyed by the family for generations. Putting our heads together helped us achieve the developments we would later pass on to our children and grand children. The descendants of those who helped in the realization of the family goals and those who refused to co-operate would benefit alike. In this world there are people who make things happen and those who watch things happen, standing at safe distance. To those who helped in the reconstruction, I say thank you very much!

―――

From the mid-seventies, when I started my legal practice, lawyers faced several challenges, which a budding lawyer had to confront and overcome. It was not easy for the ambitious, dishonest and lighthearted. The challenges were enormous and put paid to many lawyers legal practice.

The country had just gained independence fifteen years earlier. The transition from colonial rule to self-rule was still ongoing. Most judicial officers were not Kenyans. Even on the economic front, foreigners still controlled the economy. There was very little in the Kenyan pockets. Many Kenyans could not afford fees for legal services. In the countryside—where my business was—it was more pronounced than in the city and towns. For one to get legal services, he/she had to sell cattle or sometimes a piece of land, if he/she could not get assistance from a son or daughter working in some town in the country. Sometimes one had money but because of ignorance he/she still suffered. We had to help people understand legal help was available!

Sometimes lawyers who stabilized and had good business had to beware of intoxication and the temptation to put their hands on money that did not belong to them. They had to learn to live within their means. Some of those who were in a hurry to get rich ended up in jail or were struck off the Roll of Advocates.

In the eighties and beyond, the greatest challenge changed to be corruption, impunity and ambulance-chasing. Justice was on sale to the highest bidder. If you had money and got in trouble with the law you did not need a lawyer, you needed to see the one who was going to preside over your case. Once you saw him there was no need to see a lawyer. Lawyers started losing business to presiding officers. The trend continued until presiding officers started being bribed with impunity. No amount of clinical cleansing would eradicate corruption unless we changed our attitude.

The lawyers who were not ready to taint themselves by engaging in this filth ceded a lot of ground to their corrupt colleagues, who were sly and knew their way in the corridors of power. With the powers that be behind them, they could put their hands on your money and you had no chance on earth to get it. Most of the upright practicing lawyers just shut shop and looked elsewhere for a livelihood. I would later belong to this category.

The other challenge was posed by ambulance chasers. This was a situation where lawyers traversed the country looking for accidents and their victims. They promised to get compensation for the victims, which they did, but the victims ended up with peanuts. As matters stood, insurance companies became their own worst enemies. They should have looked inside not outside regarding their woes and took appropriate measures to stabilize the industry. They needed to stop hiring corrupt officials and made it a corruption-free industry. This was the only way to drown out corrupt lawyers and ensure victims got their rightful compensation.

And just where was the Law Society?

CHAPTER 14

TANZANIA

My brother Haggai Okech was born, according to him, in 1927. He was the second born. He was 5feet6, dark in complexion and had his six lower incisors removed. He was a serious guy. He never laughed, but joked a lot. He was very harsh, sometimes unreasonably. He was physically fit and hard-working. He was educated at Maliera and Kamagambo, where he dropped out because of lack of school fees. He came back to Maliera and taught with Ephraim Odero. His main hobby was playing *orutu* (an African musical instrument with one string) with Godia Omach. Being an introvert and having kept to himself, it was hard to tell his religious inclination. But one thing was clear, he neither drank alcohol nor smoked.

He married Sellina Ayier, daughter of Edward Mriga, with whom he got four kids—Caleb Ohon, Christopher Odhiambo, Loice Omol and Auma. They also had an adopted child called Akinyi. Their last work station was Moshi, in Tanzania, where his wife deserted with the kids and married an indigenous Tanzanian. My brother became a rolling stone. All his wealth, including his trucks, disappeared or grounded. Mzee Edward would later go to Tanzania to fetch his daughter and would find her married to a Tanzanian. He would thus decide to come back with Okech's children. Meanwhile Okech went into the business of fish-mongering. He moved fish from Tanzania to Kenya. One day he was arrested and charged with the offence of trading in fish without a license. He was found guilty and jailed. When he was transferred to Bondo, he escaped and came back home. That was in the early sixties. Father worked hard and got him money for transport back to Tanzania.

As part of plans for our family, I went to Tanzania in 1973 to look for Okech. I went through Namanga and Shelui and was with Cousin Odongo Okello, who knew the Tanzanian terrain well. We started tracing him from Shelui, where we briefly stopped to get direction. We were told he could be traced from the next town. Coming back to the main road, we failed to get transport. A Good Samaritan, in a pickup, gave us a ride to the town. At that town we were directed to an Arab shop owner who knew him.

The man was sympathetic. He was surprised to hear we were Okech's brothers. "Kumbe Haggai ana mandungu—Does Haggai have brothers?" he asked.

We nodded.

He served us tea and *mahmur*, the only food we had in twelve hours. He then directed his househelp to take us to Okech's place. We had gone halfway when he called back his househelp. When the guy came back, he had a mat.

A mat? Wait a minute!

First that remark and now a mat? I immediately sensed things were not rosy. We were headed for a surprise.

We passed all the houses on the way and on the outskirts of the town I saw something like an anthill ahead of us. Surprisingly, that was where the househelp was headed. On reaching the structure, we noticed fire burning inside it on a spot that looked like a hearth. The househelp called and a guy who, for all intents and purposes, could pass for a mad man emerged. The guy was lean with a sheepish look. He was smoking along *kiko* (pipe). He appeared not to have eaten anything for a long time. The househelp told him we were Haggai's brothers and excused himself and left. He spoke in Luo and beckoned us to crawl into this Kraal, with our mat. That is where we stayed from 9:00 p.m. to 2:30 a.m. The guy told us our brother had gone fishing at Mbugani, which was 35 miles from Igunga, which was the next town. He said we could not walk to Mbugani because it was far and there was no road. We had to access it through Igunga, where we could hire a truck to take us there.

But again, to reach Igunga we had to catch a Dar-Mwanza bus, which passed at 3:00 a.m. That being the case, at 2:30 a.m. we were on our way to the road. We waited and waited but the bus never came. In fact not a single vehicle came. When we did not see any by seven we started walking towards Igunga in the hope that any vehicle could give us a ride. But our dress code would later betray and almost caused us our lives. My cousin wore a brown suit and had a portable radio strung across his shoulder. I had a Chinese suit, the attire of choice for most Tanzanians. The people around that place were cousins of the Maasai of Kenya. Their clothes were *shukas* and blankets.

At around nine in the morning we saw a lorry approaching. As it passed by we tried frantically to stop it but it just continued on its way. Suddenly, about 100 yards away, it stopped and we ran towards it. As we neared the passenger side of the driver's cabin two people came out with AK 47s and demanded in Kiswahili to see our identifications. I did not have any. Of course I had one but I did not remember to carry it from Kenya—but I had my driver's license.

The men shouted again in unison demanding IDs. What worsened the situation was when the little Kiswahili I knew deserted me at the time I needed it most. With my Kiswahili gone I uttered something in English. This made one of the guys mad. He cocked his AK 47 and pointed the nozzle right at my heart. I knew I would be dead in seconds. My cousin wasn't doing any better; he too did not carry his identification. He tried to explain to them that he was a Kenyan, but a resident of Tanzania. The guys weren't buying that. We were already put on a squatting position with my cousin pleading with them in flawless Kiswahili to spare our lives. He had lived in Tanzania for a very long time and spoke good Kiswahili. But just as they were about to tell us to say our last prayers, the lorry driver jumped out of the lorry and approached us hurriedly and addressed my cousin, "Do you come from Singida?" he asked.

My cousin was puzzled. "Singida?"

"Aren't you the guy who owns a bar in Singida?"

"Not me; it's my brother, Ochieng'"

He said, "*Huyo Ndugu yako ni mtu mzuri sana*—That brother of yours is a very good man."

On realizing that the driver knew my cousin's brother, the gunmen relaxed. Ochieng' had saved us from eminent death. They agreed to give us a ride in their *Jeshi La Mugambo* lorry up to Igunga. I arrived in Igunga before my heartbeat had stabilized. We immediately started looking for a truck to hire and got an Arab with a Toyota Stout. He agreed to take us to Mbugani. After taking his gun and a twelve battery spotlight, we set off. We drove through the wilderness because there was no road; he just followed animal tracks and appeared to know the route very well. He occasionally stopped to shoot game.

Later we arrived at a place called Abdalaqueque, which was like the Port of Mbugani. The driver refused to proceed farther, arguing, and rightly so, that the truck could get stuck in the mud. Mbugani was an expanse extending as far as the eye could see. We were told that during the rainy season it turned to a lake teaming with mudfish. During draught water in the lake dried up leaving patches of water scattered all over the expanse. Man and animals invaded the place in search of water, pasture and prey. Lions, zebras, elephants, rhinos and hyenas became the new settlers of Mbugani—the Maasai cousins with their flocks of cattle too.

The Arab refused to drive any farther, but we were determined to see my brother. The people we found at Abdalaqueque knew my brother very well and knew where he was as they were fishermen who had brought catch ashore to be transported to Igunga. The fishing grounds near the shore had been depleting, so fishermen pushed farther inside the lake in search of fertile fishing grounds. The people told us they dug fish from mud, killed them, cut them open and dried them in the sunshine. It was the dry fish that was ferried to Igunga.

We decided to walk to trace him. But just as we were about to start the trek, we got three warnings—two from the fishermen and one from the Arab. The fishermen warned that we could not go into the expanse by ourselves because once we were clear of the shore we would get lost and would not find our way back. They also warned of animals like lions, leopards and hyenas. We would not be able to know what to do if we encountered any of them. Our Arab driver warned that he would drive off at 5:00 o'clock whether we were back or not. The fishermen with whom we had by then struck a friendly rapport offered to give us a guide at small fee. That would take care of the two concerns. As we walked deeper into the expanse we started to realize how stupid we would have been to make the trip by ourselves.

Twenty minutes into the journey we could not tell where we had started from. There were so many footpaths crisscrossing each other that it was hard to tell which was the correct one. One hour into the journey we came across what the guy called the first station. It was a stockade for cattle, measuring 300 by 300 feet or thereabout. It was circular in shape and had an open gate. Surprisingly neither people nor cattle were around. On the horizon we could see what looked like a pride of lions playing with their cubs under the watchful eyes of the hyenas. The heat was so unreasonable there was no need to wipe sweat from our faces. The guy told us that there were seven other stations before we could reach the point where fishing was done. He said he had made such a trip a couple of times, either as a guide or simply to bring his brothers' load of catch on shore. He told us what to do in case we came across hyenas—the intimidating type.

The second, third and fourth stations were like the first one—an enclosure, heaps of fish and a fireplace with nothing else.

But the fifth one was different. For the first time we encountered some women in the manyatta. They could speak Kiswahili, so we asked them for water. One of them reached under her Shuka and pulled out a gourd and handed it to me. I was so thirsty that I thought I could drink anything from this gourd. But I was unable to drink. When I opened and lifted the gourd to my mouth I almost threw up. The stench emanating from inside the gourd was so strong that I quickly replaced the lid and handed the gourd to my cousin Odongo, who with his eyes closed took a few sips. He then handed back the gourd to the woman, thanked her and off we went.

Our guide was used to this weather. The heat did not bother him at all. He advised us to just let the sweat flow. "It will stop at some point and then start again and stop and start again until you reach your destination, where you can rest."

By the time we reached the sixth station we had run out of time. If we did not start our journey back right now we would miss our ride. So we told the guide we must go back. He tried to persuade us to persevere and make the four miles left, but we declined after weighing options. If we pressed on the Arab would leave us and we would have to walk the 35 miles back to Igunga. Since we were not prepared for this we just had to turn our back on my brother only four miles away. Although we had travelled more than 1000 miles, we were regrettably going back without seeing him. One thing I was sure of was that he was alive and I knew where he was. I decided to make him know that I was around looking for him. I wrote seven notes directing him to come home as Father was still ill and wanted to see him (I lied). I fixed the note on one load of fish at each station and left the seventh and enough money to enable him make the journey home, with the beach leader. I asked them to persuade him to come home as soon as possible before Father passed away.

When we arrived back at the shore we found our driver restless. He said there was a section along the route that we had to pass through before dusk otherwise wild animals would not allow us through. He hit the pedal as soon as we started off. He was driving too fast for the condition of the paths. This must have dented the fuel tank which developed a leak.

Midway through the journey we ran out of fuel in the middle of the jungle. For close to five minutes we stayed put and mute inside the truck as we did not know what to do. Petrol was 17 miles away. There was no truck we could hire to go and fetch petrol. To me it appeared there were no people living nearby, but even if there were, would they have petrol? It was the driver who broke the silence. He said, "You guys will have to wait for me here."

I coiled. "Wait?"

"Just leave the headlamps on and lock the doors and windows."

My God!

With his gun and spotlight he disappeared into the darkness. In that sweltering heat we waited in the driver's cabin. When we tried to open the window for cool air a swarm of mosquitoes gushed in and we quickly closed the windows and started killing the ones that got in with our hands.

One hour after he had gone we noticed a strong spotlight coming from our rear. But this cannot be him, we thought.

It turned out it was him. He was carrying a tin of petrol. When he reached us he said he had failed to find petrol at the only shop in the trading centre, which was 15 minutes away—but he got kerosene.

I asked if the truck would move on paraffin.

He said, "Yes, but it will force me to open up the engine and clean the piston rings and bearings."

Whatever!

It was 11:00 p.m. when we finally made it back to Igunga. We booked into a hotel, had a cold bath and went to bed.

Later I would be parting ways with Cousin Odongo. He would be going back to Kuteka and I would be on my way to Kisumu via Mwanza. I asked him to wake me up at 2:30 a.m. to enable me to catch the Dar bus, which we had missed the other day. He gave me a few tips on how to be safe in Tanzania at night.

He said, "If you hear someone say *usiku* reply *mchana*."

"Why?

"Because if you keep quiet or reply differently the person will raise alarm and people will come out of their houses to administer mob justice on you," he warned.

"I got it!"

At 2:30 he woke me up. I had difficulty waking up because I was exhausted. Apart from the shopkeeper's *mandasi* and tea at Shelui, we had not eaten anything. I was hungry. The walking in Mbugani was more than my daily share of the exercise. I pushed my body to the limit. And with no food in two days I was doing my body a disservice. Whatever the case, later we bid farewell and made straight for the bus stage.

My cousin, Clement Odongo, had lived in Tanzania for many years. He knew many parts of the country like the back of his palm. He was fluent in Tanzanian Kiswahili and when speaking would pass for one of them. He had been coming home to Kenya and passed information to me that he had been meeting my brother Okech in markets and he could help me locate him. While in Kenya he stayed in Nyalenda, in Kisumu town, where I was also working. Nyalenda was like his first home. He had lived there all his life. In Tanzania he was a fisherman. He was not a pauper. He had made good money out of the many businesses and had used his wealth to develop his home in Nyalenda. He would later build his own homestead in Lundha, Gem, where he would be attacked by robbers who would beat him to near-death.

This time the bus came. I got a seat and fell asleep. I must have slept through the journey because when I woke up we were already in Mwanza. I had to alight and take another bus to Isibania via Tarime. It was 6:00 o'clock in the morning and there was very little time for the change over, so I did not get time to go to a restaurant. I made do with a soda and samosas from the hawkers. And since I was still exhausted, once I got the seat and paid the fare, I went back to sleep. Even the ticket examiner did not bother to wake me up to examine my ticket. It was 6:00 o'clock in the evening when the bus stopped and everybody was asked to disembark. We had reached Mara River Crossing and we would take a ferry to the Tarime side of the river. The bus was driven into the ferry and all of us boarded the ferry. Mara River, at this point, was one and a half kilometers wide and only a couple of kilometers to the lake. It meandered into Lake Victoria and formed part of the many rivers which formed the source of River Nile, the longest fresh-water river in the world.

I had never used this road before. I had wanted to watch things—the road, the people, the scenery, everything—but I did not, as I was too tired and slept throughout. When the ferry reached the other side we quickly boarded the bus and were on our way. Night was fast approaching. I must have been awake for only a couple of minutes then fell asleep. When I woke up, the bus had stopped and there was nobody in the bus. I thought I had reached our destination, Isbania.

I took my handbag and alighted and started walking, looking around for a hotel to lodge in for the night and have my first meal in three days. I entered the first building I came across, which looked like a hotel with lodging facilities. After inquiring about the rates, I asked when the first bus leaves for Kisumu.

The guy I asked said, "To go to Kisumu you have to take a matatu from here to Isbania, 50 miles away, then catch Kisumu vehicles from there."

"What? Then where am I?"

"Tarime," he said.

I knew I was in real trouble. I had left the bus I had paid for up to Isbania thinking I had arrived, yet this was Tarime. I was still 50 miles away! I ran back to where I had left the bus but there was no bus. I asked a guy I found standing nearby where the bus was. He told me it had left 5 minutes earlier for Isbania. I was doomed. Exhaustion had put me in a quagmire. But my troubles and tribulations were yet to start. This was but the beginning!

I resolved to look for a place to sleep and make the Isbania trip the following day. I walked and walked looking for accommodation but none was available. All the hotels and lodgings had been booked for the Tanzanian army. There was war going on between Tanzania and Uganda and Tarime was the outpost for the Tanzanian army. And suddenly things started falling in place. Our harassment by the Tanzania security personnel along Shelui-Igunga Road was not for nothing. They must have thought we were in the country as spies for Iddi Amin. When they saw our clothes—Clement in a suit with something strung on his shoulder like a communication gadget and I in Chinese attire with a bag which was big enough to carry grenades—they were aroused. Their sixth sense told them they had in their grip a big catch. The two soldiers wielding and cocking their AK 47s must have been disappointed when their driver emerged and declared he knew Clement's brother, the bar owner in Singida. Maybe they were making their way to Tarime. But would I get somewhere to sleep? That was my preoccupation. I had forgotten about my hunger, which had now dissipated, when I realized that the bus to Isbania had left. So now what?

In one place where I was rebuffed was a young Maragoli boy with a small baby. Being a Kenyan, I decided to pay him a second visit to plead with him to see how best he could help me. On my first encounter with him he had told me he came from Migori in search of a job and after securing a job where he was, he got entangled with a Tanzanian girl who got pregnant and claimed he was the father. A week earlier the girl came and dumped the baby at his place of work and disappeared. Out of sympathy his boss allowed him to continue working and even the soldiers who patronized the place, when they heard the story, were sympathetic towards him and bought him gifts for the small baby. He was a double parent for his son.

I went back to the young man and pleaded with him. I told him how the bus inadvertently left me as it proceeded to Isbania. He felt pity, but how could he help? All the rooms were booked. Even my presence there, if the soldiers discovered, would be disastrous, not only to me but to him too. I felt I was putting this young man in danger; the danger of losing his job and the danger of going to jail for harbouring and aiding an alien. I decided to leave before the soldiers, who were away drinking could come back. But as I walked away he called me back.

He said, "Gentleman, you are indeed from my country but I don't know how I can help you. Maybe you can help yourself. If I offered you a place under my bed would you take it? I won't charge you anything."

Like a drowning man I took this opportunity and within seconds he had a blanket. On the floor, under the bed I dived like lightening.

He warned that I could sleep but not snore. If I had to pee, he gave me a bottle of soda for the purpose. He told me he would wake me up after five o'clock, and only after confirming that all was clear. I asked him to help me with the snoring bit. I was very tired and when I fell asleep I would not be able to control snoring, so if he heard me snore he should prick me with a stick which I saw he had.

But under the bed I could not fall asleep for fear that I would snore or even cough when the soldiers were around. Matters were not helped by the constant crying of the baby. As I lay there I realized I had not eaten a proper meal in three days and suddenly I started feeling the pangs of hunger again. I could hear soldiers come in one by one or in groups, most of them drunk and some with whores. Some would exchange pleasantries with my Maragoli friend; one or two would yell at him when they found the baby crying. He did his best to nurse the baby to prevent him from crying. The soldiers who spent the night there never knew they had an alien in their midst.

At five in the morning he woke me up after giving me the clear signal. I got out and reached into my pocket and pulled 200/= Kshs, which I gave him in appreciation. He accepted the money with humble thanks.

*

Here in Tarime it was not possible to detect foreigners by the manner they dressed. People dressed in more or less similar manner. This helped me walk to the bus stage undetected. I did not meet any security personnel on the way. By 6:00 O'clock I was in a matatu to Isbania. I made it to Kisumu by noon. I had a shower and a nice meal and went to bed. I slept soundly until the following morning. Later in the day I went home to report to Father how things had turned out.

I will always be grateful to Cousin Clement Odongo Okello, who made it possible to locate a brother most people thought was dead. Without him I would not have made this adventurous journey. It was my first trip to Tanzania, but it would not be my last. I had to make another trip when my brother didn't come. This time I made sure I carried my driving license and identification card. I took my brother's son, Mambo Yote, along. We set off from Kisumu in the morning and had lunch in Migori. It was going to be a long drive to Mwanza, where we intended to rest overnight before proceeding to Igunga via Shinyanga and Nzega.

It was midnight when we reached Mwanza. With the help of a passenger we had given a ride, we located the Railway Station. Cousin Wilfred Indakwa had relocated to Mwanza from Kisumu and we had arranged to spend the night in his house. We knew if we located the Railway Station we would be able to locate Wifred's house. One of the security guards knew his house and led us to it. Wilfred and his wife Nyalego were extremely happy when they saw us. They made our brief stay with them as comfortable as they could.

At 8:00 o'clock, the following morning, we left for Igunga. From Igunga we would proceed to Kiteka to pick up Clemet. He was the one who would help us find out whether or not my brother was still in Abdalaqueque. But as we were on our way to Shinyanga the state of the road became deplorable. It forced vehicles to drive off the main road. Then as we drove along the side road we hit a trench—dug to drain water from the culverts—full throttle. The vehicle got airborne and landed heavily in front. Luckily, it did not overturn. I managed to control and stop it. The mud guard was smashed, three blades of the fan were completely severed and the radiator was dented in several places and was spewing hot water. We put the radiator stop leak and added water in it then limped on.

We reached Shelui by night fall.

There, we found someone who was going to Kiteka. We rode up to Kiteka and located Clement's house. Clement was away on business but his wife Nyakendu was present. She did the much she could to see to our comfort. The following morning we left for Igunga. We expected to be in Igunga by 9:00 o'clock, but that was not to be. After completing the meandering climb of the road, we found ourselves on a flat countryside road with thick heaps of sand. We hit this section as suddenly as we hit the trench the previous day. The car swerved uncontrollably and hit the kerb and stopped. On checking the radiator, it was gone; one of the three blades of the fan was gone too. Only two blades remained. The radiator had a gaping hole at the bottom where water was jetting out. We used the remaining stop leak but it didn't stop the flow. If the car was going to move, it was going to do so without water in the radiator. If we didn't move, we would be stuck there and I didn't know until when. We still had five gallons of water. We decided to drive on, filling the radiator and driving as fast as we could then stopping at the sign of overheating until the engine cooled down. We repeated this process several times until we ran out of water. We made very little progress in the process. Without water we decided to drive for short stints and stop to allow the engine to completely cool. We allowed 30 minutes between runs of 1 minute.

Luckily, or so we thought, we came to a pond and decided to fill our cans with water. These would enable us to move much faster. We moved with the 2 cans to the pond but as soon as we started to draw water a man clad only in a *shuka* emerged from behind us and demanded to know what we were doing. We were perplexed by the question because as far as I was concerned, he was not blind. He could see us and what we were doing. He moved menacingly near us. He was armed with a spear and had a bow and arrows in a holster hung on his shoulders. Feeling threatened, we abandoned our quest for water and pulled back. We tried to plead with him to allow us just take one can instead of two, but he was adamant, demanding we vacate the scene at once. When we hesitated, he took a posture, with his spear uttering war cries, suggesting he was going to attack us. We hurriedly left the scene without water.

We continued to torment the car the way we did before discovering the pond. By the time we reached Igunga it was well past 5:00 o'clock, in the evening. We went straight to the marketplace and met a very welcoming boy from Nyakach. He offered to get us a mechanic who filled the holes in the radiator and got us another fan. We heard from the traders in the market that my brother passed by saying he was headed home. That was the first inkling that my brother received my message and was on his way home. The Nyakach boy got his wife to prepare food. She even slaughtered a chicken for us. We rested well and left for home the following day. Janyakach offered to show us shortcuts to the main road from Shinyanga to Mwanza. Once we reached the main road, we put him on an Igunga-bound bus and we proceeded to Mwanza. Our plan was to be in Mwanza before 11:00 o'clock and leave for home the same day. That was our plan, but God had his own plan—or was it the devil this time?

Twenty miles into Mwanza the car developed a mechanical problem. It was the fuel system. The Engine would run and just stall by itself. This impeded our progress so much that instead of arriving in Mwanza at eleven we made it there at 5:30 p.m. A delay of about six hours. Our plan to travel home that day flopped, so we spent another night at Wilfred's. In the morning he got a mechanic to look at the car and by noon we were on our way home.

Considering our time of departure I had to drive furiously in order to catch the ferry at the Mara River—the ferry did not operate after six pm. I pressed the pedal hard and arrived just in time as the ferry was about to make its last trip to Tarime. I reasoned that if I maintained the same speed when I hit the tarmac in Isbania I would be in Kisumu by eleven p.m.

I drove the car into the ferry and disembarked. People were not allowed in the vehicles once they were inside the ferry. When we reached Tarime I cranked the engine and drove out of the ferry but did not go far before the car stalled again. It was already night and I did not know where to find a mechanic, so I applied the tactics I used between the time the problem started and the time we arrived at Mwanza. I would start the car and allow it to move at its own speed without pushing it to attain a certain speed. This way I managed to make some progress. We moved slowly until we got to Isbania. On the tarmac the car allowed us good speed but not good enough for my liking. I was comfortable with ninety to one hundred miles per hour, but the car could not pass seventy miles per hour. We, however, made steady progress and arrived in Kisumu at 4:00 a.m.

Yes, my brother had come and called at my Kisumu home before proceeding home. From what he told his in-laws in my house, the night I spent in Mwanza on my way to Kiteka, he was in Mwanza waiting to board a steamship for Kisumu. Both of us spent the night in Mwanza!

Later the car got fixed and I was finally on my way to meeting a brother I had last seen many years ago!

When I arrived home, I did not see my brother. The person I saw was the pipe- smoking old man I found in an anthill in Tanzania. The only difference was that he did not smoke like the old man in the Kraal. I was told children ran away when they saw him coming, thinking he was insane. They had to be calmed down and assured all was well. They even had to be told that he was the father of Lebo, Mambo Yote and Omol. When I set my eyes on him I pitied him. I was, however, elated that I had brought him out of the hard life in Tanzania. His comfort and health were now the biggest challenges I faced. After exchanging pleasantries, I drove back to Kisumu to collect clothes and beddings for him. Upon my return I found out that Father had arranged for him to have a haircut. With the haircut, descent clothes, bedding and shoes, he now looked like one of us!

Later I built for him a cottage and arranged for him to marry a girl from Imbo. As days turned into weeks and weeks into months, he started feeling dejected, moody and completely restless. He wanted to go back to Tanzania. Meanwhile I had talked to the Town Clerk of Kisumu Municipality to secure a position for him in the council and he agreed. I had also planned to give him capital to start a business of his choice, but this did not convince him to stay. He asked for fare back to Tanzania, for himself, his wife and his son. Although I had the money and could afford the much he wanted, I was reluctant to give it to him. I was not going to to allow him take an innocent wife and son to the life I saw with my own eyes.

I gave him enough money for his fare back to Tanzania.

After arriving in Tanzania, he wrote a few nasty letters to Father and I, making sure he did not write a return address through which we could reply his letters. We never had from him again.

Fourteen years later Father died!

The young wife my brother had left behind stayed with my family at my Milimani residence for one year and later went back to her home. I later found her working in Siaya as a bar maid. She was in this trade for the rest of her life.

*

After they parted ways, the mother of Lebo, Mambo Yote and Omol got married to a Tanzanian with whom she had other kids. It's amazing how some women bring kids into this world and refuse to take care of them. Our God, who sympathizes with the underdog, the trodden down and the neglected will protect my brother Haggai Okech's seed for posterity.

CHAPTER 15

VISION

When my mother was alive our home was a beehive of activity. Throngs of people visited every day. Some came to consult Father on a variety of issues, from cultural to political matters. This was because Father was in local politics. Others came to talk to Mother about church activities; others simply to request for small assistance. The home looked lively and habitable. After Mother's death in 1958, things changed drastically. The home became bushy; my brothers' houses got dilapidated and some fell completely. The euphobia fence got overwhelmed with shrubs and bushes. The home became a shadow of its previous self. My brothers' wives deserted with children— Ng'onga with two, Abiba with two and Selina with four. Absalom's only wife, Sylvia Awiti, was in Nairobi with her kids. My father had no grandson or son except me, living at home. All my sisters had been married and were staying in their marital homes. Do you catch the drift?

The situation was so bad that if Father had to spend a night outside the home he had to make arrangements with someone to come and sleep at home to protect and keep me company. Those were the days when being left alone at home was frightening. The lockable gate was no longer there, since all the logs had been split and used as firewood during the funeral. It could be a snake crawling from nowhere or a leopard hiding in the thicket. Danger loomed all around.

The home was gradually becoming desolate. James had just flown out of the country and although I was at home, I was far too young to do anything about the deteriorating situation. This downward trend would continue till 1974. My father's remarriage did not do much to improve the situation; it helped my father to recover from the shock of losing his wife and helped me in having someone to provide me with food and a semblance of parental care, but that was it.

My elder brother's death in 1968 and the catastrophic events of 1971 worsened the situation. Any hope of my graduate brother lifting the home from the quagmire was dashed with his death and that pushed us further into desolation. Someone in the home had to do something to arrest the situation. It could be Haggai Okech, my other brother who was still alive yet nobody had heard of. But wait. Even if he were around, was he made of the stuff that could turn this home around? Did he have a heart and the resources to do it? Nobody actually had answers to these questions as nobody knew much about him. But if it was not him, who? Could I rise to the occasion? The answer was definitely no, because I was still too young. My qualities were unknown. So could it be Father or even my step-mother? The answer was negative. They were old, lacked ideas and resources. Both of them were not committed to saving the home with the same gusto. Saving the home would wait until my adulthood and would depend on my status in life. That was just it!

In 1974 God revealed a fifteen-point vision to help me salvage our home. If followed to the letter and with prayer, these steps were bound to bear fruit. They were not going to be easy, but I vowed to work on them diligently if they were going to give me the desired results.

- To bring back home all my brothers' children, who had deserted home with their mothers. You cannot have a home without people. I had to bring home those who were supposed to be in the home. This task started in 1965, when I brought home Thuthu and Dunga. In 1968 I brought in Obuga. In 1969 Lebo, Mambo Yote and Omol came home.
- To bring back the estranged wives of Absalom—Ng'onga and Abiba. I knew this would be an enormous task but I was determined to do it. These were women who had left home over fifteen years earlier. In the case of Ng'onga she had been remarried in Ugenya and had children there. She lost her Ugenya husband and was taken in by a levirate husband who also died. At the time of my scheming to bring her home she was on her third husband and her daughter Odinga had children. Abiba however was living in Kisumu. She was not as lucky as Ng'onga so she did not have a husband. Her case was easy. I had only to talk to her and once she accepted that was it. She was the first to return home. Her husband had died six years earlier but she did not attend the funeral. She came and I arranged for a house to be built for her in my father's homestead where her husband was buried. I provided her with food until she was able to have her own from the farm my father showed her to till. Later I arranged for her to have her own homestead where her sons built their cottages and she took charge of them. In terms of food and other necessities of life, my load was reduced by the two. Both sons got married and had kids and lived prosperous lives. Thuthu however was ruined by alcohol.
- Later I tackled Ngong'as case, which was a bit tricky. I involved his son Obuga and her brother to talk to her. Surprisingly she agreed and I arranged how to smuggle her and her team out of their Ugenya home. We agreed on a date and time. I had to drive my car to Ambira at midnight, pack along the road and wait. I drove to Ambira as agreed and packed. Within five minutes they emerged from the bushes on the roadside and headed to the car with Ngong'a in the lead. They were eight in all—two adults, Ng'onga and Odinga, and six children. As they appeared to be in hurry, I bundled them into the car and off I drove. I arranged for their accommodation, gave them food and took the children to school. It was at this time that we took Job Odhiambo (Sir Job) to be one of our own. Sir Job, along with Achieng' and Akinyi, were Odinga's children—grandchildren of Ng'onga. Ngo'ong'a's other

children who came were Okoth, Manga and Awino. Only Sir Job and Okoth managed it to form four. The rest dropped out on the way.

- ➢ I arranged for Sir Job to train as a teacher and later he got married to his lovely fiancée Josephine. They were blessed with kids and lived a prosperous life—she as a nurse and he as a teacher. Awino was later married in Sakwa, Akinyi was married in Ulugano and Achieng' in Kakamega. Both Akinyi and Achieng' had children and led prosperous lives. Okoth later got married and had kids. He later migrated back to Ugenya where he, his wife and children died. Manga absconded school and went to Mombasa. He later got married several times and had kids. Odinga remarried and had a bunch of kids whom we helped her educate. They too prospered. This group, because of their number, added the burden but I did not shy away; I faced the challenge as a man. On reflection I feel proud that I did what I did to rescue my brother's family from extinction.

Later I arranged for Ng'ong'a to have a homestead where she stayed with her children and grandchildren, except Sir Job, whom we adopted as our son. This was in line with what I had done earlier with Abiba.

- ➢ Education was key to my plans. Without it we were not going to achieve anything. Every kid of school-going age had to go to school. I gave everybody, including my own children, equal opportunity to learn. I was responsible for all expenses, so failing to go to school was one's choice. I made sure nobody dropped out of school because of fees. Those who passed national exams well, including my children, I took to tertiary institutions. But education, as part of the plan posed the biggest challenge to me because it required a big capital outlay and meticulous planning. I managed singlehandedly—with help from God of course—without which I would not have succeeded.
- ➢ To buy as much land as possible for settlement, property development and farming was a core requirement of the plan. Since our numbers increased we needed farming land to enable the multitude to grow crops for their food and surplus for sale. I needed more land to settle my brothers' three wives. Each had to have a homestead where she could live with her children and look after them during school holidays. I also needed land for development. I embarked on purchasing land—farmland, developed plots and land for development. Because of financial constraints, I bought very little land, some of which I sold later to enable me to pay school fees. I was able to settle Abiba and Awiti. I was also able to develop two market plots and buy two houses.
- ➢ With land available, I was able to farm extensively to produce food. In the year 1974, I stopped everybody from tilling their respective portions of land and took it upon myself to plough all our land and planted maize, millet, cabbages, onions, carrots and kales. The yield

was bountiful. We got so much maize that I had to construct a special structure for storage. We were not able to consume or even sell all the cabbages we produced. We gave out so much to villagers that they did not want them anymore. We were not able to sell because there was a slump in the price and we could only sell in Kisumu. By the time I reached Kisumu with cabbages, sold them and came back, I had already used more money on transport than my sales. Most of them just rotted in the shamba. With that bumper yield, we kicked out famine from our home.

- ➤ To provide dependents with food, good clothes and other necessities of life was the seventh point of the plan. With food available in abundance, this multitude was able to eat comfortably. Most of them refused to eat cabbages. I was able to redirect some of my resources to the provision of good clothes, Kerosene and other necessities of life.
- ➤ To lead all dependents to church and make them stay there. You can lead a cow to the stream but you cannot force it to drink. I took everybody to church but I was unable to make them stay there. Only a few remained and are strong in the faith and the difference between those who dropped out and those who remained is quite clear. Those who remained are well read and prosperous, while those who opted out returned to their old habits like smoking, drinking and immorality and have suffered from the fate that bedevil those of their ilk who take part in those activities. Most are dead, the rest are firewood choppers, herders or diggers of graves in the villages. Their fate was sealed the moment they turned their back on the church.
- ➤ The ninth step was to start income generating ventures and businesses. I knew I needed lots of money, which I could not get from my business of advocacy alone, so I had to start things that would generate funds, which would boost income. I did retail shop, butchery and even off-license bar. But the venture that opened ways for me was the school repairs and supplies. I floated a company called Soto, together with Thuma Onyonge and Ayub Ohon. In fact the name SOTO was an acronym of our names. The money I made from the venture enabled me to buy two matatus. This time I got sufficient money from my business, which enabled me to pay fees for all dependants in school and helped in further investments. I remember that when I started the butchery business there was no other butchery in our small market. I could slaughter only on Sundays. Weekdays I was in the office and Saturday was my rest day. So when I slaughtered on Sunday at around 10:00 o'clock, when folks came from church long queues formed, snaking almost twenty yards from the butchery. I was not able to cope with the speed at which the customers wanted service. Some people waited and when they were not served fast enough left. One day a friend came by and took over from me. Within one hour the long line was no more; he had served everybody. John Ong'ayo was a born businessman who

started business as a hawker and went on to own a retail shop. I knew him casually during our herding days but came to know him better when he started retail shop at Mutumbu. John could sell you anything. He was such a good talker that he could talk you into buying even what you had intended not to buy. He ran a shop next to mine at Mutumbu, the only retail shop of substance at the time. One day when I came from Kisumu I was told John had been forced to vacate the shop he rented at Mutumbu. When I asked why he was evicted, I was told my people did not want him there because he was getting rich and he was not one of us. This upset me very much. The tribalism I was fighting to eradicate was being practiced by my own people. I termed it reverse tribalism. Our people had suffered a great deal because of tribal oppression and so when they started to practice tribalism I decided to fight that too. If I allowed them to succeed Mutumbu market was going to close down and we were not going to have an outlet through which we could develop and prosper as a people. That evening I asked where John had gone to. Dudi, I was told. I came from Kisumu in my truck (pick up) which I had bought to help me with farming. I drove to Dudi and found John cleaning up the shop he wanted to occupy. I asked him what the matter was and he told me exactly what I had been told and already knew. I asked him if he would go back to Mutumbu if he got an alternative shop to rent and he said he could. I then told him to pack his stuff if he was serious.

Around this time I had completed building a shop at Mutumbu and one side was ready for occupation. I drove John and his stuff back to Mutumbu and allowed him to occupy my shop building. I did not regret my decision to bring John back because of his efforts and business acumen. Mutumbu developed, just as I thought, into a town. That is what brought John and I close and we became friends.

So when he came to help me in the butchery he was still occupying the very shop I let out to him, where he was running a prosperous retail shop. He came four consecutive Sundays before I asked him if he could team up with me. Butchery business, during that time, was a money spinner. What you lost on meat you made up for in hide. If it were possible I would have been slaughtering every day, because I had the money to buy cattle, but I could not because I had an office to run during the week days. So when I asked John if he could join me and he agreed, we sat down to work out the modalities. We agreed I would by five bulls for slaughter on an experimental basis. John would slaughter and sell during the weekdays and I would team up on Sundays, which was still our busiest day. We would share the weekday profits two to one in my favor as the provider of the butchery and the capital and all Sunday profits would be mine. We embarked on this business under this arrangement and made some money out of it. When we exhausted our five-bull stock, I left John to continue because I had other pressing matters to attend to. He continued to pay my rent, both for the retail shop and the butchery. John would later make a fortune from the butchery business. I was glad God used me to help him stabilize. He later gave up drinking and raised his family successfully. I had a short stint in the butchery venture, made quick bucks and left. John's butchery and retail shop helped develop Mutumbu Market and was therefore proud that I was associated with its inception.

From butchery I ventured into the business of hides and skins. I bought a running business of hides and skins from Sirega Onduro. I purchased not only the business but the building and the land the building stood on. He misrepresented to me that he had bought the land on which he built the hides *banda*. I would later learn that what he said was not true. I first rented the *banda* to my cousin Ofula Kwasu but when I realized he could not pay the rent as agreed I ceded the business to him and he ran it until his death. When he died I gave the business to my stepbrother Edwin Omondi Wanyanga for free. I was happy he was able to use the income he got from that business to bring up his family of two wives and several kids. He was later evicted from the original site and moved the *banda* near his home.

Another venture I started was that of off-bar and lodgings. I had beer stocked in the retail shop side of the building. The retail shop business boomed but the off license bar didn't because already there was a bar in the market where customers preferred to patronize. I made some money on the retail shop until it was run down by the person I later left to run it.

I tried yet another business. The *busaa* business was booming at the time and I decided to try my hand on that. I was trying anything that could give me money to help me run the big family. I arranged to start the business at the building where the butchery was started. John had moved the butchery elsewhere and the building was vacant. When the building could no longer accommodate this business, I brought in my nephew Dalmas Orago to help secure land adjacent to my plot from his relatives for business expansion. To get additional capital, I brought on board my cousin Wilfred Indakwa who injected much-needed funds. This business boomed. Dalmas later died and his wife Awiti took his place. We left the business when the government banned *busaa* clubs. Awiti and Wilfred were duly compensated for their contribution to the business in kind and cash.

But the most important agro venture I undertook was poultry. I realized if I could have five hundred hens producing eggs at eighty percent daily I would have four hundred eggs daily and this would give me a lot of money. I made up my mind to construct a poultry pen that could house one thousand five hundred hens (layers). I bought the first batch of five hundred, eight week old chicks and built my stock to one thousand two hundred layers. With that number I collected nine hundred and sixty eggs daily. This was an enormous amount of eggs. It needed full time attention, particularly the sales part, where I had the greatest challenge. Whenever I failed to sell a day's collection I was in trouble. I thus arranged for my salesmen to travel far and wide looking for market. I supplied Kakamega, Kisumu and Siaya. Breakages during transport were enormous; kids were unable to eat all of them. In fact some of the kids stopped eating eggs altogether. God blessed us with abundance. Whatever I touched God blessed. Around this time everything seemed to be moving in the right direction. I lingered in poultry farming for years and it formed the backbone and mainstay of the family for several years—until I started matatu business.

Matatu business was quite lucrative during that time. I acquired an old Peugeot 404 matatu which I reconditioned and put on the road. Although I did not make much from it, I made enough to enable me to have good food on the table and to buy another Peugeot truck. Because of their condition, they were on and off the road but they served the purpose for which they were bought—provided the resources to finance the marshal plan. As God blessed everything I touched, I later proceeded to acquire two new matatus, which literally lifted us a notch higher and made us measure favorably with my contemporaries.

With the Matatu business came post office mail deliveries. I was contracted by Kenya Post and Telecommunication to convey mails from Kisumu to Maseno, to Luanda, Yala, Dudi, Mutumbu, Sidindi, Rangala, Ugunja, Ng'iya, Siaya, Uranga and Nyadorera. Although the net payment was peanuts, it added something to the kitty. I was glad I got the contract.

Meanwhile I had been allowed by the Kenya Post and Telecommunications Cooperation to operate a sub post office in Mutumbu at a fixed rent. This also helped me in generating funds, as were the two houses I bought in Kisumu.

- ➢ Point number ten was to instill discipline among all dependants, including adults. I believed in discipline and ultimate unquestionable authority. You had to be obedient and comply with orders, no questions asked. I was harsh, uncompromising and unpalatable. Nobody could push me around. I did not run the home, I ruled the home. My word was final. I am glad God gave me the wisdom to overdo and overstretch my powers. Everybody in the home, including my parents, were disciplined. Kids called me Idi Amin Dada behind my back. I later came to know about it and laughed it off. My wives were alert and were compelled by circumstances to take a low profile. It was under this environment that my kids, my brothers' kids and the village kids I was helping during that time grew up. Those, who at that time thought they were being persecuted, later came to thank me for shaping them for the future. They became prosperous courtesy of my iron hand. This helped my stepbrothers and sisters who were old enough at the time to be included in the regimen. The dose was the same for everybody. My wives benefited too, they didn't have to deal with disobedient and rebellious kids. There was no room for that in our home. Father, being a disciplinarian himself, liked it a lot and gave me every encouragement and support along the way. God helped to discipline folks and those who persevered harvested handsomely.

- The eleventh point was to use all available resources towards the maintenance and upbringing of all our dependants. The resources from my salary—and later income from my office, business ventures, shares, and rents from my properties, income from Rose, to a very limited degree, income from Jane and farm produce—were all utilized for one single purpose: the welfare of Wanyanga family. This was the funding base that made and reconstructed Kawanyanga.
- The twelfth point was to construct my own home and develop it. Why God gave me this as a plan would be known to me later in life. I had many reasons for wanting to vacate my father's home. One, I wanted my step-mother to assume responsibility for her kids like my brothers' widows, Ng'ong'a, Abiba and Awiti Sylvia did. When I lived with them, I provided money, food, clothes and fees. I wanted my step-mother to take over food, clothes and the discipline part. Two, I had reached the end of my patience with her antics, like speaking behind people, eavesdropping, setting people against each other. I needed a break. Three, I needed to develop in my own home. I would plant fruit trees, build good houses and plant other trees for shade, timber and fuel. Four, my kids, when home, would not be exposed to certain traits that would destroy their moral and religious aptitudes. I needed to protect them. Five, I needed to protect my wives too. They had been in constant fear of embarrassment and indignation by eavesdropping by my step-mother and some of her kids at night. I wanted to protect them not only from that but also from theft of their pants, utensils and clothes. We had to move out and this we did on the twelfth day of December 1978.
- Thirteenth point was to build a second home in Siaya and plant trees therein too. Siaya was my work station for twenty seven years. I had been living on rented houses and had at some point commuted home or Rang'ala. As commuting and renting was expensive I decided to plan and build a home in Siaya. It was in 1986 July when I commenced the work with only eight thousand Kenya shillings contributed by Rose. I went on to build a multi- million house which would save us commuting and rental charges. The house was huge. It had four bedrooms, one en suite and a self-contained guestwing. We had to sell one of Peugeots to be able to complete it.

The house was ready and on the 31st December 1986 we moved in. As we were doing so, we received information that my beloved Aunt Dursila Onjare was dead. We completed the moving and hired a watchman to watch things as we went home to make funeral arrangements. Later Aunty was buried with decency and after the burial I took my cousin Pastor Tobias Otieno Ayayo, elders Justo Wamboga, Isaac Ochieng and Musa Achual, together with my entire family, to Siaya to pray for us in our new home. I arranged for the entire group to be ferried back home via Rang'ala, where they had to drop Jane, the Kids and Pastor Otieno.

- ➤ Fourteenth was to bring all kids to live under one roof. With the completion of my Siaya home, the stage was set for bringing together all my kids. Previously they had been living in Kisumu, Maseno, Gem, Rang'ala and Siaya. I brought them all to Siaya. One of the reasons for building a huge house was to be able to accommodate my kids, who together with the adopted ones, now numbered twenty. At first Mama Rose stayed with them, as she was working in Siaya, but she found the task too demanding and gave up. She could come back from work tired and literally lock herself in the bedroom and expect the kids to prepare food and take to her in the bedroom. The kids had to come from school, go to the market and bring food home to cook. She was completely oblivious to the happenings in the house. This, to me, was strange because as a mother her primary duty was to ensure that food was in the house, and that food was cooked well. She did none of these. When she failed to change after talking things out, I asked her to go stay at home. She reluctantly went home, leaving the kids in Siaya, under my care.
- ➤ To get help for Rose to assist with the upbringing of the dependents was the fifteenth point. She already had assistants in Ng'ong'a, Abiba, Awiti, Jane and would soon get another one—Pamela—to complete the pentagon and launch me into a polygamous life. When I brought Jane into my life chances were that I would not reconcile with Mama Rose. In fact, if it were not for my kids with her, whom I loved very much, there would not have been any reconciliation at all. But I considered the welfare of our kids and decided to allow her back in spite of our differences. *Live and let live* was my motto, which I did not just live by, but lived.

With these austerity measures in place, God helped me turn the destiny of our family around and they became the foundation upon which Kawanyanga became a home again. Putting more emphasis on education, we went on to have more graduates than any family in the village. Our standard of living became among the best in the village. Kawanyanga became a home again, just like it was during my mother's life time. I know I made Mama proud!

CHAPTER 16

POLYGON

Before the advent of the Europeans with the Holy Bible in one hand and a gun in the other, Africa was ravaged by diseases, some of which were alien to the Europeans. Leprosy, chicken pox, small pox and elephantiasis were particularly prevalent. Malaria was a menace too, but our people had a cure for it. Although tetanus did not kill en mass like the other plagues, it had no known cure. Cholera could be treated—and because of a sparse population it was not a menace.

Famine also contributed to annihilation of populations. Climate and locusts did not help matters either, both brought famine.

I remember witnessing the dramatic landing of locusts. As they approached they blocked the sun completely. At first I thought clouds had formed and blocked the sun, but I soon heard a growing murmuring sound. I was told it was a swarm of locusts. Everybody ran to the house because they were going to make landfall in our village. But not all of them landed. People came out once they landed and started collecting them for food. They made a delicious meal. Stronger folks who could climb the trees and shake the branches to make locusts drop on the blankets below collected sacks and sacks of them. They were then killed and stored. The following morning there was not even a single leaf or blade of grass remaining. Everything green had been consumed. Little things but the destruction they left in their wake was unimaginable. When they landed they would cover one up and cause gradual suffocation. That's why guys sought shelter as they approached.

The African lived in perpetual fear of animals, diseases and other calamities. They started devising ways of self-preservation. They had discovered that they could prolong the life of a lock-jaw victim by removing six lower teeth to enable him get food down the gullet. They learned they could reduce the menace of tse tse flies and mosquitoes by clearing the bushes. They learned to make treaties, thus reducing inter tribal wars. My tribe had been on the move for years, migrating from one place to the other with livestock. But now they wanted to settle down and farm. The Europeans had introduced maize and they wanted to try it out to see if it could be a supplement or a worthy replacement for millet and sorghum—the two staples of the time. They needed strong young men in their midst to fend off attacks by poachers when they settled.

So how were they going to survive? They discovered one thing. That *yadh siko en kend*—if you want to have descendants marry!

So they decided to marry; not one or two but many wives. Those with many wives (polygamists) had lots of advantages over those with one wife (monogamists). First, they could acquire more land. During this time wealth was measured by the number of cattle one owned and size of his land. People settled on the land and one acquired as much as one could till. If you had one wife, you and your wife could only till a fraction of what a polygamist with ten wives, for instance, would till. The latter could acquire ten times more land than the monogamist. And whatever land one acquired this way remained his forever.

Second, a polygamist had the potential to have many kids. Many girls meant wealth coming into the home by way of bride price. Dowry then was no less than fifteen heads of cattle per girl. If only ten out his many daughters survived and were married, a polygamist would be one fifty heads of cattle richer. A monogamist could not match this wealth. And because my tribe is a patrilineal, ancestry is determined through the males. A polygamist's chances of having sons surviving and continuing his lineage were better than a monogamist's; and he was assured of security. Many sons had a better chance of fending off attacks directed at the home than fewer sons.

A part from security, many sons helped bring food home; they could plough, plant and weed with the bulls. They also looked after cattle and helped with harvesting and milking. The more one ploughed and planted, the more he harvested. This is why there was likely to be more food in a polygamist's home.

But to be a polygamist you had to be a good administrator; your impartiality had to be beyond reproach. You had to be a capitalist, a socialist and a democrat at the same time. You were to tamper this with a little dose of dictatorship. Polygamy taught one to be just, considerate and honest. It taught one to make tough and unpopular decisions, to ensure high standards of discipline were maintained.

Are we together?

Let's carry on then. Polygamy and immorality were strange bedfellows. You could hardly find a polygamist with a chain of mistresses. You could never find him in a *kabuti* (heavy raincoat) at 10:00 pm behind a widow's house or the house of a wife whose husband is away, waiting for kids to sleep before he enters to be entertained by the widow or the wife of that absentee husband. He was content with what he had and if, for any reason, he needed a new acquisition he discussed it with his first wife. His wives also watched each other's back and it eliminated any immorality on their part. The fear of being discovered by a cowife and reported forced moral uprightness on women. In fact, this act of *watch me I watch you* is how my nephew knew when his son one night invaded his step-mother under the influence of alcohol and tried to rape her. The following day it was hot news in the home and the father had to banish the son from the home.

In another story a monogamist turned his son's wife into a lover. It took two years for his only wife to know that her husband sneaked out of their bedroom to make love to her daughter-in-law. When the matter came to light, the son declared the wife *persona non grata* in the home. Even when his father died years later he never came home for the funeral.

In a polygamous home, food is prepared and brought to a central eating place. This can be in the *duol* (the owner of the home's private cottage) or under a tree in the upper part of the homestead, or even in the first wife's house. A polygamist must have a *duol*. All the wives prepare food and bring it to the *duol* or at a special place designated for that. The food comprises a variety of dishes—sweet potatoes with sour milk or *magira*, *ugali* and *sukumawiki* (kales), or even nyoyo with *nyuka*—porridge. The variety created an air of instant celebration in the *duol*.

Once food was served the sons, male workers and any male visitors, including the owner of the home himself, would report to the cottage to eat. More often than not the food would be more than the diners could consume. The leftovers would then be kept in a special place in the *duol* for the use of any unexpected guest or any orphan who happened to come to the home.

This was the method the owner of the home used to discharge his communal responsibility. It was a method through which orphans were helped to get food. The head of the household also used the leftovers to reward kids who were obedient and did not grumble when sent on an errand.

Polygamy also promoted the act of giving. When food was plenty it was easy to give to the poor. The orphans, widows and widowers were all covered. The act of living together—minding each other's affairs and sharing ideas, values and valuables— was the benchmark of polygamy. Children were brought up together and given equal opportunities for advancement. Sons were supposed to relate with their fathers as daughters were to be under the watchful eye of their mother. The owner of the home did not shop for only one wife; if he had to he shopped for all the wives, each according to the number of kids and dependants she had. He could not favor or be seen to favor any of them. He had to treat them equally. He had to watch what he said and where he said it. He could not talk about another wife or other wives with one wife. This had proved to be the main cause of breakage of many polygamous marriages.

Before the sudden advent of Christianity in Africa, polygamy was commonly practiced across the continent. It was considered an economic investment and a matter of prestige—a status symbol. If one had a large piece of land and a great number of cattle, it made sense to have a large working pool composed entriely of one's own wives and children. This system worked well and was accepted as an integral part of the people's way of life. With the coming of Christianity, however, things changed. The church condemned the practice of polygamy and declared that those who had more than one wife would not be admitted into the full fellowship of the church—of course with minor differences from one denomination to the other.

If those already married to more than one wife wanted to become Christians, the church demanded, perhaps with few exceptions, that they divorce one or the other of the extra wives. Indeed, certain churches insisted that a man should give up all his wives before he could become a Christian. In present day Africa, however, polygamy is very rare. This is perhaps mainly due to the churches' determined campaign against it. But it is also due to the changed pattern of today's life and the inexorable economic pressures of the modern world.

Whereas in the past children—and many wives—were an economic asset, it no longer is the case in today's individualistic, materialistic and competitive life. In the past one did not have to send kids to school, so there was no fees to pay. Now we all have to pay a great deal of money for children to go to school. We also have to worry about what type of school our children go to. This is determined by how much we can afford by way of fees. At the end of each year fees go up and uniforms get more expensive. Things are a lot more different now!

The African has thus acquired such a taste for the modern ways of life that he would much rather forgo the luxury of a second wife. In this, if in nothing else, the love of money, which the Bible says is the source of all evil, has at least come to the aid of the church. In short, it is a question of the standard of living. Instead of marrying another wife and having more childern, one would much rather work towards raising one's standard of living.

That said, there are those who in spite of these reasons feel they must have a second wife. Such a case may be that of a married couple who haven't had any children after a long period of marriage and where the man may feel tempted to marry a second wife. There may also be the case of a couple who only have girls and the husband feels he must have a boy. Then there could be other reasons that influence a man's thinking with regard to polygamy. This is just stating the facts.

Whatever the reason for a decline in the practice of polygamy—and in view of the reasons that may exist for wanting to marry more than one wife— the question is whether the church is right in condemning it as a matter of principle. *Is the church right? And where does the church derive its authority?*

It is interesting to note that polygamy is nowhere condemned in the Bible. In deed most Old Testament figures, including such great men as David, Solomon, Abraham, Jacob and others, had more than one wife. And Solomon, the most polygamous of them all, is reputed to have had more than seven hundred, not to mention the hundreds of mistresses and concubines he kept. What's more, at least some of these men had direct contact with God and God often commended them for the uprightness of their life. The Bible tells us how before Abram's marriage to his second wife, Hagar, God appreared to him and said, "Get thee out of thy country, and from thy kindred, and from thy father's house, unto a land that I will shew thee and I will make of thee a great nation, and I will bless thee, and make thy name great; and thou shalt be a blessing. And I will bless them that bless thee, and curse him that curseth thee; and in thee shall all the families of the earth be blessed" Genesis 12: 1- 3 (KJV).

And later, when Abram, for want of a child, took Hagar as a wife, and she was forced to leave his house because she could not get any with his first wife, Sarah, the Bible tells us that, "…an angel of the Lord appeared unto her" and after prevailing on her to go back, said, "I will multiply their seed exceedingly, that it shall be numbered for multitude" Genesis 16:10. (KJV).

But if there's still any doubt about God's attitude towards Abram's marriage to Hagar (or polygamy), it should be dispelled by God's appearance to Abram on a later occasion when He said, "I am the Almighty God, walk before me and be thou perfect. And I will make my covenant between me and thee; and will multiply thee exceedingly. And Abram fell on his face, and God talked with him saying, '...as for me, behold my covenant is with thee and thou shalt be a father of many nations. Neither shall thy name any more be called Abram but thy name shall be Abraham; for a father of many nations have I made thee'" Genesis 17: 1 – 5 (KJV).

In all these there was no condemnation; indeed God baptized Abraham, thereby bestowing on him the ultimate seal of His approval. The same could be said of David, Solomon, Jacob and others—how they found favor "in the eyes of the Lord" in spite of their polygamous nature. And if Solomon subsequently fell from grace, it was not because of his polygamy, but because he served "other gods."

The New Testament, on the other hand, says nothing about polygamy. All it says about marriage is more on divorce since that was the question Christ was asked... "Is it lawful for a man to put away his wife?"

Christ answerd thus, "What therefore God hath joined together, let not man put asunder" (Mathew 10:2; 9).

Although Christ, Paul and the apostles spoke out against many of the evils in the society of their time, polygamy was not one of them. Indeed, Paul, in his epistles, acknowledges the fact that there could be church members with more than one wife when he talks of those who could serve as elders. He says they should be members with one wife. Could this not mean that while the Bible is gainst divorce it is not necessarily against polygamy? On what grounds then is the church opposed to it? Is it perhaps simply because polygamy does not conform to the monogamous concept of marriage as practiced in the West? And can that concept be automatically taken as ideal for all societies?

One of the key reasons advanced by the church against polygamy was that complete love was not possible between more than two persons in the sense that Paul envisaged it to be when he said husbands shall love their wives "as Christ loved the church and gave himself up for her." But is such love always possible even in the case of a monogamous marriage? If it is possible then why are there so many divorces in the West, with all the dire consequences for parents and children? Would it be far-fetched to assume that the high incidences of divorce in America and Western Europe are at least partly attributed to the sense of rebellion felt by the husband against the ideas of being tied down forever to one wife—which if he had the alternative of marrying another wife could possibly be averted?

In such circumstances would a married African woman—for it is with her I'm concerned—be acting in her own interest by divorcing her husband for marrying a second wife? Or is the church well advised in continuing to exclude such a husband from its fellowship? Isn't it possible that even if the woman opted for the invisible polygamy of a monogamous marriage, she would still in effect continue to suffer from the fate she is trying to escape?

Perhaps the church should revise its stand on polygamy. It should be more honest, more humane and more "Christian." I'm neither for nor against polygamy on the basis of Christianity because I cannot judge. I believe, though, that Christ will judge polygamists and monogamists with grace. But I'm certain of this—that God will not bar me or anybody else from entering His heavenly kingdom on the basis of being a polygamist. That just won't be His approach!

Still, there are negative aspects of polygamy that it would be a huge disservice not to mention, because they make practicing it untenable today.

First, it is shunned by a section of Christian churches as being unchristian although this may be debatable.

Second, polygamy is economically ruinous. Those who plan to have *wives*, and I speak from over 40 years experience, be warned, you will not manage. You will not have enough food on the table for your big family. Your kids will not get the quality education you may wish them to have. In some cases you may even fail to give them any education at all. At this time when even being monogamous is expensive, you will strain to be able to keep your kids off the dustbins. Your kids will turn out to be diggers of graves and choppers of wood for fuel in the village. If they venture out of the village, they will be the pickers of tea and coffee and cleaners of toilets. They will not have acquired any education because of your inability to give it to them. They will curse the day they were born!

A polygamist is an irrational, unreasonable and intolerant guy. He will kick out a wife simply on suspicion. He cannot tolerate immorality on the part of his wife yet it is that immorality on his part that made the woman his wife in the first place. Need I say more? I think you get the picture. Run away from this practice!

The extended family is not an alien concept to an African. It is a concept practiced and observed since time immemorial. It is based on the fact that all children belong to the community. When it comes to discipline, upbringing and a roof over the head, an African child belongs, first and foremost, to the parents and close relatives and then to the community. It is based on the notion that the child's primary responsibility, when grown up, would be to the parents. It is parents, siblings, then the community. So when a brother helps his brother's children, he is morally obliged to do so. When he is doing a Project for the community he is paying back the moral support he got from the community while growing. This is the bedrock of an African family. Those who were not able had their children helped to achieve success by their brothers, uncles or other relatives. Talk about magnanimity and order!

It was this extended family concept that I inherited when I was still at the law school. It shaped what I would be and the kind of life I would live in future and helped me take care of the twenty seven plus folks I inherited. God gave me a 15-point plan which included getting assistance, helpers and aides. This took me along the path of polygamy, though I was monogamous by nature.

"But why did you elect to go polygamous, couldn't you have gotten helpers, assistants, and aides who were not your wives?" someone may ask.

Yes I could have, but those were not the only reasons I became a polygamist. I had ten reasons which pushed me into polygamy:

Unbearable marital problems
I had been pushed into a corner and had decided to walk away from my first marriage. Had it not been for the catastrophies which befell the family and the intervention of friends and relatives, this would have become a reality.

The accident of 1971, where my brother perished along with his wife, child and our daughter, drove home my own posterity worries
I was determined to have as many kids as I could, just like it was with our fathers and forefathers so that should a catastrophy strike, I would have survivors to count on. How right I was. A tragedy would befall my first wife's family where we would lose all our sons, after my wife was past *birthing* age. If I had not married again I would have been without a descendant. We lost our sons in 1982, 1994 and 1997. The first and last we lost through natural causes and the middle one we lost through vehicular accident. That would have been the end of my family—as our lineage is patrilineal.

Nature hates a vacuum
Nyasondu did not leave just physical space in my life when she ran away from time to time—and when due to circumstances beyond her control she would not join me fast enough as I was in Kisumu—she also left space in my heart. Space that had to be filled if I had to survive and see my future plans take root. Had she stuck with me and worked to retain her rightful place in my heart, had she ceased attempts to bring down my intellect to her level instead of raising hers, things, perhaps, may have been different. I wanted to run, she insisted we crawl. I had to resist. Nyairo occupied the space left by Nyasondu, and Nyamwalo got the space left when Nyairo was at the university. All of them got space because of my dislike of bastardizing children. I hated the idea of my children being taken by someone else. I wanted all my children, whether born in or out of wedlock, to be with me.

Looking for my rib
Jacob, of the biblical times, worked for Rachel for 7 years, but was cheated into marrying Leah, not out of love, but out of the observance of Laban's customs. Jacob had to serve another 7 years to get Rachel. That was his

rib—the one he loved and sacrificed 14 of his prime years to get. Sarah was Abraham's rib. David went round looking for his rib. He probably didn't find her until he saw Uriah's wife. Solomon was born out of Uriah's wife and David's union. Perhaps Nyasondu was not my rib and I went out and got Nyairo. And perhaps she too was not my complete rib and I got Nyamwalo. Perhaps Nyamwalo was not a complete rib too. Later Nyasondu regained a space, Nyairo and Nyamwalo both retain their spaces. There is no room for any other, unless one of them vacated. If any one of them left, the rib would not be complete. But it is too late in the day for any last minute desertions. So they will be in my heart to stay until God do us part.

I wanted a helper and a friend

I did not just want a wife; I needed one who was also a friend. A friend in need is a friend in deed. I needed one who could provide, not a sucker—one who had the heart to accept and embrace the many dependants I had and provide for them. I wanted a friend who could protect me through thick and thin; a friend who could put her life on the line for my family and I.

I needed a wife who could trust and be trusted

If your best friend, helper and assistant cannot trust you she ceases to be your wife and turns into an enemy. A wife should not only be trusted, but should trust her husband too. I needed a wife I could entrust with school fees for the children; one I could trust to collect rent from tenants and account for it; one that would not run down a successful business; one who would take good care of our property and maintain discipline among the kids. Was that too much to ask for?

I needed a wife with a strong character whose mind could not be swayed like a pendulum

If a wife has a mind that can be manipulated by anybody she is not worth being a wife. She becomes dangerous and lethal. She can kill without knowing. She can leave her husband on faulty grounds. She is usually the talk of the village. She would be mocked by other women without her knowing and sneered at once she turns her back. I needed someone who knew children were a gift from God and should be nursed, brought up in Christianity and educated, not one that laid her hands on the children's school fees. Not one that could not provide for the children even when she was capable of doing so. Not one that could not prepare food for her family when she was the mother of the house. A wife who knew what to say and where to say it. A strong-willed woman. That was the woman I needed!

I needed someone smart, fearless and less talkative

A smart woman is an asset in the family. The children would emulate her smartness and try to perfect it. She goes about doing her things with less pomp. She retains a natural defense mechanism against the manipulative tactics of malicious women and men who may wish to derail her marriage. She can think on her feet and be ready to confront situations as they arise. God did not give us two ears and one mouth for nothing. He expected us to listen more than we talked. A good listener makes a good instructor, and the children would definitely benefit from her wisdom. I also needed a team-player, not a lone ranger who pulled sharply left when every member of the family pulled right. To sum it up, I needed someone who did not shy away from her parental responsibilities.

I needed a wife who could talk about issues, not people

Simple minds discuss people, great minds discuss issues. I couldn't agree more. When every discussion in the home is about people, over time you run out of people to discuss. If you have discussed everybody in the home, village, work place, school and church, you soon find out you have nobody left to discuss and start the same people over again. I hate discussing people because it adds nothing to my knowledge. I like discussing issues. With issues you will never run out of what to discuss because issues regenerate. If you discussed politics today, there will still be politics to discuss the following day.

I wanted to discuss things affecting our family, how we could provide for them; things that affected our relationship with the church and the community. I wanted a wife who engaged me in discussing topical issues, not one that engaged me in cold pettiness. Is it any wonder I resisted most of such women?

I wanted to preempt the possibility of not having patrineal descendants

According to the culture of my people, failing to have patrilineal descendants was a failure to have descendants at all. Ancestry is determined through the male off-spring. So if one had no son it would be the end his family. This was true even if one had daughters with kids, some of who were sons. It was one's own sons that counted. Guys with wives who could not bear sons were compelled to take other wives to try and get a son.

In my case, when I took a second wife, I already had two sons by my first marriage, so looking for a son did not arise. But through a sixth sense or premonition, the possibility of losing my two sons crossed my mind. This was because I saw what befell my brother James. I thus made up my mind to have another wife in the hope that she would give me sons.

These points influenced my decision to go polygon. I have no regrets about that decision because it gave me a lifeline.

A polygamist had to have a very large homestead where his wives' and sons' houses could be built. There was to be space for his special cottage and pens for goats, sheep and calves. He had to make provision for *kul* (Kraal), where his many cattle could be kept. The first wife's house had to be built at the extreme end of the home from the gate. As you faced the gate, the second wife's house had to be on the right and the third wife's on the left. Their houses had to alternate in that order until all the wives were accommodated.

The boys had to build their cottages left or right of the home, depending on seniority. The first born built his *simba* (son's house) on the right as you faced the gate. All the first born sons of all the wives built on that side. Their followers built on the left side. They had to alternate that way until all the boys were accomodated. If a grandson wanted to build a *simba* in his grandfather's homestead, he had to build it along his grandmother's house. Daughters were not allowed to build in their father's homestead; only sons did. The owner of the home had his cottage built right in the centre of the homestead, and within the sight of *duol* (pen for sheep, goats and calves, where fire burned perpetually). When and where to build was strictly monitored by *wazee* (elders). For instant, a younger son cold not build a *simba* before his senior brother—and building co-wives houses had to observe seniority.

There were no cemeteries within the homestead, but there were rules to be followed in burials. If the owner of the home died, he had to be buried on the right side of his first wife's house as you faced the gate. All the wives had to be buried on the left side of their houses as you faced the gate. Sons were buried in front of their mother's house.

Prior to this era, when houses were merely temporary structures, when the owner of the home died he was buried right inside his wife's house. If he had more than one wife, he was buried inside the first wife's house.

When a member of the household died outside the homestead, his body was not to be brought into the homestead through the gate. The fence—away from the gate, or alongside the gate, depending on where his house was—had to be breached to creat space for the body to pass. This was a noble idea by our ancestors, but it is today abused by those who don't understand its origin and purpose.

Around the time this practice started, people still walked naked. The system of building houses, where sons built houses towards the gate and parents away from the gate area, was in effect because the vast ground in front of Grandpa's house was where grandchildren played, supervised by their parents. One was likely to find the wives of his sons around that area. For this reason, if a parent died he or she could not be brought into the homestead through the gate. His/her children and grandchildren couldn't see him/her naked even in death. It was a taboo. To avoid this, the fence was opened at the rear of the home to let the body in. A cockerel was killed and roasted on a fire made at the point the fence was opened (*mbuga*) and eaten by those who breached the fence and those who carried the body through it. Other than to prevent exposure of the deceased's nakedness, *mbuga* served no other purpose. But note that if it was a son who died outside the homestead *mbuga* was still opened behind his mother's house, where the body would stay, awaiting burial.

A polygamist had a cottage in his homestead where he lived alone, and his wives had separate houses where they lived. When he fell sick and realized he would not survive, he called his wives and all his children to talk to them and let them know his wishes. He told them what to do and what not to do—and which cattle to be inherited by whom. He distributed his wealth to his children. Each wife already knew her piece of land. But children eventually automatically inherited their mother's land. And the homestead, when finally vacated by senior sons, had to be inherited by the last son of the wife who was present when the home was built. If on the other hand the homestead was built when all the wives were present, the homestead belonged to all of them and the last of the last sons inherited the homestead.

After *Mzee* had made his wishes known, he would be moved to his first wife's house, where he was supposed to die. The first wife would be the first to scream—*goyo nduru* (wail aloud) to alert the other people of the death of the old man. If the first wife was not physically present when the old man died, *goyo nduru* would wait till she came back. Other wives would only wail but not *goyo nduru*.

The day following the burial, people of all walks of life, young and old, would gather in the morning at the bereaved home armed with spears, *rungus*, *kwodi* (shields) and any other item of war ready for *tero buru* (driving away evil spirits). They would be in battle gear and battle mode. Some would paint themselves black, red or white with ash—*ochre*. Others would carry twigs and tree branches. They would then set off singing and running out of the homestead as if chasing something. They would do the running and the singing until they arrived at a water point where they would smear themselves with more mud. They would then return home.

As they approached, people would give way in order not to be trampled on. Others would literally be forced out of the way by the sheer numbers and war-like behaviour. They had not been known to beat up people on their way, but had been reported to have trampled on people who did not get out of their way.

On reaching the bereaved home, they would simply disperse. This they did to chase away the evil spirits which they believed had caused the death of the old man. They believed the spirits lingered on after the burial of the body and had to be chased away. It was also intended to cleanse the home and the surviving inhabitants. This ceremony was never performed for a deceased woman or a deceased young person; it was strictly for elders, particularly heads of household.

In the evening of the day of the burial, elders prepared firewood with which they lit fire locally, known as *magenga,* in front of his wife's or in his first wife's house, if he was a polygamist. A cock was slaughtered and roasted on the fire and eaten with *ugali* prepared by older women. Children and women were forbidden to eat this food.

These practices and ceremonies are dying out as people embrace Christianity in Africa. In non-christian and atheistic communities, however, they are still practiced and are not about to disappear. When a person died in the water, he or she was to be buried on land abutting the water, near the place his body was found. A suicide victim's body, however, was buried outside the homestead whether he or she died in or outside the homestead. This was also the case with the body of a daughter who as a result of estrangement or any other cause left her husband and died, but the husband refused to take the body for burial.

Someone might have died in war in circumstances that make it impossible to retrieve the body. The person might have drowned in water and the body is eaten up by sea creatures. In the part of the country I came from, when a deceased body could not be traced, they dug a grave just as if the body was there. They performed all the burial rites including those that are to be done by the first wife if the deceased was a polygamist. In place of the body, the fruit of *yago* (an African tree with oblong fruit like pumpkins) would be lowered into the grave and buried just as if it was the body of the deceased. All other funeral rites, formalities and ceremonies would be performed, including *tero buru,* if the deceased was a male elder. In other situations, including where the deceased body could not be physically retrieved, for example the case of somebody dying in a fire, the ash would be collected and buried as if it was the actual body of the deceased.

In the part of the country where I come from, a person was more respected in death than in life. This came about as a result of the belief that only the body died but the spirit lingered around, watching over people. They believed that unless the body was given a decent burial, the spirit would return to haunt the relatives by bringing misfortunes or even death in the family. They also believed that the body of a married daughter being buried in her parents' home brought misfortunes to the other daughters in the homestead who had not been married. They could fail to get husbands. These fears came to pass because when prospective suitors heard about it, they gave girls from that homestead a wide berth. Christianity and modernity have changed these.

By 1978 I had decided to put up my own home. During that time Nyasondu and I were not staying together. We lived separately and nobody cared what the other was doing. I was the last born in our family. My brothers never put up homes. Traditionally, I could not build my home when my older brothers hadn't. Secondly, my first wife was away. It was a taboo which could not be circumvented. If I built my home in her absence, I would lock her and all her kids out. So I had to consult widely before making a final move. I loved my kids and didn't want to alienate them.

On consultation, I started with my sisters Pelesia Aduda Awinja and Lewnida Choka Abayo. At that time only the three of us were believed to be alive—nobody really knew what had happened to my brother Haggai Okech in Tanzania.

I later consulted elders, church leaders; anybody I thought could have helpful knowledge or advice. My father was not left out either. He could not let me do something that could jeopardize my prosperity. I was his only son of substance and he attached a lot of importance to the success of this project, so he too consulted widely. That I had to build a home was not debatable, though. How to do it in a safe manner was what everybody was consulting about.

Pelesia Duda Awinja—popularly known as Pelly—was born around 1932, according to her calculations. She never went beyond primary school. She was married to John Awinja Adede, who was the son of a headman, Adede Okwaro, from Kalanyo. She married in 1949. Her husband paid handsomely for her and the cattle received was used by Absalom as dowry for his wife, Abiba.

Pelly was blessed with many kids, but most of them died, leaving Peres Abaja, who later married Mr. Okelele, a son-in-law and a friend who helped me educate my kids and dependants. They were blessed with smart kids and grand kids. She later died when she joined a church which forbade taking the sick to the hospital for treatment. My sister had another daughter, Akinyi, who also married and had children and grand children. She had two sons, Fredrick Onyalo and Loice Omol. Onyalo and George Diemo were among the first dependants. Mr. Okelele helped me get a good secondary school. He got married and was blessed with kids after completing high school. I secured a job for him with Siaya County Council, where he worked for the rest of his life. Omol did not do very well in school but proved to be a good businessman until he got mental breakdown, which inhibited him for the rest of his life.

For a long time Pelly's husband, John, worked in Jinja, Uganda, as a cobbler. One day, when I was still young, he arranged for me to visit him. As this would be my first bus ride to Jinja, I looked forward with eagerness. I made it safely to Jinja and on my return he did a little shopping for my sister, which I carried a long for her. At my sister's house, I stayed one week. There was a soccer ball which was in her house which I really wanted to take home with me. It was the first rubber ball I was seeing and was smaller—just the right size for my small legs. I begged my sister to let me have it and she agreed. But when I went to collect the ball from the bedroom, where it was kept, I found it punctured. I was so annoyed and disappointed. I cried for so long that my sister got worried. Regardless, I left for home.

A day later I got so sick I had to be taken for treatment at Malanga Dispensary. My nose was blocked. I couldn't breathe well. And when I tried to sneeze nothing came out. But when I was recuperating, I sat in the yard in front Mama's house with her. I felt a sudden strong urge to blow my nose. Previous attempts of that nature had produced no mucus, but that morning a big chunk of mucus came out of my right nose and with it a live beetle. My mother and I were surprised. *A live beetle?* Had I been bewitched? When it landed on the ground my mother looked at it closely, thinking it was dead, but a second later it shook off the mucus and crawled away in our view. A few minutes later it flew away.

Pelly later lost her husband. She too fell sick and with no one to take care of her, her condition deterioriatated fast. When Lewnida went to see her she was half dead. Her house had not been cleaned for ages. Jiggers were all over her body and she had not had a bath because there was nobody to bathe her—and she had not eaten for a week! Lewnida informed me about this and I arranged to take her to the hospital. I had to do it. It was payback time—this was the sister who had shared her food with me when I was on the rocks, when I had no one to turn to. She turned around my life and I lived to talk about it. I had to be there for her on her death bed.

I took her to the hospital, where she received treatment and got well. For the next two years she stayed with me at my Siaya home, under the care of Nyasondu. This sickness left her incontinent, though. She lost her ability to control the bladder and the bowel. She had to be kept on diapers and taught how to walk again. She ate well but the more she ate the more came out in human waste. Eventually she got well except for her mental retardation.

Everyday, in the morning before she went for work, Nyasondu, assisted by our daughter Violet, bathed, groomed and washed her soiled linen. The maids and I helped in feeding, cleaning and grooming her during the day. Nyasondu could not take that anymore and she called it quits. I tried to plead with her not to abandon me with the patient, but she insisted she had to go.

And she did.

Later, when I had to travel to the States, I left my sister in the hands of Nyairo, in Gem. This would be the last time I saw her alive. Perhaps if I had been home she would not have died. At the time of her death she was seventy one years old. Not bad, but she was still stronger even in sickness and I believed with better care and good food she would have lived to be ninety.

My sister Lewnida is said to have been born in 1938. She was named after my father's sister, Rosebela Choka, who was herself named after a great famine (*Keej Choka*) which ravaged our area in the early part of the twentieth century. Her highest educational attainment was class five, in Sawagongo. She shared with my mother the credit for bringing me up. While my mother brought me into this world, suckled me and took good care of me in infancy, Lewnida took over from the moment she carried me to school until she went to Sawagongo. She loved me and nursed me like a baby. I also loved her so much—there was nothing I could do without consulting her.

In 1955 she got married to Wilson Abayo Ochieng. They were blessed with three children: Esther, Samuel and Peres. She later got grandchildren and great grand children. She took a prominent role in the reconstruction work. Dunga lived with her at some point and her advice and encouragement was extremely helpful to me. Pelly and her were the first that I ran to for advice on how I could put up my own home. Both had built their homes so they knew a thing or two about this matter.

*

From Pelly and Lewnida I learnt that I could not build a home in the absence of Nyasondu. But on building before my brothers, they advised that there was no real prohibition. As long as my father had built a home, I could not be held back by my brothers' inability to build homes. I was disappointed and encouraged by the advice. Disappointed because I was inclined to build, Nyasondu's absence notwithstanding, but they were now urging me not to unless she was present. Encouraged because they had assured me that my brothers' inability could not impede my progress. To me, making a home was the first step to progress and prosperity. They also advised that there were two ways I could go about making a home—traditional or modern (Christian way). They told me I could choose either, but not both. They, however, strongly urged that given the circumstances under which I was going to operate, it would be better to go the Christian way. I obliged.

But there were issues. Let me explain. As a traditionalist if one wanted to build a home he had to have an axe and a cock. Nobody, except the builder and his father, had to know the site where the new home would be erected. A cock would be sent to the site on the eve of building and left tied their overnight. If something ate or killed it that would not be the right place to build. The suitability of the site was determined by the survival of the cock. Very early in the morning, before sunrise, the builder, his father or in his absence any of his uncles who had himself built a home, and the builder's son carrying an axe, would walk to the site and if they did not find the cock or found it dead the whole operation would be called off and new arrangements made. If the cock was found alive work would commence.

If the builder's son was a teenager or an adult, weather married or not, things would be a lot tougher than when the eldest son was still young. He would put up a small structure/house where he and his son would stay for the night, making sure that the son didn't fall asleep—and that he vacated the structure by cock crow. This would continue for four nights. His mother would come and spend the night on the fifth day, during which the son would go and look for a place to sleep. Father and Mother would take four days from the fifth day, building a bigger house where the family would move into. Once the family was in the new home, the eldest son would then build his own *simba*, followed by his followers in a descending order.

If the first born was a minor, the builder would move into the new structure with his wife and the kids on the same night. The rest of the steps would be the same. But if the builder was a polygamist, the first son of the first wife was the one used when building. The rest of the steps would be the same, except the houses for the other wives would be built one after another in a descending order until all the wives had houses.

Simply stated, it was hectic!

When building a home the Christian way, however, things are a lot more relaxed. Traditional rules are suspended. One only needs a pastor, workers and his family. No axes, no cocks and no temporary structures. One just goes straight to the real thing—the home!

I opted for the Christian, but I still had a snag. Nyasondu was away. I told my brothers, cousins and uncles, including my father, that I was going to build a home in her absence. Everybody I talked to did not like the idea. My cousins, Wilfred Indakwa, Michael Meso and Nelson Juma took it upon themselves to look for Nyasondu and bring her home. I didn't know what they told her, but eventually she yielded and returned home. Since she did not know why I wanted her home so badly, and how I was to go about doing it, she started bringing in taboos and traditions. I resisted and gave her an ultimatum. She either had to do it my way or she had to opt out and go back to wherever she came from. She toned down and agreed to do it my way.

On the twelfth day of December 1978, Pastor Azaria Ombura took me to the place where my new home would be built and blessed the place. Given the controversy which had proceeded this day, I invited all the elders in the village to be in attendance so that if any of them saw us do anything unbecoming he had to tell me right there and then or else forever shut up. The pastor, the church elder, elders from the village, my parents and my entire family, except our little daughter Betty who had been admitted in a hospital with meningitis, were present. The pastor led the prayers and groundbreaking and work started. I was building three houses at the same time. I had a team of *fundis* (builders), one for each house. They were houses with corrugated iron sheet roofing. The following day we embark on the fourth house, which would accommodate the kids and serve as the kitchen. We went on to fence the home and provided a temporary gate.

And finally the stage was set. In 1990 I demolished the structures in the home, except two toilets, and started building modern houses in their place. I'm grateful to God for having made provision for me to start and continue building these houses. As He continued to provide, we managed to complete them. My sons later built their cottages in the homestead, following a descending order.

From an African perspective there is an element of prestige in having a home. One attracts instant respect because this is the point where one crosses the line into adulthood. In modern times, having a home gives one an opportunity to own property—livestock, chicken, and even trees. One gets a chance to plan his home in the way he deems fit. It is also where one can eat a rump of chicken which is served only to the head of the household.

I crossed that line and became an elder, with peace prevailing in my home, where close to thirty persons lived. I became a role model to many. Among my peers, I was the first to have a homestead. This was one among the many firsts I scored. My polygamy was admired by many for its tranquility and unity. My children carried themselves around as if they were all products of a single mother. The children carried this unity into adulthood and I believed if maintained it will be the foundation upon which their prosperity will be anchored.

CHAPTER 17

DISASTERS

Mzee Barnabus Oigo Miser, my father-in-law who had been ailing at the New Nyanza General Hospital, passed on. His death came as a big shock to his family. They had never handled a big funeral before. Their disadvantage was that they were many. *Oyieyo Mathoth ok Kuny nga Bur*—too many rats can't dig a hole. In the midst of their confusion, I stepped in to make funeral arrangements. I arranged for the coffin, paid the bills and provided transport for the body to Nyakach. The family was left with only food, which they provided in abundance. But apparently my efforts were not appreciated by a section of the family—going by the scanty attention shown to my team. I didn't know why. If you are asking how we knew that, let me explain. I'd thought that if I did what I'd done these folks would take care of responsibilities like building the grave and ensuring everyone who attended the funeral ate. But this was not to be for my team. And since I was at the peak of popularity in my village, when news of my father-in-law's death reached home, everyone wanted to attend the burial. So on burial day, because of the number of folks who wished to come, my nephew, John Okeyo Muger, the only son of the village, apart from I, with a car, helped ferry the people to Nyakach.

And this is where things would start to go wrong. You see, at the burial of a father or mother-in-law, sons-in-law who helped in taking care of funeral expenses were special guests—the guy and his team were given full attention. He was served the best food and was provided the most comfortable place to sit. Traditionally, they are not even supposed to see the corpse or the grave, so they were kept away from it. Now, at my father-in-law's burial there was a special *siwandha* (sitting structure) prepared for the three of us. If my brother James had been alive, we would have been the four of us—I mean sons-in-law. This is because there was Enos Obunga, Janet's husband, who was our seniour, Justo Omolo, Risper's husband, and then I. There were other girls in the home, but all of them were still young—not married. Since James was survived by a child, however, his position among in-laws had to be recognized. But the in-laws, in their confusion, did not appreciate James. They did not even appreciate my presence, leave alone my efforts. It was amazing!

To make matters worse, on burial day only Justo Omolo and I attended. We sat in the same *siwandha* with our teams. But whereas the in-laws were fully prepared for Justo and his team, they were not prepared for us at all. Sharing this same *siwandha* would prove to be our embarrassment. Justo and his team were served tea with bread and plenty of *mandazis*. In fact, they had so much that they could not eat even a quarter of what was served. There we were—yawning, visibly hungry and following how many times they picked mandazis and bread by the corner of our eyes. On their part, Justo's team took tea in a manner that suggested they were mocking us. We ended up being served no tea at all. But we calmed down and tolerated the mockery.

It turned out to be just the beginning!

The bite of the embarrassment came when lunch was served. The servers came and arranged our tables. Others arranged Justo's table. They started bringing food in big bowls and placed them on our tables, as well as Justo's. Fried beef, fried mutton, fish stew, beef stew, tripes, and even vegetables. There was also *ugali*, *chapati* and rice. But just as we were about to be ushered to the table, a fat woman, wearing a serious face as if she had had a fight with her husband, came and removed food from our table and placed the whole lot on Justo's table. No apology, "no *pole*," nothing. Without talking to anybody, and in that serious mood, she just proceeded to remove food from our table and went away. When Justo's team started eating, Justo said to me, "*Sange, sudi mondo wachiem*—Brother, come let us eat!

I cringed, but kept quiet.

"Sange, karibu!"

I did not respond. Why couldn't he realize I had a right, in fact double right, to be served food in the home just as he had. To invite me to eat with him, food that had been removed from my table, was an insult. But I kept my cool. My people, though, were beginning to read from a different script. What they were watching was hatred and an orchestrated scheme to humiliate my wife and embarrass us—a scheme they succeeded in implementing. We later realized my wife was not in control of the happenings; things were done without her knowledge. But eventually we ate remnants of the food and even had tea served. We vowed that should any big funeral occur at that home again, we would carry everything to enable us prepare our own food. We learned a lesson we would never forget.

We went home.

Later I asked my wife what the problem was. She explained that it was agreed that sons-in-law's food be prepared at one spot and distributed to the guests. She was assigned to make food for other guests and those who were supposed to serve us hatched that scheme to humiliate her. She was very sorry and apologetic and promised never to allow such a thing to happen again. I never noticed such neglect again as I attended other funerals there. It was after attending this funeral that my brother Okech traveled back to Tanzania.

After losing my father-in-law, we never experienced any immediate death of in-laws. My mother-in-law, Martha, was still strong and healthy when her husband died. With her older children, William, Thadayo and Nyasondu all working, she did not feel the burden which other widows felt after the death of a husband. She lived twelve more years before she died. She started ailing five years before her death. Her problem was her back, which got worse as it defied treatment. Coupled with other old age illnesses, she succumbed to death on the 21st December 1996. But since the burial was done in a hurry, I attended the funeral later, with my family, and we spent the night singing. During that time, our kids were many and old enough—Lydia and Kenneth were oversees. Betty,

Florence, Bernard and Kazee were dead. The kids entertained us with Christian songs through the night.

A few years later, we lost Nyairo's father, Francis Musando. Nyairo and I took full responsibility of funeral expenses and laid Mzee to rest in peace. Those who refuse to give their daughters quality education because they will be married are naïve and myopic. If it were not for Nyairo, there would have been no funeral to write about. We took charge and everything went as planned.

Nyairo's mother, Eba Adhaya, was a polite and humble mother. She loved her children dearly, especially Nyairo. One time, when Jack was down with Meningitis, she offered to stay with him in the hospital. She attended all weddings—those of her granddaughter Evelyn and her grandsons Erick, Jack and James. Whenever she attended such weddings she had something unique and of sentimental value as a gift to present. Nobody knew she was ailing. Then in 2008 she fell ill while I was in the USA and there was a delay in taking her to a good hospital for diagnosis and treatment. When she eventually made it to a good hospital, it was too late. She died as suddenly as people learned about her sickness. Again, Nyairo took charge, and with assistance from her grandchildren in the USA, Lydia and Anthony, she was able to ride at the crest of the wave. I later attended the funeral when I returned from the USA. When I attended the funeral, it was not only the funeral of my mother-in-law I had to attend, but that of her two co-wives who died while I was away.

The last of the co-wives, popularly known as Nyalang'o, fell sick while I was home. Like my mother-in-law, her ailment was not attended to in good time. When she finally reached the hospital it was too late; she died a day later in the hospital. Immediately she died I was called and told to go and organize how her body should be transported back home. On arrival we realized that since she had died only a few hours earlier her body had not stiffened. I discarded tradition and put the body on a sitting position on the front passenger seat of my car and drove her body home. After two days we buried the body with three quarters of the funeral expenses borne by us.

Wuoyi siro—a boy is a pillar. That is what the sages say, but there are some pillars which do not support anything. They are as useless as a reed erected to support a roof. A girl is a pearl; educate her as you never know where your luck will come from. Nyairo was educated by her parents and was unshakable in her resolve to help them and her brothers and sisters. Like me, and with my assistance, she was there for them until the end. Her step-brothers, step-sisters, nephews and nieces who saw the inside of a classroom did so through her financial and other assistance. In most cases she took and lived with them while they went to school.

———

I had gone to court in Bondo when at around 10.00 a.m. I received a call from Rose that my step-brother, Eliud Gordon Ondunga, had died along the Turkwell-Kapenguria Road. The circumstances surrounding his death were scanty at the time. I sought court permission and drove home to find out more and make arrangement for bringing the body home. I passed through Siaya to alert people in my office and to track my *matatu* because we were going to need it to ferry the body. I also passed by my Gem home on my way to Kisumu because I had decided to fetch the coffin, then proceed to the Kapenguria mortuary, where the body lay.

As I arrived home the details of his death started filtering in. I was told he had gotten a job as a turnboy hardly a week earlier and was on his first assignment to help ferry cement to Turkwell Gorge, where a dam was being constructed. They delivered the cement, but as they were going back to Mombasa the driver stopped the lorry at a certain market to buy cigarettes. He left the engine running. Eliud, who was his turn boy and was left in the driver's cabin, got into the driver's seat and started driving the Lorry. He had never driven before. His driving knowledge was restricted to watching the driver drive. As the lorry gained momentum down a slope, he had absolutely no idea how to stop it. He panicked and left the vehicle to hurtle downhill. With the passengers in the lorry screaming, I was told the vehicle plunged one hundred feet into the gorge and all passengers, including Eliud, died.

At four o'clock in the morning we set off for Kapenguria. On the way we stopped to see the owner of the lorry. He was a businessman in Kitale. I went into his office with my two cousins. The guy had a large table in front of him—full of money. I had never seen that much money just left lying on the table. Some more were still coming in. He never showed us any sympathy when we told him we had come for the body, instead of saying *pole* to us, he loudly lamented that he did not know how he was going to replace the lorry. We were not surprised because if I were in his shoes, I would feel the same. His driver allowed an unlicensed person to drive the lorry. No insurance company would pay for the lorry. He probably already knew that we were relatives of the guy who caused the accident.

He was right and had every reason not to talk to us. I would do exactly the same if I were him. We, however, proceeded to Kapenguria to collect the body. The mortuary was a small building with a morgue big enough to accomodate five bodies. As there were over ten people who died in that lorry alone, most of the bodies were on the floor. Some had been on the floor for months and the elements had consumed the flesh. Only bones and a heap of ash (dust) were left. When we heard about the accident a day earlier we were told it had happened three weeks earlier and was reported in the local dailies. When we checked the particular daily we got the report but his name was written in a manner that could not make us know it was him. So we were looking for a body that had stayed in the mortuary for three weeks. My cousins Ananaia, Jack Ogero and I entered the mortuary first and what we saw was chilling. All the bodies on the freezer and on the floor had decomposed beyond recognition. We realized his mother could not take this and decided to ask her not to get in. The search for the body was not going to be easy. We had absolutely no clue which among the bodies was that of Eliud. All the bodies were unrecognizable. What were we going to do? We decided on features he had that could enable us to identify him. Someone said he was hairy, but we found three or four of them hairy. Someone floated a brilliant idea—why not look for someone not circumcised? He was certain Eliud was not circumcised. The reason for coming to that conclusion was that people who lived in the area where the accident had happened were circumcised. After a check, the only one whose anatomy looked like it had not been through the process was the one we settled on. He was hairy too. This body was terrible. The head was so big that we feared it may bust any time. The eyes had been gorged out by maggots. The lips had been eaten up by the same maggots or their cousins. The body, like the head, was so swollen that clothes had to be cut free from it.

But the hard part was yet to come. The body looked bigger than the coffin. A normal adult would have fitted in it without any problem, but this was a decomposed body swollen to twice its normal size. The clothes we carried to dress him were too small. We persuaded the attendants to see what they could do to get the body into the coffin. They brought some medicine and sprinkled onto the body, but this did not help except to make our eyes teary. After they had removed patches of clothing still stuck on the body, we helped them lift the body and put it into the coffin. They literally squeezed it in but the lid couldn't close. They brought a hammer and with four of us standing on top of the lid to squeeze the body into position, they nailed the lid to the coffin. After thanking them we set off for Gem. The stench emanating from the mortuary could be felt a kilometer away.

We arrived home after the grave had been dug and immediately half-buried the body to await official burial the following day. To my surprise one of my step-sisters was heard wailing that I killed him. This didn't bother me because I didn't. As far as I was concerned he died as a result of motor vehicle accident five hundred miles away from where I was at the time. I could not have been involved in killing him. All indications were that he had died as a result of his own misadventure, his own actions for which he could not blame anybody.

The following day we buried his body. But to this day I cannot swear an oath that the body we buried, which we brought from Kapenguria, was that of my step-brother Eliud Gordon Ondunga.

―――

We lost our daughter Betty in the tragic accident of 1971. I had several accidents between then and 1982, but none involved our kids. In 1980, however, my late brother Absalom lost his son Otieno in Nairobi, not from accident but from illness. Otieno, along with his seniour brother Ogeya and Omondi together with his sister Loice and Achienge, stayed with their mother in Ziwani, Nairobi. A neighbour overheard their plan to bury Otieno in Nairobi and conveyed the information to me. That day we had a special visitor at our home. Nyagot had come to visit us. She was a secretary at the Siaya County

Council offices and a family friend. Immediately she told me what was going on, I left for Nairobi. I did not want to waste time because I feared I might find the body already buried. I arrived in Nairobi the same day. What a relief it was to the neighbours. Each of them was opposed to the idea of burying Otieno at Lang'ata. Only Silvia Ogeya and her brother Odero were for Lang'ata. Omondi and his uncle, Henry Ouma, the little girls and the neighbours were for home burial.

The situation was tense because both sides wanted to go physical. I had to use a lot of diplomacy to cool things down. Sylvia, in particular, was very fiery. She did not want to hear anything to do with Kawanyanga; she was all the time plotting and inciting those on her side to violence. Sometimes fire, when used wisely, can put out a burning fire. I decided to try that option. I went to Mama Pamela Mbolo and Mama Julie Ogwel whom I knew had between them enough firepower to neutralize Sylvia. Pamela was huge and had a strong personality. She was what would be called obese. Julie, on the other hand, was of Sylvia's size but younger. Both had sharp tongues. During the meeting, the duo did not allow Sylvia to manipulate matters. They shut her up and even threatened to beat her up. They reminded her how lucky she was to have a brother-in-law travel all the way from home to come and collect the body of his nephew at his expense. With Sylvia contained, her supporters were roped in too.

That night and the following two nights we were able to raise enough money to pay all expenses, including transport costs for the body. After three days, we were ready for the trip home

We had three vehicles in the convoy. The *matatu* carried the body, all family members and neighbours who wished to travel with the body. Pamela Mbolo's Peugeot Estate carried other people. My car, with a capacity of four, carried the rest. As Sylvia's house had collapsed, we pitched a tent for her for the duration of the funeral. In her mind she thought she was coming to a home she last saw twelve years earlier. She could not believe her eyes when she saw how the home had developed. It was a modern home with a barbed wire fence—with clean environment. She was stunned and was heard saying, *"Mabe en Kawanyanga adier*—Is this really Kawanyanga?"

We buried the body and most of the people who escorted the body returned to Nairobi in the matatu. Sylvia and her kids remained and traveled later. One of the neighbours who accompanied the body sought me out. He thanked and commended me for my insistence that the body be brought home for burial and also for the respectful manner I and my family treated them during the funeral. He said he had learnt a lesson on humility and meekness, which he would never forget in his life. He urged me to continue looking after my brother's house with the same spirit and that if I did, God would reward me abundantly.

Our son, Barnabas Oigo Miser (popularly known as Kazee), was born in 1975 in Kisumu. He was Nyasondu's sixth child, but third son. At birth and even during his infancy he was quite healthy. He was born big like his maternal uncles and had three quarters their features. His mother moved with him to Maseno when he was only five years old.

One day the mother came home to attend my victory party. As chairman of Siaya County Council, I had won a midterm election against a perennial opponent. It was an election I knew I would fight hard to win. I had a majority of the councillors on my side, but councilors, like any human beings, were easily swayed with money and my opponent was not in short supply of the stuff. I knew I had to device a winning strategy. The plan comprised of making public a rendezvous where all other councillors would converge the night prior to elections. We planned to use the leaked announcement as a ruse to mislead my opponents into believing that they would come and buy out our councillors at our hideout. Not even my supporters knew the planned venue was just a ruse. At the eleventh hour, I sent out two cars to collect my supporters with instruction to drive them to a venue. I told them the venue would be merely a collection point before we proceeded to the actual venue; but there was no actual venue. Like the leaked venue, the actual venue was also a myth to confuse and mislead my opponents. Unknown to my supporters, the collection point was the actual venue.

Meanwhile my opponent sought and obtained the backing of one Member of Parliament from his area who had no time for me. I was informed later that he got sufficient funds to buy every councillor in my camp. But he failed to use the money for two reasons. One, as he was making his way to the leaked venue, he forgot the briefcase with money in a *matatu* which immediately left for Kisumu. This incident gave me two clear steps ahead of him. On my part I had no money to give to the councillors. The little I had was for fuel, food, drinks and lodging. If my opponent located us and the councillors agreed to take his money, I would be doomed. Instead of trying to find our hideout, after discovering we were not at the leaked venue, he was busy chasing the *matatu* which went with the money. It was at night when he returned at Siaya and was the only councillor who spent the night at our leaked venue, I was later told.

The following day we drove in a convoy, thanks to my cousin Juma Chiama who offered me a *matatu* to ferry the councillors to Siaya from Ugunja for free. We agreed to arrive at exactly one minute to ten o'clock in the morning and proceeded to the Council chambers, the venue for the elections, without talking to anybody. We agreed not to be distracted by even a call of nature. Everything proceeded precisely as was planned. Within ten minutes the elections were over. My camp had taken all posts available—the chairman, vice chairman and all committee chairmen. My opponents were humiliated. I knew they had one or two questions from their sponsors and financial backers to answer. My opponents had the support of two MPs, one of whom was my local MP. I had the sympathy of the remaining 2 MPs in the District. This polarization of Siaya politics would continue for a long time, with I and my supporters supporting Jaramogi and my opponents supporting Jaramogi's haters.

It was the party for this victory that Nyasondu had come all the way from Maseno, where she was working and living, to attend. My friend, Hon. Oloo Aringo, MP Alego Usonga, and the Siaya Urban councilors, among whom were Hausi Odada and Odongo Watula, came to congratulate me. We dined and wined.

At around one o'clock in the afternoon a woman came to our home looking for Nyasondu, but luckily Nyasondu was in the kitchen preparing food. The woman met Nyamwalo first. When Nyamwalo jokingly inquired from her where she came from and why she wanted to see Nyasondu so urgently, she said she came from Maseno where Nyasondu worked and that she had bad news for her. When pressed by Nyamwalo to say what the bad news was, she said Kazee was dead. Nyamwalo was shocked and led her to Nyairo's house away from where Nyasondu was and warned her not to mention it to anybody else. Nyamwalo sent for me and broke the sad news. Nyamwalo and I agreed that the guests should not know we had death in the family and that Nyasondu should be kept in the dark too. We had to try by all means to sneak the messenger away from home before Nyasondu saw her. I went to talk to her to find out if she knew how he had died, but she said she didn't have details; but that according to the maid under whose care the kid was left, he just collapsed, foamed in the mouth and died. I gave her transport back to Maseno. I called my cousin Silas, who was present, to take my car and drive Nyasondu to Maseno, take the body to New Nyanza General Hospital Mortuary and arrange for a post mortem. Meanwhile we had to find a way of sneaking Nyasondu from home without her or the guests knowing or suspecting that something was amiss. This was exactly what I did and she left home without knowing what had happened in Maseno.

Silas did as was instructed and was not back by the time the guests left at nine o'clock in the evening. We kept this sad news wrapped up among the three of us: Nyairo, Nyamwalo and I. Not even the women who were helping with the preparation of food, and the elders who were then at my home, knew what had happened. When, immediately after the guests left Nyamwalo started wailing, everybody was surprised. They could not believe that we had known about the death of Kazee since one o'clock in the afternoon. My step-mother and Father in particular said we did well to keep the news from them. They would not have afforded to pretend everything was in order. Others shared the same sentiments. They said we had to be truly strong-willed to have kept quiet in the face of such sad news. Our guests were equally surprised that all along—as they were at our home—we'd had news of the death of one of our loved ones and had kept it to ourselves.

I suppressed the news because I did not want a connection made between the death and the cutthroat election I'd just won the previous day. If our guests were to disperse because of the death, news was going to spread like bushfire in Siaya Town that I had sacrificed my son at the alter of the election. As a family, we believed it was just a coincidence. We buried him after two days in a burial ceremony that resembled a dignitary's.

*

I received information of Obuga's death with consternation. Ever since he left school and ran away to Mombasa, he had been home a couple of times. He'd appeared to have been in good health as I never heard of his illness. Indeed, he had married into a family to which his father and I were related. The mother of my mother was a blood relative of his wife. We tried to talk him out of that marriage, but he refused. We let him have his wish, but I never got to do to him what a father would do when his son or his brother's son he was taking care of got married. I refused to go to his wife's place or send any dowry. His marriage was, however, blessed with two boys—Otieno and Odongo. At this time only Otieno was old enough to follow what was happening. Odongo was still young.

At about the time I received word of his death, our relatives had brought another body to our area from Mombasa, so I decided to talk to the guy in charge of the mini bus to give me a ride to Mombasa. He agreed, so Nyamwalo and I prepared to make the journey to bring home the body. The mini bus picked us up and we set off for Mombasa. On reaching Luanda, we picked up another guy who I would later learn was a co-driver. He was visibly drunk and carried another twenty litters of that illicit brew—*chang'aa* in four, five-litter containers. He kept the *chan'gaa* under the seats. When we reached Kisumu, we stopped for a while to allow other passengers to shop around for fresh fish and greens. Right from home, Nyamwalo and I sat next to the door of the mini bus. But just before we left Kisumu, the guy in charge came and told me to leave that seat and move to any other seat of my choice. He said that the seat was reserved for someone else. He also said there would be no room for Nyamwalo in the mini bus. Although I did not like his tone, I obliged and took Nyamwalo to a bus headed for Mombasa and on my return moved to a seat next to a window four rows away but on the right side. In Kericho the driver on the wheel stopped and insisted that his co-driver, who to me was drunk, drive. The guy in charge and other folks tried to persuade him to persevere and drive to Nakuru. He refused. Meanwhile the drunk driver, on hearing that his ability to drive was being questioned, insisted on driving. He even threatened to shovel his co-driver from the driver's seat if he was not going to leave the seat on his own.

It was drama!

The drunk driver took the wheel. About two miles into the journey, we started feeling the left tires of the mini bus run off the tarmac. The guy in charge left his seat to plead with him to stop because it was now clear to everybody he was incapable of driving, but he refused and continued to scurry downhill, oblivious to the dangers the many curves and bends posed.

Everybody in the mini bus was dead silent. I believed, like me, they were praying. A couple of minutes later, the mini bus lost control and overturned. The inside of the mini bus was plunged into darkness. There were wails and commotion as people tried to exit the bus. A certain woman who was conscious like me literally stepped on my head to reach the exit overhead. Realizing she made it out, I also made my move and was out in no time. Anybody who exited the bus moved away from it. My reason for moving away was that I strongly believed it would explode into flames and I wanted to be as far from it as I possibly could. Later, we lernt tht the driver had lost his arm. His stubbornness had cost him dearly!

Two passengers died.

The police had been called. When we saw them coming those of us who were not injured rushed back to the vehicle and poured out all the *chan'gaa* that was in the bus. We didn't want any trouble after what we'd already been through.

My attention then focused on how I was going to reach Mombasa. Nyamwalo and I had arranged to meet at the Coast Bus office at nine the following morning. With this accident intervening, I did not know if I would make it. I started flagging down buses from Kericho in the hope that they could put me in Nairobi before midnight for a connecting ride to Mombasa. None stopped. I then remembered that I could catch the Mombasa bus I put Nyamwalo in. This was my last hope. When it came and didn't stop, I knew I was doomed. I got desperate and started flagging any vehicle that passed by. It didn't work. And I could not use the police to help in stopping the vehicles because they were busy arranging the transportation of the injured to the hospital. Finally a *matatu* stopped and when I told them my problem they agreed to help me. Once inside the *matatu*, I realized they too had come from a funeral and the driver was tired. We did not go past Nakuru. The driver stopped and rested for three hours. We made it to Nairobi at 6:00 o'clock in the morning. I would be twelve hours late for my rendezvous with Nyamwalo. She did not know anybody in Mombasa but as she was an intelligent adult, she would be able to take care of herself.

I got a bus to Mombasa that morning and arrived at 5:30 pm. When I arrived, Nyamwalo was not at the Coast Bus offices. If she had not learnt of the accident she probably thought the vehicle had a mechanical breakdown. As I was walking towards the Municipal Market where I thought I could find someone I knew, I met Ohando. He was the son of my cousin and he knew me quite well. He had heard about the death of Obuga and had general knowledge where his residence was. He led me to Kwa Jomvu, where Obuga resided and believe me Nyamwalo was already there. After she failed to connect with me, she went to the post office to inquire if there was anybody from our area and found Enock Oyange, Lewnida's brother-in-law. Enock took her to Emanuel, Lebo's maternal uncle, who strove to find Obuga's place. Emanuel was the vice chair of *Dwond Maliera,* which was a welfare organization for people from my place in Mombasa. Ferrying Obuga's body home fell within their mandate.

That night we spent at Cousin James Opiyo's place, where we plotted how to involve our big shots in Mombasa in the effort of raising money for expenses.

The following day I personally visited and talked to the big five: Okoth Waudi, Sam Okello, Edwad Otieno, Clifford Wahonya and Ibrahim Onyango. They agreed to have a fundraising over the weekend. At the fundraising they and their friends raised more money than we needed to take the body home.

Obuga lived in the same area with Cousin Israel Okoth, so on our second night we decided to be closer to the bereaved to console them and let them know we were with them in their grief. While Nyamwalo helped herself in Okoth's house, I was taken to a desolated room with gaping holes big enough for a fox to get through. The fear of being attacked by one of the many nocturnal beasts kept sleep away. I remained awake for the duration of my stay there, having day time naps only.

At the home of the bereaved, *Dwond Maliera,* under the chairmanship of Mr. Isaac and his vice, Emmanuel Miriga, did their best with their friends in raising funds. We bought the coffin, hired a Nissan and paid hospital bills and other incidentals.

As they insisted Nyamwalo and I should not travel with the body in the same van, we granted them their wish and took a bus back to Kisumu. We all made it to Gem safely. But I later learnt that the driver who lost his arm died. And of the two dead passengers, the boy was from my tribe and the girl was from Nyamwalo's tribe. What a coincidence. There are things in this world that are simply inexplicable!

As we struggled to find money, Obuga's widow and her children became very uncooperative. Most of what we suggested they did not want to comply with. As they refused to pool whatever they raised with what we raised, we had to budget with what we raised only.

After the burial the widow was advised not to go back to Mombasa, but against that advice, she and her kids went back. She would later come back to Gem sick and at the point of death—where she died a few months later. Meanwhile the son, Otieno, after returning to Mombasa could not continue with his education because of lack of finances. He got odd jobs here and there and married. They were blessed with one child. He too became ill and died in Mombasa. Dunga, with friends and other relatives, ferried the body home for burial. His wife would later be taken in levirate by my driver whom she later deserted. We did not know where she went to with Otieno's young child. We do not know whether she is alive or dead. The responsibility to go after the child rests squarely on Dunga, Ogeya and Omondi. I hope they will discharge that responsibility responsibly.

Our son, Bernard Onyango, was born in 1970, in Kisumu. A part from the incident which forced us to rush him to New Nyanza General Hospital, in Kisumu, at midnight, shortly after his birth, he had no known childhood ailments. He attended Victoria Preparatory School, in Milimani, Kisumu, and later moved to Ojijo Oteko Nursery. He did his class one and two at M.M. Shah Primary School before we moved him to Mumias Boys Primary School, in Western Province, where he did his Kenya Certificate of Primary Education examination. He passed very well and was called to St. Paul's Amukura High School, also in Western Province. It was at St. Paul's that he perfected his soccer skills. During his tenure there, St. Paul's became a formidable soccer power in Western Province. He did his Kenya Certificate of Secondary Education and obtained a university entry grade. While waiting for his KCSE results, he played soccer for Siaya Medical Club, which was a provincial team. His talents were noticed and he later joined Kenya Breweries, in Kisumu. It was at the Siaya Medical that he met and fell in love with Agneta Wayayi, with whom he sired a baby boy—Mark Oile Onyango Wanyanga.

When he was invited to join Egerton University, Laikipia Campus, he looked for a Super League Club close to the campus, which he could play for and still have time to study for his bachelor of education degree. He wanted to be a teacher.

During his soccer career in Siaya, his fame spread far and wide because of his artistry. It was at this time that his fans coined a name for him. They called him "Benah." The fans loved him; and the girls were not left out. For him, girls were not in short supply.

One Monday morning, as I woke up I found two men and a girl in my living room in Siaya. I knew one of the two men. He was a driver with the Department of Trade in Siaya. I had known him for a long time because my office was on the same floor as their office. I also did some legal work for the department and knew all the employees. I did not know the other man and the girl. The driver introduced his two companions. The man was the father of the girl. The driver explained the purposes of their visit that early. The girl was carrying Benah's child, so she claimed, and the father wanted Benah to accept responsibility. He was in a combat mood, and since I had also woken on the wrong side of the bed, the serenity in the room was broken. It was like a shouting competition with the one who shouted the loudest being heard. I am not good at bickering and shouting so I allowed him to shout himself hoarse while belching out what he had in his chest. He was tactless and appeared not to have sought advice from anyone before coming to my home.

He was a guy I could not do business with. Frankly if his daughter was like him, I could not do business with her either—and neither could I see her fitting in my home. When he cooled down, I told him I could not take his daughter in before I talked to my son. Besides, my son was still at the university and could not be in a position to take care of his daughter and the baby. I further told him that as an elder, he knew tradition prohibit a younger son preceding an older son in marriage. My eldest son was still overseas and his kid brother could not take a girl in marriage. These sound reasons only helped to infuriate him more. All this time the daughter was quiet, so I ventured to ask her how she came to know Benah. She said she was in a team of girls who used to cook for Siaya Medical players and that was how she knew Benah. As the father started becoming abusive, I excused myself and left for work. That was the last time I saw him and the daughter, but it would not be the last time my emissaries interacted with him.

When Benah came home on holidays, I asked him about the girl and her claim that she was carrying his child. The child was later delivered safely and named Mark Oile. He denied halfheartedly and I suspected he might have had a chance to father the child. Because of its closeness to Laikipia Campus, Benah joined KCC Football Club of Eldoret, for which he played soccer for the rest of his stay in Laikipia.

One day Benah returned to Siaya when he was in his third year at Egerton University. It was a Friday and I had to go to our countryside home in Gem to pay the workers and also deliver some materials. Since I was running out of time, I left him and his cousin Mambo Yote to load the materials in the van (pick-up) and let him drive the pick-up and deliver the materials in Gem. He had learnt to drive and used to drive well and with confidence. I took a matatu to Gem to enable me arrive before the workers dispersed. During this period his mother was in postal training in Nairobi. I arrived home and did what I came to do. Bernard also came in the van with Mambo Yote. He did not stay for long at home. He came home, packed the van and left to say hi to his grandma at my father's home. When he returned the van had been emptied. The two were joined by Antony, Erick and Manja drove off to Siaya leaving me at home.

At nine o'clock I heard someone call at the fence on the southern part of the home. As I kept fierce dogs, nobody could come to my home at that time in the night unless the dogs were first tied. Since I had identified his voice I moved to the fence where he was. He told me he had received a phone call from Nyamwalo that the boys who went to Siaya in the van had an accident and one of them was in a critical condition. The guy had come from Mutumbu market. I was dumbfounded and for a moment I just stared blankly in the air. When I gained strength, I asked if he'd left anybody with a car at the market. He said he was not sure but he was going back and if he found any he would come back and take me to Siaya. He was gone hardly ten minutes when I heard hooting from the gate. When the gate was opened, it was him. He had managed to convince a guy with a car to bring me to Siaya.

I left immediately.

On reaching Siaya, we went straight to the hospital where the injured were admitted. Out of the five riders, four had minor injuries and were treated and discharged but one was in a coma fighting for his life. His neck had been smashed at the base of the head and had epileptic-like convulsions. He sounded like he was crying and was spewing blood through his mouth. That was Benah. From the look of things, he did not want to die; he was fighting death visibly, but because of lack of equipment and expertise, the doctor on duty, who was a good friend of mine, admitted to me that he could do nothing to save his life. He advised us to take him to Aga Khan Hospital, in Kisumu, where there were equipment and expertise. He agreed to let us use the hospital ambulance—a dilapidated ramshackle. I had known we were fighting a losing battle. The words of the doctor in Siaya still echoed in my ears. They were, "The neck is smashed at the base of the head."

At Aga Khan Hospital, a specialist was instantly summoned and came within fifteen minutes. Meanwhile the Aga Khan nurses took over from the Siaya nurse who had accompanied us. He was immediately wheeled to the Intensive Care Unit. Nyamwalo and I were allowed to sit on a bench directly in front of the ward. The doctor briefed us every five minutes. From his briefings, I learnt that Benah had other injuries too. The doctor took a bit of time sucking blood from the chest cavity. The boy had massive internal haemarrage into the chest.

We arrived at the Aga Khan Hospital at around 1:00 a.m. and Benah left us at around 3:00 a.m. that morning of the 24th June 1994. I was shocked. Only ten hours earlier I had talked and joked with him and now he is gone for good. The devil had hit me below the belt. Only two days earlier we had chatted as we sat on the doorstep of my Siaya home discussing the viability of businesses in the town. According to him, transport was the most viable and urged me to explore the possibility of starting the business. Little did we know that my business van would take his life after 48 hours.

When Benah died, I had absolutely no money. The body had been moved to the Aga Khan Mortuary, which was more expensive than New Nyanza Mortuary. I reasoned that his funeral was likely to be so big that even if I were to die, mine would not match his in numbers. With the help of Nyamwalo, who ensured I never went out of her sight, we decided on our priorities. First, we had to look for money. Second, we had to transfer the body from Aga Khan Mortuary to NNGH mortuary. Third, Nyasondu had to be informed. The first two were intertwined but the third was the easier one. On being approached, my friend and professional colleague Naphtali Hawala agreed to lend me some money. With the money borrowed, I paid the hospital bill which was high because it ran into thousands of shillings although the patient was admitted for just two hours. When I complained, the doctor waived part of his charges. I was able to pay the mortuary and we transferred the body to NNGH mortuary and sent a telegraphic message to Nyasondu in Nairobi. It was then that I went home and Nyamwalo went back to Siaya.

Funeral Arrangements were made. We moved the body from Kisumu to Siaya home to enable Siaya friends who could not travel to Gem to pay their last respects.

*

On the day Benah died my nephew, Martin Omondi, had been ill and had been admitted. His father, Pastor Tobias Otieno Ayayo, had come to see him. Pastor was in my house on the day Benah died. While I was home in Gem, making burial arrangements, Pastor Otieno was in our Siaya home representing me in every aspect— making preparations for meals for our kids, organizing meetings for harambees and prayer sessions and other matters. I will forever be grateful to him for this kind gesture.

On the burial day we had a huge crowd, but had prepared for them with the help of my brother-in-law, Shade Mukanda. He organized bouncers from Nairobi with whom he took charge of security at our home. In attendance were the entire soccer teams and their officials from Siaya Medical, Kenya Breweries from Kisumu and KCC of Eldoret. Also in attendance, and most volatile, were the Egerton University students. People of all shades of life—the clergy, politicia... and everybody—was there; but there were no ugly incidences as peace prevailed.

I had never seen a mammoth crowd like the one I saw at his funeral. I believe I will not attract even half the crowd at my own funeral.

*

Now, about five years after Benah's death we remembered the child he was alleged to have sired and decided to make a follow up. We went looking for the brother of the child's mother who was reported to be working at Siaya District Hospital. I sent my emissaries—Nyasondu and Martin Audi. They found him and he referred them to the grandfather of the child, who was living somewhere in Western Province. They proceeded to his home but the child was not there as it was reported to be with its mother in South Gem, where the mother was married. We never pursued this matter further. I felt it was no use.

Our first son, Kenneth Otieno, attended Victoria Preparatory School, and Ojijo Oteko Nursery in his formative years. He did class I, II and III at M.M. Shah Primary School before we moved him to Mumias, in Western Province. He sat his certificate of Primary Education Examinations but did not do that well. So I took him to Mwer Secondary School, where he sat for KCSE. Again he did not do well, but I was determined to push him on because I believed, as my primary school teacher once said, that "Education is a piece of soap that washes away ignorance." I wanted to open his eyes further and give him a piece of soap which my parents and brothers had struggled and gave me. I took him to Kamagambo High School for Higher School Certificate. He left Kamagambo ignominiously when he was expelled from school. I did not know what to do with him after that. All his life he had been troublesome. He was a live wire as his nursery teacher described him. He was a slow learner, argumentative and defiant. He tended to do things his way. He was the odd one out of all our kids. He was the one with questionable morals and a drunkard. He was capable of doing better but chose to take a destructive path.

Since I still wanted to give him quality education, on the advice of a friend, I arranged for him to go to India for further studies. He enrolled at

AGRA University for a Bachelor of Commerce degree, but he later moved to Punyab University, in Chandigar, where he completed his degree in 1996. When he arrived home from India, I could not at first recognize him. He was emaciated and the color of his skin was too light to be normal. He was a pack of bones. I knew immediately something was wrong with him. I recollected the day of his departure from Kenya, when I gave him money to go and change into dollars for his use on arrival in Bombay. On his way from changing the money, he must have passed by a brothel. His demeanor and apprehension suggested thus. He was embarrassed at the farewell party hosted by my friend and colleague, O.M.T Adala, at his house. If he did not pick up the virus at the time, he must have picked it up elsewhere, even overseas. For when he returned he was visibly sick. We would later learn that his drinking habits had gone overboard. He had become a full-fledged drunkard.

As he looked for a job he was ailing. Sometime in 1997 the doctors and nurses in Kenya were on strike. This coincided with Kenneth's sickness. There was no hospital he could be taken to and we asked that he be brought home from Nairobi. From home we took him to a private hospital where at first he was treated and allowed to go back home. I left him overnight under the care of his mother in Siaya while I went home to look for money. That night a guy came to the house and sweettalked his mother that there was a witchdoctor who could treat the kind of problem Kenneth had. In desperation the mother allowed the guy to bring the witchdoctor in that night. The witch made several cuts with a razorblade on Kenneth's body, ostensibly to drain germs from it. Since part of Kenneth's diagnosis was anaemia, draining blood from his system was going to hurt him. When I returned in the morning and discovered what happened, I told his mother bluntly that she had killed him. His condition worsened during the day and was rushed back to the hospital, where he died that night.

Once he had taken to drinking, his fate was sealed. My grandfather had forbidden us from drinking alcohol and he knew about the curse, yet he elected to defy. Look at the timing of commencement of his terminal attack. All the health services were grounded in the country. Look at my absence in Siaya that night and this guy coming from nowhere with a witchdoctor. Those were not just coincidences, but a fulfillment of destiny. His burial was not eventful. We mourned because we had lost yet another son. That was it. He became the first HIV/AIDS victim in our family and the second university entrant after Benah to die. We mourned the more because he was the fourth child and the last of the sons Nyasondu and I had lost. Losing four of our senior children was devastating. It was never easy on our part. Nyasondu almost cracked. On my part I consoled myself by the fact that Nyasondu and I still had our daughters. God was still preserving them although some of them had turbulent lives. We had given the daughters as good education as the boys and we expected consolation from them. They did not disappoint.

But it was tough!

One day I was driving from Rang'ala going for court work in Kisumu. Since I was late, I was driving fast to enable me to arrive on time. During the time *wananchi* were thronging chief's offices for new-generation identification cards (popularly known as IDs). On reaching Mutumbu chief's office, which is situated along Kisumu-Busia Road, I suddenly noticed, as I emerged from a hillside, a large crowd of people on both sides of the road. I slowed a bit, but on seeing the road clearly again, I hit the pedal. Then just as I neared the entrance of the chief's office, a cyclist riding on the right side of the road toward the direction I was coming from suddenly decided to make a right turn into the chief's office. I braked and swerved to my left to avoid running him over. I missed him narrowly and instead his bike hit the driver's door and smashed onto the roof of the car, but he was not hurt. But two, among the people who were on the edge of the tarmac, weren't that lucky. I hit the two simultaneously and one landed on the wind shield and the other was thrown onto the kerb of the road. Both were injured badly. I was not hurt, but the car suffered extensive damage. In saving one life the two got injured. *Wananchi* apprehended the cyclist and frogmarched him to the Chief's Camp. The injured were rushed to the hospital by volunteers.

Ironically, the accident happened five hundred meters from my countryside home in Gem and the victims were people I knew. Nyamwalo heard about the accident and immediately rushed over. I sent her to Kisumu to adjourn my cases while I awaited the police who had already been alerted. The police arrived, secured the scene and took the measurements. They also took the names of a few potential witnesses just in case the matter reached court. Virtually everybody present, who witnessed the accident, blamed the cyclist and commended me for saving his life. Knocking down the two victims was inevitable. They in a way contributed to the accident because instead of sitting on the edge of the road, they elected to sit on the edge of the tarmac. They didn't stand a chance once I swerved to avoid hitting the cyclist.

Later there were attempts at civil litigation against me, but these became a cropper as negligence on my part could not be established. That was the only accident I had where someone other than myself was injured. Unfortunately for the victims, one of them lost his leg, the other had less serious injuries.

After the accident the car was driven to the Police Station and I went home. It was while at home that the traditionalists really scared me. They came up with a list of don'ts. They said that because I had shed human blood, I should not eat with anybody, I should not sleep in my wives' houses or any house at all. And if one of the victims died, then a hut had to be built for me where I would stay for one week while being cleansed. Volunteers who claimed to have the right cleansing potions were on hand, waiting for a nod from me to start their work. They were disappointed when I did not respond and when none of the victims died.

Otherwise a medicine man would have been summoned. A goat and chickens would have been slaughtered and potions prepared for me, while staying in a makeshift hut. This would have been too much for me. I would not have survived a whole week in a makeshift hut with the rains pounding and the sun hitting my body directly. God spared the lives of the accident victims for my sake, although they carried permanent and physical scars on their bodies, a stark reminder to the seriousness of the accident.

A part from the deaths of the members of my immediate family, the only death I have space for, because of the foresight of the deceased when he was still alive, is that of Edwin Mijema alias Phinehas Otieno Ogola (popularly known as Congo. He was my cousin. His father and Pastor Silfano Ayayo Mijema were step-brothers. We were not that close though. In fact, from the time of Mutumbu Primary School books days, we had given each other space. We could help each other whenever any of us had a problem, but that was it.

I remember one day I fell ill in 1994 after the death of my son Bernard. He was on hand to help rush me to the hospital. When his son became ill and he wanted transport to take him to the hospital, I took him in my car. But whenever he had an opportunity to hit me, he did it in style. One such occasion, which will linger in my memory for a very long time, was an incident which involved Mrs. Owino Okola and I. Mrs. Owino had sold a piece of land to me to get money to take kids to school and also for provisions. We completed the transaction, but because the title deed was still held in the bank as security, we could not process the transfer of land. Congo later conspired with her to take back the land without refunding my money. This land transaction was presided over by his father, as the village group leader. The contract was written in the group register kept by his father. It was signed by the parties and the witnesses. After his father and all the witnesses had died, they hatched this plot and went to the group register and plucked off the page containing this agreement. This action, together with the death of the witnesses, goaded Mrs. Owino to step back from the agreement. So one day, when I came to my country home in Gem, I found she had been settled on a part of this said land by her levirate husband, Osoma Otina, who was privy to the conspiracy. I later allowed her to retain that portion in spite of failing to refund the purchase price. Such was my relationship with Congo.

He and his wife later became ill and the wife died before him. She was survived by the husband, two sons and four daughters. He had worked hard and constructed a permanent house for himself and his family. Despite the fact that he had children and was still alive, needing shelter for himself and his kids, he demolished his permanent house, hardly three weeks after the burial of his wife. Since he was working in Siaya at the time, he moved there and rented a tiny room. It was at that time that he converted to Islam and attended a mosque regularly. He had a few Muslim friends, who knew where he lived. Nobody else knew his place.

One day one of his Muslim friends came to my office and left a message that Congo was seriously ill in his house and had nobody to take care of him. I immediately proceeded to the mosque and got the guy who knew his house to take me there. The Muslim friend, my cousin Ondielo and I went to his residence and took him to the hospital. He stayed in the hospital for three weeks at my expense. When it became clear his illness was terminal, the doctor advised that we take him home with medication. But since he had no house in Gem, and had nobody to look after him at his Siaya house, I decided to take him to my Siaya home, where I could personally take care of him. During his stay in my house, we had plenty of time to talk. He apologized for having been antagonistic to me and gave me explicit instructions on what I should do in case he died. He told me to organize commemorative ceremonies for his deceased son, wife, father and mother. These would involve a lot of money. I asked him where money would come from and he said, "Don't worry, God will provide."

"God?"

He nodded somberly. "Yes, God!"

For someone who never went to Church, I found this astonishing. Might he have been transformed by Islam? Little did I know that he had registered me with his employer as his next of kin giving me the sole authority over his entire estate.

His condition got worse by the day and I started worrying that he would die in my house. I sent for his brothers who came as soon as they received my message. That night, in my home in Siaya, a decision was made to take him to Gem to stay at the home of his elder brother. I took him there the following day and one week later he passed on. Immediately after his death, I assumed financial responsibility over his infant orphan. His wife, who had died a few months earlier, had left a one month old baby, who was taken in by her mother (the grandmother of the baby); who was old and was unable financially. The child lived!

A couple of months after his death, his employers released benevolence fund. I divided this among his children. Two of the children, who lived with their elder brother, had just dropped out of school and my priority was to get them back to school. I gave enough money to their uncle for their fees and uniforms and the balance of the total I received I gave him to take to the grandmother for upkeep of the baby. None of these was done. The kids neither got uniforms nor went back to school and the grandmother's share never reached her. When I learned about this, I convened a meeting of the baby's grandmother, the brother I gave money and some elders to resolve the issue of non-remittance of the money and failure of the kids to return to school. The meeting degenerated into name-calling between the grandmother and the brother, and I had to end it before violence broke out. Although the issues were not resolved, it was quite clear that the brother had sat on all the money—no wonder the deceased had denied them the opportunity to look after his estate.

The next payment was from a co-operative. With it I organized the ceremonies he asked me to. All the commemorative ceremonies—his father's, mother's, son's, wife's and his were organized according to tradition. For each deceased a ram, or a goat and many chickens were slaughtered. There were traditional drinks of all types. All relatives attended these ceremonies, which were staggered in such a manner that each deceased had his or her day—a total of five days back-to-back.

When his sons reached eighteen, I handed over collection and administration of their father's estate to them; to pursue collection of the remainder of the estate. I went out of my way to ensure his wishes were carried out. Despite the strained relationship that existed between him and I, and the backstabbing he perfected and used on me whenever he had an opportunity, I still came out and helped him at his hour of need. When he was sick and had nobody to turn to, he remembered that I was the only one who could help and promptly sent for me. I did not disappoint him. He, however, warned me about his children. He told me he had bad mannered and criminal-minded sons who had to be kept at arm's length. If any of them came to me for help or advice, he said, I should help or advise but I should not bother myself with the stubborn and defiant ones. I took note of the advice and kept my relationship with them strictly on that advice. It helped.

So much for death!

CHAPTER 18

NUPTIALS

Lydia was our fifth-born child and our third daughter. She did not elect to be fifth or third; that was a biological fact about which she could do nothing. She was also the second to obtain a degree in my family, being beaten to first by her brother Kenneth. Except for her fifth, third and second position, she had also scored first in my family; she was the first to join a national high school, the first to turn down Nairobi University admission, the first to go to the USA, the first to obtain a masters degree, the first to work and compete for work in the corporate world in the capitalist country, the first to become a USA citizen, the first to enroll for PHD and the first to be married. Lydia was married to an American in Copenhagen, Denmark, on the 23rd day of July, 1993. Nyasondu and I did not attend the wedding because we were not invited, but her fiance wrote a letter requesting her hand in marriage. Initially I refused to give consent and consulted far and wide. My cousin, friend and mentor, Mr. Martin Audi Otieno, was the guy who persuaded me to accept it. He had a convincing reason. What would stop her from proceeding with the wedding without your consent if she wanted to, he said. If you declined to give your consent to something you had no power to stop or prevent, like this marriage, you would alienate your daughter forever; she would hence forth consider you an enemy. This is something you cannot afford, he said.

My eyes, which had hitherto been blinded by rage, opened. I had sacrificed a lot and borrowed heavily to let her go to Germany. She had convinced me her stay there would only be temporary—she was there to polish her German and return or if she got a good university and a scholarship she would continue her education. She wrote letters to me a couple of times telling me she was getting on well and the family she was staying with was wonderful. When we informed her she had been invited to join the University of Nairobi, she wrote back to say she had secured a good university in Germany, where she was majoring in Mathematics and was not ready to abandon that for the University of Nairobi. We caved in and allowed her to pursue her dreams. Little did we know that these dreams included getting a husband.

I gave my consent to the marriage courtesy of Martin Audi. This would not be the last time Mr. Audi came to my assistance. After marriage, they went to the USA, which was the home of her husband. In 1994, she and her husband came to Kenya to visit us. We took the opportunity to organize *kisera* for them; we did everything that is done for a daughter except the part where she says, "I do." My daughter had sent money earlier, with which a heifer and a goat was bought and brought to me as dowry. As part of the dowry, he paid some little money in cash. He got into Nyasondu's house officially. A bull, a ram and chickens were slaughtered. A multitude congregated to see them and to dine and wine. Here she also scored a first—the first to recreate a wedding scene successfully.

After the recreated wedding, I arranged for them to visit places like Lake Victoria, Kisumu, Homabay, Migori and Achuth. We stayed with them in Gem and Siaya for over one month, during which time we went out of our way to make their stay as comfortable as possible. They later returned to the USA. Little did I know that my daughter bore the greater part of their travelling expenses to and from Kenya and from her resources purchased the cattle that was paid as dowry.

The second wedding in my family was that of Edyth Atieno. Edyth was our fourth child, but second daughter after Florence Beatrice Akinyi. Before she even knew her fiance, she met and befriended a boy from around my village. The boy's home was two kilometers away. They became great friends and even had baby Brian out of wedlock. When she invited him home to meet us, he came but realized he could not measure up to the standards we expected of a son-in-law. Edyth later lost interest in him when she joined Kamagambo Teachers Training College. At Kamagambo, Edyth met and fell in love with a young man we later came to know as Joshua Oloo Wambore. Joshua later asked the hand of Edyth in marriage. When Edyth told us about it I refused. The boy was still too young and immature and did not exhibit a strong character. He lacked charisma, and danger was written all over his face. We told Edyth we did not approve. It was tricky because it was going to be back-to-back disapprovals of her choices. We had to be careful. But what we later heard of the family of the fiancé made us dig for a fight. The more we dug in, the more Edyth insisted he was her last and best choice. We gave in and allowed him to bring dowry. Everything necessary to complete the process of marriage was done and wedding set in 1994.

On the eve of the wedding, the boys came in the company of the groom for *kisera*—they were sixteen in one Nissan. During a wedding, when the groom comes for *kisera* on the eve of the D-day, he must come with vehicles to carry the bride and her team. But these boys came in a full Nissan, not even a flower girl could fit in. The groom, perhaps, did not seek good counsel over that. They were ill-prepared for *tap maro* (food especially made for the groom and eaten only on payment of money). These were things that with good counsel should not have caused any problem at all, yet they caused operational problems. At the eleventh hour I had to look for extra vehicles to ferry the bridal team to Kamagambo Teachers College SDA Church, the venue for the wedding; one fifty miles away. Mrs. Juma, Mr. Ongon'ga Sigar, Doctor Obimbo and Mr. Musa Agina provided the extra vehicles we needed.

On my team was my nephew Aima Demba. Aima had not been to a wedding before and was looking forward to his first wedding experince. We arrived safely in Kamagambo. To officiate at the wedding was the presiding pastor, Tukiko Koyo, who was my teacher during my days in Kamagambo. He was elated when he heard he was going to join in matrimony a daughter of his student of thirty years earlier.

Just as the procession started moving, Aima decided to go relieve himself in the toilet outside the church; to be sure nature did not force him to interrupt the proceedings. Now listen. The door to the toilet locked Aima in from outside when everybody was already inside the church. Aima called and banged and yelled, but nobody heard him, so nobody came to open the door. He stayed in the toilet until the church function was over.

Gima ogen Jabare!

Aima had looked forward to experiencing his first wedding ceremony and had travelled one fifty miles to do so but failed at the last minute. He, however, attended the two receptions, one at the school and another at Mwalimu Meshack Dawa's home. The wedding was first-class by standards of those days and was a talking point for many years thereafter. But the marriage later failed dismally and resulted in a divorce as a result of the couple's irreconcilable differences, which included attempts on my daughter's life.

The third wedding was for our adopted son, Sir Job, who was the son of my niece Edda Odinga and her estranged husband from Kanyikwaya, in East Gem. Nyamwalo and I took him as one of our own when he was still a toddler and lived with, educated and trained him to be a teacher. He later met and married his sweetheart Josephine in a colourful wedding at Jericho SDA Church. He was the first son from Nyamwalo's house to get married. In allowing him to marry and even attending and participating in his wedding, we again defied traditional beliefs. Traditionally it was a taboo for a son who is not your biological son to marry before your biological sons. Once we decided to discard traditions, we never looked back. His family continued to be blessed and mine too in spite of our defiance of tradition. Over time, after embracing Christianity in earnest, I discovered that if I stayed faithful to Christian beliefs no matter what people said, nothing would hurt me because the Lord would always be my shepherd, protector and saviour.

Sir Job's marriage was blessed with three lovely kids. He and his family stayed in the faith and was enormously blessed and endowed. Later in life, his attempt to locate and bond with his father failed when the father became uncooperative. He could not provide even a small portion of land to his son.

Nyagoro was our fourth child and third daughter to wed. Her wedding, along with two others, were set in motion while I was in the USA. We returned to Kenya in July 2005 to organize the three weddings. Since we had little time, we planned for the three weddings to take place in August 2005. Nyagoro had been married under customary law earlier and needed a church ceremony to formalize the marriage. She had been married to Kennedy Ochieng, with whom she had two handsome boys.

On 7th August 2005, at New Life SDA Church, in Nairobi, Nyagoro and Kennedy were lawfully wedded in a ceremony that exceeded our expectations in excellence. The wedding committee, under the chairmanship of my son-in-law, Mr. Rajoro, the husband to my niece Perez, gave us the best wedding inside the church and at the reception, where a band in attendance was wonderful.

Nyagoro was given away by my cousin, Justo Ouma. Normally I would have been the one giving my daughter away in marriage. But like the previous two, she was given away by my cousin—a tradition I maintained in all subsequent marriages of my daughters.

Everlyne Akinyi's wedding was the fifth and the second in that month. She and her husband met at Bugema University, in Uganda, where both were students. She kept their cool until after graduation, then decided to tie the knot with Haron Kadieda, from Rusinga Island, in Lake Victoria. He was the son of Mr. and Mrs. Olela.

Everlyne was the first daughter of Nyairo and the second graduate daughter in my family. All arrangements preceding the wedding including *kisera* went on as planned and on August 14th 2005, at Victory SDA Church, Everlyne and Haron tied the knot. She was given away by my cousin, Pastor Tobias Otieno Ayayo. The couple was blessed and got children. We, as her parents, later arranged and went to Rusinga to visit her at the new home. We met Haron's parents, Mr. and Mrs. Olela; a very loving and receptive couple. We enjoyed our visit with them. What struck me was the fact that our church, where Everyline came from in Gem, is called Magunda SDA Church and Haron's church, where Everlyne was now going to fellowship, was Gunda SDA Church. Magunda and Gunda mean more or less the same thing in the local dialect. While there, we had the privilage to attend the church on the Sabbath. It was a wonderful congregation and we loved every minute spent with them.

Violet Akinyi's was the sixth wedding. She met her fiance in Nairobi, where she was a teacher at Genesis Kindergarten, a school owned by the Rajoros. She did so well in drama that for three successive years she led Genesis pupils to the National Music and Drama Festival and won trophies for the school. She was Kamagambo Teachers College trained and beside drama, she was an athlete and participated in girls' soccer for her high school, Nyawara Girls, up to national level.

She fell in love with Fred Oyola and presented him to us. Fred was the son of Mr. and Mrs. James Ndweyi, from Seme.

After all the wedding formalities had been completed, they tied the knot at St. Peters ACK Church, in Kisumu, on August 27th 2005. She was given away by my cousin, James Opiyo Opondo. Like previous ones, this wedding was equally colourful. We matched Joseme blow for blow in showing our love by way of gifts to the groom and the bride.

Although her husband and family were ACK, we prayed that God would restrain the couple or any third party from forcing one or the other to fellowship in a church other than their church of birth. I knew the church issue would cause a problem; that was why I accepted the marriage after receiving an assurance from Fred that Violet would be allowed to pursue her faith as long as she wished.

****

The subsequent weddings were for our sons. I planned them while still in the USA. My initial plan—because of the pressure of time—was to have four weddings on the same day. I reasoned that this would save us time and money. We would use one church and one reception venue for all four weddings.

That was the plan.

But when I arrived in Kenya from the USA and put the idea to the grooms and their brides, it was shot down. They did not want a mass wedding. In spite of my protests that what I had envisioned was not a mass wedding, they held on to their guns and forced me to back down. Following tradition, the weddings would have been James', Victor's, Erick's and Jack's, in that order, but this was not going to be because James was not ready. We were going to defy tradition once again.

Erick was ready, so we started with him. He had met Betty in Nairobi. Betty was the daughter of the late Senior Chief Michael Opere and Mama Mary Opere, of Siburi, Kandiege, Rachuonyo District. Part of the arrangements involved a visit to the home in Kandiege, which I did with pomp. Mama Mary Opere received us well and she was happy to host us. We paid part of the dowry and left the following day. Erick later went to visit and paid the balance of the dowry agreed upon.

The wedding was conducted at New Life SDA Church, in Nairobi, and was presided over by Pastor David Churu on the 19th day of August 2007. The wedding committee was headed by Mr. George Okite Rajoro and he did a marvelous job. They retained the same band which entertained the guests during Nyagoro's wedding. The gifts were in abundance and had to be carried in two pickups.

Erick was our fifth son and James' first follower. He was a graduate of Mysore University, in India, where he obtained a Bachelor of Science in Biochemistry. Betty was a P1 Teacher, a graduate of Kabarnet T.T.C. She would later join Nairobi University for a Bachelor of Education Degree. Betty led the way in showing that high school education was only a stepping stone, a launching pad for a successful career. She and Erick also showed the example of what a committed young couple could do before being bogged down by family commitments. Erick, who already had a degree, would later enroll for post graduate diploma in education at Kenyatta University.

*

Jack and Millicent were members of Kariakor SDA Church. Jack was a deacon while Millicent was the church treasurer. Both were devoted Christians. I remember one day buying a suit for Millicent while I was still in the USA, which she refused to accept. According to her, it was an inappropriate dress because it comprised along trouser and a jacket over a blouse. Jack and Millicent met in the church and having been attracted to each other decided to tie the knot. I visited Millicent's parents and paid dowry. Jack later visited and paid the balance of the dowry and completed all the ceremonies necessary prior to the wedding.

On the 14th day of October 2007, at Jericho SDA Church in Nairobi, Jack and Millicent were joined in holy matrimony in a wonderful wedding. Jack's wedding was the eighth in my family. Jack was a higher diploma graduate of Nairobi University, in Human Resource Management. He would later enroll as a degree student at the same university, same discipline. Millicent was a holder of CPA I certificate and later strove to complete CPA's remaining sections. The couple was blessed and had children. Millicent was the first daughter of Mr. and Mrs. John Odhiambo, of Kamreri, Migori District. We share the same faith with them and her father shares a little more with me. The gifts were overwhelming.

*

The Ninth wedding was James'. He was my first son with Nyairo, and having lost his senior brothers, he was now the eldest son we had. He and his fiancée, Eunice Kelly, were at law school in India, where they met and fell in love. Although James returned to Kenya earlier, he vowed to wait for his sweetheart to return. In the face of pressure from his brothers to get a wife to enable them to also get wives, he refused to be hurried and made it very clear that it was Eunice or none. He set his kid brothers free that whoever was ready should just go ahead and marry. That was exactly what his brothers did. With his meekness, when Eunice returned to Kenya, James couldn't gather courage to introduce himself to her parents, who were at the airport to meet her. But step by step things fell in place for them and Eunice's parents allowed me to visit them as was my practice. I had never been to a family that was so united and loved one another as Kelly's family. Kelly and I shared many characteristics. He had many kids, he educated all of them, he loved them, he was of SDA faith, he was a polygamist, and He was a disciplinarian. So when I went to his home, we struck an immediate rapport. Things were arranged quickly since I had to reurn to the States.

On the 28th day of July 2007, James and his team, comprising Cornell Masimba, Victor and Gordon, left my home in a car. Victor was driving and they were supposed to pick Dunga in Oyugis. At around eight o'clock in the evening I received a call from Cornell that they had had a minor accident in Ringa, which they were trying to fix then be on their way. They were expected at 4:00 p.m., but by 8:00 p.m. they were still on the way. Cornell assured me they would call me as soon as they were through with the police, who he said would be there soon. 9:00 o'clock, 10:00 o'clock, 11:00 o'clock no call came through and my attempts to reach them were unsuccessful. I thought the call I received was just a ruse to calm me down. The accident must have been more serious or even fatal, but they didn't want to tell me. When by midnight no call came through and I couldn't reach them, I sneaked out of bed, leaving Nyairo sleeping, wrote a note of things I wanted done and left home for Kodiaga. My intention was to get a vehicle to Lwanda, where I could catch a ride to Kisumu; where I could hire a taxi to Ringa. At Kodiaga I checked all the bars and shops but there was not a single car in the shopping centre. I decided to go to Mutumbu. It was on my way to Mutumbu that I realized I was in my pajamas and sandals. I, however, proceeded to Mutumbu in the same attire and failed to get a vehicle. On my way back a thought crossed my mind. *Why don't I go to the chief's camp and talk to the policeman on duty to help me flag down any vehicle going toward Kisumu to give me a ride?* But first I had to change from my pajamas into heavier clothes to fend off the cold.

Earlier, I had taken a strong over-the-counter anti-depressant I came with from the USA to help me sleep off the stress and shock of the accident. The effects of the medicine were kicking in as I walked home. I remembered the heavy jacket which was in Nyasondu's house and decided to go for it. I opened her outer door, went into the bed room, picked up the jacket and as I sat on the edge of the bed to put on the socks and the shoes, I passed out. It was at 3:00 p.m., the following day, when I woke up to find the home quiet. There was nobody home. Maybe what I had feared had happened. But I had lost a daughter and a son in vehicle accidents and was not prepared for another one.

Where was everyone?

I made my way to Nyamwalo's house, where I found Mwana Iddi seated on a chair alone, in the verandah (Mwana Iddi was my granddaughter). Since that was the only person around, I took her in my arms and placed her on my lap. I was a worried man. Maybe the people at home had received the information about the accident and had gone to Ringa. Maybe they were just busy on their own errands. I did not know what was happening. I needed someone to talk to.

The first person to see me was Loice Auma. When she saw me as she was returning home, she ran back shouting *Daddy oduogo, Daddy Oduogo* (Daddy is back, Daddy is back). I did not know where she ran to, but when she came back she was with a throng of people anxious to see me. It was as if I had risen from the dead. When I was told what happened, I realized the enormous panic which had gripped everybody in the home was because they thought I had vanished.

Nyairo was woken by a call put through to me from Cornell. She took the call when she discovered I was not in bed. She started wondering where I was. On the table was the note I had written. Because of panic, she did not even bother to read the note. She hurried to Nyamwalo's house to see if I was there. After narrating to Nyamawalo what happened in Ringa and that I was nowhere to be seen, they embarked on a frenetic search for me. I was told they searched every inch of the home but could not find me. They went out to wake up neighbours who wondered where I might have gone. Everybody was worried because only a few months earlier a neighbour had disappeared. His body was later found on the bank of River Yala. He had drowned. By daybreak people had started imagining such things about me. They started habouring the notion that perhaps I had taken my own life. They searched all the bushes around and asked anybody who passed by if they had seen me. They even opened a disused well in front of the home to check if I plunged myself into it. Soon the crowd increased and the search widened. Nobody in the home had slept since midnight and nobody except Mwana Iddi and Siwi ate anything.

By 2:00 p.m. they resolved that my disappearance be reported to the police. It was while sorting out who should report to the police that Loice went to where they were gathered in front of the gate shouting Dad is back. On realizing I had resurfaced, everybody rushed to where I was. Very few people spoke at that time. It was when I told them that I had been dead a sleep in Nyasondu's house that they realized they overlooked checking Nyasondu's house. On my part I was refreshed and full of vigour and vitality; the medicine had done what I wanted it to do. As for the crowd, everybody dispersed and went his or her way.

That night, around 11:00 p.m., James and Victor returned home. They narrated what had happened. They said Victor was driving when they went to pick up Dunga. As they were making a right turn into the road that led to the Kelly's, an oncoming vehicle rammed onto the passenger door. The damage to the car was light—a dented front mud guard and a jammed door. When the police arrived and listened to both sides, they insisted both drivers were to blame and that if they had to prefer charges they would charge both drivers. This is what scared the other driver to back off and leave the damage as it was. Meanwhile it had been raining heavily as the argument raged. The road to the Kelly's was at some point impassable after a downpour. After battling the accident driver for close to five hours, they still had a fight on their hands before they reached home. They had to do battle with mud. The expensive suits they wore to impress the girls were all muddy from shoving and pushing the car. They finally made it home at 1:00 a.m.

On the twentieth day of April 2008, James and Eunice tied the knot at New Life SDA Church, in Nairobi. It was one of the best weddings I have ever attended. It was presided over by Pastor James Ouma Owuor, who was himself a student with James and Eunice in India. The gifts were awesome. The honeymoon was arranged for Malindi by a friend of James, Ben Owino. All is well that ends well. In spite of the trouble and mishaps on the journey, the result was a well-attended wedding, with our usual band in attendance with their latest hits. Three days after the wedding, I fell sick and had to fly out urgently to the USA for treatment.

We did not get to arrange Victor's wedding. This was not because of my illness, but because of minor complications at his in laws' home. We still look forward to Anthony's, Ken's and Edwin's weddings.

It is my prayer that all my kids—both girls and boys—wed and remain faithful to their spouses.

CHAPTER 19

BENEVOLENCE

I inherited some of my mother's most enduring traits. Chief among them was her benevolence. My magnanimity was far beyond human expectations. I helped friends as well as enemies. People came to me looking for school fees, clothes, employment, money, a roof over their heads and a night's accommodation. I was at their service twenty four seven. They needed those services and they needed them there and then. Saying no or some other time was not an option. They came for help as if it was their right; and help they got without a frown. Listen to the Bible"

> *A generous man will prosper; he who refreshes others will himself be refreshed.* Proverbs 11:25

I did not help people for prestige. I did not do it to be praised or to be great or because I was rich, which I was not. I did all these to help mankind.

Take the case of my cousin's wife. She was pregnant and was expecting to deliver anytime. My cousin was a drunkard and had no money to feed the family. The little he got he used on alcohol. Just a week before, he had come home drunk. As was his habit, demanded to be served only meat, chicken or fish. He was demanding food he never brought home—and demanding it from a wife eight and a half months pregnant. The wife, in rage, decided to cook *ugali* made from ash. Although he was drunk, he was able to detect that the *ugali* was not from millet or maize. What he did not know was that this was prepared for him to teach him a lesson never to ask for food he never brought home.

Let's move the story along.

His wife was in labour and the kids rushed to me for help. I took her to a hospital, where after a blood transfusion she delivered a baby boy. The husband was last seen three days ago. I took care of the medical bills and other provisions mother and child needed to get on with life. On the next pregnancy I did the same—only this time the hospital was in Siaya, not Kisumu.

*

Then there's the case of this widow who used to come to our country home every weekend, looking for food. She would be given maize, money to grind it and to buy *mbuta* or *omena*. As her sickness deteriorated, she started asking for chicken. On three occasions Nyairo gave her chicken, but on the fourth she said no. I prevailed on her to give the widow the chicken. I said, "You never know, this may be the last time she's asked us for a chicken."

Nyairo shrugged. "You may be right."

"If we refuse to give her now," I warned, "it will wipe out all the good we have done."

"Fine, I'll give her the bird," Nyairo said and gave her the chicken. She died a few days later and we were glad to have given her the chicken.

*

While in Thika one evening, at eight o'clock, a strange guy came to our house. He was strange in the sense that his hair was bushy and unkempt. He had very dirty clothes. He was certainly hungry. We concluded that he was not normal. Nyasondu prepared a meal for him and while at the table, I discovered he was indeed insane. He had long dirty nails and his hands appeared not to have seen water in ages. We had to give him food to eat by himself, because he refused to wash his hands. We put some bedding on the floor for him to sleep on. In the morning we found an army of lice on the bedding, but he was gone.

*

Chiero mithiedho ema gawi—your friend is your worst enemy.

When a person you help turns against you and becomes your bitterest enemy, it's not worth helping anybody. A number of times I suffered for helping people. Take the case of this boy who was kicked out of school for failure to pay school fees. His father came to me and pleaded that I give him money to take his son to school. I did not have money at the time and I told him so. He went away and tried several other people, from what he told me, but failed to get anything. When he returned and offered me his land to buy, I knew he was desparate to get his son to school. So I told him I would borrow money and pay his son's school fees on the strength of the purchase of his land. After agreeing on the price, I looked for money and paid the fees for his son in forms three and four. Although the asking price for the land was less than the school and examination fees, I paid the extra amount to enable him clear both fees. But since his son was troublesome, he was later suspended from school. His father came and pleaded with me to go and talk to the head teacher. I agreed and the boy went back and completed school. After his high school, he could not get a job. I went out of my way to secure him a job, which he later abandoned.

This guy is now an adult. He is over forty five, but the irony is that he wants to take back the land his father sold me to enable him complete his high school education. By sheer force, he has prevented my people from tilling the land. Can you believe this?

*

Another guy sold me land and later changed his mind on the eve of the day I had to settle Abiba on that very land. I had put off settling Abiba for a long time while looking for land elsewhere. He refunded a quarter of the amount I paid him as purchase price and still owed me ¾. I have no hope of receiving this money from him anytime soon. He is a guy I have helped along with his wives on very many occasions and still continue to help, despite his kicking me out of his land.

*

A client came to the office when her properties had been attached. She needed legal assistance to get her stuff released. I prepared the necessary pleadings for filing for release of the properties. I sent my assistant with the papers to court. Unknown to me, the client and my assistant were friends, so when he went to file the papers he managed to sweet-talk the advocate to strike a consent order, to the effect that our client's properties be released subject to our client making a specific monthly payment and that if she defaulted we would pay. My assistant never brought this to my attention. Our client defaulted and the creditor enforced the consent order.

I was surprised one morning when brokers descended on properties in my home. They cleaned the houses in Siaya and in Gem. It was when I enquired that I was told about this. I fought back with all my might and got back my properties through a High Court order.

From these incidences, I learned two lessons. One, *ahsante ya punda ni mateke*—the gratitude of a donkey is a kick. Two, don't be too good or too wise and don't be too wicked either, for all your efforts are meaningless.

I continued to render selfless services to my people and the community. I devoted my time, energy and resources to the service of the people. I did not want to be the only one living a good life. I wanted to lift other people, to improve their standards of living too. I knew that if I was the only person whose living standards were high amidst people wallowing in poverty, I was not only jeopardizing my security and that of my family, but was exhibiting an acute lack of humility. I was determined not to let this happen. Whatever God gave me, I shared with other people, either by giving or by rendering services for free. The only area I had not done was to share what I knew with them. I had learnt that if you wanted a guy to be selfsupporting, you must not just give, but teach him or her to be independent. In this connection, I organized villagers and members of the community into groups of poultry keepers, tree nursery managers, horticulturalists, fish keepers, microfinance and small traders. I organized aid for them from NGOs and the government. Many women groups, which were rated successful, like Mutumbu Women Group, Rindwa Women Group and Lisriga Women Group sprang from these initiatives.

Mutumbu women group later embarked on a successful tree nursery project and I later helped them start Mutumbu Youth Polytechnic, which trained the local youths in masonry, carpentry and tailoring. With government assistance, we helped them acquire carpentry tools, sewing machines and masonry tools. Many youths enrolled and graduated as artisans, having passed government trade tests. They got jobs after completing their training.

I helped Rindwa Women Group reclaim public land on which they dug fish ponds. The fish met their protein needs and they got money from their sales.

I helped Mukhwana Group get government funding to sink shallow wells for water for growing off-season horticultural crops. The water from these shallow wells was used by cattle, poultry and people for drinking, and also for irrigating farms. They were credited with being the first group to take advantage of the governments Cockerel Exchange Programme, where the government gave a high-breed cock to a family in exchange for a local cock. With this, the government believed, as I did, that the third generation of an offspring of a crossbred hen and a high grade cock would be pure breed (high breed).

For the purpose of educating members of this group and the community, Mrs. Mary Adams, Ayub Ohon and I organized a seminar at which we invited the villagers and all the relevant government department heads, provincial administrators, the chief, Jared Nyawade, and assistant chief, Oscar Owiti—and prominent local people who attended and participated in the seminar. The following week, the District Livestock Development Officer was at the chief's office in Mutumbu with grade cocks. People flocked to the office to exchange cocks. We also helped Mutumbu Women Group acquire grade cows for milk. Initially it proved successful, but later flopped due to management problems.

*

Another area where I did a lot of community work was in secondary schools and tertiary institutions. Between 1980 and 2003 I served as a board member in a total of nine secondary schools and two tertiary institutions. I failed to be reelected only in one. My membership expired when I ceased to be a councillor in one of them and on the third one I ceased being a member after reconstituting the board. In the remaining ones I ceased being a member either when I resigned due to pressure of work or left when I went to the USA. I served in the boards of Usenge, Hono, Ngiya, Siaya Institute of Technology, Bishop Okoth Mbaga, Mutumbu Girls Secondary, Holy Cross, Riat and Maliera. After constituting the board in Argwings Kodhek Secondary school I left for other people to continue.

Only a few of these schools and institutions reimbursed expenses. Most of them were starters and had no money. It therefore compelled me to use my meager resources to fuel my car to and from board meetings.

Then in 1983 I was elected Chairman of the Board of Governors of Maliera Secondary School. This was a position I held for twenty years. In addition I was elected Chairman of Bishop Okoth Mbaga Girls Secondary school. I was expected to attend and preside over all executive committee meetings, board meetings, Parents Teachers Association meetings, and parent meetings. These, together with my civic duties, took a toll on my time and eventually my health.

After shaking off some of the boards, the remaining load, although still heavy, was manageable. I served these boards with determination and dedication. We provided the necessary infrastructure, learning aids, laboratories, libraries, teachers, and all that were necessary in a good learning environment. I managed to help create good working relations between teachers and the boards. We did not have to deal with any major strike or defiance of authority; the few minor ones were detected on time and nipped in the bud. We instilled discipline across the board. We were strict but not vindictive, harsh but not malicious. With God's help, we were able to steer these institutions to greater heights of development. These institutions would later become powerhouses of higher learning.

But I would not have managed were it not for the selflessness of the head teachers. The work Mr. Moses Warom did in Usenge High School was worthy of noting. I worked with him in two institutions, as head teacher of Usenge and Chairman of BOG of Maliera when I was a member of both boards. At Usenge, Mr. Warom was instrumental in putting up the physical plant seen at the institution to date. Discipline was his middle name. Students and teachers obeyed him. He was a good administrator. At Maliera, he set the school on the path to being taken over by the government. He retired to his farm in Gongo, where he later died.

In Ngiya Girls High School, I worked with Mrs. Oluoch. She was a no nonsense head teacher who knew how to get her teachers to do the right thing. During her tenure, especially the part when I served in the board, Ngiya was at the forefront of academic excellence. She left a good legacy at Ngiya, which Mrs. Margaret Juma inherited. I served in all, but three years of Margaret's stewardship of Ngiya Girls High School. She was an administrator per excellence; a good listener, a good orator, fearless but tough as steel. She was not a manipulator and harboured no grudges against anybody. She was a straight talker, did not wait for one to turn his or her back to say what she wanted to say about him or her. Her tenure saw the academic stakes of Ngiya rise to compete with the best schools nationally. She retired to her farm in Ahero, Nyando District.

Mr. Odundo was not far behind. After Hono was run down, I was in the team, headed by Dr. Meshak Oluoch, which was selected to clean up the school. Mr. Odundo was transferred to Hono to add firepower to the team. Later, long hours of meetings and deliberations, ability of the head teacher and the chairman of the board to blend and bond, the excellent contribution of members, the cooperation of the Hon. Oloo Aringo, MP Alego Usonga, all made it possible to pull Hono out of quagmire and thrust it on a path of success. Mr. Odundo made it work!

The head teacher I worked with longest was Mr. T.T. Were Apudo, a docile and humane administrator who never wanted to harm anybody. He was head teacher of Maliera Secondary School from 1987 to 2001, when he retired.

He was an affable and amiable person. He took people's problems as his own and went out of his way to try and help. He was also a family man. He loved his wives and kids dearly. He was a disciplinarian but this was restricted only to students. He found it hard to take harsh disciplinary action against teachers and supportive staff; for this reason discipline among teachers was at its lowest, particularly in his last years. He also oversaw the installation of water tanks, electricity and connection of piped water from the Malanga Sidindi water supply. He later retired to his home in Uyoma.

The two head teachers I worked with at Bishop Okoth Mbaga Girls Secondary School were sisters. Under Mr. Joseph Kwengu as chairman of the board, we worked with Sister Symprose Atieno as head teacher. Mr. Kwengu was a sober man who knew his way around the corridors of Catholic Church, the sponsors of the School. He took the school from a very humble beginning to greater heights. If it were not for pressure of work and the opposing forces between the sponsors and the management, which he and most of us had seen emerging, he would have still offered himself for reelection at the end of his term and would have been reelected.

When the election was called, however, I was unanimously elected to take Mr. Kwengu's place as chairman of the board. A couple of weeks after the election, I ran into a vicious and vitrolic battle from the sponsors. They said I was ineligible to be chairman of the Board of Governors of a catholic-sponsored school. They knew I was a Seventh-day Adventist and for that reason they did not want me. The battle was fought at the school, where teachers and board members rallied to my support. The battle went to the District Education office, where they were shown several non-Catholic school boards chaired by Catholics in the district. Not satisfied, they took the battle to the Provincial Director's office, where they were reminded that my election was unanimous and that I had the support of the entire Mbaga Girls Secondary School fraternity. Mr. Muga Ayoya, who was a member of the board and knew the Catholic Church system, was behind me full force.

Still not satisfied with the PDE's interpretation of the law, they sought audience with the Ministry. When they revealed the name of the person they wanted to take my place, it turned out to be the one who had proposed my name. They finally let the matter rest and I served my full three-year term with distinction, this time with Sister Adipo as the head teacher.

Sister Adipo was the opposite of sister Symprose. Sister Symprose was a fearless, aggressive fighter who would stop at nothing to achieve what she thought was right. She was also secretive and kept certain things to herself or within the precincts of very close people to her. Sister Adipo was an introvert of sorts. Careful and calculated, she would easily pass as a weakling but inwardly she was as tough as steel. When she said yes it remained yes whatever the circumstances. The two ladies of God cooperated with me to uplift Mbaga. I'm sure Mr. Kwengu found my work less disappointing. He was the yardstick by which I measured my success. A dormitory, a laboratory and library were built and a mini bus acquired during my tenure.

At the Siaya Institute of Technology, Mr. Tindi Mósi was the principal. I worked with him for the duration of time I was a member of the board. Membership of the board comprised who was who in Siaya. It had prominent academicians, politicians, engineers, doctors and lawyers. It was a powerhouse and it didn't disappoint. The board members helped propel the institute to be the biggest in Siaya District, with over one thousand students.

The only disappointment we encountered was the loss of our Ndere Campus. I was privileged to preside over an ad hoc committee looking into ways of reviving it, but this failed for three reasons.

- The building the board had painstakingly built there had partially collapsed and most of the materials had disappeared. The cost of repairs would run into millions. The board had no such funds. Although donors had financed the construction, they could not help because it had collapsed as a result of substandard workmanship.

- The land on which the building sat—indeed the entire institute land— was alleged to have been bought from iindigenous owners. No such thing took place. They gave their land in anticipation of being paid later, but they were never paid; so most of them reclaimed their land.

- The surveys, which were alleged to have been done on the land, were fake. They were merely intended to hoodwink donors into releasing the funds. In fact, when we visited the owners at Ndere they were bitter at the betrayal and blamed a former Member of Parliament for having taken them to a wild goose chase. Some were still willing to part with their land for the institute, but they insisted the institute had to pay for it at current market value and only after a proper valuation. The institute could not raise the kind of money anticipated and the matter rested there.

In one of my trips back to Kenya, I passed by and saw a secondary school had sprung up on the institute land at Ndere. The collapsed building had partially been repaired and now housed four classrooms for Ndere Boys Secondary School. Based on that, I concluded that the fate of Siaya Institute of Technology, Ndere Campus, had been sealed. At the Siaya Campus, the then Principal, Mr. Tindi Mosi, was not there; someone else had taken his place.

Argwings Secondary School was started as a self-help project. It was started by the community of North Gem, first as the Anglican Church's instrument to fight the emerging influence of Maliera Secondary School, which was started by the S.D.A. Church. Its progression to stability was easy compared to what Maliera went through. Immediately it started as an offshoot of Malanga Primary School, Teachers flocked in from Sawagongo and other nearby secondary schools to prop it up. With teachers in good supply, the students flocked there and this made Maliera struggle and stagger for a long time.

As years went by, a prominent fellow from Malanga sub-location saw gold, not a school, at Argwings and started conspiring to take it over as private property. With the immense of wealth he had, nobody could stop him. Within a short time he turned the school from harambee to private. It would later take a titanic battle to dislodge him. When I was elected Councillor for North Gem, my first duty was to face this fellow and get the school back to the community, where it rightly belonged. It was a battle of David and Goliath—after all, what could a young, penniless councillor do to a millionaire? I had to prepare my battle well and use surprise. I checked whether registration of the school was still public as opposed to private as was the case originally. My inquiries confirmed that the original registration had not been changed. That emboldened me. That was the armour I needed to face the adversary. I then sought the views of prominent elders like Simon Odera, Samson Rading and Richard Otieno. I got them on my side and with their assistance we arranged to evict the head teacher the fellow had put there. It worked. We had staged a successful coup against him. His head teacher and teachers sympathetic to him were pushed out.

I then embarked on constituting a committee to help run the school. The head teacher of Malanga Primary School, Mr. Nyawade, helped a lot. And the irrepressible Melkazedek Omolo was there too. First we asked Mr. Eliazar Ouma to chair the committee. He started with vigour and vitality until one day he got an anonymous letter slandering him, calling him names and threatening him with dire consequences should he continue chairing the committee. This was too much for Eliazar, a born-again Christian. I asked him to show me the letter. When I read it, it was in a similar handwriting as the ones Aima Demba, Margaret Ragen and I received—only the details were different; but all were slanderous and abusive. I gave him our letters to see that his, like ours, was just intended to scare him but he was too frightened and he quit.

I had to scout for a strong character who could withstand the local intrigues and clanism. Eliazar was forced out because he did not come from the ruling clan. The letter he received suggested so. I was determined not to get somebody from the ruling clan because I believed that would be a recipe for the school's failure. I wanted an outsider strong enough to face the challenges and weather the storm. I settled on Mzee Barrack Okeno Osare, a fearless former Provincial Commissioner who served the government with distinction and had fought more formidable wars than this. He was an outsider and the right guy for the assignment.

He did not disappoint.

Even some of his detractors came to like him. He faced challenges as a man. I liked him a lot and I learned from him the value of keeping time.

One day he told me, "Look, Jakom, when you say the meeting starts at ten o'clock, it must be ten o'clock."

"But I'm not that late; just a few minutes," I protested.

Firmly, he said, "Late is late!"

From that day on, he never beat me. We either arrived at the same time or I arrived earlier. If Kenya could have one hundred Barrack Okenos Kenya would be a developed country. He also taught me the importance of farming and living in a decent environment. He spent most of his day on his farm and his nights in a magnificent, storeyed and tiled house, which could compete any house in the neigbourhoods of any city. He was a gentleman per excellence. It was a pity we never had him as an M.P., not because he did not try, but because he did not come from the right clan—and because that was the year we were using someone else to dismantle the ruling clan.

He put Argwings Kodhek Secondary school on a path to success and left, ironically, by way of abandonment when a prominent politician from the ruling class, in an effort to get a foothold at Argwings Secondary School, frustrated and pushed him into abandoning the school. But the school never wavered. It moved from strength to strength to become one of the leading schools in Gem. I would later team up with Barrack, Eliazar and Melkazedek in other areas of development.

Barrack later died while I was in the USA. In his death, the country lost the doyen of progressive elitists in Gem.

Malanga Dispensary was built around 1927 by the colonists, according to the inscription on one of the walls of the original building. The original building comprised one room, with open roofed space like a hide banda in front. For many years it served the purpose for which it was built. I am a living testimony to that. If it were not for the dispensary. I would not be alive today.

Immediately after independence, a serious effort was made to expand the dispensary into a full health facility. The political ruling clan supported the idea as it was spearheaded by one of their sons. Because it was the idea of the ruling clan, instead of my people embracing it, they shot it down. The other reason they shot it down was because they were not involved in the planning stages and were suspicious of the ruling clans' motives. They thought the health facility was only a ruse the ruling clan was using to snatch their land. So they refused. The ruling clan had oppressed my tribe so much that there was perpetual bad blood between them. Anything emanating from the ruling clan was an abomination to my tribe and vice versa. So Malanga remained a dispensary when other facilities built long after it progressed and became health centres.

This was an unacceptable situation.

The ruling clan was not going to help us develop the facility because they got their hand burned once. The elite in my tribe, having lived in an oppressive environment, were too scared even to think of coming home to build *simbini* (plural of *simba*). Most of them were educated in towns and didn't frequent home for fear of being bewitched. I had no such fear. I was born, brought up and educated in the countryside. I lived and worked in the countryside. I interacted and bonded well with the people they feared and above all I feared no witches or quacks. Well, I decided as was going to do something about the dispensary. Malanga Health Centre was thus conceived, my brain child for which I was very proud and was prepared to fight for to death.

I mobilized the masses and came up with a few dedicated guys whose only brief was to see the project succeed, not to line up their pockets with harambee money. The team comprised of Elisha Ojera, Melkazedek Omolo, Jotham Owino, and later Eunice Ng'onga, Barrack Okeno, Simon Odera and Onyango Ochieng. During those days, harambees were the in thing; so we organized our first one in 1978, which was presided over by the District Commissioner and friend, Mr. Stanley Thuo. With the money raised, we paid for the building plan. The two owners of the land we acquired, Ohindo Majera and Richard Otieno, were paid and construction of the health centre started. Meanwhile I approached Siaya District Development Committee, through the DC, which approved our application for a government grant. The DC helped us push our application through the Provincial Development Committee, where Kshs 450,000/= was approved and disbursed to us. The expenditure of this amount was controlled by the District Supplies Officer, Mr. Saggia, who procured the material for us. We completed the building of this huge structure with the money, but the hard part was yet to come.

I started the process of getting government approval for upgrading of the facility to health centre status. This was no picnic. It made me remember what our Member of Parliament said when I sought his assistance in this regard, and in securing a guest of honor for our harambee, which Mr. Stanley Thuo later agreed to preside over. I wrote to our Member of Parliament thus.

```
                                    MALANGA HEALTH CENTRE,
                                    P.O. BOX 60,
                                    YALA.


                                    5th September, 1978


Hon. Omolo Okero, M.P,
Minister for Information and Broadcasting,
P.O. Box 30025,
NAIROBI.

Dear Sir,

                    RE: MALANGA HEALTH CENTRE:

        The members of the Community of North Gem Location have embarked on
an ambitious Self Help Project at Malanga Sub-Location. They have started
the construction work of expansions to what is now known as Malanga Dispensary
but what will be Malanga Health Centre when completed. This project has the
blessing of the District Medical Officer of Health and the District Commission-
er, Siaya.

        We are going to build a block comprising Treatment room, office,
Lecture Room, Ante Natal Clinic, Maternity, Kitchen and sanitary facilities
and to begin with 3 staff houses. We are also going to furnish and equip
the Health Centre and provide water and light to the same. All these are
estimated to cost Shs. 600,000/=. We will of course ask the Government to
provide the personnel to man the Health Centre.

        The Project Committee to which our am the Chairman in conjunction with
the Local leaders have requested me to arrange an appointment with you
at your home in Uluwbi so that they can call on you and liaise with you
in connection with the Project.

        I shall therefore be very grateful if you could spare sometime from
your busy schedule to meet us. Kindly let me know when this can happen.

                            Yours sincerely,


                            S.C.C. WANYANGA
                                (CHAIRMAN)
                    MALANGA HEALTH CENTRE PROJECT COMMITTEE
```

And he replied thus:

Hon. I. E. Omolo Okero, M.P.
Minister for Information & Broadcasting

Ministry of Information & Broadcasting
Harambee Avenue
P.O. Box 30025
Nairobi.

MIB/PER/27

11th September, 1978.

S.G.O. Wanyanga, Esq.,
Chairman,
Malanga Health Centre Project Committee,
P.O. Box 60,
YALA.

Dear Sir,

Re: Malanga Health Centre.

    I herewith acknowledge receipt of your letter dated the 6th inst., in connection with the above subject. However, the Minister, the Hon. I. E. Omolo Okero, M.P., has directed me to enquire from you, if you have a written commitment from the Ministry of Health, with regard to the provision of staff for this Health Centre.

Yours faithfully,

E. Williamson

(Mrs.) E. Williamson
Personal Secretary to the Minister

And I wrote back to him thus:

>MALANGA HEALTH CENTRE,
>P.O. BOX 60,
>Y A L A.

>19th September, 1978

The Hon. I.E. Omolo Okero, M.P.
Ministry of Information & Broadcasting,
P.O. Box 30025,
N A I R O B I.

Dear Sir,

>RE: MALANGA HEALTH CENTRE:

Thank you very much for your Personal Secretary's letter reference MIB/PER/27 dated 11th September, 1978.

I tabled the said letter in our Project Committee Meeting where I was directed to ask you to give the Committee Members audiance to discuss this matter fully with you and to explore spheres where you, as our representative can assist us.

We have not obtained any written commitment from the Ministry of Health with regard to the staffing of the Health Centre but we approached the Medical Authorities at Siaya who assured us that since the project was not a new one but only an extension to the existing one, the Government would not stand in the Wanainchi's way if they wanted to provide better facilities to what is already existing. They sanctioned the project to start off.

In the circumstances it is important that we sit down with you and discuss matters pertaining to this project.

Please let us know when you can be available home to meet us.

>Yours faithfully,

>S.G.O. WANYANGA,
>CHAIRMAN,
>MALANGA HEALTH CENTRE PROJECT COMMITTEE

On the day of the harambee he did not attend our day function, but was kind enough to grace our night function, where we had a live music band as part of our fundraising efforts. Whether or not the gatekeeper charged him entrance fee I did not know. If he did, we were grateful for getting something, however, little from our MP.

The reply I received from him at first upset me because he had downgraded our request by directing his secretary to reply my letter instead of himself. He was, however, right in wanting to know if I had the government's approval. Events to secure the government's approval would later prove him right.

Let me explain.

Every time I discussed this with the relevant authorities I was assured approval would follow, but nothing happened. This went on until one day I was tipped that no approval would be given until the government secured money for supplies like beds, mattresses, beddings and other necessary items like microscopes. I revised my approach and concentrated my efforts in pursuit of the items (equipments). When we finally secured the equipments, I was told that a high-ranking government official must come to declare the facility upgraded. When a permanent secretary came without the authority to approve and said the Minister would come to declare the facility upgraded, we were disappointed and even thought we would never get approval.

Meanwhile the equipments we had secured were stealthily carted away by the government to another facility under the pretext, ironically, that we were not ready. This made me almost give up. But tolerance and persistence paid. Eventually we received the approval after the new M.P. stepped in. We were given other equipments and to date the modern facility is fully operational. I also applied for grants to pipe in water, which was approved. Ironically, on the day I was finishing the laying of pipes for water to be turned on, we received word that Honorable Horace Ongili Owiti, our M.P., had been murdered in Siaya. I almost passed out and never recovered from the shock for a very long time. The man was a dear friend and dedicated leader.

Later I had a gigantic battle with the councillor who took my place, Councillor Dickson Indakwa. The road to his new home passed through the health centre land where a shallow well had been sunk to help the facility with water before it was connected to the main line. His plots in Mutumbu Market also abutted the health centre land and trucks supplying beer and other merchandise passed through the land to off load. Then the Youth Polytechnic in the neighbourhood, which had been constructed and was supposed to be owned by Mutumbu Women Group, had been taken away from the women group and was being run by him and a few cronies.

The polytechnic occupied a piece of land that belonged to Malanga Nursery, because it had no land. Councillor Indakwa approached me to talk to Malanga Health Centre management committee to allow the polytechnic to build a store cum hostel for female student boarders. I agreed to talk to members of the committee because both the polytechnic and the health centre were community projects which could prop up each other. When the matter came up for discussion at the committee, he and his two cronies were present. The committee gave its approval on two conditions.

- That the construction of the building should not be used as a pretext to take health centre land to give to the polytechnic.
- That the building would be used by the polytechnic as well as the health centre when completed.

Unknown to me and members of the committee—including the two cronies—was the fact that his request was double-edged. He wanted to kill two birds with one stone. Not only did he want to acquire land for the polytechnic but he also wanted a buffer zone between the health centre and his plots, which could give him unhindered access to his home and provide off-loading space for his plots. His cronies and supporters were too myopic to see this trick.

Later I contributed money in harambees for the construction of the polytechnic building. When the building was completed he started his second move (he wanted the health centre fence to be opened to provide a gate for the hostel), I refused because I was now aware of his intrigues.

Like I said earlier, when one succeds where others have failed, envious people will come after you. That was the case with me. I was reported to government offices to be investigated for misappropriation of funds. The goal was to remove me from the chairmanship of Malanga Health Clinic. These schemes were orchestrated by the councillor. But this was one of the times I was detrmined to fight things out. The normally wise and open-minded D.C., Mr. Samwel Oreta, later came in the company of the district hospital personnel. Members of the community attended in large numbers. Many were my opponent's supporters, including women who were brought to specifically sing praises of him if he triumphed over me. The two pastors were conspicuously present. People stood in clusters of twos or three's talking in low tones as they waited for the meeting to commence. I thought I even saw two guys with *rungus* standing under the shade of the only big tree in the compound, which had escaped our axe.

It was tense.

The D.C., Mr. Oreta, called the meeting to order and gave us time to plead our cases. His supporters present were Silas Mayienga, Ongoma Waudi, who was also a member of the Health Center Management Committee. The rest were Isaiah Olang', Isaiah Odit, Elijah Okech, who were his cronies, and of course the two Pastors. On my side was the rest of the management team, including Mr. Onyango, Mr. Osare, Mr. Odera, and Mr. Jared Nyawade. I did not bring any outsider into this because in my view it was an internal problem. He misadvised his cronies to stand on the soil of their great grandfathers who acquired the land and bequeathed it to the generations down the line and lie that at some point during the adjudication of the land part of the health centre land had been registered to the polytechnic—a shallow and stupid argument that even an imbecile could see was a lie. Telling white lies like these was a taboo in our culture and had serious repercussions.

When proceedings were not moving fast enough, I stood up to reply and went full blast—both barrels blazing. I tabled copies of land registers, called green cards, for the original dispensary land and for the land we purchased from Ohindo and Otieno. I also produced another copy for Malanga Nursery plot. Those who claimed there was land registered for polytechnic had nothing to show as proof. While still presenting our case, I let off a secret I had kept for a very long time.

Wanna hear it?

When Councillor Indakwa took over from me as councillor for North Gem, I handed him health centre documents which including a letter of consent granted to the health centre to enable Ohindo Majera to transfer the portion of the land the centre bought from him. Instead of following up and registering the health entre portion, he used the approval to transfer to himself the portion he bought from Ohindo.

Seeing that we were right, the D.C. did not spare them. He blasted them hard at some point even threatening to lock them up. They were crestfallen and subdued. Their supporters started leaving one by one or in couples. Women who and been fed and wined to come and sing *Mwanawamberi* wished they had somewhere to hide; they too left in shame. Those on my side were elated. They were happy that it ended the way it ended. The D.C. left and the following day the sun rose and set as usual, but the problem never went away as it would resurface once again in the future.

In 2002 I flew out of the country to the U.S.A. shortly before the general elections. The councillor recaptured his seat of North Gem ward from Jared Nyawade. As soon as he knew I wasn't returning, he started messing up the health centre all over again. He frustrated the nurse-in-charge, Mr. Shem Owiti, until he left. He then influenced the firing of Eunice Otieno and Benson Okong'o, who were my relatives, but left Odundo Odhiambo, who was his relative; whom I employed along with the other two. But his attempts to renew efforts to grab health centre land were thwarted by a smart Chief Naboth Kosanya, of North Gem.

My selfless service to the people was turbulent and intriguing. It helped some people and destroyed others. To those who wronged me, my motto was, still is, and will always be, "Evil is overcome with good." I will continue to serve irrespective of my being wronged. I will continue to be good to my friends as well as my enemies and detractors. That is what greatness is made of!

CHAPTER 20

BLACK MAGIC

In the world there are two opposing forces—white or black, positive or negative, going or coming back, going up or coming down, yes or no, day or night, light or darkness, good or evil, the list is endless. Man is the only specie in the universe that God gave a mind to choose; all other animals work and live more or less by instinct. Man can choose to be stingy or benevolent, cruel or docile, immoral or upright, foolish or wise, bad or good. But God warns man that for him to earn the right to inherit His kingdom, where he will live forever, he must choose good over evil, day over night, light over darkness. If man chooses right, he will love God with all his heart and love fellow man as he loves himself. Clear and straightforward, right? But how many of us abide by or do as God commanded? More often than not we take the easy way out, which is the devil's way, since the path to God's kingdom is narrow and demanding. Whoever follows it to the end is worthy of being called a man of God and qualifies to inherit the kingdom of God.

Let's now move on. After I witnessed the tragedies that befell my family in quick succession, I started wondering whether or not the forces working to decimate the family were good or bad ones. People started getting loud that I should do something otherwise my entire family would be annihilated. They even started pointing accusing fingers at the alleged evil spirits. I was still bitter, but more so naïve and inexperienced. I started thinking that perhaps these people were right and that I should do something.

But what?

People came to me with all sorts of suggestions. Why don't you invite one of the Evangelical members to pray for you? What about the Legio Maria Sect; they are good at exorcism; they will sniff off all the evil spirits from the home. Oh, wait, what about consulting a witchdoctor? You know, if these problems emanate from evil spirits you must fight fire with fire. You get the drift, don't you?

I was desperate and knew I had to do something to survive. I remembered my own near-fatal accidents at Nyalenda, the one along Kisumu-Busia Road, and the one in Mutumbu and reasoned that *apwoyo ok tony ga e oro ariyo*—a hare does not survive two successive droughts. For a moment I forgot who had been my protector all the time. I forgot the very force which had saved my life when I got airborne and flew through the windscreen of the car at Nyalenda and at Simenya. I forgot the person who saved me from the Kericho mini bus accident. I forgot the hand which reached out to me and pulled me from the jaws of death in the Mutumbu and N'giya accidents. This was the person I should have run to as fast as I could, but did I?

No I didn't.

I was persuaded that there was another greater force than Him who could save our family from decimation. I was determined to try this alternative force. We human beings have very short memories indeed, but mine was at this time the shortest. I had forgotten how my deceased brother had tried this alternative option but failed and ended up losing not only his life, but also that of his wife and child. It was too recent to be forgotten, that's why I say I had a very short memory indeed. I was also myopic and foolish. Leaving a tried and tested option for an untried and untested one didn't reflect favorably on my level of intelligence.

However, as a result of these proddings I visited witchdoctors, quacks and sheikhs. Each one of them had one message for me—that there was someone in my village who was after our blood and would not rest until all of us, my father's family, were in the grave. But I did not believe them. What made me doubt was the identity of that 'someone.' They said he was a tall, light-skinned man from our village. Others said he was a black, short person and yet another said it was a woman. Taking all these three scenarios as an example, who could I believe? And even assuming I believed one of them, who could I say was the culprit? In my village there were many light-skinned men, many short black people, and women were the majority.

So, who to believe?

The efforts to hypnotize me failed. I had learnt the trick of disarming them by looking them straight in the eye and by answering their questions in the negative. My size, physique and attire helped put them off even more. During those days, I wore on my right wrist a bangle which Nyamwalo had picked on the road and which I snatched from her. With this bracelet and the sheikh's ring, which I had on my middle finger, together with the fixed look, sent terror through the spine of all the witchdoctors I encountered. They believed I had seen more prominent and stronger magicians than them. I never received any help from them. May be, like Thomas, I doubted their ability to rid my family of the evil spirits.

There were, however, some of their actions and deeds that were beyond my comprehension. I personally observed all the incidences narrated herein when I took a friend or relative to consult, and when some were performed in my presence. I took many people to consult these guys. I will narrate a couple of incidences to illustrate the power which some of these witches, had which enabled them do such wonders. I will not mention names to protect the identity of the people involved.

One day I was traveling from Kisumu to Homa Bay. An elderly man with a bike boarded the mini bus. There were many passengers in the bus. The old man had to squeeze himself through a crowd of young men to be able to get in. He got in and stood on the isle of the bus, next to me. When he was asked for bus fare, he reached for his wallet from the pocket, but it was missing. He checked other pockets, but he couldn't find it. He then shouted hysterically, "*Gimaya!*—they have robbed me!"

One of the turnboys, the most talkative, asked the old man where he had kept his wallet. "Was it in your pocket?"

"Yes, right here," the old man said.

The turn boy then told him sarcastically that he should not have kept his wallet in the verandah; he should have kept it in the bedroom. The innuendo was clear. He was telling the old man that he was careless.

As a result of this derisive remark, the old man demanded to be dropped off, which at first the driver ignored. But when the old man got mad and began saying he did not have any money for fare, the driver stopped and the old man alighted. The talkative turnboy quickly lowered his bike for him from the rack of the minibus. Immediately his bike touched down, he told the driver to wait until he retrieved his wallet. The driver tried to resist, but he told him, "You won't go far, my son, just let me get my wallet first then go in peace."

I frowned. *Get the wallet?*

At first I didn't comprehend what he was talking about. How was he going to find this wallet? May be the person who had pickpocketed him had alighted the bus. Was he going to demand that each of us be searched?

He insisted the person who took his wallet was still in the bus.

The talkative turnboy got mad and shouted to the driver to drive off, but the driver refused. Then in the hearing of all passengers, the old man said, "I'm giving whoever took my wallet the last chance to return it to me or else he will regret."

Nobody volunteered.

The old man got hold of his bike, stood it upright and deflated the front tire. Then he reached for his pressure pump from his bag and started putting pressure back into the deflated tire. As the tire filled, the stomach of the talkative turnboy started swelling. As the old man continued to pump pressure into the tire, the turn boy's tummy continued to swell. When his buttons burst, some passengers started telling him to give back the wallet to the old man. He ignored and the old man continued to pump. I was convinced his tummy would burst if he didn't give back the wallet.

I was sure he must have taken the wallet. Or why hadn't anybody else's tummy swollen? Why him?

When his eyes started bulging out, the driver intervened and told him, "*Bwana, mrudishie buda kibeti*—Mister, return to the old man his wallet."

At that point, the turnboy reached to the right pocket of his trouser and took out the old man's wallet, to the bewilderment of everybody. It contained over 2000 Kenya shillings and the old man's ID. Then it was the turnboy's turn to plead with the old man to spare his life. The driver and the passengers pleaded with the old man to yield and spare the life of this stupid young man.

He eventually agreed.

As he deflated the tire of the bike, the turn boy's tummy deflated until it got back to normal. The old man then warned him to stop pickpocketing or any other criminal activity if he wanted to live his full life. The turn boy dropped off at the next stage and we continued with our journey together with the old man who was given a free ride. Talk about mystery!

My uncle had lost a couple of cattle. It was not the first time. On two previous occasions his home had been cleaned by cattle rustlers. They usually waited until he raised his cattle well and had a good stock then struck. In the neighborhood too people had been losing cattle to them and the neighbors collectively decided it was time they did something about it.

But what could they do?

The rustlers' intelligence network was far more superior to the local security personnel, who had failed to stump out rustling. When they had youths patrolling at night, the rustlers knew it and never came. When, as individuals, they decided to take charge and watch over the cattle at night, the rustlers would strike the night they called off the watch and went to sleep. Prior to my uncle losing his cattle, a clever chief had sought the help of the villagers to help stamp out rustling and one very able and intelligent person stood in the chief's baraza and said that only fools get their cattle stolen. He said nobody could steal his because he was on watch 24/7. Later, he turned out to be more foolish than those he branded fools. Two months later, his home was cleaned. All his cattle were stolen!

When my uncle's cattle were stolen he reported the theft to the authorities, as he would later narrate to me. One of the security personnel, after a stupor of alcohol, was heard saying that people from that area—meaning our area—were the most stupid people he had ever met. They take their chickens into the house at night and leave their cattle outside, then complain about cattle theft. Which is more valuable, a hen or a cow?

During the time my uncle lost his livestock, rumors abounded about someone who, from magic, was able to detect a livestock thief. My uncle got interested and started making inquiries. He soon got wind of a person from Sakwa who had that magic. He and his neighbors pooled resources and sent for the person. The chief, the assistant chief and the police were informed to be present when the person did his thing. I also arranged to attend and see for myself what was going to happen. I attended together with many other people.

The medicine man prepared a potion which he got everybody present to drink. Village elders had been instructed to tell everybody from the village to attend. Whoever evaded the exercise automatically became a suspect. After a short time, 3 young men started vomiting. All of them were in their mid-twenties and one of them was the son of my uncle's biological brother. In between vomiting, the trio started eating grass. They mimicked how they went and untied the cattle and how they drove them. When they started speaking, they named all their accomplices, whose names were taken down by the security personnel present. They also revealed where they took the cattle. The witchdoctor said they would eat grass the rest of their lives unless he was paid to reverse the effects of his medicine. He also warned that the longest they could live was three days. When asked by relatives of the victims what he wanted in payment he said "A head of cattle for each culprit!"

The relatives of the culprits hurriedly left the place to look for payment. They were, however, warned that reversing the effect would be conditional on recovery of the stolen animals. So under police escort, the rustlers went where they had hidden the stolen animals and all were recovered. The witch was paid and left. The rustlers were tucked away in a jail to wait a date with the magistrate.

I was stunned.

But the most bizarre and scaring incident of black magic was at a house my sister and I visited one afternoon. I had seen magic and magicians, but all were a pale shadow of what my sister and I saw. I had seen an inflated tummy, men eating grass, bundles of paraphernalia from nowhere, and believed I had seen it all.

Was I wrong!

As we were walking to the house, for some strange reason, my sister and I were not talking. As we got closer, we noticed the door was ajar and there were people inside. We could see them, but because they were talking, they did not notice us approach. Suddenly we were at the door.

Inside, we noticed a man sitting on a chair facing the door and the woman, the owner of the house, was talking to him.

"Hodi", we said to announce our presence at the door.

We appeared to have surprised them because on realizing our presence, she quickly jumped from the position she was in. She was holding the laps of the man and talking to him in a low tone. As she jumped, she did not know whether to offer us seats or simply order us out because she was confused. We were surprised at her attitude. Normally she would have welcomed us with open arms, particularly my sister whom she hadn't seen in a long time. She hurriedly walked out without a word to us, as we stood there transfixed.

I decided to move closer to the man sitting on the chair to say hallo. It was at that point that a strange thing happened, which I will never forget. Just there in our view, the body of this seemingly normal person started shrinking. The limbs, both legs and both hands started disappearing at the same speed from the fingers and the toes upwards. To me it was like a dream. The head, the torso, the thorax and the rump. The whole body just melted and disappeared in our view. The chair became empty. I was so frightened that I never spoke a word. My sister, on the other hand, was shaken because she believed, as I did, that we had seen a ghost. I led her out of the house and back home. The rest of that day she never uttered a word. It took me two weeks before I told my family what I had witnessed.

During those days rumors, were doing rounds in the village that the woman kept *jinnis*, but I did not give much thought to the rumors until that day, when I saw what I considered evidence in support of that rumor.

But more would follow later, which surpassed this sheer wizardry. I met the owner of the house a day later. When she saw me, she just smiled and walked away. She later confided in me, when she knew I had not made known to the public her secret. She admitted she kept *jinnis* and that she was tired of them because they wanted blood every month. She said she was running out of the goats which she kept for that purpose and that when she did, the *jinnis* will revert to her children and kill them one after another for blood.

"At night," she said, "they turn me into a wife, sometimes entertaining up to five of them. I am going to get rid of them."

"But how," I asked.

"I know someone who wants them. I'll transfer then to him!"

"Transfer?"

"I have no choice!"

Up to six months after she disposed of them, people walking along the road behind her home claimed to see tall figures walking along the road at night. She lived a couple of years thereafter then died of natural causes. Being a Muslim, the leader of that faith came to bury her. Astonishingly, he preached from the Bible that day.

But boy, the one who beat them all was this pastor who did his wizardry with a Bible. I'll conclude with it because I believe you get the point. I did not know him before my magistrate friend asked me to give him a ride to his place. This friend gave me an impression of how he hated magicians. He was a devout member of the Legio Maria sect, which claims to have no room for wizardry and magic. He swore that he could not consult witchdoctors, not only because it was against his faith, but because he hated them. His car had been totalled and since he needed to see this pastor, he asked me for a ride. I drove him and his wife to Kisumu, where the pastor lived.

We were lucky to find him, he said, because he was planning to go to church which was 2 hours walk away. He said he would suspend going to church to attend to us. His was a 2-roomed house which served as a bedroom and sitting room. Right in the centre of the room was a coffee table covered with a red table cloth. On top of it laid a Bible. He brought water in a basin and asked my friend and his wife to wash their hands. He put the basin and the water, after they had washed their hands, under the table for a while. He then removed the Bible and the table cloth from the table and put the basin with water on top of the table and covered it with the red cloth. He placed both his hands on the table cloth and started praying. As he prayed, things dropped loudly into the water in the basin. This went on for close to five minutes. When he was done, he removed the table cloth and inside the basin were wraps of clothing tied in small sizes. When opened, they contained snails, a bic, some papers with writings on them, human hair and small bones. What surprised me was not what I saw or how they got there, but what my friend said. He said that the bic belonged to their son, that he had previously lost it and looked all over for it but could not find it. I did not understand how he knew the bic belonged to their son. Bics look alike and the mere fact that he was seeing one did not make it his son's lost one; unless there was a specific identifying mark. I tried to scrutinize the bic to see if it had any unique mark on it, but I failed to trace any.

As the pastor's work was only to extract paraphernalia from where they were hidden, he directed them to go and see a Legio Maria clergy who knew what to do for them. He also said that there were some items he could not extract because they were well protected and he could not retrieve them in the house. He told him to return the following week, without his wife, so he could take him to a desolate area where he would try to extract the remaining items.

The following week I gave my friend a ride to Kisumu again. We picked the pastor, who said my friend should identify an isolated place, where we could go to extract the items. My friend, having lived in Kisumu, knew where we could go. We carried his tools of trade—the coffee table, the basin, a jerican of water, table cloth and the Bible. We left the car and penetrated the thicket. We came across a clearing, which he said was the best site. He then gave my friend water in a basin to wash his hands. The basin, this time, was put under the table and the table covered with the red cloth. He placed the Bible on top of the table and asked us to move away from the table.

He knelt beside the table and uttered some inaudible words, then hurriedly left to join us. He said we should focus our attention on the table. As we watched, something like a whirlwind developed and grew in intensity. As the wind passed the table, a big pot dropped on the table from above and smashed it into pieces and from it came a black mamba, throwing its head menacingly before it disappeared into the thicket. I was frightened, but I did not want to show it. We moved closer to the touch down area, where we recovered more bundles of small wraps containing a variety of things. He said that the snake was put there by the sorcerer who bewitched my friend as security to prevent anybody accessing those items. Again he sent my friend to the Legio Maria clergy for more treatment. I regretted later not having accompanied him to the clergy to see how his treatment was progressing. I would have known whether or not the magic Bible worked.

I took my friend back to his work station and would on two more occasions meet with him as clergy and as magistrate. He later became a clergy with Legio Maria sect, but continued to be on the bench until he retired. Through my association with him I came to know many members of Legio Maria sect—some became my friends and others my clients. I would later get a chance to see their spiritual leader at work, and even have prayers in my house.

*

There are many more incidents I'd like to mention, especially my encounters with the Legio Maria—incliding their spiritual leader Ondeto—but my point is made about the prevalence and ability of black magic in Africa. But what science do magicians, witches and sorcerers use in doing these amazing things?

Let me say this. I don't know what manner of power such people used. I would suggest that research be done to explain the source of their power. I know that Christianity has answers to some of these issues by contending that the devil has power to pull off feats of these nature, but I still believe that if that were the case, it should be made known that Christ's power is far greater than the power of these questionable forces and the people who propel them.

CHAPTER 21

CHURCH

Having tried the black magic option and failed to get satisfaction, I sought to go back to my roots. I remembered my parents. For the 13 years I lived with them, I never saw them invite or entertain a magician at home. I never saw Father come home with charms and other magical stuff to administer to us or to themselves. I never saw them slaughter chickens, rams, goats and offer them as sacrifice to the spirits. I never saw them lick or sniff ash as medicine. They were straight forward Christians, devoted to their faith. They did not attempt to mix good with evil. Even when the temptations of death abounded, my father never wavered. Even when I fell ill, and these were many occasions, they never took me to witchdoctors; they took me to a hospital and I got cured. They held my hand and led me to the church where they expected me to stay. But unlike them, I veered off the proven path and almost tumbled into the devil's abyss.

Let me announce this—*I am happy to be alive.*

I am happy to have realized my folly and pulled away from the trail of risk and destruction. I was determined not to have a self-imposed destiny. I decided to be a master of my own fate, to be above things and to exercise my God-given right to choice positively. I knew I had been knocked down by the devil, but I was not out. Like in a boxing match, I got up before the full count to face the devil once again. This time, with the armour of the Holy Spirit, I went back to my roots.

Back to the church!

It happened gradually. I remembered how I grew up with God as maker in an S.D.A. home, my father and mother being pioneer members of the church. Their moral standards were beyond reproach. This contrasted sharply with the traditionalists or even the rest of Christian churches at the time. What made them stand out was their observance of the Sabbath-day as commanded in Exodus 20:8 – 11. They went to church on Saturday instead of Sunday. This was the atmosphere under which I was brought up. During my formative years, wherever my mother went to church she took me along. I enjoyed children's programmes; the stories were captivating. I enjoyed going to church or church gatherings.

My mother was my role model. Whatever she did to me was the right thing to do. So I tried to ape some of her characteristics and behaviors. These would help me in days to come. When I returned home from Maranda, my mother got me back into the church, but only for the duration of the remainder of her life. I remember during one of the camp meetings, I had been psyched a whole week for the day. When the D-day came, my father insisted I go and shepherd the cattle. I obliged, but I made sure I returned them home one hour before the scheduled time.

And so the time had come to abandon my dark, sinful and devilish past and clothe myself with humility and righteousness. I had been ensnared by the devil for far too long. I had worshipped idols, committed adultery, embraced polygamy, visited magicians, coveted, lied and even failed to honor my parents. I had committed all the known sins. Above all, I had abandoned my faith and church. I decided to be like my mother. I wanted to match her devotion to the church. I wanted to match my father's resolve to be a good Christian parent. I wanted to be everything right. I had seen the blessings those who worked for the Lord got. I had seen successful and prosperous Christian homes. I never saw a genuinely Christian home where the Lord was the light and his name constantly mentioned that was not prosperous. I decided to work for the church.

With that I made a big decision, a big shift which would affect my life and relations considerably. Top on the list was how I could effectively work for the church. God had given me good and well behaved children. With God's help, and if I acted right and became a good role model, my children would not only become good citizens, but also good role models as parents. I was determined to make this happen. I wanted to give God an opportunity to help me and my family. What better decision to make than decide to start working for the church!

I directed all my extra resources to working for the church. This was an area help was required. Around this time, Nyairo, who had hitherto refused to embrace the faith, suddenly started showing a lot of enthusiasm for the church. Buoyed by the cordial relationship which existed between my cousin Japheth Ojwang's family and my family at Rang'ala, Nyairo was finally baptized. The day she was baptized we had a big party which was attended by many people, including my father. What a joyous occasion it was. Nyairo never looked back. She became one of the pillars of my family's strong Christian foundation. She henceforth started playing her role as my helper more vigorously. We managed to mould a home of twenty five members into a formidable heaven-bound Christian machine.

We started encouraging our children to join kindergarten and other youth programmes of the church. We sent them to camporees, camp meetings, crusades and all youth gatherings. Our motto was *Keep the child in church for the first seven years of his or her life and he or she will forever remain in church*. Our efforts paid off almost instantly. The children's grades in school improved tremendously. Their character improved and ability to stand before a congregation and speak was remarkably enhanced. We started reaping the fruits of God's blessings. We attended church every Sabbath and never let go.

We then moved to our next stage of our strategy. A family that eats together and prays together stays together. We introduced evening prayers, first at Rang'ala, then at Siaya and later at our country home, in Gem. At this point the names of Nyasondu, Nyairo and Nyamwalo were changed by none other than our children to Mama ma Siaya, Mama ma Rang'ala and Mama ma Madala respectively. These names were derived from the places they lived at the time. These would henceforth be their lasting names.

These prayers were conducted every evening after supper. Each child, beginning with the youngest, was asked to prepare a sermon to preach every evening and they preached in ascending order till all of them preached, after which a parent or parents also preached one after the other and the process was repeated. At Mama ma Siaya's house, the process went on and off depending on the mood or who was visiting and how long he or she stayed. To her credit, I must say, she maintained her personal morning and evening prayers. A product of our plan initiated after Mama ma Rang'ala's baptism. When I returned to the U.S.A in 2009, I found she and two Overtone Park members had a three-way phone prayer session every morning, except Saturday and Sunday. She was also a member of a group of selfless women devoted to serving the Lord, led by Mrs. Lilian Gitau and Joyce Rwambwa. Their objective was to help their members spiritually and materially. I was privileged to attend one of their sessions and I enjoyed it a lot.

At Mama ma Dala's house, the session has been on and off depending on her mood and disposition during the day. With constant mood swings, the sessions have not taken root and unlike the other two houses, they have not had a ripple effect and spilled to her children. The surviving children in other two houses are stronger in faith and I believe they practice devotional prayers in their houses. I would urge all the parents and children wherever they are to take the faith, the church activities and the devotional prayers more seriously. As the wise men say "The locusts that are not in the main park are the ones eaten by birds—*Bonyo moweyo ban'g wetene ema winy chamonga*. So, children, continue fighting the good fight; keep the faith and finish the race."

> *For everyone who asks receives, and to everyone who seeks finds, and to everyone who knocks the door is opened.* Mathew 7:8

The third stage was to figure out how best to contribute to youth development in the church. As a family, we encouraged them to unite and work together. When they had a function outside the church, I provided transport and meals to enable their trip be as comfortable as possible. Most of the youths who were in this programme are strong in faith. Some of them are preachers, church elders and even wives of pastors.

As part of our efforts to help our children and those of the village, we decided that instead of striving to move them closer to the church, we should move the church closer to them. This was a brain child of my father, but he did not live to see it through. Mrs. Christabel Diemo, Mr. Henry Ndukwe and I put our heads together to plot the initiation of a church in our village of Magunda. We roped in Mrs. Jane, Trufena Okelo and Prisca Misango. We got everything in place except land to put up a building. I then remembered that my cousin, Prof. A.B.C. Ochola Ayayo, whose father was credited with the advent of

S.D.A. in Central Kavirondo had a piece of land in our village which he was not using because he had migrated to Achuth, in Migori. We approached the overseer of the land to let us build a church on that piece of land, which he at first agreed but later changed his mind. I also talked to the professor over the matter. He told me he had no problem with the church building, but he did not have a title deed to it. He asked if I could assist him get it.

I processed this title deed at the Lands Office and sent it to him. We were caught in a situation where the owner of the land agreed to have the church built on his land, but the overseer refused. The church is a Sanctuary of the Lord. We were not going to build it at a place where someone may decide to get physical to prevent us from doing the work. We dropped the idea of building the church on that piece of land just as suddenly as it was conceived.

We started looking for another piece of land. Nobody was willing to cede a portion of his land to us. When it was obvious we were not going to build a church because we lacked land, I remembered another piece of land that was still under my domain. It was my late brother Absalom's. I had applied for permission to administer this estate. I obtained the grant and got the land transferred to my name. After striking a deal with Absalom's adult children to allow me to use part of Absalom's land to build the church in exchange for the land I bought from Joka Okola, where I had settled them, they allowed me to do so. I did the sub divisions through the Lands Office and got the portion we needed transferred to the church. We quickly regrouped and arranged for a *harambee*—fund raising. On the harambee day, people of all walks of life came with all sorts of materials—corrugated iron sheets, poles for the walls and for the roof, money; anything somebody could lay his or her hands on. We raised enough money and materials to help us embark on construction as soon as possible.

Pastor Inyangala was on hand to preside over the ground-breaking ceremony. Within two weeks we had a semi-permanent church building. Magunda beat Rindwa for the name. The ensuing church was then named Magunda. Our people moved from Malanga S.D.A. Church to Magunda S.D.A. Church.

Later we got back to the drawing board to plan a proper church building and to plaster the walls and floor of the semi-permanent building. We had to come up with a strong building committee. I was elected the chairman of the building committee. A precedent was found in Maliera S.D.A. Church, where Mzee Ruben Kwasu, who like me was polygamous, was elected chairman of Maliera S.D.A. Church building committee and presided over the construction of the said church until its completion. I was also determined to emulate Mzee Ruben and preside over the construction of Magunda S.D.A. Church until its completion. But this would not come to pass because there would be intrigues, betrayal and downright infighting and insults, which would force my team out later.

The stone-laying was conducted by Pastor Tobias Otieno Ayayo, the first son of Pastor Silfano Ayayo Mijema, the initiator of Adventism in Central

Nyanza. I remember what he did. After church members congregated, he asked my step-mother, Loice Wandati, my wife, Rose Adongo, and I to bring one stone each the size used on a hearth. We brought the three stones, which he arranged in such a manner that made it look like we were going to light a fire and use the stones to support a pot. The significance was obvious—we were going to be pillars of the church however hot. So with each of us holding his/her stone, he led us into prayer and blessed the ground.

Pastor Tobias gave me a very strong warning. He said, "Now that you have laid your hand on one of the three corner stone's of Magunda Church you should never participate again in the activities of Mutumbu Sports Association." He thundered this in the presence of everybody. I never went to the sports body again.

With Pastor Boaz Otuoma, we worked hard and built the church up to the window level.

About that time, an organization known as Hands Across the World was assisting churches that met their conditions. They wanted a church which had a plot with a title deed and had started and done construction work at least up to the window level. Magunda was one of the few churches which met their conditions. With the help of the Station Director, Pastor Albert Otieno, and the Central Nyanza Field Executive Director, Pastor Hezron Sande Obuga, our application for funds was accepted. At the time the church elder was Justo Ouma and the treasurer was Jane Rose Aluoch (Mama ma Ran'gala). Since the organization needed a bank account through which to disburse the funds, the four of us—Justo Ouma, Jane Rose Aluoch, Pastor Albert Otieno and I were elected signatories to the bank account. The funds were disbursed and with them we completed the walls and the roof of the church. There was a little balance left in the account.

Later Pastor Albert Otieno left and the new pastor, with the connivance of the new elder; and Christabel Diemo, who was then the head deaconess, alleged that Justo Ouma, Jane Rose Aluoch, Pr. Albert Otieno and I had stolen money from the building kitty. I was hurt and I got very upset. I had used more resources from my family than all these people branding us thieves put together. During our struggles to build the church, before and after we received the funds, the guy who was now the church elder decided not to co-operate in anyway. In fact, he behaved, most of the time, as an infidel. If he came to the church and Elder Justo was to preach, he and his family would leave just as the divine service team entered the pulpit. When Elder Justo was elected, the guy, on a Sabbath day, took all the things he had offered to the church, including chairs, back to his home and never returned them. Christians should be a reflection of Christ. Would Christ have done that? Would He have allowed any of His disciples to do that? I doubt it, but I cannot judge; the judge sits on His throne in heaven.

From 1983, when Maliera Secondary School became a government recognized institution, under the sponsorship of the S.D.A. Church, I was nominated by the church to be its representative on the Board of Governors. I was shortly thereafter elected Chairman of the Board. I served in that capacity until the year 2003, when I left because I was out of the country. During my stewardship of Maliera Secondary School, I initiated the construction of three quarters of the structural developments in the school, including the library, laboratory, classroom, offices and water and electricity installations. I also oversaw the progression of classes from a single stream to triple streams and improvement in staffing.

Two things which were on my development list which I failed to achieve were the purchase of a school bus and changing the name of the school to Pastor Silfano Ayayo—Maliera Secondary School, in remembrance of the initiator of the school. I hope the next generation of leaders will complete those two projects. I served the church and the school with dedication and determination. Like a relay, I passed the button to a young and energetic team. With fresh ideas they would move the school a notch higher.

Allow me to wind up this segment by saying this. When the clamour for amendment of the constitution hit fever pitch, the leadership of North Nyanza Field called upon me to lead the team that would eventually compile a report on the views of Adventists. I gladly embarked on the task and went to all churches in the field, with my team. Later we submitted that report to the Field, which passed it on to the Union.

Through it all, I have learnt to trust in God in a manner that would make my Mama proud. In this church, I will take my last breath!

CHAPTER 22

POLITICS

Politics was further down the small list of professions I lined up as a career. Indeed, it never featured at all until later in my life. I was not cut for politics. I was not good at lying with a straight face. I stammered a lot when speaking. Even a village elder could speak better. Bottom line was, I could not be a politician because I didn't have what it took to be one. I considered politics a profession of failures, something one looked at after failing in other fields. But during those days, politics was not as dirty as what it later became. Only those who genuinely thought they had something to offer materially or in ideas came forward. It was a tool to help people advance economically and educationally. When the Anglican suppression had been neutralized in my area, politics took over as a weapon of choice for oppression. It determined where new schools, health centers, markets and cattle dips had to be built. It had a huge say on who was to be chief or assistant chief. It determined who got bursaries and sometimes even scholarships. It determined where and when to build bridges and construct rural roads. It affected every aspect of *mwananchi's* life.

Our detractors and oppressors used it effectively, over a long period of time, to deny us plots, administrative positions, bursaries and scholarships. It was such oppressive politics that brought a proliferation of schools in Gem. Each clan, tribe or church competed to have its own school so as not to be left behind in education. This proliferation was what made Gem the cradle of education in Kavirondo.

Politics helped my people a lot. Although they did not have an M.P., a councillor, a chief or an assistant chief, they rallied to agitate for these positions and got most of them.

From 1,974 on, I was in my country home, in Gem, every Christmas and New Year. In order to learn from the elders, I invited them to my father's home and later to my home for a treat every New Year's day. You cannot imagine how much knowledge these elders had. I learned a lot from them. They talked about virtually everything I wished to know. This became a routine I continued into the 80s. As the elders talked and shared ideas, something else was happening—their unity was being cemented and, unknown to me, I was forming a formidable campaign machine like no other in the history of my tribe. Their unity of purpose and campaign power would be manifested later when elections were called.

Meanwhile I was helping here and there with the economic empowerment of our people. Malanga Health Centre was coming up. A few plots, including mine, had been developed in Mutumbu market (which formerly was Malanga market). Mutumbu Women Group was roaring. Things looked good and promising for our people. We had even gotten a number of headmen and assistant chiefs: Philip Obonyo, Otieno Abala, Jotham Odera, John Ougo, Simon Okello, Elijah Okech, Mwalo Mumbe and Jacob Weya. We'd had a breakthrough in the religious line, economic line, administrative line and educational line. The only area we'd performed disastrously despite our superiority in numbers was the political line. Nelson Juma and Silas Mayienga had tried to break through but performed dismally.

So as soon as it was apparent there would be a general election in 1979, I called an elders' think tank. The men were: Elon Mwalo, Noah Mwalo, Ainea Chiama, Elijah Okech, Justo Wamboga and others, to strategize and shop for a candidate that would attract votes across the tribal divide. This was not an easy task. Politics did not need just the base support, but the means to reach other voters. Our ideal candidate therefore had to have money and a car. If we settled on someone who had local support but lacked money and transport, we had to arrange to get both for him. But first we had to look for someone with the triple requirements. Several meetings of the think tank yielded nothing, but eventually they settled on one of our sons. He was a prominent, retired civil servant. He had transport. His possibility of having funds was suspect. But the area he scored lowest was the ability to rally the local (grassroots) support. The elders, however, decided to summon him for an interview. At the interview, he agreed to put forward his name as a candidate for councillorship of North Gem Ward, but only on condition that the elders agreed to fund his entire campaign. I knew at once that would be a recipe for failure. The elders were not in a position to fund a campaign for even a village elder. They were not influential enough to get funding from outside our own people. I therefore advised them—and this turned out to be the biggest mistake I ever made—to continue searching far and wide if the guy they'd interviewed could not fund his campaign.

When they again convened they had a bombshell for me. *"Wuon Wanyanga, in ema wadwaro mondo imaknwa iw kwach*—Son of Wanyanga, you are the one we want to put forward as our candidate."

I instantly got upset.

What did these elders think I was? They thought I had been mobilizing them because I wanted the seat? I knew they did not understand the whole concept of my sacrifice. I could not be the mobilizer and candidate at the same time. I thought they considered me cheap. Inwardly I knew if they insisted and somewhat got me to agree, they would fail a third straight time to wrestle this seat from the hands of the ruling clan. I was not a politician and was not about to become one. Besides, I hated politics and considered it a waste of time and resources. So I bluntly refused and to demonstrate my displeasure, I ceased to be the covernor. Meanwhile, time was running out.

One morning, as I woke up, I found elders in my home—Elon Mwalo, Aineah Chiama, Jotham Odera and Nowa Mwalo. It was a weekend. Their brief was to try and convince me to accept to be a candidate. We talked and talked, but I still felt I was not their candidate. When it was clear they were not going to let go, I caved in and at 7:00 p.m., at my home, they toasted my acceptance.

It had taken over one month and more than 12 hours, that day alone, to agree to present my candidature for election as North Gem ward councillor.

The following weekend I invited them for a strategic meeting to map out our campaign plan and invited the two previous candidates to attend. I wanted to know from the candidates what they thought made them fail. I also wanted to form a campaign committee and a team. I wanted to determine what role the elders would play in the plan. I listened to the presentations of the two previous candidates and those of the knowledgeable elders and came up with a plan that was credible.

Our strategy was two pronged.

We were to fight this battle with "the navy and the army." We agreed that the elders, under the command of Elder Aineah Chiama, would take care of the submarines. The ground troops, under my command, would be headed by Elder Nelson Juma. I would look for money for fuel and other campaigns expenses. I sat back and did absolutely nothing apart from looking for money while the ground troops, in my car with a driver, were out campaigning. The plan was to hoodwink my opponents and potential opponents that I was not campaigning. So over the weekend, when I was at home, I would sit at a point where everybody passing could see me basking in the sunshine while the team was out somewhere campaigning. The elders, on the other hand, were busy with their role. They worked and achieved total support of our people. They looked into ancestral deficiencies and rectified them. They conducted prayers in all our historic sites and ensured I was protected from evil spirits. Their greatest achievement was to win over our medicinemen who previously had supported our opponents. As my main opponent was not an indigenous settler of the land, they had to use one of our guys as the owner of the land for their medicine to work against me. So by taking our people back, the elders denied my opponent a vital campaign tool and rendered him powerless.

When Parliament was later dissolved and election campaigns declared, one more candidate, Juma Oyala, declared his candidature to challenge the incumbent, Barrack Owuor Agola, and myself. At that point I was way ahead of them. If elections were done then, I would beat the two of them. As the campaigns started in earnest, we deployed our fourth plan—door to door and mini rallies in the villages. This became more effective than I thought. A few pockets of resistances were identified, invaded and neutralized. We made a strong case for a landslide.

One day as I was doing my village to village rallies, I went to a home where I found more people than I had hitherto addressed. I worked up the crowd and at the end of it an old man dashed to his house and came out brandishing a spear. He ran menacingly towards the direction I was, as if he was coming to attack me.

But no. He wasn't.

His spear was his way of appreciating what he had heard. In other words, *ne ogosira*—demonstrating his appreciation. Everybody laughed when my handlers, who actually knew what was happening, restrained me from dashing to my car to escape. I enjoyed these rallies because I used them to sharpen my skills. I got so polished in public speaking that my opponents feared sharing a speaking platform with me. I overcame my stammer and polished my local dialect, which was the language of communication to the masses.

The country was under one political party—Kenya African National Union (KANU). The party and the government were one thing. The campaigns were organized and chaired by the District Officer of the Division where the campaigns were held. We were given only a day for public rallies. One was at Malanga Chief's Camp, in the morning, another at Sirembe Market, in the afternoon.

I nearly missed these rallies.

Just as I was preparing to go to the Malanga rally, someone brought me a message that my nephew, Isaac Thuma, had died in Kisumu. Isaac was not only a relative, but was a friend too. He was the one who helped me admit Agwayo in the hospital. He helped me admit and saw to the treatment of my nephew Dunga. He was the one who organized my G.T.T. (Glucose Tolerance Test) at New Nyanza General Hospital in 1974. He had done more for me than I had done for him. With his death, how could I proceed with the rally without showing disrespect to him? I wanted to skip the rally and dash to Kisumu to arrange his funeral. My handlers refused, arguing that that was the only day set aside for rallies and that if I skipped I could as well kiss goodbye being elected.

I did not mind sitting out the Malanga rally, but the Sirembe one I could not miss. That was the bedrock of my support; therefore I did not want to disappoint them. Inwardly I was actually shaking and shivering with fright. This was going to be my first ever public rally and I did not know how the crowd was going to react to my message. Part of the reason I was wavering about attending these rallies was stage fright; not really Isaac's death. I was persuaded and I attended the rallies.

At the Malanga rally, we were the three aspiring candidates for councillorship and five candidates competing to become M.P. for Gem. The arrangement was for civic candidates to speak first, then parliamentary candidates next. Not all parliamentary candidates agreed to share the platform, though; two of them opted out. These were the incumbent and one challenger. At The Malanga rally I was the last to speak and my friend, Barrack Okeno Osare, was also the last to speak among the parliamentary candidates. It was fireworks. Opinion polls conducted after the rally showed I won the debate. I was elated.

At Sirembe, the incumbent ferried in his supporters to boost his support and heckle his opponents. Unknown to him, almost all the people he ferried were actually my supporters. When the lot was done, I was the first to speak and my friend Barrack Okeno was also the first to speak. Both of us had made a strong showing at Malanga, and if lady luck was still on our side, we expected to do even better.

And again I trounced my opponents.

After concluding my speech, none of them was allowed by *wananchi* to speak. I raised the bar so high that my opponents were not allowed to speak; only two parliamentary candidates spoke. But even they cut short their speeches because of the rowdiness of the crowd. The crowd wanted more from me and nothing from anybody else. I realized how I would have made a serious mistake had I decided to sit out these rallies. From Sirembe I knew the seat was mine. The fate of the defending civic and parliamentary candidate was sealed. One of my opponents' spouse burst into tears and loudly complained to me that I should not be saying everything. That was her reaction on how I tore into her husband's ten-year record.

Two of the parliamentary candidates were smart enough in their message delivery that they caught the attention of the crowd. One of them actually used visual aid in his delivery. He had arranged and brought a lorry load of dry sugarcane to make a point against one candidate who headed Kenya Sugar Board shortly before he declared his candidature. His message was clear and double-edged. If the candidate could not help *wananchi* have their ready sugarcane delivered to the factories, how could they be sure he would be useful to them once elected? And if he could not help them get the factories to accept their ripe sugarcane when he was the boss of the Sugar Board of Kenya, how could he help them as an M.P.?

That was the message the crowd wanted to hear.

When the rally ended, the lorry, which had made two trips to Sirembe with people, returned to Malanga empty. The candidate, after his poor showing, instructed his driver to drive back empty. His passengers had to trek back to their homes. Later, we arranged the burial of my nephew Isaac. This accorded me another opportunity to campaign by addressing the mourners.

*

On the polling day, I went to our polling station in the morning, where we found this naked guy and dealt with the situation accordingly. We took care of all loop holes in the two previous elections and left no room for any rigging or manipulation of results. We assigned vehicles to escort the votes to the vote-counting centre. This was done without any hitch.

I won!

It was a landslide. In fact, I got more votes than each of the parliamentary candidates, except the winner. When results were announced, my people were ecstatic and overwhelmed with joy. Ululations rented the air and some people went on their knees praying, others literally crying. My supporters carried me as they celebrated my victory. My victory party had just started. For two days, it was a carnival atmosphere at my home. People wined, dined and sang day and night.

The journey had just began!

After these elections, a big victory party was organized by my voters at which friends relatives and dignitaries attended. In attendance were Jaramogi, Hon. James Orengo, Mrs. Ambala, representing her husband who was our area M.P., all councillors, Dan Nyanjom, O.M.T. Adala and Ambs. Ochieng Adala; and other guests and dignitaries. Uncle Silfane Ayayo Mijema and his son, Pr. Tobias Otieno Ayayo, were present. It was a day to remember—the most important in my life, as it was more than a victory party for me. I was being installed as the Supreme Head of my tribe. In attendance to hand over the leadership was the doyen of our emancipation struggle, who himself was the Supreme Leader of my tribe. He was there in person to hand over the mantle to me. This was done in style and the ceremony was exemplary.

I was given a traditional stool like of a paramount chief; a spear, a symbol of authority; a whisk, a symbol of peace and a traditional cloak worn by kings and princes. Gifts were also given to our guests. From that day I became the de facto head of my tribe until one day I would hand over to someone.

Pr. Silfano Ayayo Mijema handed it to me.

I became an elder.

But before I could be respected, I had to respect myself and respect others. And though I was only 35, I decided to carry myself around as an elder, befitting my new status. It was during this time that I learned you must have respect if you want to be respected. That respect is earned, it cannot be forced. My names, which had hitherto been associated with terror, changed. I became Jabar or Daddy, and on the political arena I was Councillor or Jakom (Chairman). People got to respect me a lot, respect which I still relish and cherish.

I learnt that once you set yourself on the path of uprightness and righteousness the rest of the things just fall in place. I calculated my moves to avoid stepping on other people's toes. My generosity doubled. There was no way I was going to turn away a person I could see was evidently in need, even if I had to do without. I paid school fees, took patients to hospitals, provided food, clothing and sometimes even shelter to the needy. I remembered those who were in the forefront of my campaign and gave them a plot each. John Ongayo, Sila Mayienga, Nelson Juma—these guys put their lives on the line for me and I rewarded them handsomely. I rewarded others in different ways too and all were thankful.

The work of a councillor is quite tedious. He has to attend a few committee meetings and a full council meeting in a month. The chairmanship of a council is not full-time job. The chairman presides over the full council meetings and attends all committee meetings. He is expected to receive dignitaries visiting the council and attends all statutory boards and committees at the district level. He attends all national celebrations at the district headquarters or at any divisional headquarters within the jurisdiction.

But it is at the ward level that work is toughest; tougher than an M.P.'s work. He or she acts like a buffer zone between an M.P. and *wananchi*; which is why the two must bond and work together. He is all the time in the countryside and is the first person *wananchi* run to when they have a problem. Just so you get it, here is a sample of the problems:

- A child is sent away for school fees.
- A relative is sick and needs money or transport to go to the hospital.
- The family has not eaten anything for a long time.
- A wife ran away and her parents insist the balance of dowry must be paid before she comes back.

Fun, isn't it?

Since I was a first-timer and there were no orientation seminars for new councillors, I had to learn on the job; only in my case I was learning to be a councillor and chairman of the council at the same time. There were no handing or taking overs in political positions. The incumbent simply packed up his or her belongings and vacated office. But in my case I was lucky to have as a clerk a veteran in local government administration—Absalom Wambundo Ober. The guy knew local government well and took me up the ladder faster, climbing each rung carefully and cautiously until I too became an expert. I started working immediately the committees were constituted. I did not wait for my inauguration, which the Minister for Local Government wanted to attend and perform personally. Due to the minister's busy itinerary, this exercise delayed and when he finally got time to come, he combined it with the official opening of Siaya's modern market, which the government had helped the council build.

The inauguration was a watershed event in my political life. The minister clothed me with the regalia of office, a flowing robe and a glittering silver-lined chain of office. From the council chamber, we moved to the modern market. It was here that the minister said something I compared to a loaded statement I heard from one of our prominent politicians during the Lancaster Conference. The prominent politician, at the City Stadium, in Nairobi, when they had just landed at Embakasi Airport from Lancaster, said, "*Wa KADU wamekuja na punda wanadhani wamekuja na nini?*"

Wananchi roared, "*Na n'gombe.*"

"*Watajua siku ya kukamua.*"

Those were charged words. Now in Siaya, the Honorable Minister said words of similar hue. He said, *"Ninyi wajaluo hii 'n'gombe ilikuwa ni yenu mukatoroka na kuiwacha siku hizi sisi ndiyo tuna kamua—*You Luos this cow was yours but you ran away and left it, these days we are the ones who are milking it."

A loaded statement indeed, one made at the wrong place and wrong time. Besides, it was not entirely true. Not all Luos abandoned the government. Those who resigned their parliamentary seats to seek a fresh mandate were merely exercising their democratic right. They were later bundled out by schemers who manipulated and restricted their democratic space. These schemers planted the seeds of divide and rule, impunity and corruption, which would haunt the country for a long time. These, together with political assassinations, polarized and ethnicized the country so much that the country could not realize its full potential in economic, social, political and educational development. Kenya could have long joined the league of developing nations had a proper foundation been laid.

The minister went ahead and opened the market. I, as chairman of the county council, later successfully presided over the allocation of stalls there.

As chairman, I also supervised operations of the new urban councils of Siaya and Ukwala. These developed into full municipal and town councils respectively. The county council had to fight off the concerted efforts of Siaya Urban Council to take over the market and collect revenue without taking over repayment of the loan with which the market was built. It was after the modalities to take over the repayment of the loan had been worked out that the county council relinquished its right over the market to Siaya Town Council. Henceforth, the town council started collecting revenue from the market and assumed the responsibility of managing and paying the loan.

As the local government head of the district/county, I had a right to attend the District Development Committee, the body responsible for initiating, approving and overseeing all developments in the district. I articulated the county's policies and plans for the provision of health facilities and services and the development of markets.

As the Chairman, I was also an automatic member of the Ramogi Institute of Advanced Technology, which was then under the stewardship of Jaramogi. I still recall the first fundraising I attended at Riat as a member. Jaramogi had just made a fiery speech in Mombasa, tearing into grabbers of Kenyan land who refused to dish it out to the landless. This, along with other remarks he made, alienated him immediately from powerful government operatives. The President of Kenya had been invited to preside over the fundsdrive. As the president arrived, we lined up to greet him. One prominent politician refused to shake hands with Jaramogi as he stretched it. Everybody else shook hands with Jaramogi. Jaramogi took the embarrassment in stride and went ahead to give a good speech. Tension was high, but no ugly incident occurred.

But the most important of them all was membership of Local Government Staff Commission. This was a recruiting body for local government authorities. All senior staff of local authorities were recruited by this body. It accorded me an opportunity to meet the high and mighty in the local government ministry and the leadership of local government workers union. I learnt the art of conducting interviews from my membership and participation in this body. We recruited for the city council, the municipal councils and town councils.

*

At the local (ward) level, I did a lot better. I exceeded my own expectations. I helped *wananchi* start, establish and run six primary schools: Asai, Sirodha, Bar Kayieye, Miyiro, Kojuok and Mundoware. They all developed and became important schools. I also assisted the local communities to revive the following primary schools, which had collapsed: Nyapiedho, Siriwo, Malunga and Ndegwe. These too got back on their feet and developed to become important springboards for our pupils.

I assisted the local communities to start, establish and run the following markets: Sirembe Cattle Market, Regea, Kokwiri, Kodiaga and Ondisore. Apart from Ondisore and Kodiaga, which became important market centers, the rest flopped after I ceased being a councillor.

In partnership with respective communities, we planned and helped construct, of course with government assistance, the following bridges: Abir, Homba and Hundro. These were important bridges, which helped *wananchi* transport produce and sugarcane to factories and horticultural crops to the markets.

In the greater Siaya County Council, I opened a cattle market in East Ugenya, which was fought for by hardworking East Ugenya Councillor, Linus Okoth. I assisted various Councillors in other wards with their development agenda and theses helped some to be reelected.

———

On the political side, I resurrected the fortunes of the only political party, Kenya African National Union (KANU), in North Gem. The party was as dead as a dodo when I took over. As a politician I had to do something. I sought and obtained permission from the top to revive and revitalize the party. History will tell if any leader at ward level will do as much or even better than what I did. So far it has not been matched by subsequent ward leadership. Because of my exemplary efforts, the KANU big wigs asked me to revitalize party operations in the entire Gem. On this, I teamed with the M.P., the Hon. Horace Ongili Owiti.

But there's an incident I have to tell you about.

I was at the funeral of Mzee Halwenge, in Ugenya, representing the council when my friend and mentor, Hon. Oloo Aringo, M.P. for Alego Usonga, asked me to accompany him to solve a problem. He looked disturbed. I suspected he was stressed. He was not an ordinary Member of Parliament; he was a minister of the Kenyan government too, so whatever it was, it had to be serious.

I accompanied him to Agutu County Club, where he and I met Mr. Hezekiah Oyugi, Justice Masime and another guy who worked for the Department of Forestry. As the meeting progressed, I finally realized the objective. It was to persuade Hon. Oloo Aringo to denounce Jaramogi and to warn him of the dire consequences should he fail to do so. I was stunned. In those days Jaramogi had such a firm grip on Luo Nyanza that he could make or break an M.P. Why were these three men asking Hon. Aringo to commit political suicide?

Later, Hon. Aringo sought my opinion on the matter. Why he did it at that particular moment, I did not know. I did not know whether he sought it in good faith or he knew what I would say. Like him I was deep in Jaramogi's camp and confronted with a similar scenario, I would not have denounced him.

It wasn't fair!

So what would Hon. Aringo do?

He looked me in the eye and said, "*Councillor, Wachni watimo nade*—Councillor, what shall we do on this matter?"

I said, "Honorable, you should not denounce Mzee. You are still young; if you lose that flag now you can still work to get it later, but if you denounce Mzee, you will never see Parliament again."

As if that was what he was waiting for, Hon. Oloo jumped off his seat and told the stunned gentlemen, "I cannot do it!"

That brought the meeting to an abrupt end.

Through the 1:00 o'clock news—the following day—I learned that Hon. Oloo Aringo had been fired from his ministerial position. As I knew he would be sacked, this news bulletin did not shock me. I had psyched myself for this. I believe Hon. Oloo was also not shocked. The loss of his ministerial position did not, in any way, affect his M.P. status. He continued to be an M.P. and two years down the line he became a minister again. I was again instrumental in catapulting him into a position where he had to be made a minister.

*

One day as I was travelling to Nairobi by train from Kisumu, I happened to meet Hon. Alphonse Okuku Ndiege, who was also travelling first-class to Nairobi. As I was chatting with him, my M.P. burst in and started accusing me that I did not support or vote for him and that my tribe did not vote for him. The argument became so heated that he almost got physical with me.

Hon. Okuku separated us and asked each of us to go to our cabins. From that day he declared war on me. The Mutumbu Telephone Exchange, which I had negotiated with the Kenya Posts and Telecommunication Cooperation to be in my area, was switched to Sawagongo, courtesy of his interference.

Things later got worse.

Gem people began noticing the rift between the M.P. and I and they got concerned. Led by Mzee Zakayo Ochieng, a conciliatory meeting was arranged at George Luora's home, in East Gem.

At the end of the meeting elders in attendance were unanimous that he was wrong to have a grudge against me and that we should stop the war between us immediately. We wined and dined on George Luora's ram and left.

Later I learnt that my M.P.'s beef was my growing popularity. He wanted to stop my popularity because he suspected I would run against him. Since we drew our support from the same voters, he stood no chance against me on a fight for votes in Gem. That was his fear.

But hold on...

According to the law, all civic leaders, chairmen, mayors and committee chairmen had to face midterm elections. In 1982 we held those elections and my supporters were elected. I still had ninety percent support from councillors. But we did not complete our second term since Parliament was dissolved in 1983. The dissolution came as a surprise because we did not anticipate that we would face the electorate that early. The reason was the 1982 attempted *coup d'état* at which some junior officers in the air force temporarily took over government. The country's leadership later seized the opportunity to rid itself of undesirable elements they branded as *Ngorokos*. In the ensuing elections, if you were not in the good books your opponent was declared the winner even if you won with a landslide. Only those who the wielders of power wanted made it to Parliament or any elective post.

It was during this election that I got an opportunity to even scores with my local M.P., who did not want me. I shopped around for a serious candidate who could make an impact and rattle the formidable campaign machine the M.P. had put in place. I teamed up with a few friends to help.

We actually settled for Horace Ongili Owiti.

I arranged a meeting where we invited him for interaction. As a marginalized group, we wanted to know if he was going to look after our interests.

He agreed.

On that basis, we would support him against Otieno Ambala and others who wanted to contest. His campaign kitty was dry, but we agreed to help him without any remuneration. I remember I took one of his campaigners, Aima Demba, to see him over an issue. After a brief discussion, he reached into his coat pocket and took out a 500/= note to give Aima. He was disappointed when Aima looked at him and at the 500/= and told him in his face that he had decided to support him not for money but for what our people believed he could do for us. Aima castigated Horace and told him that the 500/= could not feed his family even for a day. Perhaps everybody who had gone to see him wanted money and he believed Aima was like those people. He would later talk about Aima's principles until he was killed. Anyway, I threw my full weight behind him and he won the election handsomely.

But Ambala didn't like that.

The sore looser filed a petition against the election of Hon. Ongili. I was retained by Hon. Ongili to assemble witnesses, collect and collate their statements and hand them to his lawyer in Nairobi. Later a court nullified the election and a by-election was ordered. Hon. Ongili trounced him once again and became our MP. His campaign slogan had been *Jagedo* (A builder). Even before he had declared his interest in the seat he had helped with more projects than his opponents. Hon. Ongili became a very active M.P. within months of his election. Malanga was upgraded to a full health centre and he helped me a lot in the new primary and secondary schools I had started.

He was agreat man.

Later thugs attacked and killed him at his Siaya home. It was a blow to the whole constituency. People mourned *Jagedo* like I had never seen before. He became easy prey because he was predictable. He had a thriving bakery called Sunrise Bakery in Siaya. His routine, while he was not in Nairobi, was from the bakery to his house. They got him so easily and cut him so badly that he died on the spot. Subsequently, police investigations pointed to Ambala. He was arrested and charged with the murder and remanded in prison.

On the day of the burial, just as we were lowering the body into the grave, a message was received that Otieno Ambala had died in prison. People gathered in clusters discussing the double tragedy. Two prominent sons of Gem had died within a fortnight. Ambala's death deprived the people of Gem an opportunity to know who the real killers of their beloved M.P. was because the mere fact that Ambala and others were charged with the murder did not make them killers.

It was a tragic end indeed!

In the coming elections, I defended my seat and won, but let the chairmanship go. Councillor Henry Ouma Okendo was elected Chairman of Siaya County Council. His brief was to find fault with my administration. He believed, as a result of false information he received from his moles in the council, that the clerk to the county council and I had embezzled funds. His first action was to call in inspectors from the ministry headquarters to look at the books. Siaya County Council was a poor council. Our main sources of revenue were market collections, land rents and licenses. These were not enough to finance our recurrent expenses like salaries, so when there was little money I did not take my allowances until I could go to Nairobi and get grants to help pay the workers. I could do without my allowance for up to four or five months. But when I brought the grant I would take my allowances in full.

Someone who did not know would think I was taking more than my rightful share. My reason for not taking my allowance when we were low on funds was because I had a fallback plan. I was able to earn a living from my legal practice and found it demeaning to scramble for the little the council had with workers who had no alternative source of funds. He had been warned not to bring in the inspectors, but he felt so sure that he would nail us, being blinded by envy and malice.

Inspectors know their job and this particular team did a splendid job. The first culprits were the chairman's brother, his cronies and supporters. Mr. Ober and I were exonerated after being found blameless. The chairman had to fight to save his brother and supporters from the axe. His expectations of finding fault with our administration failed lamentably. His evil schemes were defeated.

―――

On the 19th day of June 1985 my father died. The burial was attended by the clergy, prominent politicians, the new chairman of Siaya County Council, Professor Ogot and Mrs. Ogot, and Mr. Radin'g Omolo. The burial was on a Sunday and the week following the burial there was to be KANU party elections. I knew I would not do much as a part-time politician. I had already harbored a thought of vacating my council seat so why had I to bother with party posts which would not do me any good? Unknown to me, the battlelines between the principal protagonists had been drawn. During the funeral, Professor Ogot, Mrs. Ogot and I had a long discussion on topical issues. I also had similar discussions with Rading' Omolo, but none of them let the cat out of the bag. They were preparing to contest party elections and both of them either needed my support or wanted to get an inkling of my desire to contest the elections. I can safely bet they left my home that day convinced of one thing—that I was not going to contest.

On the day of grassroots elections, I did not leave my home because I had guests. At around 9:00 o'clock Mrs. Ogot sent a driver to bring me to the election venue.

I refused to go.

An hour later, she sent the driver with Mama Margret Ragen to convince me to go but still I refused. When she personally came on a third attempt and said I could go to the venue for only a short time to help, I agreed and went with her.

When I arrived at Malanga Primary School, the venue for KANU election, I saw why she so badly wanted me there. The field was full of Radin'g Omollo's supporters. Had the elections been conducted before I went there she would have gotten nothing and her political career would have ended there.

But get this. For Radin'g to have gotten the multitude to sing praises of him, he had breached the KANU constitution. He had brought in people from other sub-locations contrary to the constitution. Only residents of the particular sub-location where elections were being held could participate in the elections. The residents of Malanga sub-location present—having seen that Radin'g had the majority—flocked to him. He was on his way to beating Mrs. Ogot. And much as I wanted to help, the odds were against her and I did not know how and where to start. I told Mrs. Ogot that the situation was beyond redemption.

"Find a solution," she pleaded.

But what?

I decided to try.

I knew that if I confronted Radin'g with the law I could break his back and accede to some kind of compromise. So I sought the KANU constitution and just as I thought, the constitution forbade the importation of voters from other sub-locations. Secondly, I wanted to know Radin'g's line-up. When this was brought to me and I found out that the list contained the name of an ex-councillor I beat in the elections of 1979, and that he was earmarked for the locational KANU chairman's post where I kicked him out of during the time I was reorganizing the party, Radin'g's fate was sealed. I was going to stop him by hooks or crooks. I would use threats and a little persuasion to resolve the stalemate.

I sought Radin'g and confronted him with the law and the truth. I was the councillor of the area and therefore not an outsider. I was also a lawyer, a fact which both contestants knew well. If the elections did not conform to the party constitution, they knew I would petition Headquarters for nullification, so they had to listen to what I had to say. I told Radin'g he was wrong and in breach of the constitution for having imported voters from outside Malanga sub-location. I told him I would vet all the voters and exclude the intruders. At that point, he appeared confused. He was not sure of his strength once outsiders were excluded.

Since I was not a contestant, I immediately assumed the role of a presiding officer for the elections.

I asked both sides to call their supporters to enable me to address them. They converged and I told them that Malanga sub-location is multi-ethnic. Any particular ethnic group which tried to lord it over others would fail. I told them I had seen Radin'g's line-up and it comprised of members of his ethnic group only, which was unacceptable and would not work. I told them I had no problem with Onyango Mwalo, who Radin'g wanted to be chairman, but his deputy had to come from my tribe. All the seats had to be shared in that order for peace to prevail in the sub location. I told them to reserve four delegate vacancies for Radin'g Owuor Agola, Mrs. Ogot and I. That was exactly how elections were conducted.

Radin'g won the first round.

The second battle would be fought at the locationl level. Mrs. Ogot was thankful because I had saved her political career by playing the delegates card. But she would later behave as if she never knew me.

At the locational level, it appeared Radin'g still had the upper hand, but his candidate for chairmanship was extremely unpopular. Nobody was willing to give his or her vote to Owuor Agola. I thus devised a way of humiliating Radin'g and his candidate. I realized that with Silas they were going to beat us, so I talked Silas into stepping down for Kuyo Osunga.

The trick worked.

Mrs. Ogot and I were elected delegates to sub-branch elections in Yala.

It was at Yala that Mrs. Ogot turned against me. She was now positioned to lay claim to the right to contest the chairmanship of the sub-branch. Taking a cue from how I organized the sub-locational and locational elections, she forged an alliance with Moses Warom. They could not consider me for any post except that of delegate to Siaya branch elections.

I got upset.

True, I did not want to participate in these elections, but since Mrs. Ogot had pulled me out of my home to help her, I considered myself her ally and felt if she wanted to enter any deals she had to do it with me or at least have the courtesy of offering an office at sub-branch level to me.

But no.

She treated me contemptuously. Branch elections were due in Siaya the following day and I decided I was going to contest a post in Siaya without her support. I called my driver and a friend and started my campaign for organizing secretary of the branch. We went to Ugenya, Alego and Bondo, talking to prominent party officials and delegates and by dawn the branch organizing secretary slot was mine to take.

On arrival at the stadium, Mrs. Ogot realized I had made good my threat to contest a branch post and she got worried. To neutralize the threat, she sought private audience with the M.P. for Bondo, the one for Alego Usonga and the one for Ugenya. The four entered a Mercedes Benz and drove out of the stadium. When they returned, they had agreed on how the constituencies or sub-branches were going to share the posts. To keep me out, she had settled for the post of branch women leader as the one Gem people would go for. To keep me out, Gem had to forgo her right to contest a major branch post because of the fear that I would take it.

Was this absurd or what?

My M.P. friends tried to convince me to take the post of an executive officer of the party, but I refused because that was a full-time job which I could not do because of my professional office. I talked to Mzee Wasonga Sijeyo, who agreed to take it.

During this time, Mrs. Ogot was a nominated M.P. Hon Horace Ongili Owiti had died, but there had not been an election to fill his seat. All her political schemes and manners of using and dumping people were in preparation for the by-election in Gem. Shortly after the party elections, the by-election was called. At more or less the same time, I made up my mind to resign my councillor seat and all my political engagements to concentrate on my family and my office. So the announcement of the by-election gave me the perfect excuse to bow out honorably.

But this changed when I was called by the district security team and assured of the government's support should I decide to contest. Indeed I was the next in line after the M.P. in the political hierarchy of Gem and had worked hand-in-hand with the deceased M.P. so the government's interest in my candidature was not misplaced or ill advised. My candidature and subsequent election would be necessary to continue the policies of the deceased and to complete the developments he had initiated. It would also help in cooling the political temperature generated by his death.

Suddenly I wanted to be an M.P.

But how was I going to campaign? I didn't have money or vehicles to mount a successful constituency-wide campaign. How would I appease the impatient youth and those who would be helping with my campaign? I had only one car and no savings worth writing home about. With these odds stuck against me, I consoled myself that I had been assured of support from the only authority that mattered. I had seen paupers with similar support get to Parliament. Why not me? Besides, I thought it would accord me an opportunity to even scores with Mrs. Ogot, whom I had not forgiven for maltreating me during the KANU elections. I decided I would vacate my civic seat to contest the vacant parliamentary seat.

I resigned and started making the necessary preparations. First I had to listen to the views of my supporters. I had no difficulty securing the support of my tribe and that of my supporters in the ward. I spread out to secure key supporters throughout the constituency. Close relatives and friends came on board to help. Key among them were Mr. Ambrose Rachier, who not only helped me secure funding, but also put his money into my campaign chest. Dr. Moses Ogoye Okech not only lent me some funds, but contributed a substantial amount of money too. Mr. Dickson Sijenyi Indakwa offered me a Land Rover and a driver. Mr. John Okeyo Muger and Adams Muger offered vehicles for the campaign.

I came up with a formidable team of campaigners—rally speakers and grassroots mobilizers. The team included Owiti Ja Piki Piki and Otieno Lando, both from South Gem; Aima Demba, Nelson Juma, Mbogo Ndede, and Silas Mayienga. Shortly before the nomination I was again called by the security team and cautioned that should Mrs. Ogot resign as a nominated M.P. to to contest the by-election, they would not support me. They advised me to watch for her resignation and desist from further campaign should that happen. They, however, agreed that should Mrs. Ogot contest they would rescind my resignation and allow me to continue as councillor. I listened attentively and appeared to agree with every word, but deep inside I knew I had reached a point of no return. I was not going back to the council. Mrs. Ogot kept her decision to contest under wraps. Her decision to contest did not bother me, if it came. I knew I would beat her in a clean contest.

On the 19th of July 1985, the candidates presented their nomination papers to the district commissioner, who was the returning officer. When I got into the office to present my papers, the D.C.'s body language was clear—I should not go ahead with the nomination process. I ignored him and presented my nomination papers, which were accepted. After a short time, Mrs. Ogot arrived from Kisumu, not from Gem, in the company of women, most of them from Kisumu. She presented her nomination papers and they were accepted.

The D.C. cleared a total of ten candidates.

These were Mr. Radin'g Omolo from North Gem, Mrs. Moses Warom from Central Gem, Mr. Owiti, the brother of Horace Ongili, from East Gem, Mr. Obare Asiko from East Gem, Mr. Odenyo Lanyo from Sirembe, Mr. Anyango Jagem from East Gem, Mr. Wasonga Sijeyo from Central Gem, Mrs. Ogot from East Gem, Mr. Nyanga from South Gem and I.

Later, as I traveled home, I met Cousin John Thuthu walking in the opposite direction, toward Ondisore. I did not stop because I was in a convoy. On reaching Kodiaga, I received disturbing information that Uncle Nicodemo Ogola had passed on. His son, Ayub Ohon Ogola, was driving my car at the time. I asked him when he'd known of his father's death and he said, "While we were in Siaya."

"And you never said anything?"

He just shrugged.

Later, my cousin and I returned home. It was during this time that I received information that Uncle had left instructions that none of his sons should eulogies him, except me. I was surprised and wondered why he had to do that. And why did he decide that I was the only son (nephew) who could eulogize him? His step-brother, Silfano, who had died a year earlier had left strict instructions that when he died I be called to be at his burial. My cousin, Oluoch Okelo, while still alive, wrote his eulogy and instructed that I read it when he died. There was something they saw in me which made them trust me even in death. In all these incidences, I complied with the deceaseds' wishes. My family helped his widow until she too passed on a few years later.

Since some candidates feared sharing a rally platform, we opted for separate rallies. Mr. Wasonga Sijeyo and I were the only candidates who did not mind sharing rally platforms. When the other candidates insisted that they were uneasy and could not share platform with us, we also decided to have our separate rallies.

The campaign was intense.

It was like nine men ganged up against one woman. The woman, like me, was faulted for having left her position to come and increase the number of contestants. We knew there would be serious attempts to interfere with the election to help her. We were prepared at every stage of the campaign and on polling day I knew I would not get any assistance whatsoever from the wielders of power because I had been forewarned.

My friends Hon. Oloo Aringo and Hon. Ondiek were at my home a couple of times persuading me to step down and support Mrs. Ogot. But to me it was payback time. I declined their overtures and stuck to my campaign plan. The last time they came to my home they told me the President of the Republic of Kenya wanted to speak to Mr. Radin'g Omolo and I, and that I should go to the P.C.'s office in Kisumu at 8:00 o'clock in the morning.

Really, I wondered. *The President?*

They said they were going to pass the same message to Mr. Radin'g Omolo so that the two of us could meet the P.C. in Kisumu.

Early in the morning, in the company of my bodyguard and driver, I proceeded to Mr. Radin'g's home to inquire if the two honorable members had come to look for him. I was told that Mr. Radin'g, because of security concerns, never spent nights in his home. Since they could not divulge where he was, I decided to proceed to the P.C.'s office alone. But the P.C. was not aware the President wanted to speak with me. He said if the President wanted me, he would be the one looking for us, nobody else.

A ruse?

Whatever it was, I came back and considered my Kisumu trip a complete waste of time. I did not follow up with Mr. Radin'g to know whether they had reached him or not. It wasn't worth my time.

I campaigned hard!

But let me cut this short. The votes were later counted and obvious mischief was intoroduced in the counting hall by officials who would go on to declare Mrs. Ogot the winner. If you ask me, Radin'g had won the thing!

But the police used teargas to disperse the unruly crowd and Mrs. Ogot had to be given police escort from the hall. The first seeds of sham elections in Gem, which would extend for seven years, had been planted.

The following day I hosted a big party for my supporters to thank them for a job well done. I had beaten people I never knew I would beat in an election. They had lifted me into the history books.

What a run it was!

Between 1987 and 1989 I went into political hibernation. I avoided politics and got back to farming and other mundane matters. Indeed, the only political activity I engaged in—if it was to be called that—was to help mount a credible search for my replacement. Luckily one of our sons had just retired from service and met the two criteria on our mind. Like me before, a delegation was sent to him.

Mr. Dickson Sijenyi Indakwa.

He had been a career civil servant. He was not a politician but had dealt with politicians during the course of his job. His only handicap was his naivety in politics and inability to speak politics. He had not lived much of his life in Gem so he did not know much about Gem politics. At first he flatly refused, but when I assured him that I would coach him on the art of public speaking and Gem politics, he eventually agreed.

He won the by-election.

After his victory my people decided to organize a victory party for him, but I advised them to make it a North Gem party since Indakwa was now a leader of all North Gem people.

Later, though, due to disagreements, Aima and I dropped out of the whole matter. It was not worth it. But after half an hour, the same Aima returned and persuaded me to continue arrangements to avoid failure and embarrassment. We decided we were not going to allow our detractors to derail our focus.

We proceeded with the arrangements as planned in the committee. I had been advised by knowledgeable elders not to attend the ceremony because it would look like I was handing over to him the leadership of my tribe. I was further advised that as long as the party was in progress, wherever I was, I should be sitting on the traditional stool I was given as a mark of my status as the leader of my tribe. I did as advised by the elders. I was told the party went on well and guests received the gifts as the committee had arranged. Mr. Aima and I decided not to go to the venue of the party. We were within the vicinity available for consultation by anyone who wanted to.

Nobody did.

I sat out politics until 1990, when the struggle for multi-party began in earnest. I had been helping Jaramogi over the years, though. This started long before I was elected councillor. I was one of his close political supporters who never abandoned him. This core group was picked from across Luo Nyanza and comprised of professors, doctors, politicians and lawyers. Gem was represented in this group by Ominde Achayo and I. We strategized, brain-stormed and advised. We formed cells and ensured they functioned. We operated through informers. We kept Jaramogi out of trouble through this effective network. We concentrated on grass roots mobilization. This proved so successful that nobody could make it to Parliament or even to any council in Luo Nyanza without the tacit support of Jaramogi. This was a contribution I never stopped even after I had left elective politics.

In Gem, campaigning to be an M.P. was a waste of time. As long as the sitting M.P. was still in the good books of powerbrokers nobody, however popular, was going to be elected. People were made to believe they were participating in elections, but the winner had been predetermined. These were the years of queue-voting, where shorter queues won elections against longer queues. But now there was a new order—multi-partyism.

When activism for the multi-party structure started, I joined the movement immediately, and used my mobilization ability and experience to come on top of things in Siaya District. Section 2A in the Constitution had been repealed and citizens were now free to organize themselves into political parties. When Jaramogi formed the Forum for Restoration of Democracy

(FORD), I joined and, along with Otieno Ogonji, Dr. Obwaka, Collins Omondi, Asol Mango, Otieno Awange and others, we started to popularize the party in Siaya district.

When grassroots party elections were called in 1992, we formed a group of leadership aspirants who had support right from the sub-locations. The group was unbeatable. As we were busy mobilizing down here, our M.P.s were also busy in Nairobi helping Jaramogi to mobilize the rest of the country. Their only mistake was to think that *wananchi* would go along with whatever decision they made in Nairobi. We arranged the election in such a manner that we knew which constituency was going to take what post. We left no room for compromise or deviation from the plan. On the eve of election, our M.P.s came to the party office and told me as the interim organizing secretary that they had their lineup.

I was surprised.

I told them their lineup would not work because it was too late to undo what had been done. I told them they were at liberty to front their candidates to face ours at the elections. They must have gone back to their constituencies to assess the situation and discovered that they could not breach the plan. They got on board and participated with us in the elections.

*

Earlier, there had been concerted efforts by Dr. Okii Ooko Ombaka to shut me out of the branch elections right from the grassroots. But this wasn't gonna happen. At the sub-locational level I allowed some of his supporters to squeak through. At the locational elections his supporters lost heavily. It was at the sub-branch level (constituency) that the real fight for supremacy between him and I loomed. I had in my camp all the stalwart politicians in Gem. Orwa Apunda, Anyango Onginjo, until the last minute, Asol Mango. When we were making this line up we offered Asol Mango the sub-branch chairmanship, but two weeks into the election he switched to Dr. Ombaka's camp. While we were still pondering what to do, Mr. Joe Donde approached and asked to join my camp. I told him I could not give him a final answer until I talked to the organizing committee members. I told him to be at our last meeting in my Siaya house to get our decision.

The members accepted him.

When he came to the meeting we interrogated him to be sure he was not a mole. Once we were satisfied, we asked him if he was strong enough to fight for the chairmanship position left by Asol Mango. He said he was strong. With this agreement, the fate of Dr. Ombaka's camp was sealed.

At the branch elections, in Siaya, my camp had Hezekiah Ougo Ochieng' as chairman, and Dr. Obwaka as his vice chairman. Mr. Ougo was from Rarieda and Dr. Obwaka from Alego Usonga. I was fronted for secretary and was from Gem. At the venue, Dr. Ombaka insisted he was going to contest the post of secretary against me. His friends—and even some M.P.s tried to convince him not to stand because he would be humiliated, but he refused and registered as a candidate. Mr. Ougo Ochieng' was unanimously elected branch chairman. When election for vice chairman was done, Hon. Oloo Aringo beat Dr. Obwaka for the post. That was the decision of Alego Usonga people. Hon. Aringo had campaigned throughout the previous night to convince Alego and other delegates to vote for him. Dr. Obwaka was the only candidate from my camp to be defeated.

For election of secretary, my name was proposed and seconded. When the presiding officer called for another name, Dr. Ombaka's name was proposed, but he failed to get a seconder and I was declared elected unopposed. What a humiliation for him. Ramogi Achieng Oneko had warned him to desist from standing because he would be humiliated, but he refused. Failing to get a seconder for a guy of Dr. Ombaka's stature was a real embarrassment. The following day some local dailies captioned head news, *Siaya advocate beats Nairobi advocate.*

The elections proceeded smoothly with my camp taking all posts including delegates.

At the national level, Jaramogi Oginga Odinga was elected national chairman. Mr. Wamalwa Kijana became first vice chairman and Mr. James Orengo second vice chairman.

When the parliamentary and civic elections were called in 1992, I sought the blessings of Jaramogi to stand for the Gem parliamentary seat on a FORD-K ticket. I travelled to Nairobi and very early in the morning I was at Agip House, where FORD-K offices were. As I got in I met Ramogi Achieng' Oneko, who after exchanging pleasantries with me, offered to take me to Jaramogi's office. As early as 8:00 o'clock he was already in his office. I told him I was eyeing the Gem parliamentary seat and that I needed his blessings. He was non committal and remained so until we left his office. I suspected he had already committed his support to someone else or he had changed his mind toward me and he had no place for me anymore. As matters would turn out later, it was the former.

Ramogi took me to city hall where we had breakfast. While there, a colleague saw us and came over to say hi. He inquired the purpose of my Nairobi visit. When I told him, he retorted, "How much did you take to him?" both Ramogi and I were surprised. We demanded to know what he was talking about. He said he was privy to information that one aspiring candidate for the Gem parliamentary seat had been generous to the party and had been supporting the party financially virtually every week. Unless I could offer more than the guy I stood no chance and would be wasting my time, he said. I had been in Luo Nyanza politics long enough to know the depth of what he was talking about.

Although I did not believe my colleague right away, when the guy he mentioned presented his candidacy and got the nod, I realized his source of information was not too far off the mark. Ramogi and I discussed my colleague's comments for a considerable period of time after he left. He advised me as he had advised Dr. Ombaka during the branch elections in Siaya, to forget the idea of standing for parliamentary elections in Gem. Unlike Dr. Ombaka, I headed his advice and never presented myself for election in 1992.

Later I even campaigned with Ochieng Kabasele to help Dr. Ombaka to capture the seat.

During the 1992 elections, Clr. Indakwa was going to defend his seat on a KANU ticket. I told him if he did he would lose his seat. He resisted all attempts to persuade him to cross over to FORD-K. I finally approached and read the riot act to him. I told him the seat he held was not his, but our people's and therefore he had to do what our people wanted. I told him the people were going to lose the seat if he didn't cross to FORD-K. He pretended he did not have nomination fee to cross over. The fee was 4,000/=. KANU had agreed to pay all his expenses. Because of his dilly dallying, North Gem FORD-K selected Opiyo Ombajo to be the flag-bearer. I told him if it was lack of money I would go with him and pay all the money needed for his nomination on a FORD-K ticket. We took a bus, paid his fare to and from Nairobi. I also paid his nomination fee. He was then cleared to contest party nominations.

Part of the reason I sat out parliamentary nomination was because I would have jeopardized his chances of winning. Clr. Indakwa and I came from the same sub-location and same ethnic group. Gem being a multi-ethnic society two members of the same ethnic group standing for civic and parliamentary elections would both lose however good they were. Against this background I had to stand down in order for him to win. He went on to get the nomination and retained his civic seat.

In the 1992 general elections Jaramogi Oginga Odinga was elected Member of Parliament for Bondo constituency. In parliament he became leader of the Opposition. He served with distinction both as leader of the Opposition and member for Bondo constituency. This was the seat the Government's powerbrokers had denied him since he lost it when he was detained after the Kisumu fiasco of 1969. I was in Kisumu doing my practicals then. The Russian government had just built a magnificent hospital for Nyanza people, in Kisumu. The head of state came to open it. In 1966 Jaramogi and his supporters had crossed the floor to form Kenya Peoples Union when the country was a de facto one-party state. KADU (Kenya African Democratic Union), led by Hon. Ronald Ngala and Hon. Masinde Muliro, had disbanded and merged with KANU. The formation of KPU had upset the powerbrokers, particularly those whose intention was to grab, grab and grab. Hurdles and obstacles were placed on Jaramogi's path by the powerbrokers who looked for the slightest excuse to lock him up.

I feared to go to Russia Hospital, as it was known then. I was with my cousin Jadak at his work place, the entrance to the former Kisumu Bus Park, near Wagoi's building. Kakamega Road, leading to Russia Hospital, was full of human traffic. Suddenly we saw the director of social services, Mr. Ezra Gumbe, a huge fellow, running fast from Kakamega Road towards Kisumu's Social Centre. We then heard gun-fire from the direction of the hospital and suddenly the shots were whizzing over our heads. We decided to lie down for fear of being hit by those bullets. We then saw the presidential convoy pass as shots were fired. People lost loved ones from gunshot wounds. That evening the KPU members of parliament, including Jaramogi, were detained. Detention without trial was lawful in Kenya then. Whether this shooting incident was by design to lock up members of a budding opposition and proscribe their party or it was instantaneous, I failed to understand. What I know was that many people lost their lives. The security operatives used more force than was desirable in the circumstances. It was an incident that would have attracted a commission of inquiry in a more civilized society.

Those years in detention and subsequent house arrest took a toll on Jaramogi's health. In the early 90s, he was not the eloquent, robust and articulate Jaramogi we knew. He was elected M.P. in 1992 and in 1994 he died. His death was not only a big loss to his family, the people of Bondo, the people of Nyanza, FORD-K but the entire nation. He was the best president Kenya never had. Death robbed me of a friend, my leader and a mentor. I will forever remember him.

While there was no problem finding his replacement as M.P. for Bondo, his replacement as FORD-K chairman generated a lot of heat. HON. Wamalwa Kijana was cleared and took over the chairmanship. Hon. James Orengo, who had been second vice chairman, was elevated to first vice chairman. I attended this meeting and participated in these elections. Hon. Wamalwa then became the leader of Opposition in Parliament. But even then, the wrangles in FORD-K continued unabated. As a branch we decided to intervene. We summoned all our four M.P.s to a meeting to find out the cause of the wrangles and how they could be solved. Hon. Ramogi Achieng Oneko, Hon. James Orengo, Hon. Okii Ooko Ombaka and Hon. Otieno Makonyango attended. Also in attendance was Hon. Raila Odinga. We discussed but never arrived at a permanent solution to the problem.

Later Hon. Raila Odinga resigned from FORD-K and his parliamentary seat of Lan'gata constituency and formed the National Development Party.

He won his seat back!

When I returned to Kenya from the USA, campaigns for the 2007 general elections had started. As usual the field was crowded. The outgoing M.P. for Gem constituency, Hon. Jakoyo Midiwo, was defending his seat. With his track record of having used the Constituency Development Fund (CDF) very well, he was a force to reckon with. Mr. Rachier, who was also a contestant, represented the elite of Gem and had done his groundwork very early. He had been to virtually every village, school and church, helping in one way or the other. He had helped youth and women groups. He was liquid and propertied. He had what it took to be a leader of the people. While some of the previous contestants built homes and palaces after being elected, Mr. Rachier had all these already. He struck me as one whose principal intention was to help uplift the social, economic and educational standards of Gem people, not one who sought the seat for monetary gain. The rest of the candidates were Johnny come lately and were merely using the election as an introductory platform to Gem people. In my view the real contest was to pit Hon. Jakoyo Midiwo against Mr. Rachier.

My son, Ken, was already on the trail for Mr. Rachier.

Mr. Rachier, I don't know whether through my son's persuasion or of his own volition, came to see and asked me to help him. His style and strategy of campaign was not going to take him anywhere. He had no major opinion leaders in his fold. Most of those surrounding him were political roller coasters bent on making a quick buck but incapable of even winning even their spouses to vote in a particular manner.

I agreed to help.

It was a pity he did not follow my advice or make use of the machinery I so painstakingly put in place for him. In politics once you recruit someone to work for you, don't dump or ignore him. If you do, he will turn against you and join those hitting you. This was one mistake my friend made. The other mistake was to use the village stopovers as rallies. Even if one is a billionaire, he or she cannot afford this. Village stopovers, like door to door campaigns, are supposed to be discreet, with an element of surprise, to be effective. You don't go to them in the full glare, with blaring music from your loudspeakers. The third mistake was going late or failing to go at all to rallies and meetings. As a good politician you should never tell people you will go see them then you either fail or go late—this is political sacrilege. Otherwise he is a good man and I hope one day the people of Gem will give him the chance to prove his worth.

*

Whoever is holding an elective post should work without any fear or favor. A holder of an office should not constantly look over his shoulders for imaginary detractors or opponents; that will interfere with his focus. Every elected leader should leave the constituency or ward better than he or she found it. I didn't think the electorate expects any less.

For the six years I was a councillor—and many more when I was in militant politics—my record and performance speaks for itself. What I did was by far more than what I did not do. I didn't disappoint voters.

I left when I had to leave and never regretted being a politician or the decision to leave politics.

CHAPTER 23

LIBERATION

After the death of my mother, but before my step-mother was married, my father and I talked a lot. This was the time I learnt much from my father. One particular line of conversation which stuck in my mind was how we came to be members of the Adventist Church and not Anglicans or Catholics. The former had a large following than the latter. At that time, I wondered why people did not just go to one church to pray; after all I was taught that there was only one God. I did not realize that churches were just like umbrellas people use to shield themselves from rain or sunshine. I did not realize that churches were like a means of transport to destinations. The destination may be the same, but people may arrive there using aeroplanes, cars, trains, buses or trucks. Churches are mere vehicles to use on our journey to the New Jerusalem.

Having struck this cord in our conversation, my father opened up and narrated to me why we belonged to the S.D.A. Church. He told me that in 1906, when the white missionaries arrived in Kavirondo, they started recruiting African religious teachers and called them catechists. They taught them to read and write and, to some extent, English. The brightest of the recruits picked up fast and were trained to be teachers, evangelists, church elders, readers and pastors. The first group which came to our area was Anglicans, followed by Roman Catholics.

Those were the days of paramount chiefs.

Our area was under paramount chief Mumia, whose headquarters were in Mumias, some 30 miles away. Mumia ruled through smaller chiefs whose jurisdictions covered what would be a division today. At this critical time, Chief Ogada Odera was ruling. He developed and put in place a ruling class whose purpose was to oppress and enslave other people, particularly those who were not of their clan; whom they claimed were not pure Luos and had mixed ancestry (of mixed blood, like the U-clans).

Ironically, the U-clans were the indigenous owners of the land. They were the ones who accommodated and later gave land to those who later claimed to be pure Luos. Those among them who adapted faster became the ruling class, because they changed and harmonized faster. With the crown and the Bible, they started a crusade to oppress and dominate others. Meanwhile, the U-clans joined the Anglican Church, then operating under the Church Missionary Society. The Anglican Church was under Archdeacon Owen, popularly known as Archdeacon Owen of Kavirondo. He was also the representative of Africans in the Legislative Council.

From 1906-1930, the Anglican Church trained one, Nyende Aruwa, and ordained him padre. He was posted to serve Gem people. Padre Nyende and Chief Ogada teamed up and were credited with the mayhem visited on other people during their time. They did not want other people to go to school and be educated for fear they would be enlightened, get jobs and become wealthy. They could become tax collectors, dress decently and even dare question the malafide, lack of integrity and spiritual incompetence of the padre. They did not want people, other than their kin, to be leaders. They made sure all leadership positions, from village elder to headman to assistant chief to chief were held by their kin or their yes-men. My tribe could not be considered for anything.

Church leadership was their preserve, because that was the nerve centre of education. The church controlled who went to school and where. Pupils in standard three sat a tough government examination called Competitive Common Entrance Examination. Pupils who passed this exam joined Maseno Primary School, which was the only school around. As soon as results were released, the headmaster of the sector schools, as the schools were then called, in collaboration with the chief and the padre, sat and doctored the results. All the pupils who passed but did not come from the ruling clan had their names deleted and replaced by the names of pupils from the ruling clan, even if they failed. Their heinous game was discovered by Archdeacon Owen himself in February 1932. Can you believe this?

Let me explain.

Mr. James Walgwe, a U-clan son, had sat the CCEE in 1931 and had performed well, but his name did not feature in the list of qualifiers in the Malanga Sector. His name had been deleted and replaced by one of the ruling clan's son who did not even pass the exam. The list Archdeacon Owen and the Maseno principal had contained Walgwe's name, but his name was conspicuously missing in the Malanga Sector list. When students arrived at Maseno, the principal discovered that the best performer did not report and alerted Archdeacon Owen, who came to look for the star performer.

He found him, an energetic and brilliant boy—James Walgwe.

When the Archdeacon inquired why he had not reported, he said he did not know he had been selected to join Maseno School.

This led to the Archdeacon widening investigations, and discovered that Walgwe's name had been deleted from the list of qualifiers and replaced by a failure. This infuriated the Archdeacon, who admonished and reprimanded those concerned and took Walgwe to Maseno School. He was later the first from the U-clan who went to Alliance High School. This was the next step from Maseno School in the Anglican educational hierarchy.

And finally Makerere.

Thirty years later, these intrigues were still practiced. In 1960, I sat for passed KAPE and was called to join Maseno High School. I have yet to receive my admission letter more than fifty years down the line.

These intrigues and the violence visited on our people kept most of our brilliant minds out of school. Those who braved the violence and proceeded to class three were denied further education by a well coordinated conspiracy. The grip was so tight that our people had no immediate recourse for, but God would later find a way out for them. The solution came in the form of teachers, a school and a church. Since we did not have trained teachers or even folks to become headmasters of sector schools, we had nobody to look after our educational interests. We were thus doomed unless we figured a way forward. The top leadership of the church allowed the local leadership to be used by the local administration to oppress us. We had to adopt the good ways the whiteman had brought us. We were determined to change and whatever hurdles one placed on our way was not going to deter us from moving forward. Change is sweetest when fought for even when the fight involves blood. Nobody was going to give it to us on a silver platter.

We resolved to fight.

First, we had to get teachers.

But to get them, we had to identify our brilliant sons who were trained by the Anglican missionaries and sponsor them to training colleges. Sylvano Ayayo Mijema and Andrea Ochola were identified and taken to Butere Normal School to train as teachers and lay readers. In 1934 the duo went for a two-year course. On completing their training, both were denied permission by the padre in charge, Padre Nyende, to teach at Malanga Sector School, their only fault being *not the sons of the ruling clan.*

Brave as he was, Sylvano confronted Padre Nyende to find out why in spite being an Anglican and a trained teacher he could not be allowed to teach in an Anglican school.

What padre Nyende told him became the impetus, the catalyst he needed. The answer changed the course of a people. Let me quote the words verbatim. He said, "If you want to teach, you must find a school for your own people where you can teach them foolishness!"

You cannot believe this was said by a clergy to one of his flock. How snobbish and arrogant. No wonder it infuriated a whole tribe and the entire U-clan populace.

As a result of this rebuff and humiliation, Sylvano Ayayo mobilized the U-clans and the first ever harambee (self-supporting) sector school in the history of Central Kavirondo was planned. Then in 1938 Maliera Sector School was started. How it started and grew is outside the scope of this book. Suffice it to say it grew to be a big school, competing with the best schools in Nyanza Province in academic excellence. It provided springboard for learning for children of my tribe and the entire U-clan. The ripple effects of this school brought our people at par with our oppressors.

Andrea Ochola, on the other hand, was credited with starting Wagai and Lundha Sector schools, which became Wagai and Lundha Primary schools. These schools, along with others, led the way for our people.

But the denial of Silfano Ayayo and Andrea Ochola permission to teach or preach in Anglican schools and churches was not the only setback and humiliation our people suffered. On the 28th March 1937 our people were ignomously beaten and kicked out of an Anglican church by hired hoodlums from the ruling clan and were, as a result, forced to look for a church where they could worship in peace.

That church became the Seventh-day Adventist Church.

The S.D.A. Church therefore liberated our people from persecution and the oppression of the Anglican Church and the ruling clans in Gem.

That's why we remain in the faith!

Shortly after I had built my home, I went to Achuth to visit Uncle Silfano Ayayo Mijema. His home was large, with a large kraal for his many cattle and sheep. You can't imagine how happy he was to see me. He jumped off his seat to come and meet me. He ushered me into his big house where his wife, Esther Achieng Ayayo, was waiting for me. After welcoming me with prayer, we sat to chat. Food was brought and while I took my food with bare hands, he ate with a fork, a spoon and a knife—a symbol of affluence. To show how appreciative he was of my visit, he slaughtered a ram. Rams were slaughtered only for special guests like in-laws.

You get the point?

Now, with this visit I had the opportunity to learn everything I wanted to know and get my lingering questions answered. He had been to my residence in Kisumu on several occasions and had given me bits and pieces, mainly as answers to my questions. This time it was a narration—clear distinct and precise. This went on until the wee hours. He let it pour out. I hardly interrupted except to ask a probing question here and there. Much of our talk centered on our church, why he migrated, his life history—which included selfless service to the people and his vision for our people. On the Seventh-day Adventist Church, he reiterated what my father had narrated. The facts were the same. What I found new was the fact that Ugandans got the S.D.A. message from Maliera Mission. People from Lira and Gulu came to learn about our struggle and took the good news of Christ back to their country.

Pastor Silfano Ayayo was born in 1906, in Magunda village, which was later an administrative area of North Gem location, in Siaya District. Originally Kavirondo was divided into North Kavirondo, Central Kavirondo and South Kavirondo. North Kavirondo became Western Province while South Kavirondo became Kisii and South Nyanza districts. Central Kavirondo became Siaya and Kisumu districts. Siaya district was later divided into Bondo, Ukwala, Boro and Yala divisions. He was therefore born at what would be Magunda village, in Malanga sub-location, of North Gem location, in Siaya District, of Nyanza Province. His parents were Mijema Lugulu and Akumu. He was named after his deceased step-mother—Ayayo. My father and Pr. Silfano were brothers (in the African context). He was the son of Mijema, who was the son of Lugulu, who was the son of Muhudhi. My father, Wanyanga, was the son of Ohon, who was the son of Wadoyi, who was the son of Muhudhi. We share ancestry and he is therefore my father in the African context.

From Maliera Mission, the S.D.A. Church spread through the entire Central Kavirondo like bushfire. Later, it encompassed North Kavirondo and parts of Rift Valley, in Kenya. Today Adventism boasts a total membership of about seventeen million. Thirty one thousand and fifty of these are from Central Kavirondo, which presently comprises of Kisumu, Nyando, Siaya, Bondo and Rarieda districts. There are a total of 211 churches under Central Nyanza Field, which is equivalent to a diocese in the Anglican and Catholic hierarchical system. It has many health facilities and quite a number of sponsored primary schools.

As soon as he was old enough he sought and received literacy lessons to enable him to read the only book which was readily available then—the Bible. He also learned to write and do arithmetic. He was taught by Anglican missionaries. He saw how our people were maltreated and oppressed by the ruling clan. The patriotism inside urged him to do something to stop the lunacy. He knew he could only fight for our people from inside.

He had to get into the midst of the oppressors.

The tools of oppression were education, spiritual and secular leadership. He was determined to get all these. He positioned himself well and was selected by the Anglicans, the church to which we all belonged to at the time, to go to Butere Normal School for training as a teacher and lay reader. When he reported, his name was not on the list of those from Gem. It took the intervention of the white principal to get him in. So in 1934 he and his friend, Andrea Ochola, joined the school for two years. After completing training he returned but was denied a chance to teach or minister. He thus joined the tribunal in 1936 and became its chairman.

A tribunal was the court of first instance in the colonial court system.

He later resigned to concentrate on freeing our people from oppression. Between 1938 and 1940 he did for our people what Odera Akang'o did for his people. He forced our people to take to school every child of school-going age, and this considerably increased the literacy level of our people. As a result, our people got jobs with the Post Office, Railways and Harbors and some became teachers. The tide was turning!

In 1941 he went for a two-year pastoral training in Kamagambo, where the S.D.A. Church trained its clergy. He was later posted to Nyalgunga S.D.A. Church in 1943.

In 1944 he had an unusual transfer from one church to another.

He later worked in Kadem, Karungu, Mihuru and Wire. It was during that year that he vacated his Bungu home and left it for Maliera S.D.A. Mission Station. He took part of his family away and in 1946 built a home in Nyandago, which was still a wilderness.

In 1949 lightening struck his Nyandago house and he lost everything in the ensuing fire.

In 1950 he moved to Achuth, in Kanyamkago, where he finally settled. Then in 1959 he lost his beloved wife, Azanath Ngalo, to the cruel hands of death.

I must say that what I have written about my uncle here is not his full biography. His memoir will one day be written for future generations to read. What I have stated is what, in his wisdom, he decided to share with me. Only bits and pieces he wanted me to know. Remember he was preparing me for a task which he knew I could perform. He probably knew I had what it took to carry out the task. He was, in effect, preparing me to take up the leadership mantle of our people. He had the rod and had made up his mind to hand it over to me. Like Moses and Joshua, he had to do everything to prepare me. He handed over to me and only future generations will determine if I played my part as expected. I believe the way I handled myself as the new leader did not disappoint him during the remainder of his life.

*

From my research—and what he and Father told me—I did not bother to ask why he migrated. I learnt he was afraid he could be assassinated. Many attempts were made on his life, but God protected him.

The second reason was the welfare of his children. He had lost 2 children in Bungu under mysterious circumstances and was not prepared to lose another or others. He wanted his children to grow up, have the best education and raise families for posterity.

Thirdly, he was out there on God's calling, to convert souls to Christ. This was a calling he wanted right from his youth and strove to get. Now that he had it, he wanted to put his mind and soul into it.

Fourthly, he wanted to leave his home in Bungu for the church. Like Abraham, he left his home not knowing where he was going to or what would befall his family. His home became Maliera Mission Station. Today, apart from the mission station, there is an S.D.A. Church and a health centre there.

God vindicated him!

If you got to Achuth and compare it with Gem, where he migrated from, you will understand what I mean. Had he stayed in Gem he would have had only one acre of cultivatable land, but in Achuth he has over 50.

Before ending his narration he disclosed to me what he wanted our people to do in order not to be left behind again. He identified what caused our lagging behind as:

- Drinking alcohol
- Smoking weed and
- Keeping quails

He said our people hooked to these would never make it in life. They would neither go to school nor church. He urged our people to work hard in whatever they set their minds on. He read from the book of proverbs 14:23:

> *All hard work brings a profit, but mere talk leads only to poverty"* (quoted from New International Version).

To this end our families alone have built many churches, among which are: Malanga, Got Kayayo, Magunda, Rombe, Maliera Central, Murumba, Huluga and Regea. Two of these, Maliera Central and Got Kayayo, are on his land. He would be proud!

So who was Pastor Silfano Ayayo Mijema?

My unbiased opinion was that he was a teacher and educationalist. It was because of him that I became what I am. He was a lawgiver and disciplinarian to boot. Without these attributes, he would not have transformed a people from the down-trodden to leaders.

Above all, he was a church elder and pastor of repute. His fame and exploits spread far and wide. No wonder our people made him their leader and, like Moses, he led them out of bondage.

Time for a little story...

This happened at the Maliera Sector School.

One day an inspector of schools came while Silfano was in school. He noticed that the pupils did not stand at attention and salute as the inspector passed by. That was the standard practice those days. He attributed this lack of discipline to the teacher's ineptness. He believed that if the teachers had taught the pupils well they would have stood at attention and saluted the inspector.

After the inspector left, he summoned the whole school and demanded to know why the pupils did not stand upright and did not salute the inspector. There being no proper explanation, he reached for his whip and administered corporal punishment on the pupils. And get this—these pupils were not small boys and girls, they were in their late teens and others were adults.

Once he was done with the pupils, it was the turn of teachers. He did not spare them; he used the same whip on them. Henceforth there was no case of indiscipline in Maliera Sector School.

When it came to cleaning, it was not restricted to the school and church compounds only. The main road, in front of the school, from Kisumu to Busia, had to be cleaned too, courtesy of Pastor Silfano. This was not only done by the pupils, but the villagers too.

His word was the law!

When he said it was cleaning and sweeping time, everybody, except women and elders, was on the road. They swept two miles in both directions twice a week. The fact that he could get anybody to do anything at anytime was the basis of his power, and he used it, not only for the benefit of his immediate and extended family, but for our people as well; and this enabled our people to make great strides in educational and economic advancement. He was a disciplinarian who never allowed room for nonsense and this became his trademark.

Toward dawn, I noticed that he was visibly tired. He started yawning frequently and at some point I caught him off the corner of my eye dozing. I realized it was time to let him rest. I thanked him for the words of wisdom, then excused myself. The following day, I made it back to Gem.

I had talked to a sage!

*

Four years later, his health deteriorated and before he died he gave firm instruction that I had to be informed of his death and must be present at his burial. He died on the 21st day of April 1984 and his wishes were carried out. As soon as he died, Pastor Tobias Otieno Ayayo sent Ayub Ohon Ogola (popularly known as 'Baba') to Gem to inform me. I immediately alerted his brothers Justo Wamboga, Nicodemo Ogola, Isaac Ochieng and my father and, together with Dickson Sijenyi Indakwa, we left that same day for Achuth.

Gem mourners followed the following day.

Right there in the beautiful countryside of Achuth rests my father, my leader, my hero and my mentor.

Pastor Silfano Ayayo Mijema!

CHAPTER 24

OVERSEAS

My daughter Lydia had been in the United States for nine years when in 2002 she invited me for her graduation. She had been at the University of Memphis, doing her bachelors in Business Administration—Finance. She was a working mother of three lovely kids. Her enrollment and graduation surprised me. How did she juggle work, three kids and university work?

To many, it would have been impossible.

Not Lydia.

She was devoted, diligent and firmly focused. She was intelligent and determined. During her primary and high school days, she was a straight 'A' student. Her teachers and fellow students at Mary Hill High School discovered her leadership talent and made her a dining hall captain, German club chairlady, basketball captain and Christian Union chairlady. Those were the qualities that had enabled her to make it to the top in the corporate sector in the U.S. despite the hard and tough life of an American working mother.

My wife preceded me and was already in the country when I arrived in December 2002. There were certain arrangements I had to make before I left the country. I had to arrange how a multitude of people who depended on me for livelihood were going to survive and my office run in my absence. I also had to complete the marital rites I had not done for Mama Madala.

The first one was easy.

I had developed plots and town houses which generated income. With these, part of the school fees for children and the upkeep of dependants would be met. The main challenge would be the clearance of fees arrears, which ran into thousands of shillings.

The second one was a bit tricky.

But one of my pupils, who did his pupilage in my chambers, agreed to take over and run the office in my absence. He took over my staff, Anjeline Oloo and Joseph Ndeda Otieno.

The third I had to handle personally, before I flew out of the country.

On the 16th of November 2002, my friend, Martin Audi, my cousin, Jack Ogero, and my nephew, Aima Demba, accompanied me to Mama Ma Dala's parents' home with two heads of cattle and two goats, as tradition demanded. We also had cash in lieu of the cattle to accompany the animals. This was the last part of dowry payment, so I had to do it myself.

Their custom required that after this visit she had to return to her matrimonial home before I left the country. As we were leaving her home, she declined to accompany us back and I hit the roof. She failed to appreciate that I allowed myself to get along with these traditions for her and her parents' sake. Her decision not to play ball infuriated me and almost made me burst and say a few unpalatable things. I was embarrassed and humiliated not just because she refused to comply with what everybody was saying, but the tone and demeanor in which she was communicating it showed total disrespect in the African context. This was the fourth humiliation and embarrassment she had subjected me to in the presence of my friends or peers.

We returned home without her, but I had to send the car the following day to go and pick her up. That was the compromise arrangement.

The day following her return I went to Nairobi to look for a Visa. I had been told how hard it was to get one. I looked for people who had been to the USA to tell me how they got a visa—to steady my nerves. My search took me to a teacher who had been my neighbor in Siaya. She claimed she knew someone in Nairobi who could arrange for me to get a Visa without much ado. I caught the bait and she traveled with me to Nairobi, where she introduced me to a young, beautiful lady whom she appeared to know well because they referred to each other by their first names. The lady told me to pay her Kshs. 30,000/= to enable her to coach and prepare me for the interview.

What made me suspicious was the fact that despite my parting with Kshs. 30,000/=, from her explanations, I was still not sure I would get the visa.

Regardless, I agreed and gave her Kshs. 10,000/= upfront and the balance after the fact. She couched me a little that day and promised to do the rest on the eve of the interview. I booked an interview and went back home before I paid the visa application fee.

On the eve of my interview at the U.S. Embassy, I made arrangements to travel to Nairobi. Unfortunately I was late in making it to the bus stage and could not get a Nairobi-bound bus that evening. Very early the following day, I took a bus to Nairobi. The arrangement was to arrive by 1:00 o'clock and make it to the embassy before they closed that afternoon. The problem was—I had not paid the application fee, which was not paid to the embassy, but to a bank in the city's business district area. Only the receipt was to be presented at the embassy. Talk about stress!

When I realized the bus was not moving fast enough, I made frantic efforts to have the application fee paid before I got to Nairobi. Unfortunately my brother-in-law, Shade, who could get the money to my son Jack, was out of town. By the time he got through to his office, through the phone and gave instructions for release of the money, the bank had already closed. As a result, I missed my embassy interview that day.

But this would prove to be a blessing later.

My coach waited for me at the embassy but failed to locate me. Her calls could not be returned because I was enroute and also because I had decided to dispense with her services. I had to make a fresh appointment on my own, but I could not get a date earlier than my travelling date.

That's when I remembered Rose.

Niece Rose Achieng' Mihudhi—popularly known as Achienge—for a long time had worked at the Nairobi U.S.A. Embassy, but thank God had left shortly before the bomb blast.

I decided to consult Achienge and see how best she could help me secure an earlier interview. When I reached her and explained my situation, she agreed to try, but lamented that most of the people she knew had perished in the bomb blast. She did her best and got me an interview two days before my departure. I got things together and arranged them meticulously. When I went to the interview, I got the visa for six months and flew out of the country two days later. It was my first international flight.

I was awake and alert throughout the flight because I wanted to observe everything.

I made it to Memphis safely, where my daughter, her husband and my wife were on hand to receive me. A big welcoming party awaited me. We drove straight to her residence in Raleigh, where I met Kenyan residents in Memphis. I met mzee Wafula, a soft-spoken, straight talker. He was my age or slightly younger. Mzee Wafula would tell it to you like it was—no ifs or maybes. I met Baba Karanja and his lovely wife, Rebecca. I also met the gentleman of Memphis, Isaac Luboti—smart, neat, sly and articulate. He was a guy who was mindful of other people's problems and went out of his way to help. He loved my U.S.A. family very much and helped them a lot. I met almost the entire Kenyan community in Memphis, including Seth Giriango and Tony Mosi, who later became my best friends.

They were an interesting duo.

While Seth was a blunt, straight talker, Tony was meek and calculated. Both were members of the Adventist faith and were leaders in their respective churches. They could be Lydia's age mates. They raised themselves to my level and later we interacted a lot. They were the only guys I had a real good time with. They could come to see me in the evening and chat until dawn, covering divergent topics from social to political matters and Bible study.

The one I enjoyed most was the latter.

Apart from the duo, I also met Boyi, Nicky, Ken, Chief, Vicky, Beryl, Eddy, Mike, Millicent, Dorothy, Rhoda and Ochanda. The daughters of my late friend, Micah Amayo, Betty and Jemima, were among the first ladies I met.

A few days later, we attended Lydia's colorful graduation ceremony. It was an occasion attended by almost all Kenyans in Memphis. The reception at Madam Juanita's German townhouse was wonderful. It accorded me an opportunity to meet other Kenyans like Mr. Kariuki and their spouses. They paid glowing tribute to a mother who worked hard and graduated despite the many odds and hurdles poised against her.

In my short speech, I urged Kenyans who made it to the U.S.A. to make use of their time to achieve something. With the many educational openings, it would be a pity if they returned to Kenya empty-handed. On her part, Lydia urged everybody to work hard. If she could make it as a single mother, anybody with proper focus could make it too. The party ended and we went back to Raleigh.

A few days later my wife and I were invited to dinner by Fannie Bonner, Tyrone's mother, at her residence. She was a single mother living alone. She prepared well for our visit and received us warmly. I presented to her the gifts I brought for her from Kenya. It was at this visit that I learned American serve cold tea. When I was asked if I could have some tea I answered in the affirmative. What was brought was not hot but iced tea. I was told what they served hot was coffee. With plenty of other drinks to choose from, we enjoyed our dinner and left for Raleigh.

We were later invited by Keith and Olivette Smith, for the Thomas' family reunion. Keith and Olivette were close family friends of my daughter's family and called me daddy. Olivette availed her shoulder for my daughter to cry on while in grief; and because of my daughter's failing marriage this was quite often. She never tired to keep my daughter company. If it were not for the efforts of the Smiths, I doubt my daughter would have pulled through.

Pastor Julius and his wife—and Elder Venter and his wife—were all on hand when Lydia needed consolation and spiritual counseling.

We attended the family reunion and were presented with T-shirts for which we were thankful. By this time I had learned that my daughter's husband had walked out on her. At first I thought it was my visit that caused him to walk. I thought the house was too small and he wasn't comfortable with my wife and I around, but these turned out not to be the reasons. He came occasionally to see us, but made sure he never spent the night in the house. We could not understand what was wrong.

I discussed the situation with my daughter, but she too had no clear reason for the walk out.

I later discussed it with my wife and we agreed we had to do something as parents. We reminded each other what we would have done back home in a similar situation. We decided to summon him and his mother, who was his only parent around. Lydia and Mama prepared a lot of food, just as we would have done back home. We expected that he would not only come with his mother, but with a third party—an uncle, cousin or friend.

When he came, he was in the company of his mother.

We automatically realized very little would be achieved in the meeting. After the meals I demanded to know what the problem was that forced him to desert his family.

My daughter said her husband just changed, started drinking, stopped providing for the kids and started hating whatever she said or did. He also complained about the people she hung around with, but those were her customers. He did not want her to associate with anybody who came to visit their home. He was particularly concerned and disturbed about Kenyans. By their nature, Kenyans like to socialize, meeting and receiving visitors. When his vehemence grew worse, Lydia had to talk.

She said, "This is part of our culture!

The man didn't care.

"I'd like our kids to be brought up knowing God and this has the full support of my mother-in-law."

The man drew a deep breath. "My mama?"

"Yes," Lydia said. "She bought and gave us a beautiful Bible as a present. Didn't that tell you something?"

He said nothing.

So Lydia said, "All I want is our kids to receive the best education in Christian schools, but he won't pay!"

Since we were not in a court of law, I did not ask him to challenge what she had said, instead I asked him to state his case.

He had little to say.

He was emotional and kept on saying he did not want to stay this way anymore. "I've reached a point I can't take it anymore. It's enough. I'll never stay with her again."

He was curt, blunt and straight to the point. He'd reached the end of his tether, the point of no return with my daughter.

When I asked his mom to say something, she was all tears, murmuring things about her grandchildren. She appeared more concerned about her grandchildren than the marriage. It was over!

But I felt sad.

Sad for Lydia and the children.

Then the problem of fees for the many kids and university students who depended on me crept up. Money was needed!

So in March 2003 Lydia talked to Isaac Luboti to hire me to work in his construction company. He was in the business of renovation. He got contracts for pulling down and reconstructing or renovating houses. I put my mind and soul into this job. Isaac paid me well. Although the work was actually hard labor, to someone like me who had never done physical work in my entire adult life, it was like being jailed—but because I was paid well, I soldiered on.

Lydia did not allow me to contribute anything towards the maintenance of the home to enable me clear the fees arrears back home. I talked to Isaac, who lent me some money with which I started constructing a shop at home. I agreed to be paying him every month until the whole amount was cleared.

With the salary from this job, I cleared the fees arrears and with the loan I built a shop at our local market centre—three quarter way.

I will forever be grateful to Isaac for his magnanimity and humility. If it were not for him, my stay in the U.S.A. would have been in vain as I would have had nothing to show for it.

Toward the end of 2003, the company started getting fewer and fewer contracts and it forced me to drop out to lessen the number of people the company had to pay for doing little work.

Meanwhile we discussed and agreed that in order to enable my wife to obtain a green card, my stay had to be extended beyond the allowed six months. Lydia had applied for citizenship and was awaiting an interview. It was agreed that as soon as she obtained her citizenship she would petition, not only for my wife but, for me too. As soon as she petitioned, my wife and I received social security numbers and work authorization. I moved fast and obtained a driver's license. By the time I stopped working for Isaac, I already had the three documents the law required—driver's license, work authorization and social security number.

With these, I started looking for a job.

In March 2004 my wife, who constantly tarmaced for me, received information from my nephew, Sam Mayienga, that he would get me a job in Kansas, Missouri. I took a bus to Kansas, where I was received by Sam. Two days later, he got me a job with MHS Hospitality Group LLC as a front desk manager. I stayed with Sam and his lovely wife, Mellesa, for two months. The family had their two kids, Calvin and Carmichael, who also stayed in Kansas but independently.

It was a lovely couple.

Both were great cooks.

They accorded me the best hospitality, benefitting an uncle and my status. Sam made sure he got me a job that was not demeaning. He was himself doing a similar job. My duties included customer front desk services and night auditing. It involved extensive use of computers, which Sam quickly taught me. I learned fast enough so I was able to carry out my duties without constant supervision.

Sam and his wife were devoted Christians. Sam took me to church every Sunday. It was in their church, Tree Of Life Global Missions, where I met his friend Pastor and Founder G. Cornelius Jones. It was at this church that Sam was ordained as pastor. While their son Calvin was hard working and was at the university, their other son Carmichael was not and had taken to smocking and too much drinking. He was constantly in trouble with the law, having a couple of times been pulled up for DUI (Driving Under Influence of Alcohol). I would later try to help him and get my fingers burnt.

I'll leave that alone.

I later moved to my own apartment and bought some old furniture and a TV from a pawn shop. I also brought utensils from Mellesa. The problem was the inadequacy of what I made from my job. It was not enough to pay my bills, run the car and put food on my table. I lived on starvation diet. Sometimes I could go without food after paying my car insurance and rent for the apartment.

Not a bed of roses!

As I was living alone, I had no one to talk to. All the people I knew were either away at their work stations or were sleeping after a day or night's work. I decided to buy a computer to keep me busy. This became my companion for my entire stay. While it helped ease my indolence and anxiety, it added to my financial woes. I had to get a telephone landline in order to access the internet. By the time I paid all the bills, I had no money left. I could not afford a meal on the kind of salary I was earning. It was during this time that I lived on crumbs of bagels leftovers at the hotel where I was working. I could not afford to help my people back in Kenya and got more frustrated. Since I hated idleness, wherever I had free time I wrote letters to my kids and their mothers back in Kenya. I could talk with my wife in Memphis for long hours on the phone. I was dying from loneliness. It forced my wife to make two visits to Kansas just to check on me. Occasionally she helped me out financially from her meager resources, but this was not sufficient. The fact that I could not help dependants back home worried me but I soldiered on.

Meanwhile back in Memphis my wife and I had been invited for permanent residence interview. Our lawyer requested that my file be sent to the Kansas mission, where I was working. My wife was interviewed and got approved for permanent residency. It was not long before I was also invited for an interview in Kansas. I hired the services of an attorney. My entire Memphis family came—my wife, daughter and grandchildren. When the interviewer saw the form we had filled, our ten children's names, she was stunned.

She said, "All these are your kids?"

I nodded.

"Ten kids?"

I said, "What do you think an African couple does in an African village at night where there is no TV and no electricity?"

They burst into laughter and promptly approved my application. That was in November 2004. And in December the same year, my wife and I got our permanent residence cards.

By the end of March 2005 I was back in Memphis, and in July 2005 my wife, daughter, grandchildren and I flew back to Kenya to attend the weddings of our daughters Martha, Everline and Violet. While Lydia and her kids returned to the U.S.A. in July, my wife and I remained behind and followed them later in September 2005.

When I returned to Memphis from Kansas, I found my daughter and my wife staying with a certain woman. Mary Sellesor moved in to stay with my family as a house help. She was about 65 years old, 5' 4" with fair complexion. She was smart and intelligent. She was easily attracted to men, in the company of whom she was comfortable. She liked gossiping and this became her pass time. She set husbands against wives and vice versa, and would interfere with young men and women having their good time.

Above all, she set my wife against me all the time. She found my wife gullible to her intrigues. She would tell my wife how I took her out and had a good time with her when the only thing I did was to take her for grocery shopping. She would make up and say things to my wife which my wife misinterpreted to mean I had an affair with her. I believed she knew what she was doing, creating artificial rift between my wife and I. I later cut off all communication with her. While I was home when everybody was away, I would lock myself in the bedroom and only sneak to the kitchen for a bite when I was sure she was not there. Severally we urged my daughter to get rid of her, but she was unwilling because she had nowhere to take her. Lydia refused to release her into the streets. When I returned to Memphis in 2009, she had migrated.

Carmichael's situation really worried his parents. During the time I was staying with his parents they realized he listened to me and respected me a lot. They had tried to talk to him to change his lifestyle in vain. They tried all they could but Carmichael could not bulge. They still loved him and wanted to help him. They did not want him to get in trouble because he had not normalized his status. Given the respect they thought he had for me, his parents approached me to talk to him. They believed such an approach could make him abandon drinking and indolence.

I agreed and they gave me money to use in any restaurant I chose to talk to him.

I arranged and talked to him at length.

He complained bitterly about his parents. He thought they loved his brother more than him and considered him good for nothing. For this he also didn't have a soft spot for his brother. He complained that his father always quarreled whenever there was an issue to discuss. And he said his mother's only problem was to support his father even when he was definitely wrong.

He opened up to me!

Encouraged by this positive development, when his parents had to vacate their apartment for a home they had purchased, he asked me to take him in and I obliged.

Three months later I lost my job. I decided to return to my family in Memphis. I left the boy the apartment and most of my stuff.

I returned to Memphis to rejoin my family. After two weeks Lydia got me a job with Independent Living Assistance Inc, still in hospitality industry. I was trained by the state to take care of the mentally retarded. I received a total of nine certificates in this field, thus enabling me to rise between the ranks to become personnel and finance director of the company. This position enabled me to employ many Africans, particularly Kenyans. As the company was owned by an African American and was doing good, the authorities who still looked at things through color, did not waste time to betray it. When it was shut down by the government, I moved to Guardian, in April 2007, for a similar job.

I later resigned and made up my mind to stop working and come back to Kenya.

The reason was two-fold.

One, I was tired and needed a lot of rest. I also needed to attend to my things in Kenya, which I heard were in a bad shape. Some of my rental houses had crumbled and my Siaya home was in ruins since nobody was staying there. My boys wanted to marry and needed my presence. I also needed to pay dowry in readiness for the weddings. I could not do all these by phone.

The second reason was the more compelling one. When I lost the job at Independent Living Assistance Inc, I had good savings in the bank. In fact, I knew I could live on my savings for at least four months if I stayed for that long without another job.

———

One day I went to the grocery store to purchase provision and used my debit card for payment. I was surprised when I was told there were no funds in my account. I got furious and rushed to the bank to find out what the matter was. I was told someone placed a court lien on my account and took away all the money. I knew I was not indebted to anyone as I had been very careful with my finances. I wondered who might have taken me to court and got an order to attach money in my bank account.

I doubted it was really a court order.

I didn't receive any summons ordering my attendance in court. Courts don't give exparte orders unless a party was duly served, but failed to enter appearance or file his defense. Further inquiries revealed that my problem originated in Kansas, not Memphis.

So what was it?

Listen to this. I discovered that Carmichael, whom I had left in my apartment stayed in the apartment long past June 2005, when my lease expired and as he continued to pay the rent after the expiry of term of the lease, the landlord assumed I was staying on and continued to accept the rent. Then in or around September, Carmichael got into trouble and vacated the house.

The Landlord sued me!

The court papers were left at the apartment. Whether this was proper service I did not bother to ascertain because I did not contest the order. I considered it too expensive to contest an order of a court 800 miles away in a state whose legal system may be different from that of the state where I lived. I decided to negotiate payment terms with the lawyer on the other end. I also contacted Carmichael to let him know what had happened and ask him to arrange to pay.

He sounded remorseful.

To ensure he paid, I asked him to be remitting some money to me every month, which I would in turn remit to the lawyer—until the whole amount was paid. Meanwhile, I agreed to remit a similar amount every month to the lawyer until the amount was paid.

But did the boy play ball?

Carmichael failed to remit even a single installment. When I drew the attention of his parents to the matter, they were not sympathetic. To them it was as if I got what I deserved. It turned out to be a blame game. They totally forgot that they asked me to help them talk to their son. They forgot a whole lot of accolades they heaped on me for having turned their son around. I was being blamed for having done what they had asked me to do. At least I deserved sympathy since I was not asking them to take over their son's indebtness to pay. The good thing I did in helping the young man cost me my stay in the U.S.A. I could not stay without working and could not work when every dime I made was going to service the debt and bills. I was not going to have enough funds to pay my bills and service my debt. I called it quits and left employment in 2007.

I made arrangements to return home. I sold my car and computer for a song and flew back to Kenya in 2007.

In Kenya I visited my sons' in-laws in Ringa, Kandiege, Kamreri and Seme, in preparation for their weddings. Ringa was where James' in-laws stayed. Eric's in-law lived in Kandiege. Jack's and Antony's in-law lived in Kamreri and Seme respectively. Later James, Eric and Jack went ahead with their weddings, but Antony didn't because he was in the U.S.A. His wife and kid were in Kenya.

*

On the 31st day of March 2007, I received information that my wife had collapsed in the U.S.A. and was rushed to an emergency room. I was needed back in the States as soon as possible. My wife had not been the sickly type at all. She was strong, healthy and athletic. She could still run and play netball. She would later have a lot of health issues related to pregnancy in 1969, a couple of months after Kenneth was born. She got so ill and had to be rushed to a hospital where she was admitted and received blood transfusion. In 1976, she unexpectedly suffered miscarriage, six months into her pregnancy.

We lost the foetus.

I went to the hospital and collected the dead foetus for burial. Jadak helped me bury it in Kisumu cemetery.

In September 1977, she went to Lake Nursing Home for a normal delivery. The baby was normally delivered and named after her mother, Martha Akoth. But immediately after delivery, she passed out bleeding.

The doctors were perplexed. They referred her to a specialist at New Nyanza General Hospital, where the battle to stop the bleeding was fought. The child was placed in a hospital nursery where she never stopped crying. With her mother in a coma, I decided to take the little girl home. I took her to Gem and left her under the care of Mama Madala.

She never stopped crying.

I had to move her from home and took her to Ran'gala, where we discovered she was crying because she was not getting enough food. Once we made this discovery, everything returned to normal. Meanwhile her mother remained in the hospital for a whole month undergoing treatment.

After her discharge from the hospital, she needed a few weeks to recuperate, at the end of which I sent Martha to her. She was one among a couple of my kids who never suckled. She was named after my mother-in-law, for which reason we had difficulty calling her by her name. In the African culture you don't call your mother-in-law by name, sometimes even your mother and your father. My mother-in-law came from Agoro so she was called Nyagoro and the name stuck.

To emphasize the urgency with which I was required in the U.S.A., my air ticket followed soon after the information. I flew out to the States to attend to my wife's sickness. When I arrived, I was told she collapsed and passed out in the bathroom. The emergency services were called and took her to the hospital, where she was admitted. A growth in the brain tissues was positively diagnosed and the passing out attributed to it.

She required surgery to remove the growth.

The surgery was scheduled later in the month, so on the 28th of June 2007 she was taken to the hospital. My daughter, son and friends were at the hospital. We had psyched ourselves and prepared her psychologically for the surgery. On arriving, however, we were told her name was not in the list of those scheduled for surgery.

It must have been a mistake!

Through our insistence and the cooperation of the surgeon, the hospital agreed to work on her the following day. As soon as this consensus was reached, the hospital personnel started preparing her for the surgery. I spent the night beside her in the hospital. It was not until 2:00 p.m., the following day, that she was wheeled away for surgery. I was put in the waiting room, where I was joined by my daughter, son, Milly and a friend. They gave us updates of the surgery hourly.

They got done at 11:00 p.m.

I was the first to enter the room, then my daughter, then my son and friends. Although she was still weak, when I touched her hand she opened her eyes and she recognized me. I touched her other hand and the response was the same. I immediately realized she did not lose her sense of feeling. She also recognized me. She was then on her way to recovery. We decided, for the first time in three days, to have a sumptuous dinner. We went out to a restaurant and ate and wined well. She was still under the constant care of the nurses so we were not worried when we left her alone.

The following morning my daughter and I went to the hospital. I was fully prepared to stay with her in the hospital until she was discharged. I stayed with her day and night, helping when she wanted to visit the bathroom and when she needed a shower. I helped with the grooming too. Her right hand was weak and she could not walk, but she could speak very well.

She recovered pretty fast and regained the use of her limbs fully. She could prepare food and do the dishes, bathe and even do laundry. The only thing she could not do was drive. When it was clear she had recovered, I returned to Kenya to continue with preparations for the weddings.

On the 15th of April 2008, I left home for Nairobi to attend James' wedding. I had to be there early to help with preparations.

On the 18th April 2008, Betty Ngesa, my niece, invited me for dinner, where I ate a lot of *imondo*—gizzards.

The wedding took place on the 20th April 2008.

On the 21st April 2008, I was invited to the Ken and Ombado homes for lunch and super respectively. We enjoyed the meals. I returned to Gem on the 22nd April 2008 and on the 23rd April 2008, I fell sick. But since my sickness did not respond to local treatment, I decided to see Doctor Okech, in Nakuru, on the 29th April 2008. The x-ray revealed a swelling on the prostrate. This could only be remedied by surgery. If done in Kenya, it would cost a substantial amount of money, but would cost even more in the U.S.A. I informed my people of this new development after I had been given medication by Dr. Okech and returned home. Since my time for returning to the U.S.A. was only three months away, a decision was made to fly me to the U.S.A. to save my status—and to get treatment.

On the 30th May 2008, I left home for Achuth, en route to Nairobi. I wanted to see my cousin, Pr. Tobias Otieno Ayayo, who had been sick too, before I left the country. My visit coincided with the annual get-together of the descendants of Ayodo. Ayodo was the father of Rosebella Otieno, Pr. Tobias' wife. I was accompanied on this trip by Mama Madala.

I found Pastor quite sick, but in high spirits. He was happy to see us. I seized the opportunity to visit Martin's and Mama Bela's beautifully terraced home. We enjoyed my favorite dishes—*ugali* with *obambo*. She prepared the food just as she used to prepare for me while we were staying with them in our Siaya town home.

On the 2nd June 2008, we left Achuth for Nairobi through Narok. We rode in Atieno Ombado's car and on the way saw Rena's beautiful home.

On the 4th June 2008, I flew back to the U.S.A. through Lagos. My luggage arrived on the 10th June 2008.

Because of financial constraints, the search for my treatment did not commence until 23rd June 2008, when my daughter took me to see a doctor. Several tests were done and specimen taken for further testing. I saw him again on 7th July 2008 when he referred me to Dr. Duncan, with whom I secured appointment on 29th July 2008. That doctor also referred me to Medplex on the 7th August 2008.

On the 6th September 2008, Dr. Duncan performed a colonoscopy surgery on me at the Delta Endoscope Centre.

At the Medplex, a young white doctor looked at me contemptuously and—with a pair of dirty gloves—dipped his fingers into my bottom and proclaimed that I needed no surgery. He prescribed medication, which I bought from Walgreen. He did not tell me how long I had to use the medicine. So after one year, I stopped using them.

My problem was not solved.

I still feel the same symptoms I complained about, but the colonoscopy surgery helped me a lot. After that treatment, I went back home on the 17th November 2008, where I continued to recuperate.

*

While in the United States, my wife was involved in a near-fatal accident. The beautiful car was totaled and three other cars damaged. Luckily she never got injured. Her insurance took care of the claims, but she had no means to take her to work. It would be a long time before she got another car, through a family friend.

On the 19th February 2009, my step-mother, who had been ailing, died. Dunga had spent a fortune trying to treat her. It was a swelling of the tummy, which was attributed to smoking cigarettes.

She was treated.

But later, when it was clear she was not recovering from the malady, she asked to be brought home. On the 19th February 2009, she passed on.

Her funeral was riddled with controversy.

Let me explain.

Dunga and I decided that in order to give her a decent burial, it was imperative we take her body to the mortuary for preservation, for a week. His surviving son—Hezron Omondi, and two daughters, Anne and Miriam, under the prompting of their aunt, Sarah—refused. They said they were ready to bury at a moment's notice.

Other controversies followed...

And by the way, the events that preceded her death showed they wanted her to die. First, they refused to take her to the hospital. When Dunga decided to foot the bill, nobody was willing to go and stay with her in the hospital. Whatever food Dunga and I gave her, they made sure they took three quarters and left her on a starvation diet. And on the day she died Omondi and Anne carted away all her property including poultry, farm produce and utensils. It was pathetic!

Although we eventually won the right to take her body to the mortuary, the battlelines had been drawn. They declared they were going to have nothing to do with my family. We decided to ignore them and proceeded with the funeral arrangements as if they never existed

---

While in the United States, I visited tourist attraction sites and places of historical significance. In Memphis, I visited Martin Luther King Jr. museum.

Martin Luther King Jr. was an African American icon who fought segregation and white supremacy. He was born on January 15th 1929 to Martin Luther King Sr. and Alberta King, in Atlanta Georgia. He polished his oratory skills as a pastor in the Baptist church and used the pulpit and church congregation to get his message across. He later mobilized masses for awareness campaigns and protests. The Voting Rights Act was said to have been as a result of his efforts.

He was eloquent and made many hallmark speeches in his short life span. Speeches like:

> *I have a dream that one day on the red hills of Georgia the sons of former slaves and the sons of former slave owners will be able to sit down together at the table of brotherhood. I have a dream that my four little children will one day live in a nation where they will not be judged by the color of their skin but by the content of their character.*

No wonder they cut short his life through an assassin's bullet on April 4th 1968. Although they assassinated him, the fire he had lit continued to burn unabated. His museum in Memphis is actually an entire hotel building, where he slept on the day of his assassination, and the adjourning hotel where the assassin was. They've preserved the hotels and the rooms as they were. I toured the two hotels. I visited the room Martin Luther King Jr slept in. The bed was still made the way it was. The bedside table, the ash tray and butts of smoked cigarettes, were still as they were. All the other places within the building had pictures of his tours, speeches and the matches he organized.

As I toured the buildings his speeches thundered from small loud speakers in the rooms. The pictures on the walls showed the brutality the white man subjected a black man to before emancipation.

It was chilling!

And later, in Atlanta, Georgia, I visited Martin Luther King Jr's grave. It was a magnificent sight, right in the middle of water. The grave was surrounded by a kind of swimming pool whose depth I could not tell. Springs of water jetted around the grave, giving a rainbow appearance against the sunshine. It was marvelous to watch.

Inside the building were pictures of places and the throngs of people he addressed. Everywhere he made a benchmark speech and photos was captured, those photos were now exhibited in the rooms. One could follow the sequence of his entire life with the aid of the pictures. I was enthralled to watch them and wondered how fast the U.S.A. had moved to catch up with the rest of the world in democracy. It all began with Martin!

Let me switch gears here.

I want to commend the Americans, not for their military might, not for their economic power, not for their capitalism, but for the way they have put in place a machinery for taking care of those in their midst who are mentally retarded. It is the one country I have visited where persons with diminished responsibility and mental challenges don't roam the streets, but are taken care of by the state governments. They are put in homes where they are provided with all necessities of life and medication like anybody else. They have the same rights as normal people. They are under watch by trained and qualified personnel. The government meets all the expenses for taking care of them. With guns bought like T-shirts, if these guys were allowed out there, the situation would be chaotic. Governments would have full hands solving murder and other violence-related cases.

The other area I would commend American people is the way they treat persons with disabilities. They are given priority treatment wherever they go. In churches, cinemas, stores and all public buildings, they have special ramps for entry and exit. Authorities appreciate their ambulatory rights and have made provision to enable them to move around. They have also been educated and encouraged to be self-reliant.

I even saw persons without hands driving, doing their laundry and preparing their food.

A particular one which amazed me was a lady without upper limbs who could write perfectly using her toes. She was self-reliant and independent. She drove herself to the store and did everything that a normal person did.

I was touched!

The midgets in their midst are not left out either. They have been educated and psyched to be independent.

There is something for us to emulate in Kenya.

―――

In November 2003, we were invited by Pastor Paul Onyango Wahonya to visit in Michigan. My daughter and her kids, my wife, Seth Giruango and I went to Berrien Springs, where Andrews University was located.

Andrews is an S.D.A. university.

Although at the time it was much colder in Berrien Springs than in Memphis, we enjoyed the good food Mrs. Wahonya prepared—and our stay was fantastic. Paul was a PhD student at the university. We met his promising young family and on Sabbath he took us to one of the many S.D.A. churches within the university.

After church, Paul took us to sightseeing. He took us to every corner of the university. We later met Karl Marks and Jimmy Ayayo, Kenyans who came to see us. And in the evening, he took us to see Mr. and Mrs. Sam and Hellen Okello, who are his brother-in-law and sister. A lovely couple. We detoured to Indiana briefly, before we returned to Paul's home.

The following day we returned to Memphis.

My friend, Seth Giriango, spent a lot of time showing me places. He took me to Mississippi, where we toured a couple of casinos. I saw how they operated and even tried a few of them after Seth had shown me how to operate them. At some point I scored while he was away in the bathroom and because I did not know which button to press to release the money, I pressed the wrong button which neutralized my score.

I was so disappointed.

We visited two or three other casinos before we returned to Memphis. Seth later organized his itinerary and took me to Huntsville, Alabama, to see the NASA headquarters, particularly the first spaceship which went to the moon. We arrived when they were about to close and managed to see the spaceship, but not much else. We then proceeded to see his friend, who was a nurse in one of the hospitals. When she brought us food, I was surprised to find on the table indigenous Kenyan vegetables—*muto* and *akeyo*. In Memphis we did not have those vegetables. She said she got them from California.

We returned to Memphis that night.

We later returned to Huntsville with my wife, daughter and her kids to visit Jim Ayayo. That visit accorded me an opportunity to see Oakwood University. We met Rena, Jim's sister, and Jim's white friend and his family, whose kids immediately struck a rapport with my grandchildren. Later, as they bade farewell to each other they didn't want to let go. We enjoyed our stay at Jim's place, although I felt our numbers kind of overwhelmed him. My family could not fit into his house together with the family of his white friend. The white friend had to relocate to a hotel with his family. I was so embarrassed at the inconvenience we caused our host and his visitor.

We returned to Memphis the following day.

Then one day, as we were in our church, Overtone S.D.A. Church, we heard that the General Conference of S.D.A. was to be held in St. Louis, Missouri, five hours from Memphis. I asked my daughter to make arrangements for us to attend for at least one day. She arranged and, in the company of Dorothy and her family, Tony Mosi and Millicent Makonya, we drove to St. Louis on Saturday, the closing Sabbath. Although we were late for the morning events, we watched the choirs from each continent perform after the divine service. Of particular interest was the Conference Hall choir with a presentation in which they performed the way whites would sing and black Americans would sing the same song.

It was hilarious.

There were choirs from India, Korea, Africa and other places. It was worth the 10-hour drive. I saw people from all walks of life and from most races of the world. I saw men and women, boys and girls all united in praise of the Lord. I wished I had attended all the sessions. It was in my view a replica of what the scene would be like when the Son of God comes to take home His chosen people.

Later in the evening we drove back to Memphis satisfied that God had made it possible for me to attend the General Conference of S.D.A. which I would not have attended had I not come to the States.

Allow me to say a word about the Mississippi before I turn to Barrack Obama and the U.S. elections—in closing this book.

I'd heard a lot about this river while in Kenya. It was the longest river in the U.S.A., traversing the country for 3709 miles. It was also the 4th longest river in the world after Yangtze, of Asia with 3964 miles, Amazon of South America with 4049 miles, and Nile of Africa with 4160 miles.

At the Memphis Point, it is navigable. The East Memphis front had been developed into a recreation park with trees planted and well kept grass stretching up to the water front with tracks traversing the entire park for joggers and those who wanted to exercise by walking. There were also seats placed at strategic points for those who wanted to sit and just enjoy the breeze or watch the steamships trudge by.

It was a beautiful place to behold and the authorities charged with keeping it clean did not disappoint. Flanked by long, magnificent bridges on the east and on the west, and the train that took people for tours over the river, the entire place was scenic and picturesque. It was a scene one wished to write home about. I enjoyed the tour, walked the lanes, sat and rested and finally took a train ride over the river.

It was amazing!

Now to our Kogelo boy!

The U.S. presidential campaigns started in earnest while I was there. It pitied John McCain, a Republican, against Barrack Obama, a Democrat. Barrack Obama was born on the 4th of August 1961 to a Kenyan father of Luo ethnic group and a white American mother from Missouri. Her name was Ann Dunham. He was born in Honolulu, Hawaii. He attended various schools and institutions in Hawaii, Indonesia and the U.S.A. While at Harvard Law School, he was elected the first African American President of the Harvard Law Review, in 1990. In 1992, while teaching constitutional law at the University of Chicago, he was involved in a voter registration project. Later he worked as a community organizer for low-income residents of the Roseland and Altgeld Gardens communities.

In 1996 he ran as a state of Illinois senator as a Democrat and was elected. Then in 2000 he was unsuccessful in democratic primary election for the U.S. House of Representatives seat.

In 2004 he decided to run for the U.S. Senate open seat vacated by a Republican, Peter Fitzgerald, which he won.

That summer, he was invited to deliver the keynote speech in support of John Kerry at the 2004 Democratic National Convention, in Boston. He emphasized the importance of unity and made veiled jabs at the Bush Administration and the diversionary use of wage issues.

It was stunning!

That speech catapulted him into national politics.

In February 2007, he made a decision to run for President. He was only 47. He was going to make history. He was going to be the first African American to make a bold and serious bid for the presidency.

He got locked in a tight battle with former first lady and then U.S. Senator from New York, Hillary Rodham Clinton, until he became the nominee on June 3rd, 2008. That was Barrack's fiercest battle. Beating Hillary was no mean achievement. She was a fighter and had the unequivical support of most women and whites. Even some African Americans supported her.

It was history in the making!

The Republican flagbearer was an old veteran of Vietnam War, John McCain. Although eloquent in his own right, he only excelled with small audiences. In a rally situation he was no match for the young democrat whose rallying political slogan was YES WE CAN!

The bringing on board of Sarah Palin as his running mate to capture the women voters' disillusioned by the failure of Hillary to secure Democratic nomination backfired and did not help in his campaign at all. Sarah was a novice in national politics. She might have done well as governor in Alaska, but national politics was a different ball game that required a lot of exposure and experience, which she lacked.

Let me close this now…

On November 4th 2008, Barrack Obama, a Democrat, defeated John McCain, a Republican. Then on January 20th 2009, Barrack Obama became the 44th President of the United States of America. He was the first Luo to be president of the most powerful nation in the world.

But what did his election portend for the American people?

Let me say this—I saw God's hand in his election as the 44th President of the United States of America. God works in miraculous ways. He used Moses, a stammerer, to agitate for the Israelites to be released from Egyptian bondage. He allowed David to take over the reins of power from a powerful Saul, thereby denying Absalom, the son of Saul, his inheritance. Just like the Israelites were in bondage in Egypt for 400 years, so were blacks and native Indians in America. The time had come for the down-trodden and despised to rule—and God was on their side. The innocent blood of multitudes killed, murdered or massacred cried out from beyond the graves not for revenge or retribution but fairness.

It makes me wonder what the white man will do if he found the New Jerusalem patronized by blacks. Will he turn and walk back to hell?

The End!